REAL WORLD
ADOBE®
ILLUSTRATOR® CS3

MORDY GOLDING

Adobe

Peachpit Press

REAL WORLD ADOBE® ILLUSTRATOR® CS3
Mordy Golding

Peachpit Press
1249 Eighth Street
Berkeley, CA 94710
510/524-2178
Fax: 510/524-2221

Find us on the Web at www.peachpit.com

To report errors, please send a note to errata@peachpit.com

Peachpit Press is a division of Pearson Education

Real World Adobe Illustrator CS3 is published in association with Adobe Press.

Editor: Karyn Johnson
Production Coordinator: David Van Ness
Copyeditor: Kim Wimpsett
Proofreader: Haig MacGregor
Composition: Myrna Vladic
Indexer: Jack Lewis
Cover Design: Charlene Charles-Will
Cover Illustration: Ron Chan

ISBN-10: 0-321-49621-3
ISBN-13: 978-0-321-49621-8

9 8 7 6 5 4 3 2 1

Printed and bound in the United States of America

This book is dedicated to my wife, Batsheva,
who continues to support me in everything I do.
The words in this book belong to her
just as much as they do to me.

ACKNOWLEDGMENTS

There are two people who I need to thank first, even though words can't really describe the gratitude I owe for their sincere friendship. Sharon Steuer and Sandee Cohen helped me to establish myself in the Illustrator community, and for that I am eternally grateful.

I've written books before and when I was approached to write this title, I thought it would be an easy task. Months later, I look back and realize how much work has gone into this book, and I have a new appreciation for the team at Peachpit Press. Thanks to Nancy Ruenzel, Marjorie Baer, Nancy Davis, Charlene Charles-Will, Sara Jane Todd, and the folks at Adobe Press. I want to personally thank Kim Wimpsett for copyediting this book and David Van Ness for his work in production. Most of all, I want to thank my superb editor, Karyn Johnson, for her direction, awesome ideas, endless patience, and demand for excellence. The high quality of this book is to Karyn's credit.

I am extremely grateful to have had the opportunity to work with my good friend and colleague Jean Claude Tremblay. JC tirelessy tech edited this book and offered wonderful advice.

If you think publishing a book is a huge undertaking, I can assure you that producing an application like Adobe Illustrator is an even greater task. Special thanks go to the entire Illustrator team for their concerted efforts, and specifically to Phil Guindi, Terry Hemphill, Teri Pettit, Ty Voliter, Paul George, Ian Giblin, and Brenda Sutherland for their personal assistance and advice. Thanks also to Thomas Phinney, John Nack, Will Eisley, Lynn Grillo, Julieanne Kost, and the always-entertaining Russell Brown for their continued friendship.

I'm lucky enough to count a number of professional authors and educators among my friends. Thanks to David Blatner, Chris and Jennifer Smith, Ben Willmore, Deke McClelland, Bert Monroy, Claudia McCue, Matthew Richmond, and Barry Anderson, who continue to share advice, support, and funny anecdotes over the occasional drink.

Even though he's a die-hard SF Giants fan (I'm a NY Mets fan), I reserve a personal note of appreciation for my friend Ron Chan who created the wonderful illustration that appears on the cover of this book.

You can't write a book unless you have a clear mind, and nothing clears the mind like the smell of fresh cut grass and the sound of your golf ball dropping into the bottom of a cup early in the morning. Thanks to Jeremy, Avi, and Shimmy for putting up with my writing schedule and for getting me out onto the course. Bethpage Black next week?

Finally, I want to thank my entire family for their encouraging words of support. I appreciate everything that you do for me and hope that I make all of you proud.

TABLE OF CONTENTS

INTRODUCTION

Because I've been the product manager of Adobe Illustrator, people frequently approach me who, prior to attending a demo or workshop on Illustrator, either thought they had no need for the program or were under the impression it is used only for designing logos.

The truth is, Illustrator is essential to a broad range of professionals and hobbyists, and it has an incredible number of uses—so many that it's hard to define exactly what Illustrator does. Features such as transparency, 3D, Live Trace, Live Paint, gradient mesh, live effects, professional typography, Flash animation, and SVG support have all redefined how people use Illustrator every day. It's certainly not the same program it was 10 years ago.

My goal with this book is threefold: to teach new users how to take advantage of the technology, to help experienced users learn about features that have changed, and to give power users the understanding they need to push themselves and produce reliable files. I love showing people all the cool and productive things you can do with the product, and nothing makes me happier than seeing a designer crank out a totally awesome design using Illustrator. Throughout this book, I share my thoughts, experiences, and knowledge about Illustrator so that you can have fun with it, sharpen your skills, and make it work for you.

THE MANY USES OF ILLUSTRATOR

Look all around you.

Billboards along the side of the highway, packages of cereal and other groceries at the supermarket, navigation icons on a Web site, posters announcing an exhibit at a museum, advertisements throughout magazines and newspapers, logos and artwork on T-shirts and sportswear, animated cartoons and feature films, user interfaces on your computer and cell phones … all of these and more are created with the help of Illustrator.

Illustrator is used by creative individuals who want to express their creativity in print, on the Web, in video, and on wireless devices. The program is distributed in many different languages, and you can find millions of Illustrator users across the globe. Of course, with such a diverse user base, Illustrator is used and applied in many ways. To get an idea of what I mean, take a look at how some creative professionals use Illustrator and how this book can help them.

Creative Genius: The World of Graphic Design

It's difficult to define the job of a graphic designer because the title encompasses so many different types of design. For the most part, graphic designers specialize in a particular field of design such as corporate, advertising, direct mail, or even typography. Graphic designers work on a variety of projects and usually have experience with several programs including Adobe Photoshop, Adobe InDesign, and QuarkXPress.

For these kinds of users, Illustrator serves as a creative springboard for designs such as logos and type treatments, ad storyboards and campaigns, spot illustrations, maps, charts, and general design elements.

If you're a graphic designer, you'll find the following chapters most helpful as you read through this book:

- Chapter 3: *Objects, Groups, and Layers* (page 65)

- Chapter 4: *Advanced Vectors* (page 97)

- Chapter 7: *Typography* (page 231)

- Chapter 8: *3D and Other Live Effects* (page 261)

- Chapter 9: *Mixing It Up: Working with Vectors and Pixels* (page 333)

- Chapter 10: *Graphs, Distortion, and Blends* (page 371)

Telling a Story: Illustration and Animation

To an animator or an illustrator, Illustrator is an empty canvas waiting to come alive. In a world of animated feature films and TV shows, it's easy to understand the benefits of drawing characters and animations directly on a computer. Its ability to repurpose art for almost any need makes Illustrator the perfect environment for creating animations and illustrations.

Adobe didn't name its product Illustrator without reason. Artists create illustrations for children's books, magazine covers and articles, packages, and a variety of other products, and they use Illustrator to take advantage of the high quality and precision available in the program. A variety of tools, such as gradient meshes, blends, and even 3D, allow illustrators to translate the images they see in their minds into reality.

If you're an animator or an illustrator, you'll find the following chapters most helpful as you read through this book:

- Chapter 2: *Vectors 101* (page 29)

- Chapter 3: *Objects, Groups, and Layers* (page 65)

- Chapter 4: *Advanced Vectors (*page 97)

- Chapter 5: *Brushes, Symbols, and Masks* (page 197)

- Chapter 8: *3D and Other Live Effects* (page 261)

- Chapter 9: *Mixing It Up: Working with Vectors and Pixels* (page 333)

- Chapter 11: *Web and Mobile Design* (page 413)

- Chapter 13: *Saving and Exporting Files* (page 479)

Interactive Experience: Interface and Web Design

Web designers have a language all their own, which includes acronyms such as HTML, XML, SVG, SWF, GIF, JPEG, PNG, and CSS. Illustrator supports these and other Web-specific technologies, giving Web designers access to the formats in which they need to deliver their designs. Taking advantage of Illustrator's object-based design environment, Web designers can lay out precise navigation elements, buttons, and entire pages.

In today's fast-paced world, everyone needs a presence on the Web. However, businesses find that they also need to provide content in print format. By creating art in Illustrator, Web designers can easily use that art for both Web and print layouts, thus reducing the need to re-create art for each medium.

If you're a Web designer, you'll find the following chapters most helpful as you read through this book:

- Chapter 5: *Brushes, Symbols, and Masks* (page 147)

- Chapter 8: *3D and Other Live Effects* (page 261)

- Chapter 9: *Mixing It Up: Working with Vectors and Pixels* (page 333)

- Chapter 11: *Web and Mobile Design* (page 413)

- Chapter 13: *Saving and Exporting Files* (page 479)

- Appendix A: *Automation with Illustrator* (page 527)

Tomorrow's Trends: Fashion and Apparel Design

If you're thinking about bathing suits while it's snowing outside, either you're dreaming about going on vacation or you're a fashion designer. What type of clothes you design may directly correlate to the seasons of the year, but designing apparel is also a highly creative field that demands the most of a designer. Illustrator's object-based approach to design makes it easier to work with body shapes, apparel guidelines, and product labels.

Fashion designers can create symbol libraries of repeating objects such as motifs, buttons, buckles, and zippers. Illustrator can also create pattern fills and simulate shading and realism using transparency effects.

If you're a fashion designer, you'll find the following chapters most helpful as you read through this book:

- Chapter 2: *Vectors 101* (page 29)

- Chapter 3: *Objects, Groups, and Layers* (page 65)

- Chapter 4: *Advanced Vectors* (page 97)

- Chapter 5: *Brushes, Symbols, and Masks* (page 147)

- Chapter 9: *Mixing It Up: Working with Vectors and Pixels* (page 333)

Thinking Outside the Box: Package Design

If you're good at reading upside-down text, you just might be a package designer. That's because most package designs are created flat on one sheet, with different panels facing different directions. Once printed, the entire package is folded up so it appears visually correct. Package designers use Illustrator to define spot colors, place images from Photoshop, and apply trapping settings—all in an effort to grab a potential buyer's attention.

Because of production requirements, package designers often need to be able to make minute adjustments to colors and artwork. By building files in Illustrator, these designers can control nearly every aspect of the file and meet their deadlines.

If you're a package designer, you'll find the following chapters most helpful as you read through this book:

- Chapter 3: *Objects, Groups, and Layers* (page 65)

- Chapter 4: *Advanced Vectors* (page 97)

- Chapter 5: *Brushes, Symbols, and Masks* (page 147)

- Chapter 7: *Typography* (page 231)

- Chapter 8: *3D and Other Live Effects* (page 261)

- Chapter 12: *Prepress and Printing* (page 445)

The Science of Design: Art and Print Production

Production artists are a separate breed (I would know—I'm one of them); to them, everything in a file matters. Illustrator allows production artists to dig deep into graphics files and make the edits and changes that are necessary to print a file correctly. Whether for producing or using spot colors, using overprint commands, using transparency flattening, or generally cleaning up paths and shapes, production artists have come to rely on

Illustrator. Because they can use it to open and edit EPS and PDF files (and many other file formats), Illustrator has become a utility that is a required tool for art production.

If you cringe at the thought of an RGB file with overprints, transparencies, and spot colors, then you're certainly a production artist. You might not care much about how to create nice brush strokes, but you care about simplifying paths so that they print faster.

If you're a production artist, you'll find the following chapters most helpful as you read through this book:

- Chapter 3: *Objects, Groups, and Layers* (page 65)

- Chapter 5: *Brushes, Symbols, and Masks* (page 147)

- Chapter 9: *Mixing It Up: Working with Vectors and Pixels* (page 333)

- Chapter 11: *Web and Mobile Design* (page 413)

- Chapter 12: *Prepress and Printing* (page 445)

- Chapter 13: *Saving and Exporting Files* (page 479)

- Appendix A: *Automation with Illustrator* (page 521)

Frame by Frame: Motion Graphics

In an industry where the term *indie* doesn't refer to InDesign, the art of producing movies and motion graphics lives by its own set of rules. And although that is certainly true, Illustrator still plays a huge part in generating graphics that can help jazz up a corporate promotional video or create an intricate opening or credits sequence for a big-budget film.

Illustrator's artwork may be vector, but that allows for more options when used in a pixel-based video workflow. Used in tandem with applications such as Adobe After Effects, Adobe Premiere, Apple Final Cut Pro, or even Apple iMovie, Illustrator adds an entire dimension to the motion graphics workflow.

If you're into motion graphics or video production, you'll find the following chapters most helpful as you read through this book:

- Chapter 3: *Objects, Groups, and Layers* (page 65)

- Chapter 5: *Brushes, Symbols, and Masks* (page 147)

The Melting Pot of Design: Creativity for Everyone

If you didn't identify with any of the titles I've listed so far, that's okay. In fact, it's nearly impossible to list all the kinds of people who use Illustrator every day. Because Illustrator has so many uses, the people who use it are very diverse. They may include doctors, lawyers, architects, signage and environmental designers, video and film specialists, or even a restaurant owner who is designing a menu cover.

Just realize that Illustrator is for everyone who wants to express their creativity, and that makes for one big happy family!

Where Did Illustrator Come From?

Our past is what helps define our future. Whether you're new to Illustrator or a veteran who has been using it for years, it helps to better understand the history behind a product that helped redefine the graphics industry.

In the 1980s, during a time when the personal computer was beginning to take the world by storm, Apple Computer introduced the Macintosh with an "affordable" laser printer called the Apple LaserWriter. What made the LaserWriter so remarkable wasn't so much the price (about $7,000 at that time) as the technology that was hidden inside it—Adobe PostScript, a computer language that enabled the LaserWriter to print beautiful graphics.

John Warnock, one of the founders of Adobe Systems, invented PostScript and was trying to find a way to make more money selling it. Although PostScript was cool, graphics still had to be created by entering line after line of computer code. John needed a way to have people create PostScript files visually, and that's how Illustrator was born. In early 1987, using the Bézier curve as the basis for vector graphics, Adobe introduced Illustrator 1.1 with much success. Now, nearly 20 years later, Illustrator continues to thrive and help those in the design community innovate.

WHEN SHOULD YOU USE ILLUSTRATOR?

Good designers have many tools at their disposal. Especially in an environment where most designers have other powerful graphics applications, it can be difficult to choose which one to use for a particular task. For example, a designer can apply soft drop shadows in Photoshop, Illustrator, and InDesign—is one application any better than the other for this?

How does one know when to use Illustrator? To answer the question directly, use Illustrator when it's the right tool for the job.

In reality, using the right tool for the job is what this book is all about. When you understand the strengths (and weaknesses) of each program, you also understand when it's best to use (or not to use) a particular application. As would be expected, every design or production task you are called upon to do will require a different technique, method, or feature. When you are comfortable with Illustrator, you'll easily be able to look at any project and know how to go about implementing it.

WHAT'S NEW IN ADOBE ILLUSTRATOR CS3?

Every time Adobe ships a new version of Illustrator, users get that mixed emotion of yearning for new cool and timesaving features while simultaneously worrying about what Adobe has changed about their favorite graphics program. Illustrator CS3 certainly doesn't disappoint in either department, especially considering how Adobe has given Illustrator (and all the Adobe Creative Suite apps, for that matter) a much-needed face-lift in the form of a new user interface.

Overall, you'll find that Adobe has made many changes throughout, and therefore, I cover all the new CS3 features in the context of the book. That way, you can read the book, learn the techniques, and use the knowledge that you've learned to quickly master Illustrator CS3. However, if you're looking for a head start on learning about the new big features in CS3, here's a list that will serve that purpose well and that will point you to where you will find more detailed information in the book:

- **New user interface.** Illustrator CS3 features a new sleek user interface, with dockable panels that are easy to organize and control. Read about the new user interface in Chapter 1, *The Illustrator Environment.*

- **Live Color.** Illustrator CS3 features many new improvements in working with color, including a powerful new feature called Live Color. Read about the new Live Color feature in Chapter 6, *Working with Color,* and in the 16-page color insert.

- **Flash integration.** Illustrator CS3 and Flash CS3 Professional work extremely well together, considering they both now share the same underlying graphics engine. Learn how you can use Illustrator and Flash together in Chapter 11, *Web and Mobile Design.*

- **Eraser tool.** Illustrator CS3 features an all-new vector Eraser tool that allows you to easily erase portions of your artwork. The tool is even pressure-sensitive. Learn how to erase artwork intuitively in Chapter 4, *Advanced Vectors.*

- **New document profiles.** Illustrator CS3 features a whole new way to quickly create new documents. Efficient document profiles make it easy to maintain a variety of often-used settings. Learn more about new document profiles in Chapter 1, *The Illustrator Environment.*

- **Crop Area tool.** Illustrator CS3 features an all-new Crop Area tool, which makes it easy to quickly define and control crop areas in your file. Learn more about the Crop Area tool in Chapter 1, *The Illustrator Environment.*

- **Isolation Mode feature.** Illustrator CS3 features an all-new way to intuitively edit both groups and symbols. Now, everything is a quick double-click away from a quick modification. Learn about the new Group Isolation Mode feature in Chapter 4, *Advanced Vectors,* and in Chapter 5, *Brushes, Symbols, and Masks.*

HOW THIS BOOK IS ORGANIZED

Unlike most other books on Illustrator, this text isn't formatted to systematically cover each menu, tool, panel, and feature. Rather, it is organized based on my years of personal experience teaching Illustrator. I cover concepts such as appearances and groups long before I discuss text or brushes.

Loading and saving libraries comes before discussions about fills or strokes. In this way, you'll understand the important aspects behind the features before you actually use them. The way I see it, it's like taking a class on skydiving—you spend a few hours on the ground learning all about the physics of the jump, and then you get on the plane. Once you've already jumped, it's a bit too late to start learning.

Featured Matchup sidebars contain a set of boxing gloves.

Most chapters in this book contain a "Featured Matchup" sidebar that discusses conceptual or physical differences between Illustrator's features and technologies. These are meant to give you a deeper understanding of the tools you have at hand, and they will assist you in choosing the right tools for the right tasks. Tips and notes appear throughout the book as well and offer bite-sized nuggets of information and resources where appropriate. When keyboard shortcuts are included for Illustrator commands, I've listed the Macintosh shortcut first, followed by the Windows shortcut in parentheses.

Tips are called out in the margin with an arrow.

Notes appear in the margin with a note-paper icon.

You'll also find two appendixes at the end of this book covering automation and application preferences. The appendix on automation will give you guidance on how you can begin using actions and scripts to have Illustrator handle more of your work while you find more important things to do. The appendix on application preferences is a great reference in case you ever need to know what a particular preference setting is. During the time of this writing, Adobe made the announcement that they were discontinuing the development of FreeHand. For those in need of a guide for switching to Illustrator from Freehand, you'll find a useful third appendix available on the book's registration page at www.peachpit.com/rwillcs3. It shows feature-by-feature comparisons between FreeHand and Illustrator, discusses differences in terminology between the two, and offers general advice on making the switch. Also on the book's registration page you'll find a link to additional materials and updates.

Overall, this book serves as a great resource no matter what your experience level is with Illustrator. My hope is that you learn something about Illustrator that you never knew before. So read on, and enjoy!

CHAPTER ONE

The Illustrator Environment

Adobe Illustrator, like most other Adobe applications, contains many tools, panels, windows, menus, and commands that enable you to get your work done. Adobe calls this environment your *workspace*, and you can think of it as being similar to the surface of your desk.

At any time, you can open individual documents in your workspace and work on them. Illustrator documents are separate entities, and although you can open multiple files at once, you can't work on those files as if they were in one document together. That's okay, though, because you can easily bring Illustrator files into Adobe InDesign, QuarkXPress, Adobe Photoshop, Adobe Flash, Adobe Dreamweaver, Adobe Premiere, Adobe After Effects, and other programs if your project requires it. Before you learn how to put actual content into your Illustrator documents, you'll explore the Illustrator environment in this chapter.

EXPLORING THE WELCOME SCREEN

Upon launching Adobe Illustrator CS3, you are greeted with the Welcome Screen (**Figure 1.1**) that offers several options. You can either choose to open files you've recently worked on or choose to quickly create new documents by clicking a variety of new document profiles that are already set up for certain workflows (more on document profiles in just a bit). At the bottom of the Welcome Screen, you'll find the Getting Started, New Features, and Resources links—all of which will direct you to respective parts of Illustrator's Help system. The bottom-right corner of the Welcome screen is dynamic, and if you're connected to the Web, the content will vary.

Figure 1.1 The Adobe Illustrator CS3 Welcome Screen gives you several options for exploring this new environment, including creating new documents and learning about new features.

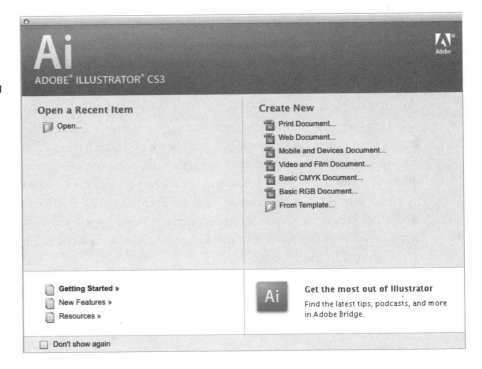

You can also open templates from the Welcome Screen. Templates are covered in detail later in the chapter.

Checking the Don't Show Again check box in the lower-left corner keeps the Welcome Screen from popping up every time you open Illustrator. You can always access the Welcome screen from the Help menu.

CREATING NEW DOCUMENTS

You can create a new document by clicking any of the new document profiles that appear in the Create New section of the Welcome Screen. A *new document profile* stores several important document attributes, including page size, orientation, measurement units, color mode, raster effects, and preview mode, making it easy to get started working on a new document for a specific workflow with one click of the mouse. New document profiles can also contain specific swatches, brushes, symbols, and graphic styles.

In addition to basic CMYK and RGB profiles, Illustrator features four new document profiles:

- **Print.** The Print profile is optimized for quickly creating artwork that will be used for print purposes. The Color Mode option is set to CMYK, and the Raster Effects option is set to 300 ppi.

- **Web.** The Web profile, optimized for Web graphics, has Color Mode set to RGB, Raster Effects set to 72 ppi, and Units set to pixels.

- **Mobile and Devices.** The Mobile and Devices profile is optimized for developing content that will appear on cell phones and handheld devices. Color Mode is set to RGB, Raster Effects is set to 72 ppi, and Units are set to pixels.

- **Video and Film.** The Video and Film profile, used for creating documents that will be used in video and film applications, includes an additional option to set Illustrator's transparency grid. This makes it easier to preview the alpha settings. This profile sets Color Mode to RGB, Raster Effects to 72 ppi, and Units to pixels.

When you click a new document profile, Illustrator will present you with the New Document dialog (**Figure 1.2** on the following page). You can also create a new document and get to the New Document dialog without using the Welcome Screen at all, simply by choosing File > New or by using the keyboard shortcut Command-N (Control-N). Clicking the arrow button next to Advanced will reveal all the options you can set as you create your new document. Although choosing a new document profile will automatically adjust some of these settings as necessary, you can always change them to suit your particular needs.

Hold the Option (Alt) key when choosing a new document profile to quickly create a new file, skipping the New Document dialog altogether. Alternatively, press Command-Option-N (Control-Alt-N) to quickly create a new document based on the same settings as the last document created.

Although you can adjust any of the settings you find in the New Document dialog even after you've already created a document, it's always better to get them right before you get started. Here's an overview of what each setting means:

- **Name.** The Name field simply lets you name your file before you even create it. Note that this setting doesn't actually save your file yet but merely saves you one step later.

- **New Document Profile.** The New Document Profile pop-up menu allows you to choose from a variety of preset profiles. Choosing a setting can serve as a starting point to adjust other settings in the New Document dialog.

- **Size.** The Size pop-up menu is populated with standard sizes that are appropriate for the chosen new document profile.

- **Width, Height, and Orientation.** The Width and Height settings allow you to customize the size of the document's artboard. You can also choose between portrait (tall) and landscape (wide) orientations.

- **Units.** The Units setting determines the default general measurement system used in the document. You can choose to use points, picas, inches, millimeters, centimeters, or pixels.

- **Color Mode.** Illustrator supports two color modes: CMYK, which is used for artwork that will appear on the printed page, and RGB, which is used for artwork that is destined to be displayed on a TV or computer screen. Refer to the "Featured Matchup: CMYK vs. RGB" sidebar later in this chapter for important information on the differences between these two color modes.

- **Raster Effects.** The Raster Effects setting controls the resolution used when applying special effects such as soft Drop Shadows, Glows, and Photoshop filters (such as Gaussian Blur). Although you can change this setting within your document at any time, it's important to understand the consequences of doing so. For detailed information about the Raster Effects setting, refer to the "Massaging Pixels in Illustrator" section and the "Featured Matchup: Illustrator Effects vs. Photoshop Effects" sidebar, both in Chapter 8, *3D and Other Live Effects*.

- **Transparency Grid.** The Transparency Grid setting is available only when you choose the Video and Film new document profile. The grid is a checkerboard pattern that appears on your artboard to help you better identify the Opacity values of objects in your document. This makes it easier to understand how artwork in Illustrator will composite with other art or video content later in your workflow. Refer to "Setting Up Your Document" later in this chapter for more information.

- **Preview Mode.** The Preview Mode setting allows you to specify the initial preview setting that Illustrator uses when the new document is created. You can leave it set to Default (which is Illustrator's normal preview setting), Pixel (for better representation of Web and video graphics), or Overprint (for better representation of print graphics and spot colors).

The New Document dialog also has a Templates button. Clicking this button will direct you to a folder containing all the prebuilt templates that come with Illustrator. For more information on templates, refer to "Creating and Using Templates" later in this chapter.

The New Document dialog is sticky, which means it remembers the last settings you used. So if you create an RGB file to create a Web graphic, the next time you create a new document, the dialog is set to RGB.

Creating Your Own New Document Profiles

Illustrator's six profiles are quite generic, and you may find it useful to create your own new document profiles to suit your own needs. The good news is that it's easy to do—just follow these steps:

1. Create a document using an existing new document profile. If you want your profile to include the transparency grid setting, make sure you start with the Video and Film profile.

Featured Matchup: CMYK vs. RGB

CMYK stands for *cyan, magenta, yellow, and black* (black is called K because some printers refer to the black plate as the *key plate*). Mixing these colors creates a gamut (range) of colors. It's easier to think of colors in CMYK because the mode seems to follow the rules that we all learned in preschool. Mixing cyan and magenta (blue and red) makes purple, mixing yellow and magenta makes orange, and so on. Today's printing presses use the four CMYK inks to produce printed material in color. For jobs you want physically printed, you should choose the CMYK color mode.

RGB stands for *red, green, and blue* and is used to display color on TV screens, computer monitors, and other electronic devices such as digital cameras. Unlike CMYK where you start out with a white sheet of paper and then add colors to get to black, RGB works in reverse. For instance, when your TV screen is off, it's dark, and when you turn it on and add red, green, and blue, the cumulative effect is white. The RGB color mode has a significantly larger gamut of colors than CMYK does, especially in the area of bright fluorescent colors. For jobs you want displayed on the Web or video, RGB is the color mode you should choose.

When creating a new document in Illustrator, you can choose between the two color modes in the New Document dialog. Illustrator conveniently indicates the document's color mode in the Document title bar. Since version 9, the artboard in all Illustrator documents is restricted to the use of only one color mode (previous versions allowed both CMYK and RGB elements to appear on the same artboard). For example, if you copy and paste an object from an RGB document into a CMYK document, Illustrator will convert the object to CMYK as soon as you paste it onto the artboard.

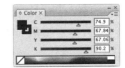

In contrast, panels in Illustrator (Swatches, Color, Symbols, Brushes, Styles, and so on) can contain both CMYK and RGB content. Content from a new document profile is copied into each new file you create, so if you create a new Web document, your Swatches panel will be filled with RGB colors. Although you can switch color modes at any time by choosing File > Document Color Mode, it's important to realize you're changing the color mode only of the document artboard—not the content that already exists in your Swatches or Symbols panels.

Figure 1.3 Odd CMYK breakdowns are almost always the result of an RGB conversion.

In a real-world workflow, it's possible that you may create an RGB document but convert the document to CMYK at a later point in time. If that happens, each time you apply a swatch color from your Swatch panel (which still contains RGB colors), Illustrator will be converting that RGB swatch to CMYK. If you ever see CMYK percentages with odd decimal values instead of whole numbers (**Figure 1.3**), there's a good chance that your document either is set to RGB or started out as RGB and was converted to CMYK. Remember that each time you make a color conversion, color shifts can occur.

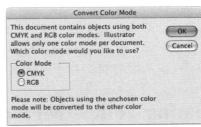

When opening Macromedia FreeHand files or older Illustrator files, you might see a dialog telling you the file contains mixed color spaces (**Figure 1.4**), and you can choose what color mode to convert to when opening the file.

Figure 1.4 Illustrator alerts you when opening a file that contains mixed color spaces and asks you to choose the color mode to which you want to convert the file.

2. Once the new file is open, adjust your document settings to match your desired profile. For example, use the View menu to choose the Preview setting, choose Effect > Document Raster Effects Settings to adjust the Raster Effects value, and choose File > Document Setup to adjust your artboard size.

3. Add any desired content to the Swatches, Brushes, Symbols, or Graphic Styles panels. You can also remove content that you don't want or need from these panels.

4. Choose File > Save, choose Format > Adobe Illustrator Document, and save the file in the following location on your computer:
Mac: *Username/Library/Application Support/Adobe/Adobe Illustrator CS3/ New Document Profiles*
Windows: *C:\Documents and Settings\Username\Application Data\Adobe\ Adobe Illustrator CS3 Settings\New Document Profiles*

New document profiles are cross-platform compatible and can easily be distributed amongst an entire design group or company.

Setting Up Your Document

There was a time when the Document Setup dialog was accessed quite frequently, but since a lot of the page and printing settings have been moved to the Print dialog, you don't have to go to Document Setup nearly as often. That being said, it's still helpful to know what options you have when you create a new document. The Document Setup dialog has three panels, which you can access by choosing File > Document Setup:

• **The Artboard panel.** This panel allows you to change some of the settings you saw in the New Document dialog, such as artboard size and orientation (**Figure 1.5** on the following page). Additionally, there's a setting for how raster-based images appear when you're in the Outline mode. By default, images appear only as empty boxes in Outline mode for performance reasons, but with the Show Images in Outline Mode option activated, raster images are visible (in black and white) in Outline mode.

Figure 1.5 The Artboard panel in the Document Setup dialog lets you specify the physical dimensions of your artboard.

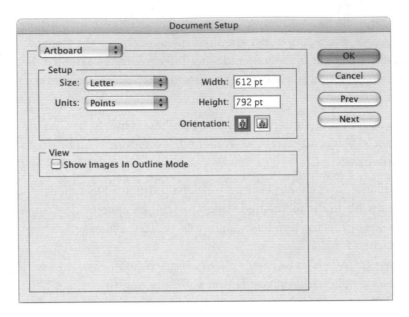

• **The Type panel.** This panel contains several important settings for how text is used in Illustrator (**Figure 1.6**). You can choose to have Illustrator highlight substituted fonts or glyphs, which can be helpful when opening files that other designers created. With these options activated, Illustrator highlights missing fonts in pink and missing glyphs in yellow so that you can quickly find where these problem areas are in a file.

Figure 1.6 The Type panel in the Document Setup dialog is where you can specify how legacy text is exported when saving to legacy Illustrator and legacy EPS formats.

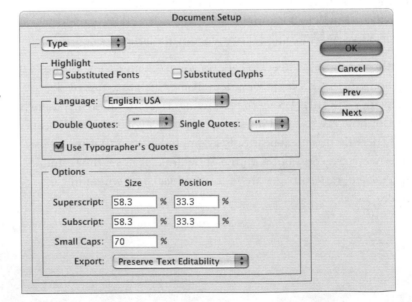

Additionally, you can specify the language for the file and how double and single quote marks should appear when you type them in your document. There's also an option to use typographer quotes, which means the correct curly quotes are automatically used instead of straight marks. Illustrator also allows you to define the size and position percentages for creating superscript, subscript, and small-cap characters. However, if you're using OpenType fonts, you can take advantage of the built-in support for these specific features, which we'll cover extensively in Chapter 7, *Typography*.

The final option in the Type panel is for specifying how text is exported when you are saving to legacy file formats (any version prior to Illustrator CS). When you choose the Preserve Text Editability option, text is broken up into individual type objects. When you choose the Preserve Text Appearance option, all type objects are converted to vector outlines.

- **The Transparency panel.** This panel (**Figure 1.7**) allows you to specify settings for Illustrator's transparency grid (which you can turn on by choosing View > Show Transparency Grid). Similar to the transparency grid found in Photoshop, this checkerboard pattern makes it easy to identify transparent areas in a file. If your file is going to be printed on colored paper, you can also have Illustrator simulate that color onscreen by using the Simulate Colored Paper option.

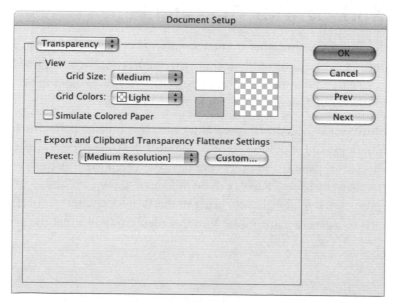

Figure 1.7 The Transparency panel in the Document Setup dialog allows you to specify a paper color to simulate what your file might look like on colored paper.

In Chapter 12, *Prepress and Printing*, you'll learn more about transparency and how it prints. For now, it's important to know that a process called *transparency flattening* has to occur to correctly process artwork with transparency in it. This flattening process has many different options, all controlled by choosing from several different presets. Specifying a preset in the Export and Clipboard Transparency Flattener Settings area sets a default preset for your document that you use when copying art with transparency to the clipboard or when exporting files to formats that don't support transparency.

LIVING IN YOUR WORKSPACE

Whether you use Illustrator an hour a week, an hour a day, or all day long, you have to feel comfortable using it. Adobe applications in general are customizable to the point that you can really arrange your work space to address your particular needs. To know what works for you, get to know the various menus and tools well and learn how to best utilize them for your particular workflow or project. We'll offer some suggestions in this book where a customized workspace can improve workflow. In addition, Appendix B, *Application Preferences*, lists all of Illustrator's preferences in one handy place.

Working with Tools and Panels

Illustrator CS3 introduces a new user interface that is similar to that found in the CS3 versions of Photoshop, InDesign, and Flash (**Figure 1.8**). You can easily configure the interface to your liking, and moving between Illustrator and other CS3 applications is a lot easier.

Illustrator is loaded with tools and panels. Each panel performs specific functions, and you'll use some of them all the time (such as the Color and Layers panels) and others not nearly as often (such as the SVG Interactivity panel). Panels can be hidden or shown as needed, and all appear listed in alphabetical order in the Window menu. A check mark next to a panel's name in the Window menu indicates that the panel is open on your screen.

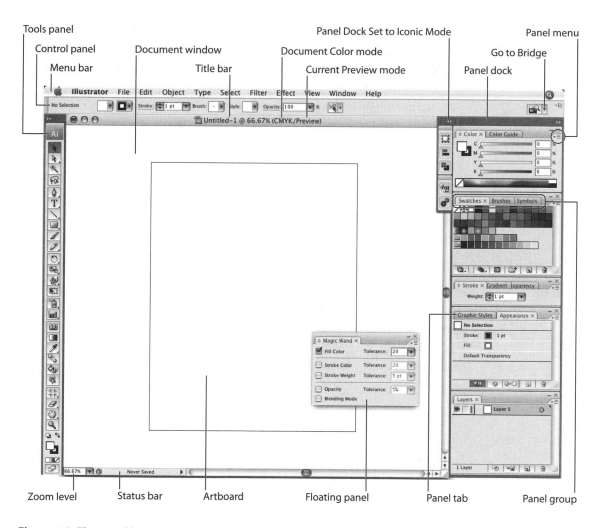

Figure 1.8 The panel-based user interface in Illustrator is similar to what you'll find in InDesign CS3 and Flash CS3.

Adobe calls these panels *floating panels* because they sit above your Illustrator artboard and are always accessible. At the same time, because these panels float above your workspace, they can get in the way of your ability to see and work with your design. Depending on the size and resolution of your screen, organizing the panels is important so that you can work efficiently.

Everything you see here about panels applies not just to Illustrator but to Photoshop CS3, InDesign CS3, and Flash CS3 Professional as well. With the exception of some small nuances, the functionality is consistent across these applications.

You can reposition a panel by clicking and dragging its tab (where the name of the panel appears) or the blank area that appears directly above the tab. You can group several panels by dragging one panel into the tab part of another one (**Figure 1.9**). You can also attach a panel to the bottom of another by dragging it onto the lower section of the other panel (**Figure 1.10**). Some of Illustrator's panels have multiple states or views to allow you to use them in different ways. For example, the Transparency panel contains a state that shows just the Blend Mode pop-up menu and the Opacity slider. Clicking the little up and down arrows that appear to the left of the panel name toggles these different states. Alternatively, you can double-click a panel's tab to toggle between states.

Figure 1.9 Dragging the Swatches panel to the Brushes panel creates a panel group. You'll notice the tab area of the panel highlights as you drag another panel to form the group.

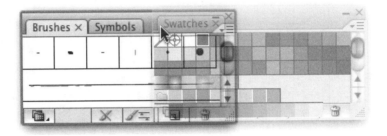

Figure 1.10 Dragging the Swatches panel toward the bottom of the Symbols panel docks the two panels. Notice that a highlight appears only at the base of the Symbols panel.

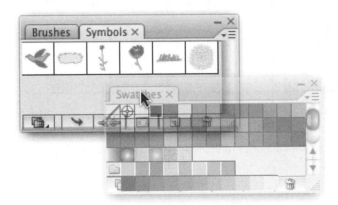

The problem with floating panels, though, is that they can often get hidden behind other panels, and constantly opening and closing these panels makes it hard to find what you need quickly. To address this problem, Illustrator CS3 allows you to organize your floating panels within docks. You can also adjust these panel docks in a variety of ways to maximize the work area on your screen, while still keeping all your panels readily accessible.

You create a new panel dock by dragging any palette toward the left or right edge of your screen. As you approach the screen edge, a blue bar appears, indicating the ability to create the panel dock (**Figure 1.11**). Release the mouse, and the panel expands to fill up the entire dock (**Figure 1.12**). You can collapse the entire dock by clicking the double arrows that appear in the upper-right corner of the panel dock, and you can drag the left edge of the dock to adjust the width of the collapsed dock (**Figure 1.13**). You can even adjust the dock so only the panel's icon appears. When a dock is collapsed, you can still open an individual panel by simply clicking its icon (**Figure 1.14**). You can add panels to an existing dock simply by dragging and drop-ping them in between existing panels within the panel dock (dragging a panel directly into another panel will create a panel group within the dock).

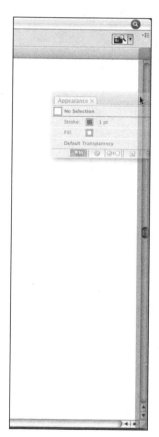

Figure 1.11 A shaded bar indicates you're about to create a new panel dock.

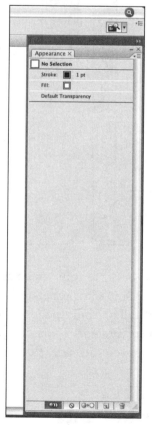

Figure 1.12 Panels expand to fill the entire dock.

Figure 1.13 If there's enough room, Illustrator will display the name of the panel when the dock is collapsed.

Figure 1.14 Clicking any panel icon in a collapsed dock will reveal that entire panel.

The Tools panel can also live within a panel dock, along the left side of the screen. Clicking the double arrows at the top of the dock toggles the Tools panel from a one-column layout to a two-column one (**Figure 1.15**).

Figure 1.15 Illustrator's Tools panel can be displayed as a single column, saving valuable screen space (left), or as the traditional two-column layout.

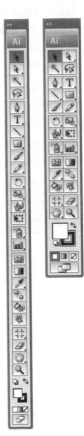

Pressing the Tab key on your keyboard will instantly hide all your panels and docks. Pressing Shift-Tab will hide all panels with the exception of the Tools and Control panels.

You can add as many panel docks to your screen as you like (you can add new docks to existing ones), and some panel docks can be fully expanded while others are collapsed and in iconic mode. By arranging the panels you use most on your screen into docks, you can set up a work area you're comfortable with and where you can easily find the functions or settings you need.

Using the Control Panel

The Control panel is a context-sensitive bar containing often-used settings from different panels. Unlike Photoshop's Tool Options bar, which is tool-centric, the Control panel in Illustrator is selection-centric, meaning it changes based on what objects are selected. Also, with the Control panel open on your screen, you can keep more panels closed to free up more screen real estate. This is possible because of some cool features you'll find on the Control panel. For example, you can dock the Control panel to the top or the bottom of your screen, or you can have it float, just like any other panel. You can also control what is displayed in the Control panel by choosing options from the Control panel menu (**Figure 1.16**).

Figure 1.16 You can choose what information is displayed in the Control panel.

At the far left of the Control panel, you'll see notification of what your targeted selection is (**Figure 1.17** on the following page). Additionally, you'll notice that some items are pop-up menus or text fields, and some labels are shown as underlined blue text. The blue underlines indicate links, and clicking them opens their respective panels. For example, if you don't have enough room in the Control panel to display all the options for resizing or position your selected artwork, Illustrator simply displays the word *Transform* in the Control panel (with a blue line under it). Clicking Transform will cause the Transform panel to temporarily appear (**Figure 1.18** on the following page). This behavior alleviates the need for you to have many panels open at once.

Figure 1.17 The active targeted selection is highlighted in the Control panel, acting as a reminder when you are applying certain effects and masks.

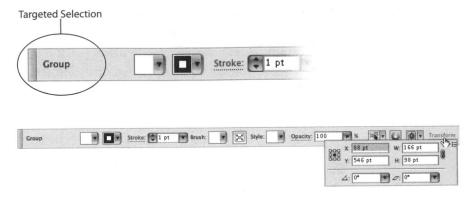

Figure 1.18 Accessing the full Transform panel from the Control panel means you can open it when you need it and it doesn't take up valuable screen space.

➡ Clicking the Fill or Stroke icon in the Control panel will open the Swatches panel, and Shift-clicking either icon will open the Color panel.

The Control panel not only saves screen real estate by relieving the need to keep certain panels open all the time but it also helps reduce keystrokes and mouse clicks by making certain menu items accessible. For example, when you select a raster-based image in Illustrator, you can apply a Live Trace preset directly from the Control panel instead of digging into the Object menu.

Setting Up Custom Workspaces

As we explored in the introduction, many different kinds of Illustrator users exist. Depending on the kind of work you do, you may need to access certain tools or panels more often than others. Experienced users carefully arrange the panels on their screen so they have access to the features they use most often. Many designers perform a variety of tasks on a daily basis and use a wide range of features. This means they are constantly opening and closing numerous panels and arranging them on the screen, which often leads to confusion or loss of productivity because they are trying to find where a particular panel is. Although big monitors may help users keep more panels open, it also takes users longer to scan such screens to find the right panel. If only there was a way to manage all these panels.

📄 Workspaces are saved in the Adobe Illustrator CS3 Settings folder in your user Preferences folder.

Thankfully, there is—workspaces. As mentioned earlier, the setup of your screen, which includes a listing of which docks and panels are open and their locations on your screen, is what Adobe calls your *workspace*. Illustrator allows you to save a workspace and then return to it at any time by choosing Window > Workspace and then choosing the name of the saved workspace. For example, you may arrange your screen to your liking for general use.

You would then choose Window > Workspace > Save Workspace to name and create a new workspace (I call my generic workspace My Happy Place). You could create additional workspaces for other kinds of tasks as well. Each time you need to perform a different task, just switch to the workspace you've already defined, and the panels that you need will appear just as you've specified (**Figure 1.19**).

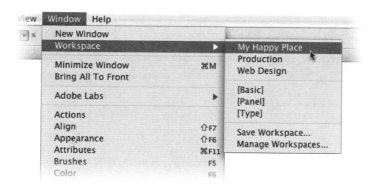

Figure 1.19 Choosing between several saved workspaces. Even having just one or two saved workspaces can save you a tremendous amount of time, especially if you're working in an environment where you share your computer with others.

Using Keyboard Shortcuts

Ever have someone ask you for a phone number and you can't remember it? Do you walk over to a phone and watch as your fingers automatically press the number sequence to remember what it is? The same phenomenon happens to many computer users whose fingers seem to know what to press without much thought. Although the mouse was a nice invention, you can get things done a lot faster by pressing the keys on your keyboard.

One of the benefits of using Adobe products is that many of them share similar keyboard shortcuts, so you have fewer shortcuts to remember. However, as you can imagine, Illustrator contains tons of commands and tools, and it's impossible to assign keyboard shortcuts to all of them. So, Adobe assigns keyboard shortcuts to the commands they believe most people will use most often. As an individual user, however, you know what commands you use most often, so it's comforting to know that you don't have to live by what Adobe considers an often-used feature. That's because you can customize your keyboard shortcuts and tailor them to the needs of your fingers.

For example, if you're a FreeHand convert, you might want to use the R key to choose the Rectangle tool. Illustrator uses the M key for that tool, but you can choose Edit > Keyboard Shortcuts to assign your own keyboard

Illustrator keyboard shortcut sets are stored in the Adobe Illustrator CS3/ Presets/Keyboard Shortcuts folder.

shortcut for that tool (or any menu command for that matter). If you try to assign a keyboard shortcut that's already taken by another feature, Illustrator conveniently alerts you to the fact, asking whether you're sure you want to give up the other keyboard shortcut (**Figure 1.20**). You can save different sets of shortcuts if you'd like, which can be helpful if you share your computer with other users.

Figure 1.20 Illustrator alerts you if you try to reassign an already-used keyboard shortcut, keeping you from accidentally overwriting other keyboard shortcuts.

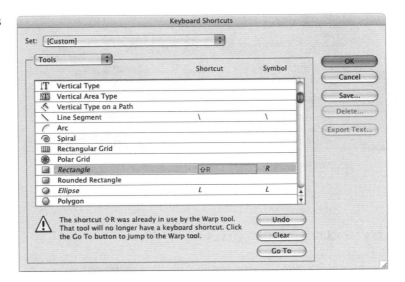

Viewing Documents

As you're working in Illustrator, you can choose to view your artwork in different ways, each offering different benefits. The most common view mode, Preview mode, allows you to create and edit art while seeing a close representation of what your art will look like when printed (**Figure 1.21**). In Outline mode, Illustrator hides all the pretty colors and shows you just the geometry of the shapes in your document. Although it may be difficult to visualize what your file is going to look like when printed, Outline mode gives you the ability to easily see whether shapes are aligned correctly, and it gives you a better idea of the structure of the file (**Figure 1.22**). Think of Outline mode as an X-ray film that a doctor reads. Although just black and white, an X ray reveals what's going on behind the scenes. Just like a doctor reads an X ray, an experienced Illustrator user can sometimes get a better idea of how an Illustrator file is constructed when in Outline mode. You can toggle between Preview and Outline modes by pressing Command-Y (Control-Y).

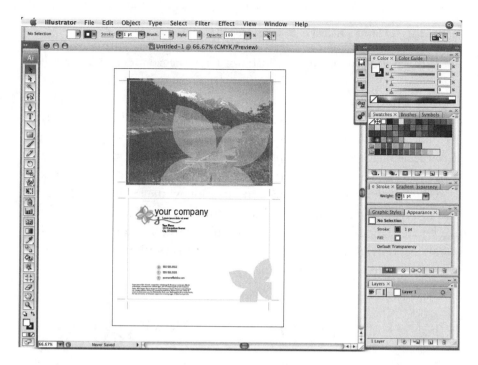

Figure 1.21 When viewing artwork in Preview mode, you can get a really good idea of what your file will look like when printed.

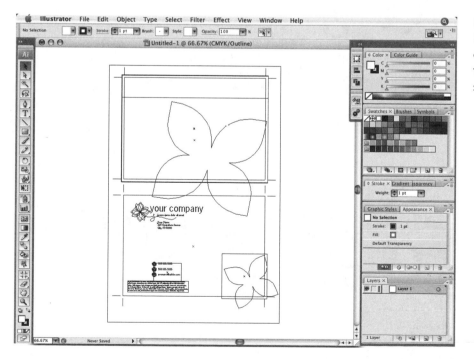

Figure 1.22 Viewing a file in Outline mode can make it easier to select objects and to identify the underlying structure of a file.

Using Overprint Preview

For those in the print business, Illustrator has a special preview mode called Overprint Preview, which you can access by choosing View > Overprint Preview. Overprinting is a process you use when creating color separations to control how certain colors interact with each other (we'll cover overprinting in detail in Chapter 12, *Prepress and Printing*). Because overprinting is an attribute applied only in the print process, designers traditionally struggle with proofing files that specify overprints. Illustrator's Overprint Preview mode simulates overprints so that you can see how they will print (**Figure 1.23**). In truth, Overprint Preview is far more accurate than Illustrator's regular Preview mode, especially when your file uses spot colors (more on that in Chapter 6, *Working with Color*). However, Overprint Preview is slower than normal Preview in redraw performance.

Figure 1.23 In the top example, the vector shape's fill is set to Overprint, as shown in the Appearance panel. In the lower example, with Overprint Preview turned on, you can see the effects of the overprint.

Not to leave Web designers out in the cold, Illustrator has yet another preview mode called Pixel Preview, which you can also access via the View menu. Illustrator, as a vector-based application, produces resolution-independent art. Most of today's printers have high-resolution settings, and modern imagesetters use resolutions upward of 2500 dots per inch (dpi). For that reason, print designers aren't worried about how good their artwork looks on their screen, because they know when output at high resolution, everything will be perfect. Web designers, however, care very much about how their artwork appears on a computer screen because that's exactly how people view their designs. Pixel Preview renders artwork to the screen as pixels and shows how antialiasing affects the art (**Figure 1.24**). We'll cover Pixel Preview and these Web-specific issues in Chapter 11, *Web and Mobile Design*.

Figure 1.24 In Pixel Preview mode, Illustrator displays artwork as it would display in a browser. Zooming in on your artwork reveals the actual pixels and the effects of antialiasing.

Using Rulers and Guides

Even though you can scale Illustrator artwork to virtually any size, it's still important to be able to create artwork using exact and precise measurements. Package designers and technical illustrators are always careful about creating artwork to scale, and even designers need to know what size a logo or an illustration has to be.

Choose View > Show Rulers to display vertical and horizontal rulers along the left and top edge of your document window. You can Control-click (right-click) a ruler to change its measurement system (**Figure 1.25** on the following page). Although the rulers can help identify the coordinates of objects that appear in a document, rulers also serve another function. You can click a ruler and drag a guide out onto your artboard. A *guide* is a line that's visible on your screen but not on your printed or exported art. Guides have

Guides in Illustrator are just vector objects. You can select any vector shape in Illustrator and choose View > Guides > Make Guides to turn that object into a guide.

"magnetic personalities," and objects that are moved or drawn near them stick to them, helping align objects and create consistent art and layouts.

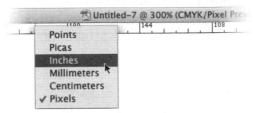

By default, once you drag out a guide, it is unlocked, and you can reposition it to your liking. You can even use the x and y coordinates in the Control panel to precisely position the guides. At any time, you can choose View > Guides > Lock Guides to prevent moving them by accident.

UNDERSTANDING BOUNDING AREAS

When setting up a new document, one of the settings available is the size of your artboard. Depending on the kind of project you're working on, the document height and width aren't that important. For the most part, Illustrator is used in two ways: to create art that is printed from Illustrator (such as a single-page advertisement) or for art that is placed into another application (such as a logo or masthead).

Every Illustrator file has several different regions, or *boxes,* that determine how the portions of a file are displayed (**Figure 1.26**):

- **Art box.** Also called the *bounding box*, this area is defined by the bounds of the combined art that appears in the document.

- **Trim box.** This area is defined by the Illustrator artboard and is the size you specify in the Document Setup dialog or when creating a new document.

- **Crop box.** This area is defined by using the Crop Area tool or the Object > Crop Area > Make command in Illustrator.

- **Bleed box.** This area is defined by the Bleed setting in the Save Adobe PDF dialog (when saving files as PDF), and it extends beyond the trim box area.

- **Media box.** This area is defined by the size of the paper on which you choose to print your document.

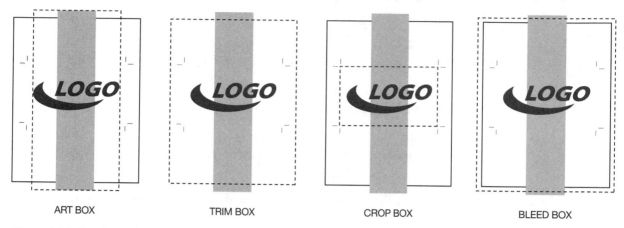

ART BOX   TRIM BOX   CROP BOX   BLEED BOX

Figure 1.26 The dotted line outlines the different boxes that are used to define the boundaries of a file.

By default, the art box setting is what is used when placing an Illustrator file into another application. However, some applications, including InDesign and Photoshop, give you the option to choose which box to use when placing the artwork (**Figure 1.27**).

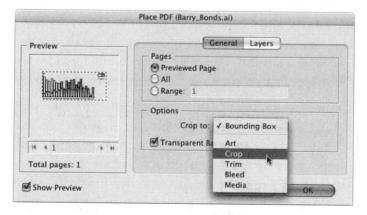

Figure 1.27 When using the Show Import Options setting in InDesign, you can choose a bounding area to use for an Illustrator file when you place it.

Defining a Crop Area

If you'd rather take control of the bounding area of your file (instead of leaving it up to the art box setting), you can define a crop area in the file. When a crop area is active in a file, it supercedes the art box and becomes the bounding area of the file. This makes it possible to specify exact sizes for files (which is useful in Web design and video applications) and also allows you to choose to export just a portion of a file without having to delete the rest of the artwork.

You can define a crop area in your file in three ways:

- With nothing selected, choose Object > Crop Area > Make. This action will define a crop area using the dimensions of your artboard.

- Using the Rectangle tool, draw a rectangle as the size and position of your desired crop area. With the rectangle selected, choose Object > Crop Area > Make.

- Using the Crop Area tool, click and drag to define a crop area.

Using the Crop Area Tool

At first glance, the Crop Area tool seems to be just a quick and dirty way to define crop areas. But there is really a lot of functionality built into the tool. For example, you can simply double-click the Crop Area tool (in the Tools panel) to open the Crop Area Options dialog (**Figure 1.28**). You can click the Preset pop-up menu to access a laundry list of print, video, mobile, and Web dimensions, or you can specify your own Width and Height settings. You can also enter x and y coordinates for the center point of the crop area. These coordinates match the rulers on your artboard. The dialog also contains several Display options, which are useful for video workflows. Once you've specified your settings for the crop area, click OK.

The Crop Area tool doesn't cut or remove any content from your file but rather indicates which parts of a file are visible when exported and viewed in other applications.

Whenever you select the Crop Area tool, the current crop area becomes highlighted on your screen, at which time you can also use the settings available in the Control panel to adjust your crop area. You can simply click a crop area and drag it to reposition it, and you can start dragging elsewhere on your screen to delete the first crop area and define a new one.

You can hold the Option (Alt) key while dragging with the Crop Area tool to create additional crop areas to your document. Each crop area can contain different settings, and you can delete specific crop areas by holding the Option (Alt) key and clicking the close box that appears for each crop area. Only one crop area can be active at any one time, though, and you can make a crop area active by holding the Option (Alt) key and clicking the desired crop area with the Crop Area tool. Alternatively, you can move between the crop areas by using the arrow keys on your keyboard. Maintaining multiple crop areas in a single file can be useful in Web and video workflows but less so in print workflows.

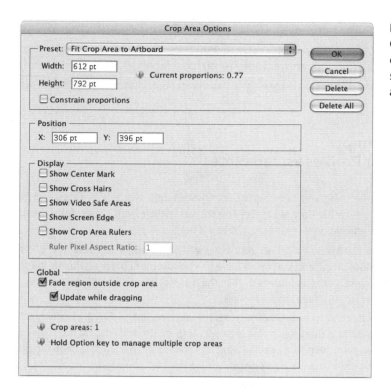

Figure 1.28 The Crop Area Options dialog gives you complete control over the size, position, and appearance of your crop areas.

CREATING AND USING TEMPLATES

For repetitive work, use templates, which allow you to set up a file with certain settings and attributes—even actual artwork and layers—to create more consistent files in less time. Illustrator templates are really just regular Illustrator files with one difference—you can't save them. You can only perform a Save As function with them (so you don't overwrite the template).

To create a template file, start by creating a new Illustrator document. Draw guides, add content, place artwork on the artboard, add layers, and adjust your document settings as you'd like them to appear in the template. When you're ready to save your template, choose File > Save As, and specify the Illustrator Template (AIT) format in the dialog. Template files contain a flag in them so that when they are reopened in Illustrator, they open as untitled documents.

Illustrator actually ships with hundreds of professionally designed templates, which you can access by choosing File > New from Template. Illustrator's templates are stored in the Adobe Illustrator CS3/Cool Extras/Templates folder. You can also browse the template files using Adobe Bridge so you

If you're a professional designer, you might not want to use any of Illustrator's prefab templates, but it's helpful to open the files and explore them to see how they were created. One of the best ways to learn is by reverse-engineering what someone else has done. One of the techniques you'll learn in this book is how to pick apart an Illustrator file; Illustrator's template files are perfect for this because they employ many different features and techniques.

can see previews of what the templates contain. Before you wrinkle your nose about using "clip art," you'll be happy to know that Illustrator also includes an entire folder of blank templates. These blank templates contain trim marks, and you can use them to create print- or Web-ready work.

 Featured Matchup: New Document Profiles vs. Templates

When you create a new Illustrator file, you'll notice that several swatches, symbols, brushes, and graphic styles are already present in the file. How did they get there? The answer is, they were copied from the file used to define the new document profile you chose when you created the file.

This means if you use certain swatches or symbols frequently, you can simply edit these new document profiles (or create your own custom ones), and you never have to load another library again. Although this is true, the more content you have in your new document profile, the more content you will have in every file you create, making for larger files (which also take longer to open).

Templates, on the other hand, can also contain content. Additionally, template files are really full Illustrator files that can contain paragraph and character styles, artwork on the artboard, crop marks, layers, and more—something new document profiles can't do. It may be more efficient to keep a small startup file but have a set of rich templates that you can open at any time to get a running start on your design work.

If you ever do edit your new document profiles (instead of creating your own new ones), be sure to first create and save a backup of the existing files (save it somewhere where you can find it and not accidentally delete it). This way, if you end up doing something crazy, you still have a way to return to the original default files. You can also simply delete a profile from its folder, and Illustrator will automatically generate a new one in its place.

ADDING METADATA TO YOUR FILES

If you go to a popular stock photo Web site, you can enter a keyword or a description of the kind of image you're looking for and instantly see a list of images that match your criteria. Have you ever wondered how this works? How does a search engine know what the contents of a photograph are? The answer is metadata.

Using Adobe Bridge CS3, you can even add metadata to a file without having to open the file. Simply highlight a file in Bridge, and choose File > File Info. You can add metadata to multiple files simultaneously by highlighting several files and then choosing File > File Info.

Metadata is information about a file, and it can be just about anything. The creation date, author, creation application, keywords, and copyright information are all examples of metadata. Adobe applications use an XML-based standard called Extensible Metadata Platform (XMP) to store this metadata inside files. The metadata resides in an XML header at the top of each file, and Adobe applications can read this data.

In Illustrator, you can choose File > File Info to open the File Info dialog, where you can enter a variety of metadata for your file (**Figure 1.29**). When you save the file, the metadata is embedded within the file.

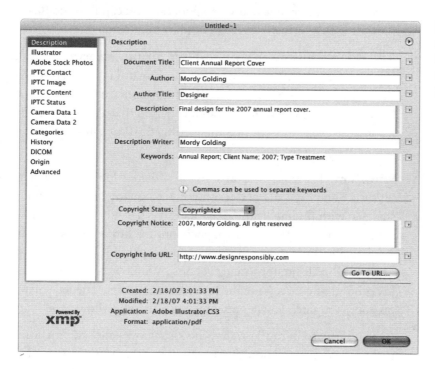

Figure 1.29 The File Info dialog in Illustrator stores keywords and other metadata using the XML-based XMP standard.

Adobe takes metadata a step further in Illustrator CS3, and certain information is already added to each file automatically. For example, each time you save your file, Illustrator adds a list of fonts, swatches, color groups, and color separation plates in the file's metadata for you.

FINDING HELP

Although Adobe's documentation usually leaves much to be desired, it does get better with each new version. You can launch the Adobe Help Viewer by choosing Help > Illustrator Help. The Adobe Help Viewer allows you to search across all Adobe applications (not just Illustrator), and it's easier to navigate than in previous versions.

Online you'll find some wonderful resources on Illustrator as well:

• **The Real World Illustrator Blog.** An up-to-date companion to this book, the Real World Illustrator Blog offers insights, tutorials, and interesting information about the use of Illustrator and other Adobe applications. Readers of the blog (and this book) are welcome to submit questions and participate via commenting on the blog. The blog also features a regularly updated video podcast. You can find the Real World Illustrator Blog at http://rwillustrator.blogspot.com.

- **The Adobe Illustrator User-to-User forum.** An extremely valuable resource, Adobe's own User-to-User forum is a great place to ask questions, get advice from other Illustrator users, and share your own knowledge. The forum has a search function that acts as a tremendous resource as well. You can find the forums for Illustrator (and all other Adobe applications) at www.adobeforums.com.

- **knowhow.** There's a division at Adobe called Adobe Labs, which works on future and experimental technology. Knowing how users often struggle with finding help, Adobe Labs has developed a new way to get contextual help within an application. Luckily for Illustrator users, Adobe Labs chose to test this new technology with Illustrator first. From within Illustrator, you can choose Window > Adobe Labs > knowhow. After accepting the terms of using experimental software on your computer, you're presented with the knowhow panel.

As you select tools in Illustrator, the knowhow panel automatically updates with information about how to use that tool (**Figure 1.30**). The three buttons that appear near the top of the panel allow you to search Adobe's Help and the Web for links and information about the tools, view keyboard shortcuts used with the selected tool, and view options for the selected tool (if available).

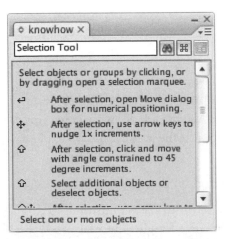

Figure 1.30 The knowhow panel displays context-sensitive help for every tool and feature in Illustrator.

CHAPTER TWO

Vectors 101

You've heard people describe Adobe Illustrator as a vector graphics application, but what does that really mean? How do graphics created using vectors behave differently than, say, graphics that are made using Adobe Photoshop? When does it make sense to use Illustrator to perform a task instead of another program such as Photoshop? Answers to these questions will become apparent in this chapter. More importantly, you'll learn how to create vector graphics and understand their attributes.

In addition to learning how to draw basic shapes using a variety of drawing tools, this chapter will also introduce you to the different types of fill and stroke attributes you can apply to objects. You'll learn how to create two kinds of type objects (called *point text* and *area text*) as well. To round out your introduction to the world of vector graphics, the chapter concludes with a task you'll be doing quite often in Illustrator—selecting objects. Are you ready?

WHAT ARE VECTOR GRAPHICS?

What would the world be like if we didn't have both vanilla and chocolate ice cream? We'd probably all be a few inches smaller around the waist, right? Seriously though, just as there are two main flavors of ice cream, there are two main flavors of computer graphics. One is *pixel-based* (these graphics are also referred to as *rasters* or *bitmaps*), and the other is *vector-based* (also referred to as *object-based*). Pixel-based graphics and vector-based graphics are different conceptually, and each has its own strengths and weaknesses. For example, Photoshop is primarily geared to working with pixel-based images and is great for photographic content. Illustrator, on the other hand, is primarily a vector-based drawing application and excels in creating illustrations.

In addition, just like a vanilla-and-chocolate-swirl ice cream cone, an image can contain a mixture of both pixel- and vector-based information. In Illustrator, you can draw a shape, which is a vector, and then apply a soft drop shadow, which is a raster. In fact, you'll find that more and more today graphics files contain a mixture of both vector and raster content (**Figure 2.1**).

Figure 2.1 Some examples of art that contain both vector and pixel content.

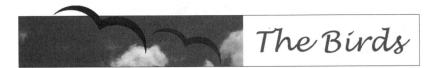

Once you've learned how these two graphic types differ in makeup (see the sidebar "Featured Matchup: Vectors vs. Pixels"), you can begin to understand how to use them and what their benefits are. High-resolution raster images can produce photorealistic paintings and actual photographs.

Control over each and every pixel in the image gives the creative professional complete freedom to change even the smallest of details. However, pixel-based images have a finite level of detail, defined by the pixels per inch (ppi) or resolution of the file. Enlarging a raster-based file is akin to viewing a sheet of graph paper with a magnifying glass—the squares simply get bigger.

In contrast, vector graphics, which are defined by plotted anchor points, can be scaled to any size with no loss in detail or quality. As the image is resized, the computer does the math and plots the points at new coordinates, and then it redraws the Bézier path that connects them (**Figure 2.2**). Instead of storing millions of pixels in a file, a computer only needs to keep track of the coordinates of these anchor points and information on how to fill and stroke the paths that connect them. Vector graphics are also easier to edit because you have distinct shapes to work with, not miniscule pixels. Keep in mind, however, that this object-based approach translates to less control because you have no access to individual pixels.

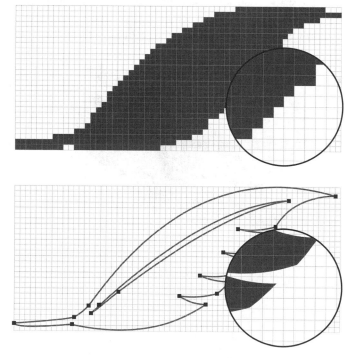

Figure 2.2 The image on top is a raster file with a section shown enlarged to 200 percent. The result is the same image with larger pixels. The image on the bottom is a vector file with a section shown enlarged to 200 percent as well, but the quality of the image remains intact.

As you go through the remainder of this book, you'll get a better understanding of how vectors and pixels work, and you'll see real-world examples of how they are used.

Featured Matchup: Vectors vs. Pixels

You might not be a huge fan of mathematics, but math has a lot to do with how computer graphics work. Raster images consist of a matrix of dots called *pixels*. If you imagine a sheet of graph paper, each square represents a single pixel. By turning pixels on or off (filling in different squares), you can create a shape. Because the squares on the graph paper are so big, the results are blocklike (**Figure 2.3**). However, if you had a sheet with much smaller squares, you'd have more control over the detail of your shape.

Pixel-based images are usually measured in ppi. A higher ppi number means the size of the pixels is smaller and the level of detail in the image can be higher. Higher ppi comes at a price, though—file size. As you increase the number of pixels in your image, your computer has to store that much more information in the file. Color adds to file size as well because instead of each pixel being either black or white, each pixel must store additional colors. *Bit depth* describes how many possible colors a file can contain. An image with a high ppi setting (referred to as the *resolution* of a file) and a high bit depth can result in large file sizes. However, because of the tiny pixels and the capability to apply different colors to each of those pixels individually, raster-based images can produce images that are photographic in nature.

Let's go back to the sheet of graph paper. Instead of coloring in squares to create a shape, map coordinates on the grid to create boundaries for the shape. Then, just as you did when you were a youngster, connect the dots to create the shape (**Figure 2.4**). This is the vector-based method of creating graphics. Instead of a collection of pixels, vector shapes are actually objects—hence, you'll hear the term *object-based graphics*.

Figure 2.3 The level of detail in a pixel-based image is tied directly to the number of pixels it contains. Larger pixels result in less detail.

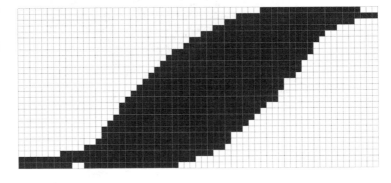

Figure 2.4 A vector-based image connects the dots to create a high level of detail without relying on pixels.

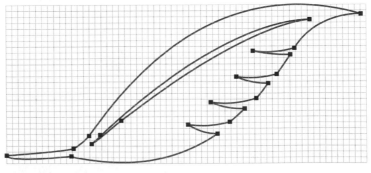

By truly understanding the benefits of these formats—and their limitations—you'll be able to achieve any look or design in the most efficient manner. For more information on this hybrid of graphics files, see Chapter 9, *Mixing It Up: Working with Vectors and Pixels.*

EXPLORING THE ANATOMY OF A VECTOR OBJECT

Now that you understand the differences between rasters and vectors, you can dissect vectors and find out what makes them tick. We mentioned that vectors are defined by plotted anchor points, and the coordinates of these points are what define the actual shape. You'll start with a simple path—a straight line—to see exactly what that means. A straight line consists of two anchor points. The first anchor point defines where the path begins, and the second anchor point defines where the path ends (**Figure 2.5**). Once the two points are plotted, Illustrator connects them with a straight line.

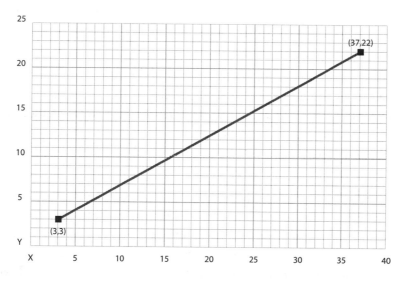

Figure 2.5 A straight vector path has two anchor points. The numbers in parentheses are the coordinates of the anchor points.

OK, you can create two anchor points to create a line, so logic dictates that you need four anchor points to create a rectangle (**Figure 2.6**). Again, focus on the four points, and remember that Illustrator connects them all with straight lines.

Figure 2.6 A vector rectangle has four corner anchor points; straight lines connect them all.

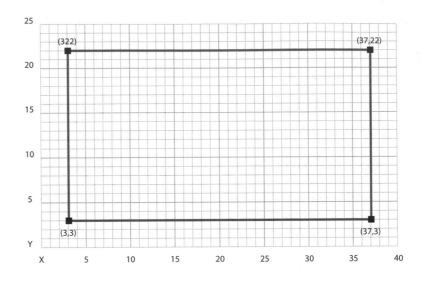

It's important to think of a line as two points, not as a drawn line, because when working in Illustrator, you often create the points, not the path itself. For example, imagine that you are the artist creating a children's connect-the-dots coloring book. You create the dots, but someone else actually connects the lines. When you think of vectors in this way, the concept becomes a lot easier to grasp.

By creating both a straight line and a rectangle, you've created the two kinds of vector paths you can draw. A straight line is an *open path*, because the path that connects the dots starts at one anchor point and ends at another. The rectangle, however, has a path that begins at one anchor point and then returns to that same anchor point, creating a *closed path*.

This all seems easy because we've been talking about straight lines. However, the line that Illustrator draws to connect two anchor points doesn't have to be straight—it can be curved. Anchor points connected by straight lines are called *corner anchor points*. Anchor points that are connected to each other by curved lines are called *smooth anchor points*, and they have some additional attributes.

A smooth anchor point has two *direction handles* (a.k.a. control points), which specify how the curved line is drawn. The smooth anchor point becomes a tangent to the drawn path itself, and the position of the direction handles defines the curve (**Figure 2.7**). For example, to draw an oval, you need to create four smooth anchor points; each anchor point needs to have two control handles that define how the curved lines should be drawn (**Figure 2.8**).

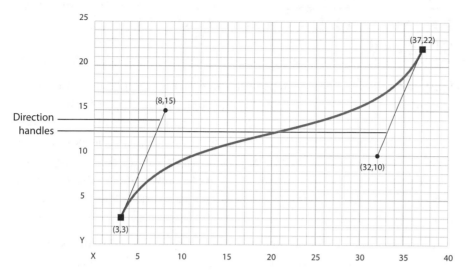

Figure 2.7 A vector path that is curved contains direction handles that define the slope of the path that connects the two smooth anchor points.

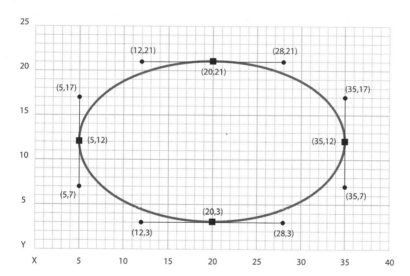

Figure 2.8 A vector ellipse, like a rectangle, has four anchor points. However, the additional direction handles define a curved path that is drawn between each anchor point.

The good news is that Illustrator's primitive drawing tools allow you to create simple shapes without having to worry about anchor points or direction handles. You won't be creating individual anchor points at this stage (we'll cover that in Chapter 4, *Advanced Vectors*), but for now, you'll be able to use what you know to start drawing.

Anchor points and direction handles don't actually print. They just appear on your screen so that you can edit vector paths. When you print a file, only the lines that connect the anchor points print.

DRAWING PRIMITIVE VECTOR SHAPES

Illustrator contains a healthy set of primitive vector drawing tools. In this case, primitive doesn't mean "something simple" as much as it means "acting as a basis from which something else is derived." Artists are taught to sketch using primitive shapes, like rectangles and ovals, so that they can build structure; you can certainly apply similar techniques to drawing with vector shapes in Illustrator. Instead of trying to draw complex shapes, try to visualize how you can combine simple shapes in a variety of ways to create more complex ones.

A simple example involves drawing a crescent shape. Rather than trying to draw it from scratch, it's far easier to create two overlapping circles and then remove the parts that you don't need, which leaves you with the crescent shape (**Figure 2.9**). In Chapter 4, *Advanced Vectors*, you'll find out how Illustrator's Pathfinder or Live Paint features make it easy to edit paths in this way, but for now, we'll explore how to create these primitive shapes.

Figure 2.9 By creating two circles and offsetting them, you can define the geometry you need to create a crescent shape. The Pathfinder panel, covered later in the book, makes it easy to create single shapes from multiple objects.

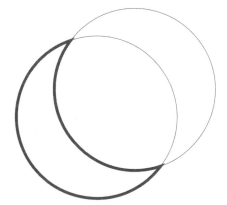

Illustrator's primitive drawing tools are split up between those that create closed-path vector objects and those that create open-path vector objects. Additionally, these tools are interactive in that you can specify or control certain settings while drawing shapes. To take advantage of this functionality, you choose a tool and begin drawing. As you hold down the mouse button, you're able to make changes to the shape you're creating, but once you release the mouse button, you commit to the shape. Let's explore how this works.

Using Closed-Path Shape Tools

The closed-path tools in Illustrator comprise the Rectangle, Rounded Rectangle, Ellipse, Polygon, and Star tools, and they are all grouped together in the Toolbox (**Figure 2.10**). To create any of these shapes, choose the desired tool, click the artboard, and drag outward. While dragging the pointer, you can add commands to interactively adjust the shape. See **Table 2.1** for a list of these interactive commands.

The Flare tool, which is used to create vector-based lens flare effects, is also grouped with the closed-path shape tools. A valid question is why the Flare tool is located here, although it's difficult to come up with an acceptable answer. We cover the Flare tool in Chapter 10, *Graphs, Distortion, and Blends.*

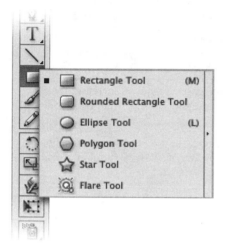

Figure 2.10 The closed-path shape tools are all grouped with the Rectangle tool in the Toolbox.

Table 2.1 Drawing with Closed-Path Shape Tools

Interactive Command	Rectangle Tool	Rounded Rectangle Tool	Ellipse Tool	Polygon Tool	Star Tool
Keyboard Shortcut	M	N/A	L	N/A	N/A
Shift	Constrains all sides to be equal, resulting in a perfect square.	Constrains all sides to be equal, resulting in a perfect square with rounded corners.	Constrains all arc segments to be equal, resulting in a perfect circle.	Constrains the bottom side to be parallel to the constrain angle.	Constrains the bottom two points to be parallel to the constrain angle.
Option (Alt)	Draws the shape out from its center point instead of its corner.	Draws the shape out from its center point instead of its corner.	Draws the shape out from its center point instead of its corner.	N/A	N/A

(continues)

Table 2.1 Drawing with Closed-Path Shape Tools *(continued)*

Interactive Command	Rectangle Tool	Rounded Rectangle Tool	Ellipse Tool	Polygon Tool	Star Tool
Command (Control)	N/A	N/A	N/A	N/A	Adjusts the inner radius of the shape.
Spacebar	Allows you to reposition the shape on the artboard.	Allows you to reposition the shape on the artboard.	Allows you to reposition the shape on the artboard.	Allows you to reposition the shape on the artboard.	Allows you to reposition the shape on the artboard.
Tilde	Creates multiple copies of the shape.	Creates multiple copies of the shape.	Creates multiple copies of the shape.	Creates multiple copies of the shape.	Creates multiple copies of the shape.
Up Arrow	N/A	Increases the corner radius value.	N/A	Increases the number of sides.	Increases the number of points.
Down Arrow	N/A	Decreases the corner radius value.	N/A	Decreases the number of sides.	Decreases the number of points.
Right Arrow	N/A	Turns on the rounded corners.	N/A	N/A	N/A
Left Arrow	N/A	Turns off the rounded corners.	N/A	N/A	N/A
Moving the Mouse	N/A	N/A	N/A	Moving the mouse in a circular motion rotates the shape.	Moving the mouse in a circular motion rotates the shape.

Using Open-Path Shape Tools

Even though they are grouped with the open-path tools, the Rectangular Grid and Polar Grid tools create a combination of both open and closed paths.

The open-path tools in Illustrator comprise the Line Segment, Arc, Spiral, Rectangular Grid, and Polar Grid tools, and they are all grouped together in the Toolbox (**Figure 2.11**). To create any of these shapes, choose the desired tool, click the artboard, and drag outward. While dragging the pointer, you can add commands to interactively adjust the shape. See **Table 2.2** for a list of these interactive commands.

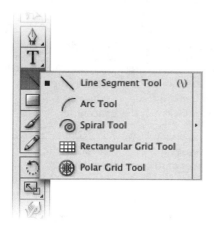

Figure 2.11 The open-path shape tools are all grouped with the Line tool in the Toolbox.

Table 2.2 Drawing with Open-Path Shape Tools

Interactive Command	Line Segment Tool	Arc Tool	Spiral Tool	Rectangular Grid Tool	Polar Grid Tool
Keyboard Shortcut	\ (backslash)	N/A	N/A	N/A	N/A
Shift	Constrains the path to angles in 45-degree increments.	Constrains the X and Y axes, creating a perfect quarter circle.	Constrains the path to angles in 45-degree increments.	Constrains the grid to a perfect square.	Constrains the grid to a perfect circle.
Option (Alt)	N/A	Draws the arc out from its center point instead of its corner.	Increases the length of the path.	Draws the grid out from its center instead of its corner.	Draws the grid out from its center instead of its corner.
Command (Control)	N/A	N/A	Adjusts the decay of the path (making the winds of the spiral more drastic).	N/A	N/A
Spacebar	Allows you to reposition the path on the artboard.	Allows you to reposition the path on the artboard.	Allows you to reposition the path on the artboard.	Allows you to reposition the path on the artboard.	Allows you to reposition the path on the artboard.
Tilde	Creates multiple copies of the path.	Creates multiple copies of the path.	Creates multiple copies of the path.	Creates multiple copies of the path.	Creates multiple copies of the path.

(continues)

Table 2.2 Drawing with Open-Path Shape Tools *(continued)*

Interactive Command	Line Segment Tool	Arc Tool	Spiral Tool	Rectangular Grid Tool	Polar Grid Tool
Up Arrow	N/A	Increases the slope of the curve to make it more convex.	Increases the number of segments in the spiral.	Increases the number of rows in the grid.	Increases the number of concentric dividers.
Down Arrow	N/A	Decreases the slope of the curve to make it more concave.	Decreases the number of segments in the spiral.	Decreases the number of rows in the grid.	Decreases the number of concentric dividers.
Right Arrow	N/A	N/A	N/A	Increases the number of columns in the grid.	Increases the number of radial dividers.
Left Arrow	N/A	N/A	N/A	Decreases the number of columns in the grid.	Decreases the number of radial dividers.
Moving the Mouse	N/A	N/A	Moving the mouse in a circular motion rotates the path.	N/A	N/A
C and X Keys	N/A	C draws the arc as a closed shape instead of an open path.	N/A	C skews the columns in the grid to the left; X skews the columns in the grid to the right.	C skews the concentric dividers toward the center; X skews away from the center.
F and V Keys	N/A	F flips the X and Y axes of the path.	N/A	F skews the rows in the grid to the top; V skews the rows in the grid to the bottom.	F skews the radial dividers toward the left; V skews them to the right.

Drawing by Numbers

If you're an aspiring artist, you can buy a sheet of paper that uses numbers to indicate where colors are supposed to go, taking the guesswork out of the design process. Although being free to create is certainly a good thing, you don't want to be guessing when you've been asked to create a shape to an exact size. The methods of drawing that we've discussed to this point are purely for those in a creative state of mind. As you create each shape, your mind is saying, "Yeah, that's about right." However, sometimes you are required to specify exact dimensions for shapes, and Illustrator can be precise up to four decimal places.

To create any shape numerically, select the tool you need, click the artboard once, and immediately release the mouse button. A dialog appears, letting you specify exact values for the shape or path you want to create (**Figure 2.12**). For most shapes, this action uses the point where you clicked the artboard as the upper-left corner of the shape. To draw a shape out from its center point from the place you click, press the Option (Alt) key while clicking.

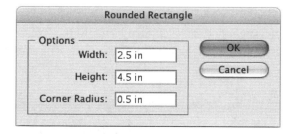

Figure 2.12 Clicking a blank area on the artboard with a shape tool allows you to specify numeric values and create a shape precisely.

In Chapter 4, *Advanced Vectors*, we'll discuss how you can use the Control panel or the Transform panel to change an existing object's dimensions numerically as well.

APPLYING FILLS AND STROKES

As we mentioned earlier in this chapter, vector shapes comprise anchor points, which control how the paths that connect them are drawn. The anchor points and direction handles make up the physical structure of a vector object, which further consists of two attributes: a fill and a stroke. The *fill* of a vector object is the appearance of the area that is enclosed by its path.

If the shape isn't a closed path, the fill is defined by the existing path and is closed with a straight line connecting the start and end points (**Figure 2.13**). The *stroke* of an object is the appearance of the vector path itself. These paths are referred to as *Bézier curves*, and because of their nature, they result in objects or shapes that have clean, smooth edges. We'll talk in detail about Bézier curves in Chapter 4, *Advanced Vectors*.

Figure 2.13 Open paths can have a fill attribute applied, and Illustrator stops the fill by creating a boundary (no physical path is created).

To quickly apply an attribute of none to an object, press the / (slash) key on your keyboard.

Fills and strokes can have a variety of appearances, and vector objects can also contain multiple fill and stroke attributes—something we'll cover in Chapter 3, *Objects, Groups, and Layers*. Additionally, a vector object can have an attribute of *none* applied to its fill or stroke. Fills or strokes with a none attribute applied appear invisible and completely transparent.

Applying Fills

There are three types of fill attributes: solid colors, gradients, and patterns (**Figure 2.14**). Each of these fill types can be stored in the Swatches panel. The Swatches panel allows you to view these attributes as thumbnails or as a named list, and you can apply these attributes to a selected object simply by clicking the swatches. We'll go into more detail on how to use the Swatches panel in Chapter 6, *Working with Color*.

Figure 2.14 Each of these three objects contains a different kind of fill: solid color, gradient, and pattern.

Illustrator's Control panel makes applying color to objects easy. With any object selected, you can specify a fill and a stroke color directly from the Control panel (**Figure 2.15**). Clicking the Fill or Stroke icons in the Control panel allows you to choose a color from the Swatches panel. You can also Shift-click the Fill and Stroke icons in the Control panel to choose a color from the Color panel instead.

Figure 2.15 When applying attributes from the Control panel, you don't have to target the fill or stroke of an object first. Instead, you can choose directly from the two separate pop-ups.

The Tools and Color panels contain two square icons that overlap each other: the fill and stroke indicators (**Figure 2.16**). Pressing the X key on your keyboard toggles the focus between the fill and the stroke.

Stroke indicator ———

Fill indicator ———

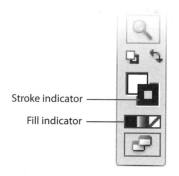

Figure 2.16 The fill and stroke indicators in the Toolbox allow you to specify whether you want to apply an attribute to the fill or stroke of a selected object. Double-clicking the indicators opens the Color Picker.

You can create a new color swatch either by specifying a color in the Color panel and then dragging the color into the Swatches panel or by holding down the Option (Alt) key while clicking the New Swatch icon at the bottom of the Swatches panel. The Swatches panel always has two swatches: one for None and one for Registration (color that separates at 100 percent on every plate).

If you thought Gradient Mesh was a fill attribute, think again. Gradient Mesh is actually a special kind of an object that Illustrator refers to as a *mesh object*. Mesh objects are treated differently and don't act like regular vector paths. We'll talk more about Gradient Mesh in Chapter 5, *Brushes, Symbols, and Masks.*

When you're using the sliders to specify colors in the Color panel, hold the Shift key while you drag one slider to get lighter or darker shades of your color.

Solid Fills

A solid color fill applies a single color to the appearance of the fill of a vector shape. For example, a rectangle can have a solid blue fill, a solid yellow fill, or any color of your choosing. There are actually three types of solid color fills in Illustrator (process, global process, and spot color), and we'll discuss each of them in detail in Chapter 6, *Working with Color*.

Because it's easy to forget whether the fill or stroke is in focus, it's recommended that you always keep the focus on the fill, and if you need to toggle to the stroke, then toggle back to the fill immediately when you're done. Otherwise, there are just too many times where you click a color to fill an object and nothing happens to the fill. This occurs when the focus is on the stroke and the color is applied to the stroke in error.

Gradient Fills

Whereas a solid color fill consists of just one color, a *gradient* fill consists of solid colors that blend into each other. A gradient can contain as few as one color and as many as—well, let's just say we stopped counting at 300. *Linear* gradients start with a color on one side that gradually blends into a color on the other side. *Radial* gradients start with a color at the center and gradually blend into a color, radiating outward (**Figure 2.17**). A gradient has four attributes:

Figure 2.17 You can use linear and radial gradients to easily add shading or perceived dimension to objects.

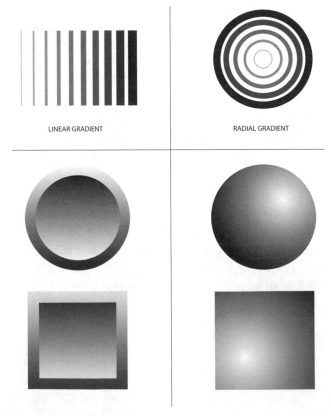

LINEAR GRADIENT   RADIAL GRADIENT

- **Type.** Either linear or radial, as just described.

- **Color Stop.** The point at which a new color is added to a gradient.

- **Midpoint.** The point at which two adjacent colors meet at exactly 50 percent of each color.

- **Angle.** The direction of the gradient (only for linear gradients).

You can create gradients using a combination of the Color, Color Guide, Swatches, and Gradient panels. You can expand the Gradient panel to show the gradient slider and the angle and location fields. To define a gradient, drag colors from the Color, Color Guide, or Swatches panel directly onto the gradient slider.

The little icons that appear beneath the slider are color stops. You can drag colors directly onto an existing color stop to change its color, or you can select a color stop and hold down Option (Alt) while you click a color in the Swatches panel. To remove a color stop from a gradient, simply drag it down, away from the gradient slider. The diamond-shaped icon that appears above the gradient slider indicates the midpoint between two colors. Drag the midpoint to the left or right to adjust how quickly one color blends into the other. Once you've defined a gradient, you can drag the preview icon (in the upper left of the Gradient panel) into the Swatches panel (**Figure 2.18**).

To replace an existing gradient swatch, hold the Option (Alt) key while you drag the preview icon from the Gradient panel over the existing gradient swatch in the Swatches panel. The swatch appears with a thick black outline to indicate that it will be replaced with the new one.

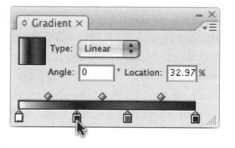

Figure 2.18 Moving a color stop shifts where color appears in the gradient. Dragging one color stop on top of another while holding the Option (Alt) key swaps the two colors.

To modify how a gradient fill is applied to an object, you can use the Gradient tool. Start by selecting an object and filling it with a gradient of your choice. Then, select the Gradient tool, and click and drag to define the start point of the gradient. The direction in which you drag the pointer determines the angle of the gradient. The point where you release the mouse button defines the end point of the gradient. When you're using radial gradients, the first click determines the center point of the gradient, and the release point determines the outside of the gradient (**Figure 2.19**).

Figure 2.19 The Gradient tool makes it easy to apply gradients at an angle.

What makes the Gradient tool so powerful is that you can begin or end a gradient anywhere, even outside the boundaries of the object you have selected (**Figure 2.20**). Additionally, you can select multiple objects and apply a single gradient across all of them using the Gradient tool.

Figure 2.20 A gradient fills the distance from where you first clicked to where you release the mouse button, even if those locations are beyond the boundaries of your selection.

Pattern Fills

Hold the Option (Alt) key while dragging artwork from the artboard onto an existing pattern swatch in the Swatches panel to update or modify the pattern.

A *pattern* fill uses a repeating art element to fill the boundaries of a path or object (**Figure 2.21**). To define a pattern, create just about any kind of art on your artboard (including raster images and text objects), and drag them into your Swatches panel. You can apply pattern fills to objects the same way you apply solid color fills—by targeting the fill or stroke of a selection and choosing a pattern swatch from the Swatches panel.

Figure 2.21 Three examples of vector objects with pattern fills. Good patterns have no visible seams.

In Chapter 4, *Advanced Vectors*, we'll talk about transformations (such as scaling and rotating objects). When objects are filled with patterns, you can choose to rotate the patterns with the objects, or you can have Illustrator rotate just the objects but not the pattern fill.

If you create a lot of patterns, check out Artlandia's SymmetryWorks 4 plugin at www.artlandia.com.

The Art of Pattern Making

In reality, an entire book could be written on creating patterns, which is an art form in and of itself. Creating perfect, repeating patterns that tile seamlessly can take a bit of advance planning, as well as trial and error.

When you drag artwork into the Swatches panel to create a pattern swatch, Illustrator uses the bounding area of the artwork that you selected as the boundary of the repeat area. In many cases, however, this default bounding box does not create a seamless pattern. In order to create a seamless pattern, you might have to position objects well inside the repeat area, or even have artwork extend beyond the repeat area. To define a repeat area for a pattern, draw a no-fill, no-stroke rectangle at the bottom of the stacking order. Even if there are objects that extend outside the rectangle, Illustrator will use that rectangle to define the repeat area (**Figure 2.22**).

Sometimes, the best way to learn is to reverse-engineer existing artwork. To get a better feel for how repeats are designed, take a look at some of the patterns that come with Illustrator. Choose Open Swatch Library > Patterns from the Swatches panel menu to view some of these patterns. To access the art that was used to define any pattern swatch, simply drag a swatch from the Swatches panel onto the artboard. In addition, see the sidebar "Pattern Thinking" in Chapter 5, *Brushes, Symbols, and Masks*.

Figure 2.22 Using a rectangle as the bottommost shape in your pattern art defines a repeat area, thus helping create a seamless pattern tile.

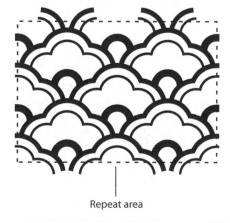

Repeat area

Applying Strokes

As you learned earlier, a *stroke* is the appearance of the vector path itself. You can specify a stroke color by choosing one from the Stroke pop-up in the Control panel or by targeting the stroke using the fill/stroke indicator and then choosing a color from either the Color or Swatches panel. You can also choose from several different settings to control the appearance of a stroke, all of which are available in the Stroke panel:

- **Weight.** The thickness of a stroke is referred to as the *stroke weight*, and it is traditionally specified in points (pt). Specifying a stroke weight of less than .25 point might be problematic for most printing presses.

- **Miter limit.** A stroke's *miter limit* specifies the appearance of corners that have very acute angles. If you find that the corner of a stroke appears clipped, you can increase the miter limit to correct the appearance (**Figure 2.23**).

Figure 2.23 The object on the left has an 18-point stroke applied with a miter limit of 2, whereas the object on the right has an 18-point stroke applied with a miter limit of 4.

- **Cap.** The *cap* setting is an attribute that affects the appearance of the start and end points of a stroke. Obviously, this setting applies to open paths only (although it can be applied to dashes as well, as you will soon see). You can choose between a Butt, Round, or Projecting cap (**Figure 2.24**).

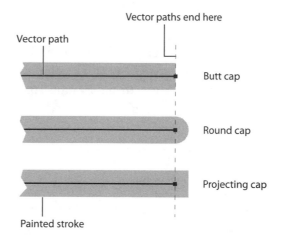

Figure 2.24 The cap setting defines how the start and end of a stroke appear. From the top, Butt, Round, and Projecting caps can also add to the length of a stroke.

- **Join.** A *join* attribute determines the appearance of a stroke as it passes through an anchor point. Miter, Round, and Bevel are the different options you can choose from (**Figure 2.25**).

Figure 2.25 The join setting defines the appearance of connecting straight anchor points. From left to right are examples of stroked paths with Miter, Round, and Beveled joins.

The Control, Transform, and Info panels all provide exact feedback on coordinates, positioning, sizing of objects, and more. By default, these panels use the actual vector path to determine these numbers, not the visual boundaries of the object. For example, you might have a shape that has a thick stroke applied to it, which is not represented in the value you see in the Transform panel. If you select the Use Preview Bounds option in Illustrator's General Preferences, however, all panels will use the visual boundary of a path as the dimensions value, rather than the underlying vector path.

Aligning Strokes

By default, Illustrator paints a stroke on the center of a path. For example, if you specify a 10-point stroke for an object, the result is 5 points appearing on the outside of the path and 5 points appearing on the inside of the path. In the Stroke panel, you can specify whether you want the entire stroke painted on the inside or outside of the vector path (**Figure 2.26**). This setting is available only for closed paths.

Figure 2.26 Use the Align Stroke options in the Stroke panel to specify whether a stroke should be painted on the center, inside, or outside of the path.

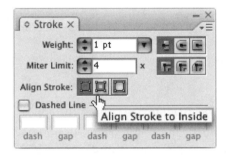

Using Dashed Strokes

Strokes don't have to be solid lines. They can have a broken appearance resulting in dashed lines. The nice feature is, rather than just choosing a preset dashed line, you can specify exactly how the dashes should appear along a stroked path.

When specifying the appearance of a dash, you can specify the length of the dash and the length of the gap—the space that appears after the dash. The Stroke panel contains three sets of dash and gap settings. If you specify a dash without specifying a gap, Illustrator creates a gap equal to the size of the dash. For most standard dashed strokes, you will use only the first dash and gap setting. However, you can use all three to create a sequence of dashes and gaps (**Figure 2.27**). When you specify the Round cap option for the stroke, a dash value of 0 results in a perfect circle, allowing you to create dotted lines.

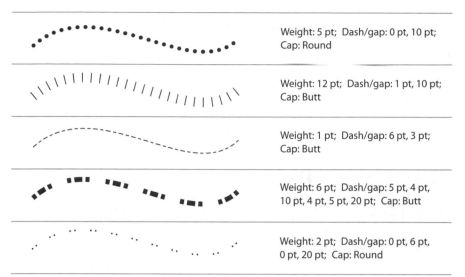

Weight: 5 pt; Dash/gap: 0 pt, 10 pt; Cap: Round

Weight: 12 pt; Dash/gap: 1 pt, 10 pt; Cap: Butt

Weight: 1 pt; Dash/gap: 6 pt, 3 pt; Cap: Butt

Weight: 6 pt; Dash/gap: 5 pt, 4 pt, 10 pt, 4 pt, 5 pt, 20 pt; Cap: Butt

Weight: 2 pt; Dash/gap: 0 pt, 6 pt, 0 pt, 20 pt; Cap: Round

Figure 2.27 Illustrator's ability to set custom dashes for a stroke allows you to create a plethora of dashed strokes, which you can use for a variety of tasks.

One shortcoming of Illustrator is its inability to ensure that dashes set on strokes match up evenly on the corners of an object (**Figure 2.28**). This is because you can specify only absolute dash and gap settings, and those settings don't always match up exactly with the size of the object you've drawn. It's interesting to note that Adobe InDesign does have the ability to stretch or adjust dashes and gaps to display consistent corners.

Figure 2.28 Because Illustrator uses absolute values for dashes, it's nearly impossible to get dashes to line up perfectly at the corners of a path.

In Illustrator, there *is* a way to get consistent dashes to appear around a shape—by using the versatile Pattern brush feature, which we'll discuss in Chapter 5, *Brushes, Symbols, and Masks*.

If adjusting dashes along a path is something you need to do often, you might want to check out a shareware ($15) plugin created by Rick Johnson called Nudge Palette. You can find Nudge Palette at http://rj-graffix.com. This plugin allows you to easily shift dashes along a path to get the most optimal appearance.

WORKING WITH TEXT OBJECTS

They say that a picture speaks 1,000 words, but you still need to type words every once in a while. Illustrator has very powerful typography features, which we'll cover in detail in Chapter 7, *Typography*. For now, it's sufficient for you to learn about the two kinds of type objects that Illustrator can create: point text and area text. Naturally, each has its own benefits.

Working with Point Type

There's really a third kind of type object called *path text*, where you can specify text to follow along a vector path. We'll talk more about path text in Chapter 7, *Typography*.

The simplest form of text in Illustrator is *point type*, which you can create by choosing the Type tool and clicking any blank area on your artboard. Once you've defined a point at which to start typing, you can enter text onto the artboard. Point type doesn't have defined boundaries, so text never wraps automatically, although you can use Return (Enter) characters to manually type on a new line. When you use point type, the paragraph alignment settings (left, right, and center) refer to the single point that you created when you first clicked with the Type tool (**Figure 2.29**).

Figure 2.29 Text in a Point Type object aligns differently depending on the paragraph alignment options you set for the text.

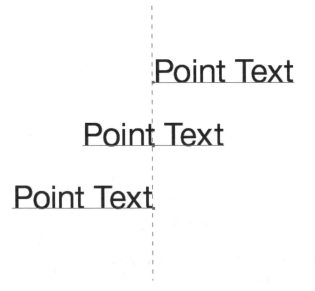

Although point type is easy to create, many of the powerful text features that Illustrator has, including the Adobe Every-line Composer, text threading, and the ability to set text in columns, are not available. However, if you want to place text in numerous areas of an illustration (such as callouts, maps, graphs, and so on), point type is the way to go.

Working with Area Type

As with most page-layout applications, you can also place text within a frame, although with Illustrator, any vector object can serve as a text frame. *Area type* is text that is enclosed within the confines of a vector shape (**Figure 2.30**). To create an Area Type object, you can either use the Area Type tool to click an existing vector shape or use the Type tool to click inside any closed vector shape (**Figure 2.31**). Alternatively, you can click and drag a blank area of the artboard with the Type tool to create an Area Type object.

At Design Responsibly, we teach technique. We teach why and when you would use a particular application. We teach best practices. Sure, features are nice, but learning how to apply them to real world design projects and customized workflows is key.

"Give a man a fish and you've fed him for a day, teach a man to fish and you've fed him for a lifetime." That's what we value at Design Responsibly. Rather than just a brain dump of feature upon feature, our training truly teaches designers and printers how to think about a project before starting, or how to best attack any

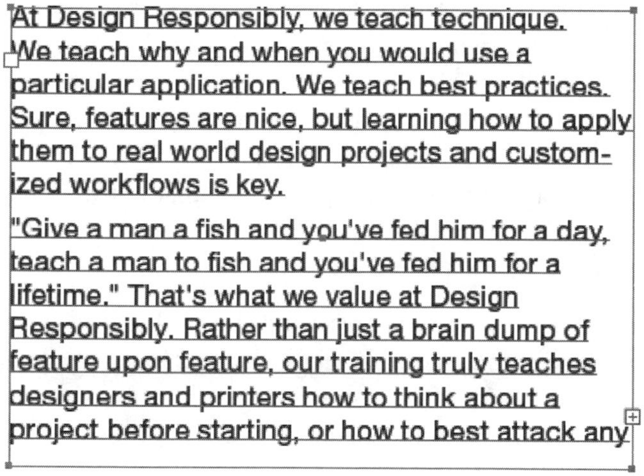

Figure 2.30 An example of an Area Type object. Any vector object in Illustrator can serve as a text frame.

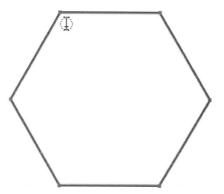

Figure 2.31 As you drag the Type tool over an object that can become a text frame, Illustrator displays the tool icon in parentheses.

Multiple area type objects can be linked to have a single-story flow across them called a *thread of text*. Text flows from line to line automatically within an Area Type object, and more advanced paragraph settings such as columns, composition, hyphenation, and indents are available. We'll cover text threading and the advanced text features that are available when we get to Chapter 7, *Typography*.

Area type might take an extra click or two to create, but for uniform layouts and longer runs of copy, you'll want to use it.

Converting Text to Editable Vectors

Earlier in the chapter, you learned about Illustrator's primary shape tools. The characters in both Point Type and Area Type objects are vector shapes too, but they can't be edited as regular vector shapes can because you can't access their anchor points or direction handles. In essence, text is a special kind of vector object. Fonts have specific information built into them, called *hinting*, which modifies character shapes slightly based on the size in which text is printed. For example, a lowercase *e* character has a small hole in the middle, and at really small point sizes, that hole might appear to close up or fill in when printed. Font hinting adjusts the size of that hole to be slightly larger at smaller point sizes.

You can select any text object and choose Type > Create Outlines to convert text into regular, editable vector shapes. Doing so allows you to perform edits on the actual shapes of the characters (for example, extending an ascender or removing the dot from an *i*) but results in the loss of any font hinting (**Figure 2.32**).

Figure 2.32 Converting text to outlines (bottom) gives you unlimited freedom to edit the vector paths.

Where possible, it's always best to leave text in an editable state and avoid converting it to vector outlines. In this way, you'll be able to make edits easily, and you'll preserve font information. However, sometimes it's a good idea to convert text to outlines, such as when you've created artwork that will be distributed or used in many different places (logos are good examples). In this way, you don't need to worry about passing font files around as well (which has legal ramifications anyway—something we'll discuss later in the book).

Older versions of Illustrator required text to be converted to outlines if the text was going to be used with certain features such as gradients, patterns, and masks. The next-generation text engine introduced in Illustrator CS allows you to use text with just about any feature while allowing it to remain completely editable. Other than the reasons given earlier for converting text to outlines, you can take advantage of using editable text in all of your design workflows.

Why Text Looks "Fatter" When Converted to Outlines

You might notice that when you convert text to editable vector outlines, the appearance of that text is bolder than text that is not outlined. There are actually two main reasons behind this (both technical in nature):

- The loss of hinting makes certain features potentially inconsistent. For example, letter strokes that you expect to be the same width might turn out to be different widths depending on how they fall on the grid of the output device. Slight differences can get magnified unexpectedly, such as rounded letters going below the baseline. This happens because the information that makes the outlines round consistently to the pixel grid has been lost.

- The change in the fill algorithm combines with the lack of hinting to make the letters look fatter. Font rasterizing uses a fill algorithm that turns on a pixel only when the center of the pixel is within the glyph outline (center-scan). Graphics rasterizing uses a fill algorithm that turns on a pixel when any part of the pixel is within the graphic outline (overscan). Given that the outline is no longer being rounded to pixel boundaries at key points, the rendering will generally be at least 1 pixel thicker and occasionally 2 pixels thicker.

Of course, how much difference this makes depends on the size and style of the type and especially on the resolution of the output device. At 2,400 dots per inch (dpi) with typical text sizes, the effect is pretty subtle. At 600 dpi with 6-point text, the effect is quite obvious.

Special thanks to Thomas Phinney of Adobe for providing this information.

SELECTING OBJECTS

In reality, the selection tools mentioned here do more than just select objects. You can use them to move selected objects as well. Moving an object in Illustrator is actually considered a transform function, so we'll be talking about the Selection and Direct Selection tools in Chapter 4, *Advanced Vectors*, as well.

By far, the tools you will employ most often when using Illustrator on a day-to-day basis are the selection tools. The power of Illustrator lies not just in creating graphics, but more so in manipulating them. In order to perform just about any function in Illustrator (or nearly any computer graphics program for that matter), you need to select something first. Without selections, Illustrator has no idea which of the objects in your document you want to modify.

If you've used Illustrator before, you're familiar with the twins: the *Selection tool* and the *Direct Selection tool* (**Figure 2.33**). These tools have been given a variety of alternative names over the years (some of which can't be printed in this book), including the black and white arrows or the solid and hollow arrows. In reality, there's a third tool called the *Group Selection tool*, although it doesn't get much exposure because of a certain keyboard shortcut that we'll talk about shortly.

Figure 2.33 The dynamic duo, the Selection and Direct Selection tools, are also referred to as the black and white arrow tools.

Making Selections

Before we talk about the tools themselves, the reason why there are two different selection tools, and when to use one over the other, let's first see how you can make a selection in Illustrator:

- **The click method.** To select an object, just click it with any of the selection tools. To select multiple objects, you can click a second object while holding the Shift key to add the second object to your selection. Shift-clicking an object that is *already* selected will *deselect* it.

- **The marquee method.** Another way to create selections is by creating a *marquee*, which is similar to drawing a rectangle, only with a selection tool instead of a shape tool. You start by clicking and dragging the pointer to specify a rectangular area, called a *marquee*. When you release the mouse button, any objects that fall within the boundaries of the marquee become selected (**Figure 2.34**).

Figure 2.34 Selecting multiple objects using the marquee method keeps you from having to Shift-click multiple shapes to select all of them.

Keep in mind that you can use a combination of both methods to make more efficient selections. For example, say you want to select all of the objects in a certain area except for one. You can use the marquee method to first select all of the objects and then Shift-click the object that you don't want in order to deselect just that object.

Sometimes, you don't want the ability to select an object at all. Especially in complex files with many overlapping objects, it can be easy to accidentally select objects without realizing what you've done (until it's too late, of course). Illustrator allows you to select an object and choose Object > Lock > Selection, which makes the object unavailable for editing. Unfortunately, it can be difficult to select objects that overlap each other (there's no easy way to click through the stacking order of objects like InDesign can), so locking and unlocking objects becomes a frequent endeavor. Learning the keyboard shortcuts to lock (Command-2 or Control-2) and unlock (Command-Option-2 or Control-Alt-2) is a good idea.

The keyboard shortcut to quickly select all objects is Command-A (Control-A), and the shortcut to deselect all objects is Command-Shift-A (Control-Shift-A).

Setting Your Selection & Anchor Display Preferences

Illustrator does offer a few ways to help you make selections through the Selection & Anchor Display panel in Preferences (**Figure 2.35**).

Figure 2.35 The Selection & Anchor Display panel in Preferences gives you greater control over how you make selections.

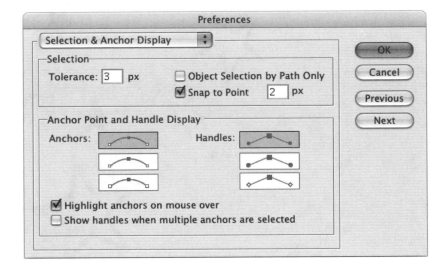

Illustrator CS3 introduces a different method for how the selection tools work. In previous versions of Illustrator, if several anchor points were in close proximity with each other, clicking with the Selection tool would choose the anchor point that was highest in the stacking order. This made it difficult to select anchor points of objects that appeared lower in the object stacking order. In Illustrator CS3, if several anchor points are in close proximity of each other, clicking with the Selection tool will select the anchor point that is closest to the cursor, regardless of stacking order.

Here are a few options you can select in the Selection & Anchor Display panel in Preferences:

• You can set a tolerance for how close your cursor has to be in order to select an anchor point or an object. You can find the Tolerance setting in the Selection & Anchor Display panel in Preferences. A higher pixel value will make it easier to select objects quickly, but a lower pixel value will give you far more accurate results, making it easier to select anchor points that appear very close to each other. The Object Selection by Path Only setting restricts Illustrator to select objects only when clicking their paths (not their fills). And the Snap to Point setting determines the distance at which your cursor snaps to other objects or guides.

- With the Direct Selection tool, Illustrator will highlight anchor points as you move the pointer over them. This can help you identify where the anchor points are and, more importantly, can make it easier to identify what you're editing. You can set this behavior by selecting the Highlight Anchors on Mouse Over check box.

- You can control the size of anchor points and control handles. On high-resolution monitors, anchor points and control handles appear very small and are difficult to grab with the selection tools. Preference settings allow you to choose from three different sizes for both anchor points and control handles, making it easier on your eyes (and your sanity).

Using the Direct Selection Tool

If there's one aspect that confuses people most about Illustrator, it's that there are two selection tools (the Pen tool doesn't *confuse* people nearly as much is it *frustrates* them). Fear not, though, there's a method to the madness—and once you understand it, you'll breathe easier. The good news is that whatever you learn here will apply to InDesign and Photoshop as well, because they use the same selection tools.

When you are using the Direct Selection tool, clicking the fill area of an object selects the entire object (unless the object is filled with None or unless Object Selection by Path Only is turned on in Preferences). Clicking the vector path either selects a segment of the path (if you click between two anchor points) or selects the anchor point that you click.

If you hold the Option (Alt) key while clicking either the fill or the path of an object with the Direct Selection tool, it selects the entire object—just as the Selection tool does. So with a single keyboard shortcut, you can make the Direct Selection tool "act" like its twin. If you are working with a group of objects, holding down Option (Alt) and clicking an object's path once with the Direct Selection tool selects the entire object. Holding down Option (Alt) and clicking a second time selects all of the objects in the group. If there are nested groups (groups within other groups), each additional Option (Alt) click results in the next level up in the hierarchy of the

With Illustrator CS3, if you have an object that is already selected, you can use the Direct Selection tool to click and release on any one anchor point to select it. In previous versions of Illustrator, you would have to deselect the entire object first and then select just the desired anchor point.

group being selected. If you ever want to select an entire group with one click, press the Command (Control) key to temporarily switch to the Selection tool.

Once you master this method of using the Direct Selection tool while using the keyboard shortcuts, you'll never think twice about the two selection tools again.

By default, the Object Selection by Path Only setting in Preferences is turned off, which allows you to select an object by clicking its path or anywhere within its fill area (if it has a fill attribute applied). Although this is convenient, sometimes, especially when you are working with complex artwork, this behavior makes it difficult to select objects. Turning this preference on allows you to select objects only by clicking their vector paths, not their fill areas.

Featured Matchup: Selection Tool vs. Direct Selection Tool

At the simplest level, the Selection tool (the black, or solid, arrow) is used to select entire objects and groups. The Direct Selection tool, on the other hand, is used to select parts of objects or individual objects within a group. For example, if you draw a star shape and click it with the Selection tool, the entire star becomes selected. In contrast, if you click one of the points of the star with the Direct Selection tool, only that point becomes selected (**Figure 2.36**).

At first, it sounds like life in Illustrator is all about constantly switching between these two tools. To make things a bit easier, when you have one selection tool active, you can press the Command (Control) key to temporarily switch to the other selection tool. To make life even easier than that, you can learn how power users utilize modifier keys with the Direct Selection tool efficiently; this practice practically negates the need for both the Selection tool and the Group Selection tool.

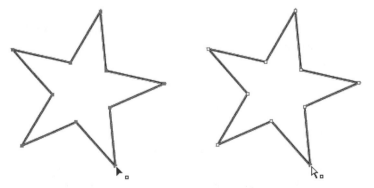

Figure 2.36 The object on the left is selected with the Selection tool. The object on the right is selected with the Direct Selection tool.

Using the Group Selection Tool

In reality, there are *three* selection tools: the Selection tool, the Direct Selection tool, and the Group Selection tool. The Group Selection tool is useful for selecting groups of objects. As you will learn in Chapter 3, *Objects, Groups, and Layers*, groups can be nested (meaning you can have groups within groups). Using the Group Selection tool, clicking an object once selects the object. Clicking the same object a second time selects the entire group to which the object belongs. Each successive click will select the next level up in the hierarchy.

Earlier we referred to Illustrator as having two selection tools because the Group Selection tool is rarely chosen. Why? It's because of the keyboard shortcut that we mentioned. When you have the Direct Selection tool chosen, pressing the Option (Alt) key toggles to the Group Selection tool, which is why you can then select entire objects.

Using Alternative Selection Techniques

Although most of the selections that you make will incorporate the use of the Selection tool or the Direct Selection tool, sometimes you might need a more specialized selection tool. Illustrator can offer a helping hand in a variety of ways.

Using the Lasso and Magic Wand Tools

Two selection tools first appeared in Photoshop but both have made their way into Illustrator's toolset: the Lasso tool and the Magic Wand tool. Although they're similar in concept to those found in Photoshop, remember that Illustrator is an object-based program, so these tools select objects, not pixels.

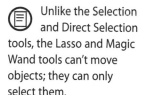 Unlike the Selection and Direct Selection tools, the Lasso and Magic Wand tools can't move objects; they can only select them.

The Lasso tool in Illustrator acts much like the Direct Selection tool in that it can select individual anchor points. Whereas a marquee is always limited to a rectangular shape, the specialty of the Lasso tool is that you can draw a marquee in any freeform shape. Where you have many objects in close proximity to each other, the Lasso tool allows you to draw a custom marquee shape to select just the objects—or anchor points—that you need (**Figure 2.37**).

Figure 2.37 Drawing a freeform marquee with the Lasso tool can be helpful when you are trying to make complex selections with art that is in close proximity to other art.

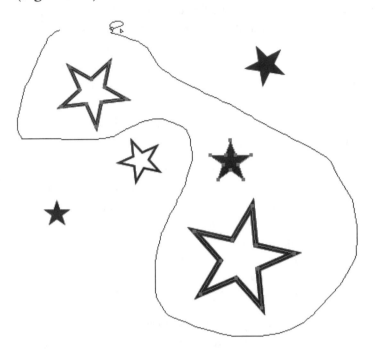

If you're a production artist, the Magic Wand tool is invaluable. By setting a tolerance of .25 point for Stroke Weight and clicking a path with a .25-point stroke on your artboard, you can select all paths in your document with a stroke weight between 0 and .5 points, making it easy to set consistent hairline stroke widths.

If you have several similarly styled objects in your document and you need to select them all, it can be tedious to manually select them using the click method. If they are scattered throughout the document, the marquee method won't work for you either. In such cases, the Magic Wand tool allows you to click one object; when you do, any other objects in your file that have the same attributes as the object you clicked become selected as well. Not bad for one click, right? If you double-click the Magic Wand tool in the Toolbox, the Magic Wand panel appears; here you can specify which specific attributes you want the Magic Wand tool to pay attention to (**Figure 2.38**). The true power of the Magic Wand tool is that you can set a tolerance for each attribute. So if your document contains several objects colored a variety of shades of yellow, you can still select them all with the Magic Wand tool by clicking a single yellow object.

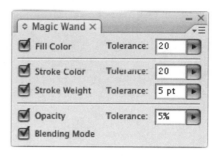

Figure 2.38 You can use the Magic Wand panel to specify tolerance levels for different attributes.

Selecting Similar Objects

Illustrator has a Select menu, which contains a variety of selection-based functions. You'll find some of the most useful ones in the Select > Same and Select > Object menus. To use the *Same* functions, first make a selection on the artboard with any of Illustrator's selection tools. Then, choose from the list of attributes to select objects based on that attribute (**Figure 2.39**). At any time, you can use the *Object* functions to select a certain kind of object in your file.

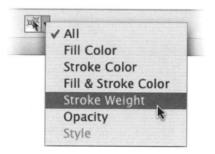

Figure 2.39 The Control panel also contains a button that allows you to select similar objects. The button becomes available whenever you have an object selected.

Saving Selections

Making complex selections can take time, and it can be tedious having to constantly make selections to objects as you are working on a design. To make life just a tad easier, you can save your selections and retrieve them later. Once you have made a selection using any of the methods mentioned earlier, choose Selection > Save, and give your selection a name. That selection then appears at the bottom of the Select menu, which you can access, or *load*, at any time. Because selections in Illustrator are object-based, a saved selection remembers objects even after they've been moved or modified.

CHAPTER THREE

Objects, Groups, and Layers

Some people have clean, organized desks, whereas others have desks that are quite messy. Likewise, some designers organize their Adobe Illustrator files using groups and layers, while many do not. And just as there are benefits to keeping an orderly desk, there are advantages to using groups and layers for adding structure to your files. In Illustrator, groups and layers not only offer a convenient way to manage objects in a file, but they can also control the appearance of your file. For example, applying a drop shadow to several objects that are grouped looks different than a drop shadow that is applied to those very same objects if they aren't grouped. You may even find that using groups and layers is necessary to create the art you need.

UNDERSTANDING APPEARANCES

As we discussed in the previous chapter, a vector path can have certain attributes applied, which can define the appearance of that path. When you print a file, you aren't seeing the vector path; you're seeing the appearance that was specified for that path. An example of an attribute might be a particular fill or stroke setting. As you'll learn later in this chapter, attributes can also be effects such as drop shadows or 3D effects.

In addition, you will learn that appearances are applied to something called a "target." See the sidebar "Featured Matchip: Selecting vs. Targeting" for more information.

Using the Appearance Panel

When you specify attributes, they appear listed in the Appearance panel. We know this sounds like an advertisement for a movie, but if you keep only one Illustrator panel open on your screen while you're working, make it the Appearance panel. In fact, the Appearance panel is probably the most important panel in Illustrator—ever.

Like X-ray vision, the Appearance panel enables you to look at the underlying objects in your file and see how they were built or created. This panel also gives you access to every attribute of an object. But before we get ahead of ourselves, let's start with the basics.

Basic Appearances

Draw a rectangle with the default white fill and a 10-point black stroke and take a look at the Appearance panel. When the rectangle is selected, the Appearance panel displays a thumbnail icon and the word *Path*, which is the targeted item. (When we discuss groups later in the chapter, you'll get a really good understanding of what the target is.) The panel also lists the target's stroke (with the weight beside it), the fill, and the transparency

Featured Matchup: Selecting vs. Targeting

As we begin to learn about appearances in Illustrator, it's important to understand a concept in Illustrator called a *target*. In the previous chapter, you learned that you can select an object. However, when you apply an attribute to an object, such as a fill or a stroke, that attribute is applied to what Illustrator calls the *target*.

For the most part, *selecting* is an action that is used to define a set of criteria that will be used for performing transformations. As we'll see in Chapter 4, *Advanced Vectors,* transformations consist of moving, scaling, rotating, skewing, or mirroring objects. You select objects because you want to move them from one side of your document to another, because you want to delete them, and so on.

Targeting, on the other hand, is an action that is used to define a set of criteria specifically to apply an attribute such as a stroke, a fill, a transparency, or a live effect.

Ordinarily, you don't have to physically target anything, because Illustrator does it for you (something Illustrator internally refers to as *smart targeting*). When you select a path with the Selection tool, Illustrator automatically targets that path so you can apply attributes to it. However, sometimes you might want to specifically target something else. For example, you can target a layer and then add a stroke attribute to the layer itself (**Figure 3.1**). This gives every object on the layer the appearance of a stroke attribute (we'll discuss this concept in detail later in this chapter).

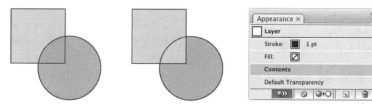

Figure 3.1 When you add a stroke to a layer, it is added to the top of the stacking order. All objects on that layer appear with a stroke. Because the stroke applies to the entire layer, even objects that are overlapping each other are stroked.

(**Figure 3.2**). The order in which the listed items appear is important, because they define the final appearance of the object.

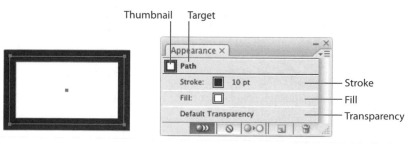

Figure 3.2 The Appearance panel displays the attributes for the targeted item.

Let's expand on what you learned in the previous chapter about fills and strokes. By default, a fill is painted first; the stroke is then painted on top of the fill. This is why you can see the entire weight of a stroke that is painted on the centerline of a path. However, you can click the Stroke attribute that is listed in the Appearance panel and drag it so that it appears listed beneath the Fill attribute (**Figure 3.3**). This ability to change the stacking order of attributes in an object's painting order becomes even more important when we talk about groups and layers later in the chapter.

Figure 3.3 The Appearance panel gives you the ability to change the stacking order of attributes. Here, the Stroke attribute appears beneath the path's Fill attribute.

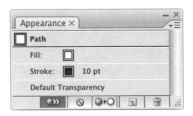

You can't change an object's transparency settings from the Appearance panel, but double-clicking the transparency listing in the Appearance panel will open the Transparency panel, where you can make changes.

You can also use the Appearance panel to target individual attributes by simply clicking them to highlight them. For example, when you click an object to select it, you can apply an Opacity setting to that object via the Transparency panel. This Opacity setting is applied to both the Fill attribute and the Stroke attribute of the selected object (**Figure 3.4**). However, if you first target the fill by clicking it in the Appearance panel (**Figure 3.5**) and then changing the opacity, you'll notice that the setting is applied to the fill only and not to the stroke. This is indicated in the Appearance panel by a disclosure triangle just to the left of the Fill entry: The Opacity setting appears indented immediately underneath the fill's Color setting (**Figure 3.6**).

Figure 3.4 The Appearance panel displays the object's transparency setting. Here, an Opacity value of 48 percent is applied to the entire object.

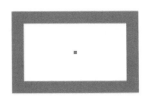
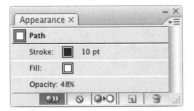

Figure 3.5 Clicking the Fill or Stroke setting in the Appearance panel targets the attribute, allowing it to be adjusted independently of other attributes in the object.

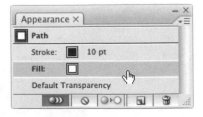

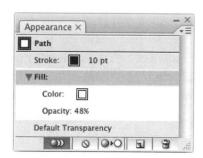

Figure 3.6 When a setting is applied to an attribute individually, it appears indented beneath the attribute.

Complex Appearances

Objects that have a fill and stroke are referred to as having a *basic appearance*. However, vector objects aren't limited to just one fill and one stroke and can contain multiple attributes. An object with more than just one fill or stroke is referred to as having a *complex appearance*.

To add an attribute to an object, choose Add New Fill or Add New Stroke from the Appearance panel menu (**Figure 3.7**). You'll see the new attribute appear in the Appearance panel, where you can change its place in the stacking order. Alternatively, you can drag a Fill or Stroke attribute to the Duplicate icon at the bottom of the Appearance panel. Dragging an attribute to the trash can icon removes the attribute from the object.

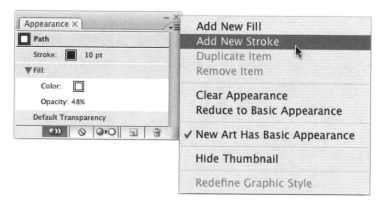

Figure 3.7 Choosing to add a new stroke from the Appearance panel menu. There's no limit to how many fills or strokes you can add to a single object.

You may be wondering what good two fills or two strokes do in an object, because one always covers the one beneath it. Earlier, we discussed the ability to target a specific attribute so that you can apply settings to each individually. By first targeting the lower fill and specifying one color and then targeting the second fill, choosing a different color, and setting that fill to overprint (or by giving it an Opacity setting or a blend mode), you've combined two inks in a single object (**Figure 3.8**). Adding multiple strokes, each with different widths, colors, and dash patterns, can result in useful borders or even stitch lines (**Figure 3.9**). There are numerous reasons for adding multiple attributes, and there's no limit to how many fills or strokes you can add to an object. Another benefit of numerous fills and strokes is that you can create a complex appearance yet edit just a single path. We'll discuss more ways in which this feature can be useful when we talk about live effects later in this chapter.

Figure 3.8 Combining two fills in a single object allows you to create interesting effects. Here, a pattern fill and a gradient fill are combined using a transparency blend mode.

Figure 3.9 Combining two strokes in a single path gives you the ability to create complex strokes and still edit a single path.

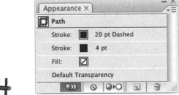

The Appearance panel also gives you control over the behavior of appearances. At the bottom of the panel are several buttons (**Figure 3.10**):

Figure 3.10 The Appearance panel contains several functions to control the appearances of objects.

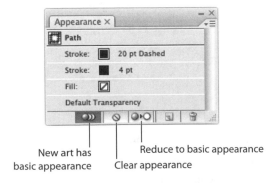

New art has basic appearance

Clear appearance

Reduce to basic appearance

- **New Art Has Basic Appearance.** This toggle, on by default, means that each new object you draw will have a basic appearance—a single fill and a single stroke. Ordinarily, Illustrator styles a newly drawn object based on the last object that is selected. For example, if you click an object with a black stroke and a yellow fill, the next object you draw has a black stroke and a yellow fill as well. However, if you select an object with a complex appearance and then create a new shape, you may not want that new shape to be drawn with multiple attributes. When this is toggled off, all new objects pick up the complex appearances of any object previously selected.

- **Clear Appearance.** This function reduces any appearance to a single fill and a single stroke, both with an attribute of None. This is a great way to select a shape and start from scratch.

- **Reduce to Basic Appearance.** This function reduces any complex appearance to a basic appearance by removing all fills and strokes except for the topmost fill and the topmost stroke.

Expanding Appearances

You'll notice that you can't select a specific attribute of an object from the artboard—the only place to access this functionality is via the Appearance panel. This makes the Appearance panel infinitely important, but it may make you wonder how an object with a complex appearance will print. After all, how does the printer or export format know to draw these multiple attributes on a single path?

The answer is that Illustrator breaks these complex appearances down into multiple overlapping paths—each path contains a basic appearance. This process, called *expanding*, doesn't happen on your artboard—it happens in the print stream or the export stream.

Sometimes you may want to manually expand your appearances to access the multiple attributes on the artboard. To do so, choose Object > Expand Appearance. Remember that once you've expanded an appearance, you are dealing with a group of multiple objects, not a single object anymore. Each of those individual objects has a basic appearance, and unless you've created a graphic style (covered later in this chapter), you have no way to return to the original complex appearance.

Although some people don't trust Illustrator and expand all appearances before sending final files off to print, we don't condone such behavior. There is no risk in printing files with appearances—they print just fine. Additionally, expanding your appearances limits your options if you have to make a last-minute edit or if your printer has to adjust your file.

ENHANCING APPEARANCES WITH LIVE EFFECTS

Illustrator has two entire menus dedicated to manipulating art and applying cool effects (such as 3D and warp distortions): the Filter menu and the Effect menu. The Effect menu differs from the Filter menu in several ways (see the sidebar "Featured Matchup: Filters vs. Effects"), but one of the most important is how effects are used in concert with the Appearance panel.

Illustrator refers to effects as *live effects*. There are several reasons for this. First—and most important—any effect you apply from the Effect menu is added as an attribute in the Appearance panel. Second, all effects can be edited at any time, even after the file has been closed and reopened at another date. Finally, when an object's path is edited, any effects that are applied to that object are updated as well. Because these effects are nondestructive, they are considered as "live" and are always editable.

The way that Illustrator accomplishes this live behavior is by keeping the underlying vector object intact, while changing just the appearance of the object by adding the effect. Think of those 3D glasses that you get at a movie theater. Without the glasses, the movie appears like any other, but once you don the glasses, the movie appears to be 3D. You can think of the Appearance panel as a pair of 3D glasses in this sense—once you add an effect, the object changes in appearance, but the original untouched vector paths remain beneath the hood (**Figure 3.11**).

Figure 3.11 After a Warp effect has been applied, a vector shape appears distorted (left). When viewed in Outline mode, you can see the underlying vector shape still exists, unscathed (right).

You can choose from many live effects in Illustrator, including those that are vector-based (such as Scribble) as well as those that are raster-based (such as Gaussian Blur). For the purposes of understanding how these effects work and how they interact with the Appearance panel, we'll discuss what is arguably the most commonly used live effect—Drop Shadow—in this chapter. The remainder of the live effects are covered in Chapter 8, *3D and Other Live Effects*.

Just as adding a second fill or stroke categorizes an object as having a complex appearance, adding a live effect to an object also produces an object with a complex appearance.

 Featured Matchup: Filters vs. Effects

You'll notice that Illustrator has both a Filter menu and an Effect menu. At first glance, the contents of these menus seem similar, and many of the items listed in the Filter menu appear to be identical to those in the Effect menu. In truth, there's a big difference between filters and effects in Illustrator.

As we mentioned, effects in Illustrator are referred to as *live effects*, and as they are applied, they appear in the Appearance panel. As you update your objects, any applied effects update accordingly. You can remove or edit these nondestructive effects at any time. In contrast, once you apply a filter, the actual vector object is changed, and the filter can't be edited or removed. For this reason, you can refer to filters as *dead effects* because they are applied to objects in a destructive fashion.

Although you will most likely use effects for the majority of your work, sometimes it makes sense to use filters instead. For example, you might need to apply a filter because it allows you to edit the vector paths right away. Rather than having to apply an effect and then expand it, you can just apply the filter, which is already expanded.

Additionally, some items in the Filter menu do not appear in the Effect menu—namely, those that appear in the Filter > Create menu. These filters (for example, creating trim marks) are usually applied once and aren't edited afterward.

Applying a Live Effect

Applying a live effect is easy. To apply a soft drop shadow, select an object, and choose Effect > Stylize > Drop Shadow. The Drop Shadow dialog appears, where you can specify the exact settings for your drop shadow including blend mode, opacity, offset (the distance between the object and its shadow), and the blur amount, which is the softness of the shadow. Additionally, you can choose a color or darkness value for your drop shadow (**Figure 3.12**).

Figure 3.12 The Drop Shadow live effect gives you the ability to control all the specifics of creating a soft drop shadow.

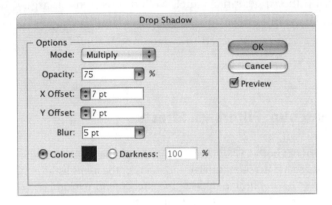

To choose a spot color for your drop shadow, you must first define the desired color as a swatch using the methods described in the previous chapter. Click the color swatch in the Drop Shadow dialog, and then click the Color Swatches button, where you'll find your custom color in the list of swatches.

Note that the dialog has a Preview option, which, when checked, allows you to see your shadow update as you make changes to the settings. This is a useful feature, and you'll find that nearly all live effects have a Preview option (yet another difference between many filters and effects). Once you're happy with the appearance of your drop shadow, click OK to apply it.

Now, let's take a look at the Appearance panel. Note that the path is listed as the target, and then examine the attributes in the object itself. Reading from the bottom up (the order in which the attributes are drawn), you have default transparency, the drop shadow effect you've just applied, the fill, and finally the stroke of the object (**Figure 3.13**). The drop shadow appears beneath the fill and the stroke of the object because it wouldn't be much of a drop shadow if it were painted above the fill and stroke, would it?

Figure 3.13 Live effects, once they are applied, appear listed in the Appearance panel.

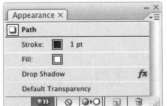

The truth is, you can use the Appearance panel to control exactly how and where your drop shadow—and any live effect—is painted. Using the method we discussed earlier to apply opacity settings to fills and strokes independently, you can click the Fill or Stroke attribute in the Appearance panel and then add the drop shadow. In this way, you can add a live effect to just the fill or just the stroke of an object (**Figure 3.14**). If your object contains multiple fills or strokes, you can apply live effects to each of them individually. Once you've already applied a live effect, you can drag it within the Appearance panel to change its place in the painting order and to have it applied to a specific fill or stroke.

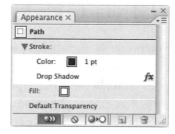

Figure 3.14 Live effects can be applied to fills or strokes of objects individually. Here, the drop shadow is applied just to the stroke of an object.

Editing a Live Effect

One of the important benefits of live effects is that you can edit them at any time. Double-clicking an effect that is listed in the Appearance panel opens the dialog for that effect, where you can view the current settings and change them at will. Many people make the mistake of going to the Effect menu to edit an effect. For example, if an object has a drop shadow applied to it, some might select the object and choose Effect > Stylize > Drop Shadow in order to change the settings of the effect. Doing so actually adds a *second* Drop Shadow effect to the selected object (**Figure 3.15**). Illustrator allows you to apply an effect to an object as many times as you'd like, and in Chapter 7, *Typography*, we will explore when that might be beneficial. The important thing to remember is that when you want to add a new effect to an object, you choose it from the Effect menu. To edit an effect that already exists, you double-click it in the Appearance panel.

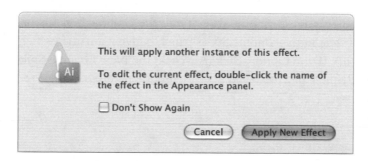

Figure 3.15 If you try to edit an existing effect by choosing it from the Effect menu, Illustrator informs you that you must edit existing effects through the Appearance panel.

⊕ You can also duplicate an effect by dragging it in the Appearance panel while holding the Option (Alt) key.

To duplicate an effect that you've applied, highlight it in the Appearance panel, and click the Duplicate icon in the panel. You can also drag effects to the Duplicate icon. To delete an effect from an object, highlight it in the Appearance panel, and click the trash can icon in the panel. You can drag effects directly to the trash can icon as well.

USING GRAPHIC STYLES

You probably already have a sense of how powerful appearances and live effects are. However, if you have several objects in your file to which you need to apply the same appearance, it can be inefficient to do this manually using live effects. Additionally, if you ever need to update the appearance you applied, you would need to do so for each object individually. Graphic styles can help.

A *graphic style* is a saved set of attributes, much like a swatch. When you apply a style to an object, that object takes on the attributes that are defined in the style. At any time, you can redefine the attributes of a particular style, and when you do, any objects in your file that already have that style applied are updated as well. The best part about graphic styles is how easy they are to use. And you'll never guess which panel plays an integral part in creating graphic styles—that's right, the Appearance panel.

Defining a Graphic Style

As we mentioned, a graphic style is a saved set of attributes. You know that the Appearance panel lists all attributes, so you already understand the first step in creating a graphic style—specifying the attributes you want defined in the style. Once you've specified stroke and fill settings and added live effects, click the New Graphic Style button in the Graphic Styles panel (**Figure 3.16**). Alternatively, you can drag the target thumbnail from the Appearance panel and drop it into the Graphic Styles panel. Double-click a style in the Graphic Styles panel to give it a name (which is always helpful). If you Option-click (Alt-click) the New Graphic Style button, you can define a new style and give it a unique name in a single step.

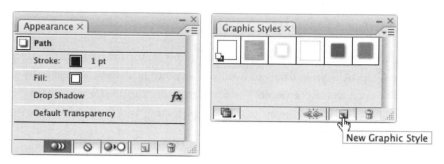

Figure 3.16 Once you've specified your attributes in the Appearance panel, you can use the Graphic Styles panel to create a new graphic style.

Notice that when you apply a graphic style to an object in your file, the Appearance panel identifies the target and the style that is applied. This makes it easy to quickly see which style is applied to an object (**Figure 3.17**).

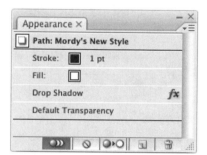

Figure 3.17 When a graphic style is applied, the Appearance panel helps you easily identify the target and the applied style.

Sometimes designers need to combine two inks to create a certain effect. For example, package designers often want to mix black ink with a spot color ink. Although you can't create a swatch that contains two inks, you can create a graphic style that contains two fills. The lower fill is the spot color; the other fill is a percentage of black, set to Overprint (**Figure 3.18**). You can then apply the style to any object with a single click.

Figure 3.18 To simulate a multi-ink color, combine two fills, and use the Overprint command. The result is a single, editable path that contains two colors.

Editing a Graphic Style

Editing a graphic style is an exercise that involves both the Appearance panel and the Graphic Styles panel, so it makes sense to position them side by side. You don't need to have an object selected in order to modify an existing graphic style, but if you do have an object selected, you'll be able to preview the changes you're making to the style.

In the Graphic Styles panel, click the style you want to edit. The Appearance panel lists all the attributes for the selected style. You can modify the style by adding attributes, by deleting existing ones, or by changing the paint order by dragging attributes in the Appearance panel. Once you're happy with the modifications, choose Redefine Graphic Style from the Appearance panel menu to update the style (**Figure 3.19**).

Figure 3.19 Once you've modified the attributes, you can update the style, which updates all other objects that have the style applied.

Any objects in your file that have that particular style applied then immediately update to reflect the modifications. Alternatively, you can Option-drag (Alt-drag) the target thumbnail on top of the existing style in the Graphic Styles panel. A heavy black outline appears around the style in the panel to indicate that the style will be updated (**Figure 3.20**).

Figure 3.20 Dragging the thumbnail from the Appearance panel on top of an existing graphic style while holding the Option (Alt) key redefines the style.

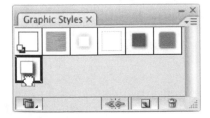

Loading Attributes with the Eyedropper Tool

You can use Illustrator's Eyedropper tool to load the attributes of existing objects quickly. This can be useful in two ways. First, if you already have an object selected when you click another object with the Eyedropper tool, your selected object changes to match the object you clicked. Second, you can click once with the Eyedropper tool to sample the attributes of an object, and you can then Option-click (Alt-click) to apply those attributes to other objects in your file without actually having to select them.

You can configure the Eyedropper tool to sample just the basic appearance of an object (the topmost fill and stroke) or complete complex appearances. To control what the Eyedropper tool can sample, double-click the tool in the Toolbox (**Figure 3.21**).

Shift-click with the Eyedropper tool to sample colors from the pixels of raster images. In this way, the Eyedropper tool works much like the one found in Photoshop.

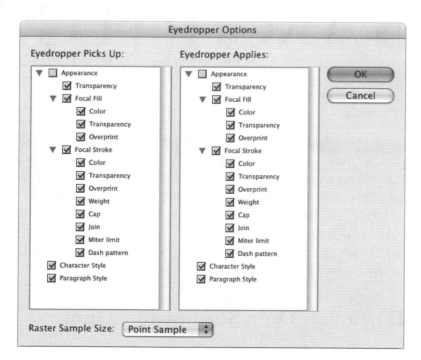

Figure 3.21 Double-click the Eyedropper tool in the Toolbox to control what specific attributes the tool uses for sampling.

WORKING WITH GROUPS

As we mentioned at the beginning of this chapter, creating groups is a way to organize the elements in a file. Most important, groups allow you to easily select or work with several objects that may belong to a single design element. You can also nest groups, meaning you can have groups within other groups. For example, you might have a logo that consists of an icon and a type treatment that has been converted to outlines. You can group the objects that make up the icon, and you can put the items that make up the type treatment into a separate group. You can then group both groups, resulting in a single group (the logo) that contains two groups (the icon and the type treatment) within it (**Figure 3.22**).

Figure 3.22 An example of a nested group, where two groups are nested within a third group.

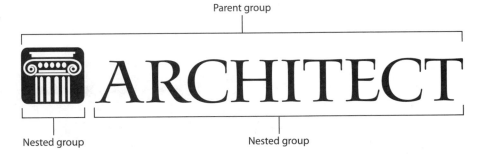

When you think of groups in this way, it's simply a matter of labeling certain objects that belong together. But now that we have appearances in Illustrator, it's more than just a concept—a group is actually an entity itself. Illustrator refers to a group as a *container*—something that contains the grouped objects within it. This introduces two important concepts: The container itself can have attributes applied to it, and the container can affect the way the grouped objects interact with each other and other art elements in your file. Let's take a look at a simple example using the Drop Shadow effect you just learned about in the previous section.

Adding a Soft Drop Shadow to a Group

Draw two overlapping shapes, a circle and a square, each a different color. Now create an exact copy of those two shapes, but in the copied version, group the two objects by selecting them and choosing Object > Group.

So, now you're looking at two design elements, each identical in appearance, but one consists of two separate objects, and one consists of two objects that are grouped (**Figure 3.23**). Select the first set of objects, choose Effect > Stylize > Drop Shadow, and apply the default settings. Now select the grouped objects, and apply the same drop shadow. Observe the results (**Figure 3.24**).

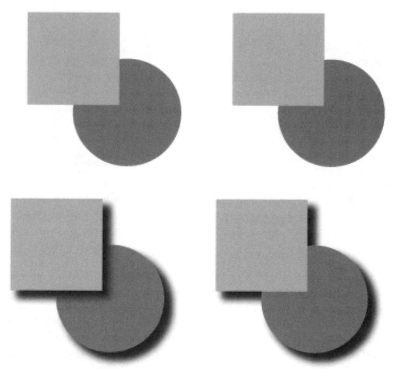

Figure 3.23 The design elements shown here are identical except for one fact: The element on the right has been grouped.

Figure 3.24 Applying a drop shadow to individual objects (left) appears different from the same drop shadow applied to a group of objects (right).

The first design element appears to have drop shadows applied to each object individually. The second design element—the group—has a single drop shadow applied to it, as if the two separate shapes were really one shape. This difference in appearance occurred because in the second design element, Illustrator applied the drop shadow not to the actual objects themselves but to the container that has the two objects inside of it—the group. Now, select the group and choose Object > Ungroup, and the drop shadow disappears! By removing the container (ungrouping), you've removed the effect that was applied to that container.

Adjusting Opacity to a Group

Let's look at another example using the same two design elements—one of which is grouped. Select the first set of objects, and change the opacity value in the Transparency panel to 50 percent. Now select the group, and make the same change to the opacity value. Observe the results (**Figure 3.25**).

Figure 3.25 When applying an Opacity setting to individual overlapping objects, you can see one object through the other (left), but when the opacity is applied to a group, the entire group takes on the attribute, giving it a different appearance (right).

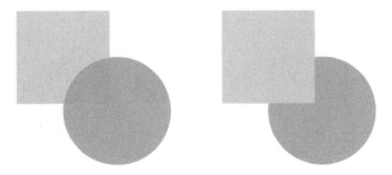

The first design element has the opacity value applied to each object individually, and each object interacts with the other, enabling you to see through one object to the one underneath it. The grouped objects have the same opacity applied, but you don't see the objects overlapping with each other. Again, this appearance is because Illustrator is applying the opacity to the container, not to the objects themselves. As in the previous example with the drop shadow, simply ungrouping the two objects removes the opacity as well.

These two examples clearly illustrate how groups can have attributes applied to them or how they can control how grouped objects interact with each other. In this context, you begin to see that grouping objects is more than just making files easier to manage. Creating groups can have a significant impact on the appearance of your art. In fact, simply ungrouping art can alter the appearance of your file completely.

The current target is also displayed on the far left side of the Control panel.

The obvious questions you should be asking are, "How do I know when I'm applying an attribute to an object versus a group?" and "How can I tell whether ungrouping something will alter the appearance of my file?" The answers lie in the all-important Appearance panel, which tells you what is targeted. If you think back to the grouping examples we discussed earlier, you'll recall that when you selected the group, the drop shadow was applied to the group because it was targeted. Had the individual paths been targeted, the drop shadow would have been applied to the paths themselves.

Text as a Group

Text is a special kind of object in Illustrator—it's actually a group. The type object itself is the container, and the actual text characters are like the objects inside a group. You can see this by looking at—that's right—the Appearance panel. Select a point text object with the Selection tool, and the Appearance panel shows *Type* as the target. Switch to the Type tool and select the text, and the Appearance panel shows *Characters* as the target.

When you select a text object with a selection tool, Illustrator's smart targeting automatically targets the Type container. You can see Characters listed in the Appearance panel, and double-clicking the Characters listing automatically switches to the Type tool and highlights the text on your artboard (**Figure 3.26**). The target is now Characters, and you can see the Fill and Stroke attributes.

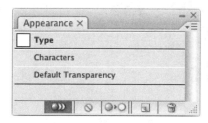

Figure 3.26 When a Type object is selected, the Appearance panel shows the Type as the container and the characters within it.

Isolating Groups

Sometimes you'll want to draw a new object and add it to an existing group. For example, say your client requests that you add the Registered Trademark symbol to a logo, which is already grouped. One way to accomplish this is to use the Type tool to add the Registered Trademark symbol to your document. Then you select the logo, ungroup it, and then select the logo and the new trademark symbol to group the objects together. This is problematic only because we know that you can apply attributes and effects to a group,

Group isolation mode is especially useful when you're using Live Paint groups, which we'll cover in detail in Chapter 4, *Advanced Vectors*.

and the mere act of ungrouping your artwork will remove that attribute or effect (**Figure 3.27**).

Flash CS3 Professional can also edit groups in the same manner.

Illustrator features an easier way to add objects directly into existing groups, using a feature called *group isolation*. Using the logo example we just discussed, you would use the following method to add the trademark symbol. Using the Selection tool, double-click the logo. A gray bar appears across the top of the document window, and all other artwork in the file becomes dim, indicating that the group is now isolated (**Figure 3.28**). When a group is isolated, any new shapes or objects that are created become part of the group. Select the Type tool, and create a text object with the trademark symbol to automatically add the symbol to the logo group. To exit isolation mode, either double-click anywhere outside the group or click the arrow in the gray bar. If you have nested groups, each successive double click isolates another level within the group. The arrows in the gray bar help indicate where you are in the hierarchy of your groups (**Figure 3.29**).

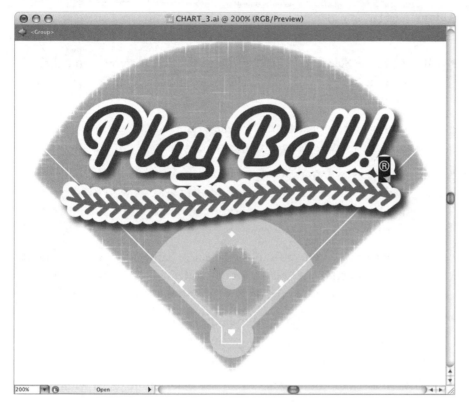

Figure 3.28 When in isolation mode, a gray bar appears across the top of the document window, and all other artwork on the artboard is dimmed. Any new artwork created is drawn directly into the isolated group.

Figure 3.29 Clicking the arrow in the gray bar will take the current group out of isolation.

In truth, isolation mode is useful for a variety of tasks, including the editing of groups. Ordinarily, you would be required to use the Direct Selection tool to move one object within a group (the Selection tool will select the entire group). However, in isolation mode, the Selection tool will select parts of a group. So to make a quick edit within a group, you can double-click with the Selection tool, make the required change, and then double-click to exit the group—all without having to use the Direct Selection tool at all.

→ Illustrator's General panel in Preferences contains a setting to disable the ability to isolate a group by double-clicking it.

Although isolation mode is wonderful, certain functions are either not available or don't work as expected when you're in isolation mode:

- If you choose Select All when a group is isolated and you then either choose Edit > Paste in Front or choose Edit > Paste in Back, you will exit isolation mode.

- You cannot edit an opacity mask while in isolation mode, and you cannot isolate groups within opacity masks when editing them.

- The Create New Layer button in the Layers panel and the Duplicate Selected Item button in the Appearance panel won't work when in isolation mode. A workaround is to choose those options from their respective panel flyout menus.

- Choosing any menu item from the Select > Same menu will select only those objects within an isolated group while in isolation mode. Artwork that appears elsewhere in the document will not become selected.

- Neither Snap to Pixel nor Snap to Point works when moving isolated objects near nonisolated ones. Smart Guides, however, do work amongst all objects.

- When in isolation mode, you cannot use the Outline preview mode.

- While in isolation mode, you cannot use the Object > Lock or Object > Hide function. You can only hide or lock objects via the icons in the Layers panel.

- Saving a view using the View > New View command doesn't preserve isolation mode.

Working with Layers

Layers are nearly identical to groups in concept, but they offer more flexibility and functionality. Whereas groups are used to combine design elements in a file, layers also allow you to organize and combine elements within a file. Just as groups can be nested within each other, so can layers. And just as groups are containers that hold contents within them, layers are containers as well. In addition, layers, just like groups, can also have attributes applied to them. As we explore the power of layers in Illustrator, all of these concepts will come to light.

The Significance of Layers

Don't be fooled into thinking that layers are just for making files neat and organized. Quite the contrary, a file that takes advantage of using layers can benefit from many other features as well:

- **Layer clipping masks.** Illustrator has the ability to make the topmost object in a layer a mask for all items within that layer.

- **PDF layers.** Illustrator can export PDF files with layers intact, allowing users in Adobe Acrobat or Adobe Reader to interactively turn on and off those layers. Additionally, Adobe InDesign has the capability to control the visibility of PDF layers.

- **Photoshop export.** When exporting an Illustrator file to a PSD file, you can choose to have layers preserved, thus making your file easier to edit when you bring it into Adobe Photoshop.

- **Transparency.** Sometimes artwork with transparency can result in files that look less than perfect when printed on a high-resolution press—if the file is built in a certain way. Using layers can significantly reduce the number of issues you might encounter when using transparency features.

- **Animation.** When creating art for frame-based animations, such as those used in GIF and SWF (Flash) animations, Illustrator layers serve as frames. Layers are also integral when you are creating art that will be animated in programs such as Adobe After Effects.

- **Cascading Style Sheets (CSS).** Illustrator layers can be exported as CSS layers when you're creating web layouts and SVG graphics, allowing for greater flexibility and better support for browser standards.

- **Scalable Vector Graphics (SVG).** Illustrator layers serve as basic building blocks when you're creating files that are going to be saved as SVG. Providing structure for SVG files can help make it easier to animate and edit the SVG files in a Web or wireless environment.

- **Variables.** Illustrator's XML-based variables feature relies on the organization of layers in your document. Object visibility and naming conventions are all done through the Layers panel.

There are plenty of other good reasons to use layers in Illustrator, and you're sure to find yourself using layers more and more.

Using the Layers Panel

You'll start learning to use layers by taking a look at the Layers panel and learning some of its simple functions. Then you'll put together everything you've learned in this chapter to take full advantage of the power found in the Layers panel.

By default, all Illustrator documents are created with a single existing layer, called Layer 1. The buttons across the bottom of the panel are used to activate clipping masks (which we'll cover in detail in Chapter 5, *Brushes, Symbols, and Masks*), create new layers and new sublayers, and delete layers. To the left of each layer are two boxes—the box on the far left controls layer visibility, whereas the other box enables locking (**Figure 3.30**). The Layers panel menu contains duplicates of these functions, as well as some other functions that we'll cover when we talk about animation in Chapter 11, *Web and Mobile Design*.

Figure 3.30 All files are created with a blank layer in the Layers panel.

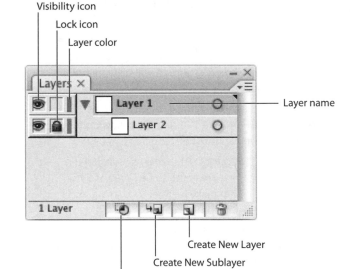

Double-clicking a layer enables you to specify several settings for that layer (**Figure 3.31**):

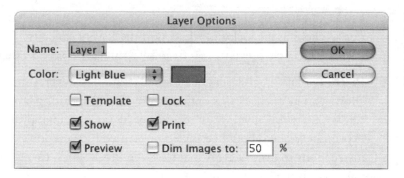

Figure 3.31 The Layer Options dialog allows you to specify settings for each layer—most notably, the name of the layer.

- **Name.** Every layer can have its own distinct name. Layer names are important when you're creating SVG files and generally make files easier to work with. Naming layers is especially important when you're designing templates. A file littered with layers named Layer 1, Layer 2, and Layer 3 can make editing a challenging task.

- **Color.** This setting is a bit deceiving because it doesn't add a fill color to the layer but instead defines the selection color used for the layer. When you select an object in Illustrator, the path of that object is highlighted so that you see what is selected. By assigning different colors to each layer, you can tell what objects belong to which layer by selecting the object and observing the highlight color. Setting a layer color to black or really light colors generally isn't a good idea because you won't be able to differentiate a selection from a regular path. A layer's color also appears along the left side of the layer name in the Layers panel.

- **Template.** This setting is used specifically when you want to manually trace placed images. Setting a layer as a template automatically locks the layer, disables printing of that layer, and sets the Dim Images setting to 50 percent. Although this makes it easier to see and draw over placed images, the new Live Trace feature makes this option less important.

- **Show.** This setting controls layer visibility (whether the art on a layer is shown or hidden) and performs the same function as clicking the show/hide icon in the Layers panel.

- **Preview.** This setting controls the preview setting for the chosen layer. By default, Illustrator's Preview mode is turned on, but unchecking this option displays the layer in Outline mode.

Option-click (Alt-click) the visibility icon of a layer to hide all other layers with one click. Option-click (Alt-click) once more to show all layers again. The same shortcut applies to the lock icon as well. To change layer visibility for multiple layers, you can click and drag across several layers.

- **Lock.** This setting controls layer locking and performs the same function as clicking the lock/unlock icon in the Layers panel itself. Locking a layer effectively prevents you from selecting any object on that layer.

- **Print.** By default, all layers in a file will print. However, Illustrator allows you to uncheck this option to create a nonprinting layer. This can be useful when you want to add instructions to a template file or to explain how a file should be folded or printed but you don't want those instructions to print. Layers that have the Print option turned off appear italicized in the Layers panel.

- **Dim Images To.** This option allows you to define an Opacity setting for how placed images appear on your screen. By making placed images dim, you can make it easier to manually trace them. This feature is often used in tandem with the Template function.

Object Hierarchy

When a layer contains artwork, a disclosure triangle appears just to the left of the layer. Clicking this triangle reveals the contents of the layer within the Layers panel (**Figure 3.32**). Every object that appears in an Illustrator document appears listed in the Layers panel. The order in which items appear has significance—it indicates the *stacking order*, or object hierarchy, of the file. Objects that appear at the bottom of the Layers panel are drawn first, and therefore they appear at the bottom of the object stacking order.

Figure 3.32 Clicking a disclosure triangle reveals the raw power of the Layers panel—the ability to view the entire object hierarchy of a file.

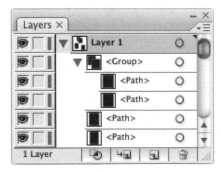

Configuring the Layers Panel

If you find that the level of detail offered by the Layers panel is beyond the needs of your simple design tasks, you can set the behavior of the Layers panel to match the functionality that existed prior to Illustrator 9. Choose Panel Options from the Layers panel menu, and select the Show Layers Only checkbox (**Figure 3.33**). This hides all objects from the Layers panel. Additionally, you can turn off layer thumbnails (which will significantly enhance performance). For documents that have lots of layers (such as maps, for example), you might also choose the Small option for Row Size (**Figure 3.34**). One caveat to these options is that they are document-specific, which means you need to change these settings for each document.

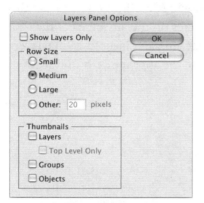

Figure 3.33 Turning off layer thumbnail previews in the Panel Options dialog significantly enhances performance in large files.

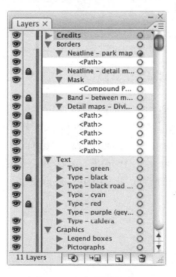

Figure 3.34 Choosing the Small option for Row Size in the Panel Options dialog can give you the ability to see far more layers on screen at once and reduce the need to scroll as often.

You can drag items listed in the Layers panel to adjust where they sit in the stacking order. Dragging an object from the bottom of the Layers panel to the top of the panel places that object at the top of the stacking order. It's important to note that each layer and each group also maintain their own stacking orders. The Layers panel basically represents the stacking order of the entire file.

In the Layers panel, layers and sublayers appear with shaded backgrounds, and objects appear with white backgrounds.

You can create nested layers by dragging one layer into another layer (**Figure 3.35**). You can do the same with groups as well, which makes it easy to organize your artwork even after the art is created. In fact, this method of dragging items within the Layers panel makes it possible to move objects from one group and place them into another group. As you learned earlier in this chapter, groups can have attributes applied to them; this becomes significant because when you're moving an object into a group that has an attribute applied to it, that object takes on the attributes of the group. The reverse applies as well, so simply moving an object from one layer to another or into or out of a group can change the appearance of the art in your file.

Figure 3.35 When you're dragging layers in the Layers panel, black arrows on the left and right indicate that you're moving a layer into another layer rather than above or below it.

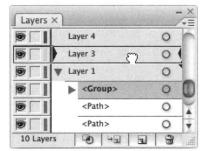

Using Layers and Appearances

If you take another look at the Layers panel, you'll notice that to the right of every item listed is a small circle, called the *target indicator* (**Figure 3.36**). If you remember, we spoke earlier about how the target controls where attributes are applied. If you take the same examples we used earlier, the ones of identical design elements of which one is grouped and one is not, you can clearly see how targeting works.

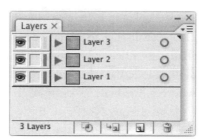

Figure 3.36 The little circles that appear on the right side of each layer are target indicators.

In the Layers panel, the ungrouped design element appears listed as separate paths, whereas the grouped design element appears as objects nested inside a group (**Figure 3.37**). When you select the first design element, a double circle appears on each of the individual paths, indicating that those paths are targeted (**Figure 3.38**). Now select the grouped design element, and you'll see that although the objects are *selected*, the group is *targeted* (**Figure 3.39**).

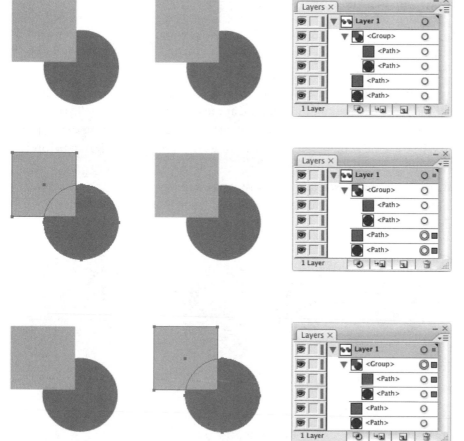

Figure 3.37 A quick look at the Layers panel reveals the hierarchy of the file. Layer 1 contains two path objects and a group. The group contains two path objects.

Figure 3.38 Selecting the path objects also targets the two individual paths. The large squares to the right indicate the objects are selected, and the small square to the right of the layer indicates that some objects on the layer are selected, but not all of them.

Figure 3.39 When selecting the group, Illustrator's smart targeting feature targets the group, not the objects themselves. Notice the double circle target indicator appears only on the group, not the objects.

Now you'll add a drop shadow to each of the design elements. A quick glance at the Layers panel now shows that some of the target indicators are shaded or filled, whereas some of the target indicators are hollow (**Figure 3.40**). Hollow circles indicate that the item listed has a basic appearance, whereas filled circles indicate that a complex appearance exists on that object (Adobe engineers refer to these filled circles as *meatballs*). Just by looking at the Layers panel, you can tell that the second design element has some kind of effect applied to the group. This is your first indication that ungrouping such a group will result in a change in appearance.

Figure 3.40 Shaded target indicators—meatballs—show where complex appearances exist.

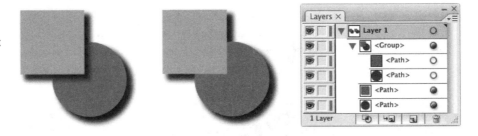

You can manually target groups or layers by clicking the target indicator for that object. For example, you can target a layer and then use the Appearance panel to add a new stroke. The Appearance panel lists the attributes for the targeted layer, and if you look at the contents of the panel, you'll see that the stroke appears above the contents of the layer. Dragging the stroke underneath the contents of the layer causes the stroke to be drawn behind each of the objects on that layer (**Figure 3.41**). When you drag a shape into such a layer, the object automatically appears to have a stroked appearance, and when you drag any objects out of that layer, that stroked appearance disappears.

Dragging a meatball from one layer or object to another effectively copies the complex appearance and applies it to the object to which you are dragging it.

Figure 3.41 With a layer targeted, you can add appearances directly to the layer. Here, a stroke has been added to the layer, and the stroke has been moved to appear below the contents of the layer, adding an interesting outlining effect.

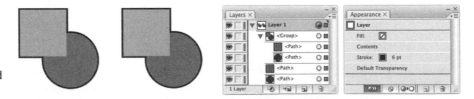

The important concept to remember is that taking a quick look at the Layers panel and scanning for meatballs helps you find complex appearances that appear in the file. In this way, you won't accidentally change a file's appearance just by grouping or ungrouping objects.

The Appearance panel is also useful in helping you understand how files are built because if you select an object that is part of a group or layer that has an appearance applied, the Appearance panel lists the group or layer above the target (**Figure 3.42**).

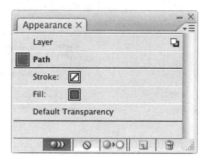

Figure 3.42 When you select an object that is part of a group or layer that has a complex appearance, the Appearance panel alerts you to this by displaying elements above the target.

PUTTING IT ALL TOGETHER

The importance of the Appearance panel is obvious. Without it, you have no way to edit multiple attributes applied to an object, you have no way to edit attributes that are applied to groups or layers, and you have no way to edit the properties of a live effect.

The importance of the Layers panel is equally apparent. Without it, you have no way to understand the hierarchy of a file, and you have no warning as to when a simple action such as grouping or ungrouping will change a file's appearance.

But it's deeper than that. The Appearance panel is like the Matrix—you can look at it and see the underlying makeup of any Illustrator file. By using the Layers and Appearance panels together, you can quickly and efficiently reverse-engineer any file you receive (**Figure 3.43**). If you're a production artist who needs to know every detail about a file or if you're trying to troubleshoot a particular file, these two panels will be your best friends.

Figure 3.43 Don't trust everything you see on the artboard. It's easy to create a single object, group it by itself, and then apply a 50-percent Opacity setting to the object, the group, and the layer. The result is an object that prints at 12.5-percent opacity. The meatballs in the Layers panel should be an indicator that you need to take a closer look.

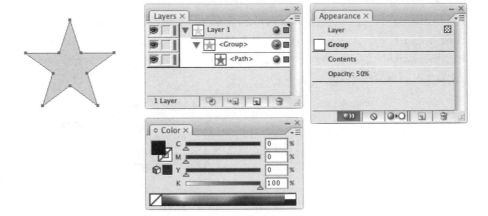

Throughout the remaining chapters of this book, you'll learn how features such as clipping and opacity masks, envelope distortions, and placed images are all easily identified in the Layers panel. You'll also learn the importance of using layers when you're creating Adobe Flash animations or SVG files for the Web.

In complex files, it can be hard to locate certain objects either on your artboard or in your Layers panel. Using the Layers panel to select objects can make it easier to find and select objects on the artboard, and selecting objects on the artboard can also quickly identify where those objects appear in the Layers panel.

CHAPTER FOUR

Advanced Vectors

Drawing rectangles, ovals, and stars is nice, but that's not why you use Adobe Illustrator. The true power of Illustrator is that you can use it to create custom shapes as you need them—this allows you to tweak a design to perfection. Illustrator comes with a variety of tools and functions, each with its own strengths and uses. Whether it's the mystifying Pen tool, the Live Paint feature that allows you to edit and color vector objects more freely, or the dependable Pathfinder and path functions that have helped make Illustrator so powerful over the years, this chapter reveals the true art of the vector path.

DRAWING AND EDITING FREE-FORM VECTORS

Strip away the cool effects. Forget all the fancy tools. Ignore the endless range of gradients and colors. Look past the veneer of both print and Web graphics. What you're left with is the basis of all things vector—the anchor point. You can learn to master every shape tool in Illustrator, but if you don't have the ability to create and edit individual anchor points, you'll find it difficult to design freely.

Illustrator contains a range of tools that you can use to fine-tune paths and edit anchor points. At first, it might seem like these all perform the same functions, but upon closer inspection, you'll find each has its use.

Mastering the Pen Tool

Just the mention of the Pen tool sends shivers down the spines of designers throughout the world. Traditionally, Illustrator's Pen tool has frustrated many users who have tried their hand at creating vector paths. In fact, when the Pen tool was introduced in the first version of Illustrator in 1987, word had it that John Warnock, the brain and developer behind Illustrator, was the only one who really knew how to use it. In truth, the Pen tool feels more like an engineer's tool rather than an artist's tool.

But don't let this prevent you from learning to use it.

Learning how to use the Pen tool reaps numerous rewards. Although the Pen tool first appeared in Illustrator, you'll now find it in Adobe Photoshop, Adobe InDesign, and Adobe Flash; if you know how to use it in Illustrator, you can use it in the other applications as well. You can use the Pen tool to tweak any vector path to create the exact shape you need, at any time. Additionally, if you give yourself a chance, you'll see that there's a method to the madness. After learning a few simple concepts, you'll quickly realize that anyone can use the Pen tool.

Usually, when new users select the Pen tool and try to draw with it, they click and drag it the same way they might use a normal pen on paper. They are surprised when a path does not appear onscreen; instead, several handles appear. At this point, they click again and drag; now a path appears, but it is totally not where they expect it to appear. This experience is sort of like grabbing a hammer by its head and trying to drive a nail by whacking it with the handle—it's the right tool, but it's being used in the wrong way.

While we're discussing hammers, let's consider their function in producing string art. When you go to create a piece of string art, you first start with a piece of wood, and then you hammer nails part of the way into it, leaving each nail sticking out a bit. Then you take colored thread and wrap it around the exposed nail heads, thus creating your art. The design you create consists of the strands of colored thread, but the thread is held and shaped by the nails. In fact, you can say that the nails are like anchors for the threads.

When you're using the Pen tool in Illustrator, imagine you're hammering those little nails into the wood. In this situation, you aren't drawing the shape itself; instead, you're creating the anchors for the shape—the Bézier anchor points. Illustrator draws the thread—the path—for you. If you think about drawing in this way, using the Pen tool isn't complicated at all. The hard part is just figuring out where you need to position the anchors to get the shape you need. Learning to position the anchors correctly comes with experience, but you can get started by learning how to draw simple shapes.

Drawing Objects with Straight Paths

Follow these steps to use the Pen tool to draw a straight path:

1. Select the Pen tool, and click the artboard once—do not click and drag.

    Clicking once with the Pen tool creates a *corner anchor point*. This anchor point is the start point of your path.

2. Now, move your pointer to where you want the end point of your path (**Figure 4.1**); click again to define a second corner anchor point.

Figure 4.1 Once you've clicked once to create the first anchor point, move your pointer to the location where you want the second anchor point.

When drawing new paths with the Pen tool, it's best to set your fill to None and your stroke to black. Otherwise, Illustrator will fill the path as you create it, making it difficult to see your work.

Holding the Shift key while you click with the Pen tool constrains paths to 45-degree increments. Additionally, you can choose View > Smart Guides to have Illustrator display helpful guides and hints as you move the pointer (see Appendix B, *Application Preferences,* for more information).

Once you create this second point, Illustrator automatically connects the two anchor points with a straight path, completing the line (**Figure 4.2**).

Figure 4.2 Clicking a second time creates the path between the two anchor points. No clicking and dragging is necessary.

For now, the first concept becomes clear: when you're using the Pen tool, clicking—not dragging—is what defines a corner anchor point.

At this point, with your Pen tool still selected, Illustrator assumes you want to add points to your path. By clicking again, you can create a third corner anchor point, and if you do, Illustrator draws a path to connect the second anchor point to the newly created one (**Figure 4.3**).

Figure 4.3 Each successive click with the Pen tool continues to create additional path segments.

Admittedly, this behavior may prove confusing because you may have been expecting to start a new path rather than add to the existing one. To start a new path, you first have to deselect the current path. The easiest way to do this is to click a blank area on the artboard while pressing the Command (Control) key, which temporarily changes your tool to the Selection tool. Once you've deselected the path, you can click with the Pen tool to start drawing a new path.

So now you understand a second concept: when drawing an open path with the Pen tool, each click adds another anchor point to the path until you deselect the path, which is how you indicate to Illustrator that you've finished that path.

You can indicate that you've finished drawing a path in another way—by drawing a closed path. Until now, you've been creating open paths, but now you can try to create a closed shape—in this case, a triangle:

1. With nothing selected, select the Pen tool, and click once to define the first anchor point of the triangle.

2. Move the pointer to another part of the artboard, and click again to define the second point.

3. Now move the pointer once more, and click to define a third anchor point (**Figure 4.4**).

A triangle has three sides, so you have all the anchor points you need, but at the moment, the object you've drawn is an open path.

4. To complete the shape, move the pointer so it rests directly on the first anchor point that you defined, and click once to close the path (**Figure 4.5**).

At this point, if you click again elsewhere on the artboard, the Pen tool starts drawing a new path.

Figure 4.4 A triangle needs three anchor points; the third click creates two path segments.

Figure 4.5 Clicking the first anchor point completes the shape. This is the shape after it has been closed.

This brings us to a third concept: when you create a closed path, the next click with the Pen tool starts a new path.

If this sounds confusing, try it once or twice, which should help—especially if you pay attention to your Pen tool pointer. When you're using the Pen tool, the pointer changes as you draw, helping you understand the three concepts you've just learned. When the Pen tool is going to start creating a new path, a small X appears at the lower right of the icon; when the Pen tool is going to add anchor points to an existing selected open path, no icon appears next to it; and when the Pen tool is going to close a path, a small *O* appears at the lower right of the icon (**Figure 4.6**).

Figure 4.6 The Pen tool shows subtle indications in its icon that let you know the function it will perform.

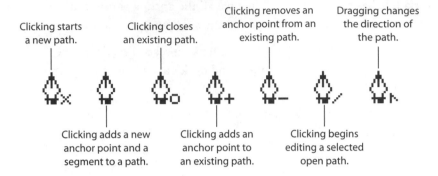

Clicking starts a new path.

Clicking closes an existing path.

Clicking removes an anchor point from an existing path.

Dragging changes the direction of the path.

Clicking adds a new anchor point and a segment to a path.

Clicking adds an anchor point to an existing path.

Clicking begins editing a selected open path.

Drawing Objects with Curved Paths

 By now, you should be able to understand the statement we made earlier about how drawing the path is the easy part of using the Pen tool. The hard part is trying to figure out where to place the anchor points to get the path you want.

The paths you've drawn up until this point were all made up of corner anchor points, which are connected with straight lines. Of course, you'll also need to create paths with curved lines; this section explains what you need to know.

In Chapter 2, *Vectors 101*, you learned that curves are defined with *direction handles*, which control how the paths between anchor points are drawn. When you want to draw a curved path, you follow the same basic concepts you learned for creating straight paths, with one additional step that defines direction handles:

1. To draw a curved path, select the Pen tool, and make sure an existing path isn't selected. Position your pointer where you want to begin your path, and then click and drag outward before releasing the mouse (**Figure 4.7**).

    This action creates a *smooth anchor point* where you first clicked and defines direction handles at the point where you released the mouse.

Figure 4.7 Clicking and dragging with the Pen tool defines the smooth anchor point and, at the same time, allows you to position the direction handles.

2. Now position your pointer where you want the next anchor point to be, and click and drag once again (**Figure 4.8**).

Using the direction handles as guidance, Illustrator draws a curved path connecting the two smooth anchor points.

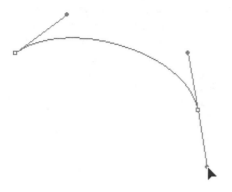

Figure 4.8 Clicking and dragging a second time completes a curved path between the first two anchor points and defines the next curve that will be drawn.

3. Move your pointer to another location on your artboard, and click and drag to create a third smooth anchor point.

4. Click and drag the first anchor point to close the path (**Figure 4.9**).

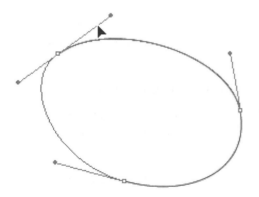

Figure 4.9 Clicking and dragging on the first anchor point completes the curved shape.

We can now define a fourth concept: clicking and dragging with the Pen tool creates a smooth anchor point and defines its direction handles.

Learning to anticipate how the placement of direction handles creates the path you want takes time, but you don't have to get it right the first time. Once you create a smooth anchor point, you can switch to the Direct Selection tool and click and drag the anchor point to reposition it

➜ Even the most experienced Illustrator artists need to switch to the Direct Selection tool to tweak the curves they create, which can be time-consuming. To get around this time suck, you can press the Command (Control) key while the Pen tool is active to temporarily access the last-used Selection tool. While the Selection tool is active, click and drag the anchor points or direction handles to adjust the path, and then release the mouse to continue creating more points with the Pen tool.

(**Figure 4.10**). Additionally, when you select a smooth anchor point at any time, the direction handles become visible for that anchor point, and you can use the Direct Selection tool to reposition those as well.

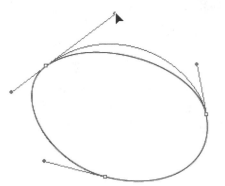

Figure 4.10 Using the Direct Selection tool, you can change the position of anchor points and direction handles to adjust a curved path.

Drawing Objects with Both Straight and Curved Paths

In the real-design world, shapes consist of both straight and curved lines. You can use the knowledge you've gained up until this point to create paths that contain a mixture of both corner and smooth anchor points. Basically, you know that clicking with the Pen tool produces a corner anchor point and a straight line, and you know that dragging with the Pen tool produces a smooth anchor point and a curved line.

Try drawing a path with both types of anchor points:

1. Select the Pen tool, and make sure you don't have an existing path selected (look for the small *X* icon on the Pen tool pointer). Click once to create a corner anchor point.

2. Move your pointer, and click again to create a straight line (**Figure 4.11**).

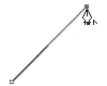

Figure 4.11 You can begin a new path by creating two corner anchor points to make a straight line.

3. Move your pointer, and click and drag to create a smooth anchor point.

You now have a single path that consists of both a straight line and a curve (**Figure 4.12**).

Figure 4.12 Adding a smooth anchor point creates a single path with both straight and curved paths.

You can use Illustrator's Convert Anchor Point tool to convert a corner anchor point to a smooth anchor point, and vice versa. To do so, choose the Convert Anchor Point tool (which is grouped with the Pen tool), and apply the same concepts you've learned. Click an existing anchor point once to convert it to a corner anchor point, and then click and drag an existing anchor point to pull out direction handles and convert it to a smooth anchor point.

Changing Direction on a Path

As you were creating smooth anchor points, you may have noticed that when you are creating or editing direction handles, a mirror effect occurs. On a smooth anchor point, the direction points are always opposite each other, and editing one seems to affect the other. Remember that the direction handles control how the path passes through the anchor point, so the direction handles are always tangential to the curve (**Figure 4.13**).

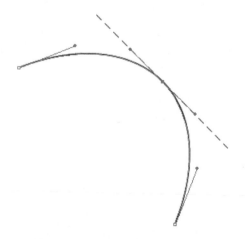

Figure 4.13 With a smooth anchor point, the direction handles are always tangential to the curve of the path.

You can, however, change the direction of a path as it passes through an anchor point:

1. Use the Direct Selection tool to select a smooth anchor point.

2. Switch to the Convert Anchor Point tool, and click and drag one of the *direction handles* (not the anchor point).

   In essence, this creates a combination point, which you can then continue to edit with the Direct Selection tool (**Figure 4.14**).

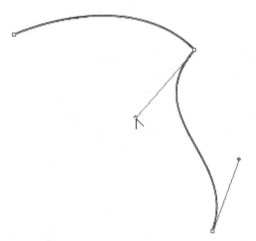

Figure 4.14 Clicking and dragging a direction handle with the Convert Anchor Point tool creates a combination anchor point.

To make life easier, you can create combination points as you draw with the Pen tool:

1. Start by clicking and dragging to create a smooth anchor point.

2. Move your pointer to a different position, and click and drag again to create another smooth anchor point and, hence, a curved path.

3. Now, position your pointer directly on the second anchor point you just created. You'll notice that the Pen tool icon shows a small inverted *V* in its icon.

4. Click and drag the anchor point while holding the Option (Alt) key to drag out a single direction handle (**Figure 4.15**).

5. Move your pointer to another location, and click again; you'll see that you've created a combination point.

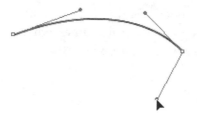

Figure 4.15 As you're drawing a path with the Pen tool, you can create a combination point by clicking and dragging the last anchor point of the path while holding the Option (Alt) key.

Converting Type to Outlines

Overall, using the Pen tool takes some getting used to, and if you're going to use Illustrator often, it's best to practice. While practicing, you might find it useful to convert some type to outlines (choose Type > Create Outlines) to see how the anchor points are positioned in those shapes (**Figure 4.16**). Try to re-create them on your own, and get a feel for when you need a corner anchor point and when you need a smooth anchor point. The more you use the Pen tool, the easier it will be to use.

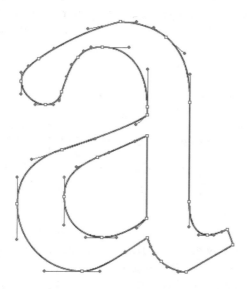

Figure 4.16 When you're learning to use the Pen tool, it can be helpful to convert some type characters to outlines so you can study the placement of the anchor points and direction handles. Choose Select > Object > Direction Handles to see the direction handles for an entire shape at once.

Adding and Deleting Anchor Points

Because anchor points are used to define paths, you must add and delete points from a path to achieve the shapes you need. You may think you can select an anchor point with the Direct Selection tool and simply press the

Delete key on your keyboard, but doing this deletes a portion of the path (**Figure 4.17**). Although this may be useful at times, what you really want is to keep the path but remove the anchor point.

Figure 4.17 Using the Direct Selection tool to select and delete an anchor point (left) also deletes the connecting path segments (center). The Delete Anchor Point tool keeps the path closed but removes the anchor point (right).

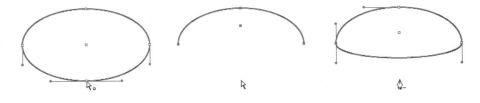

To delete an anchor point from a path without deleting the path, select the Delete Anchor Point tool, and click the anchor point once that you want to remove. Likewise, you can switch to the Add Anchor Point tool and click a selected path anywhere to add a new anchor point to the path (**Figure 4.18**). As an alternative, you can click the Remove Selected Anchor Points button in the Control panel. Note that this button will not appear when *all* anchor points of a path are selected.

Figure 4.18 The Add Anchor Point tool enables you to add new anchor points to an existing path.

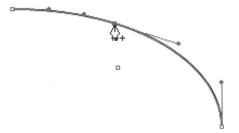

Illustrator tries its best to help you get your work done, but sometimes its overzealousness gets in the way. By default, when you move your pointer over an existing path with the Pen tool, Illustrator, thinking you want to add a point to the existing path, conveniently switches to the Add Anchor Point tool. Likewise, when you move your pointer over an existing anchor point, Illustrator switches to the Delete Anchor Point tool, thinking you want to remove that anchor point. This is great, unless you wanted to start drawing a new path with the Pen tool on top of an existing selected path. You can turn this feature off by checking the Disable Auto Add/Delete option in the General panel in Preferences, which politely tells Illustrator, "Thanks, but no thanks."

Drawing with the Pencil Tool

To draw with the Pencil tool, simply click and drag on the artboard. As you drag, you'll see a light path trail the movement of your pointer (**Figure 4.19**). After you release the mouse, Illustrator creates the anchor points necessary and creates a vector path for you (**Figure 4.20**).

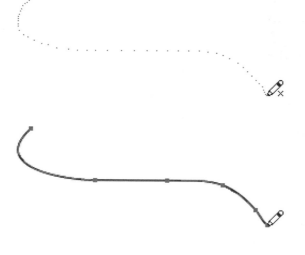

Figure 4.19 As you drag with the Pencil tool, a faint line traces the path of your pointer.

Figure 4.20 After you release the mouse, Illustrator creates anchor points as necessary and displays the drawn path. Depending on your mouse control, the path may have a jittery appearance.

Because drawing with the Pencil tool relies on how steadily you handle your mouse or tablet pen, you can employ several tools and settings to help create better-looking paths.

The Smooth tool, which you'll find grouped with the Pencil tool in the Toolbox, is a tool you can use to iron out the wrinkles of any selected vector path. Select any vector path, and click and drag over it with the Smooth tool. Doing this repeatedly makes the vector path smoother and smoother. The angles in the path become smoother, and the path itself modifies to match the contour of the direction in which you drag with the Smooth tool (**Figure 4.21**).

Pressing the Option (Alt) key with the Pencil tool selected will temporarily switch to the Smooth tool.

Figure 4.21 Using the Smooth tool repeatedly on a path can enhance its appearance.

If necessary, the Smooth tool removes excess anchor points.

Double-clicking the Pencil tool or the Smooth tool opens the Pencil Tool Preferences dialog, allowing you to specify that tool's behavior (**Figure 4.22**).

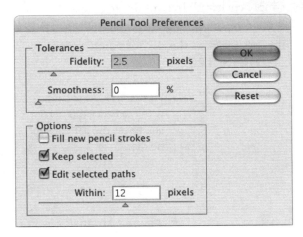

Figure 4.22 Selecting the Edit Selected Paths option allows you to easily reshape or adjust existing paths.

The preferences for the Pencil and Smooth tools are saved when you quit Illustrator so that you don't have to set these for each new file you create or each time you launch Illustrator. If you trash your preferences file, however, you'll need to reset these preferences to your liking.

- **Fidelity, Smoothness.** Available for both the Pencil and Smooth tools, the Fidelity setting determines how close the vector path is drawn in relation to the movement of your mouse or input pen. A lower Fidelity setting results in a path that more closely matches the exact movement of your mouse. A higher Fidelity setting results in a path that is smoother and less jittery but that may not match your stroke exactly. If you're good with handling the mouse or if you're using an input pen, you might go with a lower setting. If you have trouble controlling the mouse or pen precisely, you might benefit from a higher Fidelity setting. The Smoothness setting refers to how much smoothing Illustrator applies to paths as you draw them. The higher the Smoothness setting, the fewer anchor points you'll see on your paths. If you're looking for more fluid strokes, increasing the Smoothness setting will help.

- **Fill New Pencil Strokes.** By default, Illustrator creates paths drawn with the Pencil tool as paths with a stroke but no fill. In Chapter 2, *Vectors 101*, you learned that even open paths can have fills and that checking this option gives you the ability to choose a fill color and create filled paths as you draw them with the Pencil tool. This setting is available for the Pencil tool only, not for the Smooth tool.

- **Keep Selected, Edit Selected Paths.** With Illustrator's default behavior, when you draw a path with the Pencil tool, the path becomes selected as soon as you complete it. You can change this behavior by deselecting the Keep Selected option. When the Edit Selected Paths option is selected and your pointer is within the specified number of pixels from an existing selected path, Illustrator allows you to modify the selected path by simply drawing over it with the Pencil tool. This can be helpful because it allows you to tweak a path to perfection as you are drawing it, almost as if you were using the Smooth tool. Where this gets in the way, however, is when you intend to draw a new path but inadvertently end up editing a path that is selected instead. This can happen often if you have the Keep Selected option turned on. Many designers prefer to turn off the Keep Selected option but leave on the Edit Selected Paths option. This way, if they do need to edit a path, they can Command-click (Control-click) a path to select it; at this point, the Edit Selected Paths feature lets them draw over it.

 ### Featured Matchup: The Pen Tool vs. the Pencil Tool

In contrast to the Pen tool, the process of drawing with the Pencil tool mimics that of drawing with a real pen on paper. In reality, the Pencil tool is the exact opposite of the Pen tool. With the Pen tool, you define the anchor points, and Illustrator completes the paths. With the Pencil tool, you draw the path, and Illustrator creates the anchor points for you.

If using the Pencil tool to draw paths sounds a lot easier than creating anchor points with the Pen tool, remember that the mouse isn't the easiest tool to control when you're trying to draw. Although the Pencil tool is easier to use to create paths, it's not as easy to create exact or precise paths with it. However, if you have a pressure-sensitive tablet available, the Pencil tool is a bit easier to control.

For technical drawing and precise illustration work, including logo creation and letterforms, you'll most likely find that the Pen tool offers the fine control you need. You'll find the Pencil tool useful when you're working with creative illustrations, cartoons, and projects that require a more natural feel. As you'll see later in this chapter, the Pencil tool proves valuable when you're working with Live Paint groups.

You can also use the Path Eraser tool to remove parts of a vector path. It's important to realize that the Path Eraser tool is not akin to the Eraser tool found in paint programs, which you can use to just erase pixels at will (however, Illustrator has an Eraser tool that does just that, which we'll talk

→ Remember that you can use the Smooth and Path Eraser tools on any vector path in Illustrator— even those that were not created with the Pencil tool.

about shortly). You use the Path Eraser tool specifically to erase portions of a selected vector path. As you trace over an existing selected path with the Path Eraser tool, a light path appears to trail the movement of your pointer. When you release the mouse, Illustrator deletes the portion of the path you've traced.

Using the Reshape Tool

You can also use the Reshape tool across multiple selected paths.

Using the Direct Selection tool to select individual points on a path results in some anchor points moving while others remain stationary. In most kinds of path editing, this is the desired behavior, although it can result in paths that appear distorted (**Figure 4.23**). At times, you may want to stretch a path by moving selected points, but you may also want other points to move as necessary to maintain a nondistorted path appearance. The Reshape tool is perfect for this task.

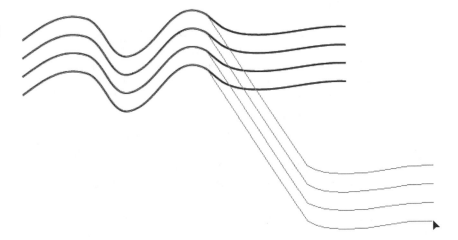

Figure 4.23 Although you can always select individual points on a path and move them, you may not get acceptable results.

1. Select a path using the Selection tool, and then select the Reshape tool.

2. Click an anchor point or a part of a path that you want to act as a focus point when you stretch the path. This way, you'll have the most control over how this focused point is moved.

   You can also hold the Shift key and select additional focus points (as well as drag to marquee-select additional anchor points).

3. Once you've selected your focus points, click and drag one of the focus points to reshape the path.

You'll notice that as the points that are in focus move, other points in the path move as well to keep the general proportion of the path (**Figure 4.24**).

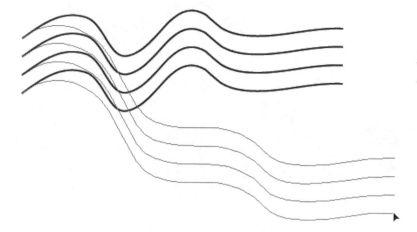

Figure 4.24 Using the Reshape tool, you can stretch paths and reshape them without telltale distortion.

Using the Eraser Tool

Illustrator CS3 features a new tool called the Eraser tool. Unlike the Path Eraser tool, the Eraser tool works as you would expect—it simply erases parts of objects. That being said, the Eraser tool has a variety of settings, and you should know about some "side effects" as well.

You'll find the Eraser tool in the lower part of the Tools panel, grouped with the Scissors and Knife tools (**Figure 4.25**). To use the Eraser tool, select it, and then click and drag over any object (or objects). If nothing is selected, the Eraser tool will erase all objects across all layers in your document, with the exception of locked layers, of course (**Figure 4.26** on the following page). For more control, you can make a selection first and then use the Eraser tool, at which time the tool will erase only those objects that are selected (leaving all other objects intact).

Figure 4.25 The Eraser tool (not to be confused with the Path Eraser tool) is grouped with other tools that cut or sever objects.

Figure 4.26 A single swipe with the Eraser tool erases all objects in its path.

It's important to realize that although the Eraser tool is cool and makes it seem effortless to quickly remove parts of an illustration, the tool still must abide by the general rules of how vector objects are drawn. This means if you try to erase part of a single closed path, the result will be two closed paths, not open ones. It's easiest to see this when attempting to erase paths that contain strokes (**Figure 4.27**). In addition, although you can certainly use the Eraser tool to erase portions of a stroke, you must reapply the strokes to each segment of the resulting path (**Figure 4.28**). In the latter case, you can get around this by first applying the Object > Path > Outline Stroke command before using the Eraser tool. The same applies when trying to erase paths with brushes applied (refer to Chapter 5, *Brushes, Symbols, and Masks*, for more information on brushes).

Figure 4.27 Although you may initially expect the eraser to simply remove an area from an object (left), the result will actually be two closed shapes (right).

Figure 4.28 If a stroke has the Round Cap option specified, the eraser may appear to create a clean break while you're using it (left), but the result will be two paths, each with its own respective round cap appearance (right).

Once you get used to the behavior of the Eraser tool, it becomes a useful (and fun!) tool to use. Even better, you can adjust some really powerful settings to get the full potential of the Eraser tool. First, you can adjust the size of the eraser by tapping the bracket keys on your keyboard (just as you would adjust brush size in Photoshop). You can also double-click the Eraser tool in the Tools panel to open the Eraser Tool Options dialog (**Figure 4.29**). You can manually adjust the numerical values for the angle and roundness of the Eraser tool, or you can click and drag the black dots and the arrow in the preview near the top of the dialog to adjust those values visually. You can adjust the size of the diameter of the eraser as well.

You'll find that the settings for the Eraser tool are quite similar to the Calligraphic Brush settings, which are covered in Chapter 5, *Brushes, Symbols, and Masks.*

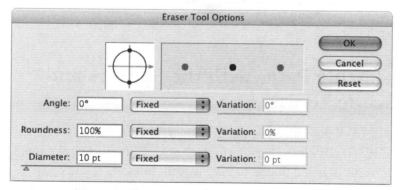

Figure 4.29 The Eraser Tool Options dialog offers control over how the Eraser tool works.

By default, all the values are fixed, meaning they remain consistent as you use the Eraser tool. However, you can choose to make the values random and select a variation for each setting. Even better, if you have a pressure-sensitive tablet (such as the one from Wacom, for example), you can choose other variables including Pressure (**Figure 4.30**). For example, setting Diameter to Pressure with a high Variation value gives you the ability to erase with more control and flexibility (**Figure 4.31**).

Holding the Option (Alt) key while dragging with the Eraser tool will allow you to erase using a rectangular marquee area. Dragging with the Shift key will constrain the eraser to increments of 45 degrees.

Figure 4.30 When choosing variable settings such as Pressure, the preview window in the Eraser Tool Options dialog displays the minimum, median, and maximum sizes of the eraser.

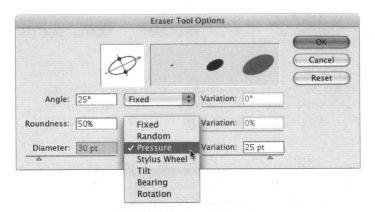

Figure 4.31 By applying pressure with a Variable setting for the eraser, you can achieve natural-looking results not possible with a mouse.

Cutting Paths with the Scissors and Knife Tools

If you find you need to cut through multiple paths at once, you should look into Rick Johnson's Hatchet tool plug-in (http://rj-graffix.com).

When editing paths, you might find you need to cut or split a path at a certain point. With the Scissors tool selected, you can click any topmost vector path (selected or not) to cut the path. In essence, you create two anchor points by doing this. The Scissors tool can cut only one path at a time.

The Knife tool is much like the Scissors tool, only you cut or split a path by dragging the pointer across a path instead of clicking it. Whereas using the Scissors tool results in an open path, using the Knife tool results in at least two closed paths (**Figure 4.32**). The Knife tool cuts through multiple paths when nothing is selected, but cuts through only objects that are selected (even if those selected objects appear beneath other objects).

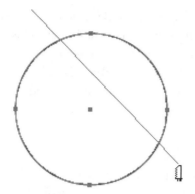

Figure 4.32 Using the Knife tool to slice a single object results in two separate closed paths.

Holding the Option (Alt) key while dragging with the Knife tool constrains the tool so that it uses straight lines only.

Using the Scissors or Knife tool is unwieldy at best, and you may find that if you're doing a lot of path editing, you'll get better results using Live Paint groups, which are covered later in this chapter.

CREATING COMPOUND PATHS

A *compound path* is a single path that consists of more than one path. That sounds like an oxymoron, no? Think of the letter O in the alphabet. It appears to be a large circle with a smaller circle cut out from its center. How is such a shape created with Illustrator? The answer is by drawing two circles and combining them to become a single compound path. You do this by choosing Object > Compound Path > Create. The result is a shape with a hole cut out of the middle (**Figure 4.33**). Compound paths are treated as one entity, and therefore, both paths that make up this compound path take on the attributes of the bottommost path. If your compound path consists of multiple shapes, Illustrator does its best to figure out which paths become hollow and which appear solid.

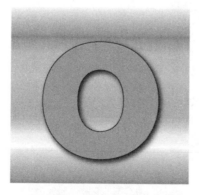

Figure 4.33 An example of a compound path. The hole in the center is actually cut out from the path, and objects that appear beneath the compound shape are visible through the hole.

When a path reverses direction in a shape such as in a figure eight, it can never be all clockwise or all counterclockwise. In such a case, the direction of the region(s) with the largest total area is what defines the results.

For more on this, refer to the sidebar "Featured Matchup: Non-Zero Winding Fill Rule vs. Even-Odd Fill Rule."

Illustrator uses one of two methods to decide which paths of a compound shape are hollow and which are solid. The default method is the Non-Zero Winding Fill Rule method; Illustrator can also use another method, the Even-Odd Fill Rule method. You'll find both of these buttons in the Attributes panel, and you can choose them when a compound path is selected on the artboard (**Figure 4.34**). By default, Illustrator uses Non-Zero Winding Fill Rule and makes the bottommost path clockwise and all the other selected paths counterclockwise.

When you create a compound path and click Non-Zero Winding Fill Rule, you can manually reverse the path direction to control whether a shape is hollow or solid. Use the Direct Selection tool to select the path you need, and click the appropriate button in the Attributes panel (**Figure 4.35**).

Even-Odd Fill Rule

Non-Zero Windows Fill Rule

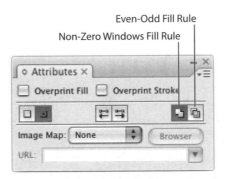

Figure 4.34 You can use the Attributes panel to choose one of the two supported compound path methods for determining hollow and solid areas.

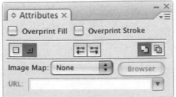

Figure 4.35 Using the Attributes panel to manually reverse the direction of a path, you can specify whether a part of a compound path using Non-Zero Winding Fill Rule is hollow or solid.

Featured Matchup: Non-Zero Winding Fill Rule vs. Even-Odd Fill Rule

More math! When you compare them to each other, Even-Odd Fill Rule seems more intuitive, and it is easier to predict which areas will be filled and which areas will be hollow. Although you have more flexibility with Non-Zero Winding Fill Rule—you can manually control the result—this rule is more difficult to understand, and the result is harder to predict.

With Even-Odd Fill Rule, every area inside an even number of enclosed areas becomes hollow, and every region inside an odd number of enclosed areas becomes solid (**Figure 4.36**). An *enclosed* area refers to an area enclosed by another path (or the loop of a path in a self-intersecting shape). The outermost enclosed area is always numbered 1, and therefore a regular path is filled (it is enclosed by a single area, which is an odd number).

In contrast, the Non-Zero Winding Fill Rule takes into account the direction of a path: An area enclosed by a clockwise loop counts as +1, and an area enclosed by a counterclockwise loop counts as –1. When the sum of these counts is zero, that area becomes hollow. When it is anything else, that area becomes solid (**Figure 4.37**). Because you can manipulate the path direction to get different results from the same shapes, Non-Zero Winding Fill Rule is more flexible, but it's an exercise of trial and error since you can't see the direction of a path on the artboard.

Although the results in most cases are the same whether you use the Non-Zero Winding Fill Rule or Even-Odd Fill Rule setting, sometimes the result is different (**Figure 4.38**).

—*Special thanks to Teri Pettit of the Adobe Illustrator team for helping explain these rules.*

Figure 4.36 When you're using Even-Odd Fill Rule, Illustrator labels areas using odd and even numbers to determine hollow and solid areas.

 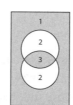

Figure 4.37 When you're using Non-Zero Winding Fill Rule, Illustrator takes into account the direction of the path when it determines the hollow and solid areas of a compound path. The arrows indicate path direction.

 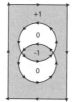

Figure 4.38 Some compound shapes appear different, depending on the fill rule specified, especially with self-intersecting paths.

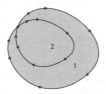

PERFORMING ADVANCED PATH EDITING

Editing paths by hand can be tedious, but it doesn't always have to be. Many times, you'll need to perform certain edits on vector paths, such as removing extra anchor points from a complex path or splitting larger shapes into smaller ones of equal size. Other times, you may need to create outlines of strokes, create duplicate paths at larger or smaller sizes, or simply clean up loose paths and objects in your file. The good news is that Illustrator has a variety of useful path functions you can use to perform these kinds of tasks.

You can find the functions covered here in the Object > Path menu.

Working with the Join and Average Commands

When you have two anchor points, you can use the Join command to connect the two points with a straight path. Although this sounds simple, you must meet certain requirements for the Join command to work:

- Only two anchor points can be selected. If you have three or more anchor points selected, the Join command will not work. Unless …

- All of the anchor points on an open path are selected. In this case, the Join command draws a straight line between the start and end anchor points to close the shape.

- The selected anchor points cannot belong to different groups.

- The selected anchor points cannot be part of a graph object.

If the two anchor points overlap each other exactly, Illustrator combines the two anchor points and gives you the option of converting the resulting single point to a smooth point or a corner point (**Figure 4.39**).

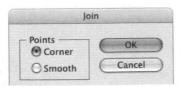

Figure 4.39 When you are trying to join two overlapping anchor points, Illustrator offers you the option of creating a corner anchor point or a smooth anchor point.

Older versions of Illustrator allow you to use the Average command to easily align point text objects. Unfortunately, that functionality is not present in Illustrator CS3.

The Average function allows you to select at least two anchor points and reposition them by evenly dividing the space between them. You can average anchor points horizontally, vertically, or both horizontally and vertically.

There is no limit to how many anchor points you can average at once (**Figure 4.40**).

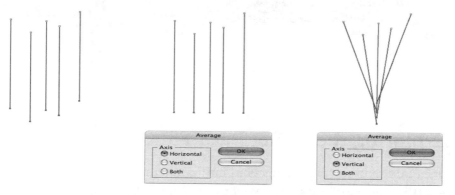

Figure 4.40 Choose Object > Path > Average, and then align multiple anchor points.

You can also select two anchor points and press Command-Option-Shift-J (Control-Alt-Shift-J) to perform a combined Average and Join function in one step.

Using the Outline Stroke Command

The stroke of a path adds thickness to the appearance of the path, but it's an attribute you can't physically select and manipulate on the artboard. However, you can select a path with a stroke and choose Object > Path > Outline Stroke; when you do, the stroke of that path expands to become a filled shape that you can then edit with the Pen tool. This allows you to tweak the path to make it appear as if the "stroke" is thinner and thicker in different places.

Sometimes you might want to convert a stroke to an outline for production reasons. If you have a final version of a logo, converting all strokes to filled paths assures that it will scale properly under all circumstances, because users may forget to turn on the Scale Strokes & Effects setting.

Similar to what happens with patterns, when you apply transformations to objects that have strokes or effects applied, the default behavior is that only the shape is transformed, not the strokes or the effects (**Figure 4.41** on the following page). Turning on the Scale Strokes & Effects option in the General panel of Preferences changes the default behavior so that strokes and effects are transformed as well. You can also find this setting in the Scale Options dialog.

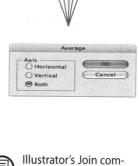

Illustrator's Join command can connect only two anchor points at a time. If you need to join several anchor points or paths at once, you should take a look at Rick Johnson's Concatenate plug-in (http://rj-graffix.com/software/plugins).

Figure 4.41 If you forget to turn on the Scale Strokes & Effects setting, you can run into problems when scaling artwork. In this example, the text of the logo was reduced, as was the path, but the stroke weight was not scaled. Outlining strokes prevents these kinds of accidents.

Exploring the Offset Path Function

One of the most useful path functions in Illustrator is Offset Path. When used, this function creates a new vector path that is offset a user-specified amount from the selected object(s). The original selected path is not affected. If you think about it, it's like a scaling function—you can offset paths to be larger or smaller. But if you've ever tried to scale an object such as an oval, you'll know that doing so creates an oval of a different proportion. If you want to create an object that is the same but that has its edges enlarged evenly across the entire object, choose Object > Path > Offset Path (**Figure 4.42**).

Figure 4.42 Scaling an oval shape results in a distorted shape (left). Using the Offset Path function results in a nondistorted result (right).

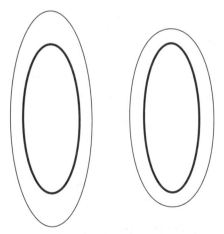

You can use Offset Path with negative values as well, which allows you to create paths that are offset inside existing paths.

Offset Path works a bit differently depending on the kind of path you have selected. On a closed path, it seems to work as expected, by creating the new path at the offset you specify. On an open path, however, the Offset Path command creates a new closed path, appearing on both the inside and outside of the original path (**Figure 4.43**). Depending on the task, this might mean you need to take an extra step to delete the part of the path that is not needed.

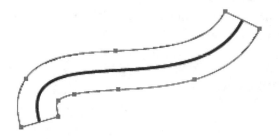

Figure 4.43 The Offset Path function, applied to an open path, results in a new closed path. You have to delete a portion of the resulting path if you want an open path.

Simplifying Vector Paths

Earlier in this chapter, you learned how to use the Remove Anchor Point tool to delete existing anchor points from a path. Although that tool is useful for removing a point or two from a path here or there, it's quite another story when you're trying to remove a lot of anchor points from a path.

You may find that some vector paths contain unnecessary anchor points. By unnecessary, we mean you might be able to create the same path with fewer anchor points. Too many unnecessary anchor points on a path translates into more complex files that take longer to print and that are more difficult to edit (**Figure 4.44**).

 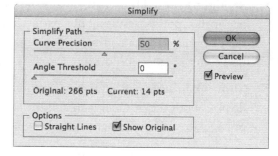

Figure 4.44 Paths with numerous unnecessary anchor points are harder to edit and take longer to print.

You'll often come across this problem when you're importing files from CAD applications or when you're using vector tracing programs such as Adobe Streamline (the Live Trace feature in Illustrator, covered in Chapter 9, *Mixing It Up: Working with Vectors and Pixels*, does not suffer nearly as much from this problem).

To reduce the number of anchor points on a path, select the path, and choose Object > Path > Simplify. You can use the Preview option to see the results as you change the settings. The Simplify dialog also gives you real-time feedback on the number of anchor points on the original path and the number of points using the current Simplify settings (**Figure 4.45**). The dialog also offers the following settings:

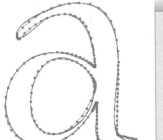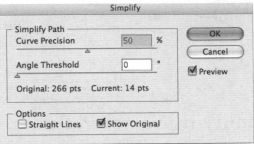

- **Curve Precision.** This controls how closely the simplified path matches the curves of the original selected path. A higher Curve Precision setting results in a path that more closely matches the original but that has fewer reduced anchor points.

- **Angle Threshold.** The Angle Threshold setting determines the smoothness of corners. If the angle of a corner point is less than the Angle Threshold setting, the corner point is not changed to a smooth anchor point.

- **Straight Lines.** This setting forces the simplified path to only use corner anchor points, resulting in a path that is far less complex. Of course, the path may not match the original that well, but this option may be useful in a creative mind-set.

- **Show Original.** With the Show Original option checked, Illustrator displays both the original path and the simplified result, allowing you to preview the difference between the two.

Using the Split Into Grid Feature

The Split Into Grid feature is wonderful for creating layout grids and for creating columns you might use for text threads or even tables.

The Rectangular Grid tool is great for creating quick grids for illustration purposes, but with it you lack fine control, especially if you want to create gutters—space that appears between columns and rows. Illustrator's Split Into Grid feature takes an existing shape and splits it into a specified number of equal-sized rectangles.

With any vector object selected, choose Object > Path > Split Into Grid to open the dialog. Select the Preview check box so you can see the results as you enter the values. Add rows and columns as needed, and also specify a value for the gutter. Illustrator automatically calculates the width and height values for you as you change the other values. At the bottom of the dialog is an Add Guides check box, which draws guides at the borders of the rows and the columns (**Figure 4.46**).

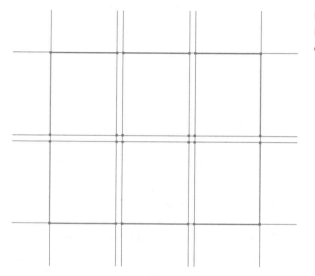

Figure 4.46 Using the Split Into Grid feature can make it easy to set up layout grids.

Removing Unnecessary Elements with the Clean Up Feature

While working on revision after revision of a file, your document may become littered with stray anchor points, empty text objects, or unpainted objects (those that have neither a fill nor a stroke applied). Having these objects present in a file can be problematic for a variety of reasons. Empty text objects may contain references to fonts, and you, thinking that those fonts aren't there, may forget to include them when you send source files to prepress. Additionally, stray points in a file can cause files to export with unexpected size boundaries (refer to Chapter 1, *The Illustrator Environment*, where we spoke about bounding boxes) and could lead to corrupt files.

Choose Object > Path > Clean Up, and choose which of these elements you want to automatically remove from a file (**Figure 4.47** on the following page). Beware that to Illustrator, a stray point is a single anchor point with no path. Some designers use Scatter brush art by using the paintbrush to click just once to place a single instance of a brush. Running the Clean Up command to delete stray points deletes these Scatter brush objects from a file as well. In reality, it's better to use Symbols rather than Scatter brushes for these designer tasks, something we'll discuss in Chapter 5, *Brushes, Symbols, and Masks.*

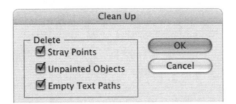

Figure 4.47 Illustrator's Clean Up feature makes it easy to remove excess elements from a document.

INTRODUCING THE LIVE PAINT FEATURE

Although you can appreciate the power and precision that vector graphics have to offer, you can also appreciate how easy it is to use pixel-based paint programs such as Photoshop or Corel Painter to easily apply color to artwork. In a paint program, you can perform flood fills, in which you choose a color and use a paint bucket–like tool to fill areas of the illustration with color. When working with vectors, you know that you have to create distinct paths and shapes in order to apply a fill to add color. In other words, you can't just apply a fill to any arbitrary area on your artboard; rather, you need to select a distinct object to which to apply the fill. This need to create distinct objects can make drawing in Illustrator seem nonintuitive or time-consuming at best.

Live Paint introduces a new concept of working with vector paths, where you can colorize vectors and edit them without having to follow the traditional vector rules that we've been covering up to this point. This feature makes it a lot easier to draw (and edit) in Illustrator. Let's take a closer look.

Using Live Paint to Color Paths

First you'll create something using Live Paint to get a feel for what the feature is all about. Then we'll discuss how the feature works, and at that point, you'll better understand how to use it in a meaningful way. Select the Line Segment tool, and draw two parallel vertical lines and two parallel horizontal lines to create a tic-tac-toe board. Don't worry if the lines or spacing aren't perfect—for this exercise, you just want to make sure the lines cross each other (**Figure 4.48**).

Select the four lines, and select the Live Paint Bucket tool. As you move your pointer over the four paths, the paths become highlighted (**Figure 4.49**). Click once to create a Live Paint group. Now, choose a fill color (a solid color, gradient, or pattern) from the Control panel, and move your pointer over the center area of the tic-tac-toe board. The enclosed area in the middle becomes highlighted in red, which indicates an area that you can fill with color (**Figure 4.50**). Click once with the Live Paint Bucket tool to fill the highlighted area (**Figure 4.51**).

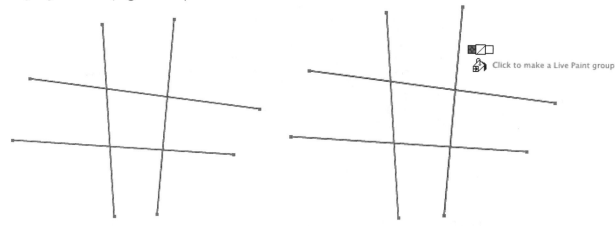

Figure 4.48 Using the Line Segment tool, you can create a simple tic-tac-toe graphic.

Figure 4.49 If you have the Live Paint Bucket tool selected, Illustrator shows a tool tip to create a Live Paint group when your pointer passes over a valid selection.

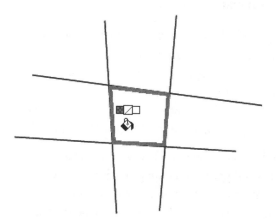

Figure 4.50 Illustrator's Live Paint Bucket tool highlights areas that can be filled as your pointer moves over them, even if the Live Paint groups aren't selected.

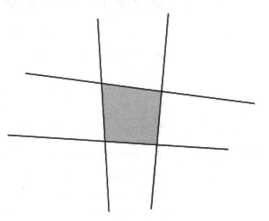

Figure 4.51 With one click of the Live Paint Bucket tool, you can fill areas that appear to be enclosed, even though there is an actual vector object there.

The resulting behavior is very Photoshopesque—you've filled an area that is enclosed on all sides, but you didn't fill an actual object. Choose the Direct Selection tool, select one of the paths, and move it just a bit. Notice that the color in the area updates to fill the center (**Figure 4.52**). If you move one of the paths far enough to the side so that it no longer touches the other paths, you'll find that the fill color disappears, because there is no longer an enclosed area to fill (**Figure 4.53**).

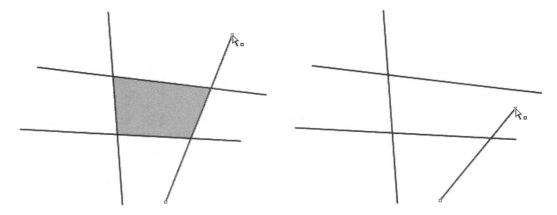

Figure 4.52 The fill areas in a Live Paint group update automatically when you're moving the paths with the Direct Selection tool.

Figure 4.53 When editing the paths in a Live Paint group, creating an opened area results in the loss of the fill.

Understanding Live Paint Groups

If you move a path so that an enclosed painted area becomes unpainted, Illustrator doesn't remember that the region was filled with a color prior to the edit. Moving the path back to its original position will not bring back the fill; you'll need to reapply the fill color.

Let's take a moment to understand how Live Paint works. When you select several overlapping paths or shapes and click them with the Live Paint Bucket tool, you are creating a *Live Paint group*. This is a special kind of group in which object stacking order is thrown out the window. All objects in a Live Paint group are seemingly combined onto a single flat world, and any enclosed area acts as a closed shape, which can be filled with color.

Although clicking several selected paths is the easiest way to create a Live Paint group, you can also select several paths and choose Object > Live Paint > Make to create a Live Paint group. Once you've created a Live Paint group, however, you may find that you want to add paths or shapes to the group. To do so, draw the new paths, and use the Selection tool to select the existing Live Paint group and the new paths. Then choose Object > Live Paint > Add Paths. The new paths will become part of the group, and any intersecting areas will act as individual areas that you can fill with color.

Live Paint groups can also utilize the Group Isolation Mode feature that enables you to draw objects directly into existing groups. Using the Selection tool, double-click an existing Live Paint group to enter Group Isolation Mode. Now switch to any shape or path tool to add paths directly to the Live Paint group (**Figure 4.54**). This ability to add paths directly to a Live Paint group is extremely powerful because it allows you to define regions for color in just a few quick steps. Using Pathfinder filters to create multiple overlapping shapes is no longer required for such tasks.

You can use the Live Paint Bucket tool to color multiple regions with a single color in one step by clicking one region and dragging the pointer across additional contiguous regions.

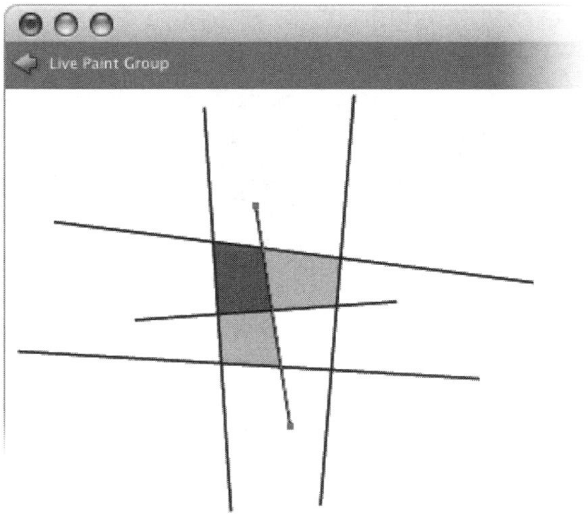

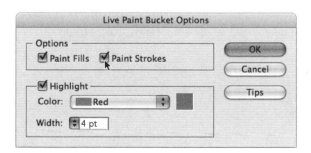

Figure 4.54 In Group Isolation Mode, you can draw new paths in an existing Live Paint group to instantly create additional regions that can be filled with color.

In the Toolbox, double-click the Live Paint Bucket tool to change its behavior. By default, the Live Paint Bucket tool affects only the fill of a path, but you can also set the tool to apply color to strokes as well (**Figure 4.55**). Additionally, you can specify the color that the Live Paint tool uses to highlight closed regions.

Unfortunately, the Live Paint feature doesn't work with paths that have brush attributes applied. If you do try to turn paths with brushes into a Live Paint group, the appearance of the brush will disappear, leaving just the appearance of the stroke.

Figure 4.55 You can set the Live Paint Bucket tool to apply color to strokes in a Live Paint group as well.

When using the Live Paint Bucket tool, you can press the Shift key to toggle between painting the fill and painting the stroke.

Using Gap Detection

Until now, all the regions you were filling with color were completely closed. But what happens if your paths don't exactly meet each other? That's where the Illustrator Gap Detection feature can really make a difference. You need to choose Object > Live Paint > Gap Options to control the settings for this feature (**Figure 4.56**). If you don't have any Live Paint groups selected when you choose this option, the settings you choose become the default settings for all new Live Paint groups. You can specify different gap options for each selected Live Paint group in a document as well.

Figure 4.56 The Gap Options dialog makes it possible to fill areas in a Live Paint group even if they aren't completely enclosed.

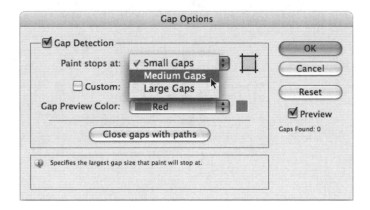

Using Gap Options

With Gap Detection turned on (**Figure 4.57**), you can specify that paint will fill areas containing small, medium, or large gaps. Additionally, you can specify an exact amount for how big a gap can be before Live Paint considers it an open area instead of a closed one. Illustrator previews gaps in the selected color, and you can also choose to have Illustrator fill any gaps in an object with physical paths (Illustrator always uses straight paths to do so).

Figure 4.57 With a Live Paint group selection, you can choose to open the Gap Options dialog from the Control panel.

Gap Options

Releasing and Expanding Live Paint Groups

Live Paint groups can be expanded, at which time they behave like ordinary vector paths. The appearance of an expanded Live Paint group remains identical to the original, but it is split into multiple objects for both fills and strokes. This is similar in concept to expanding live effects. To expand a selected Live Paint group, either click the Expand button in the Control panel or choose Object > Live Paint > Expand.

From a production standpoint, you don't need to expand Live Paint groups in order to prepare a file for print. Live Paint groups print perfectly, because Illustrator performs the necessary expanding of paths at print time (similar to live effects).

Additionally, you can choose Object > Live Paint > Release to return a Live Paint group to the original paths used to create it. Where expanding a Live Paint group results in objects being broken up in order to preserve appearance, releasing such a group preserves the geometry of the original paths, but the appearance or colors are lost.

Merging Live Paint Groups

If you have several separate live paint groups, you may want to combine them to edit them as one entire group. You can do so easily by selecting the different groups and clicking Merge Live Paint in the Control panel. Alternatively, you can choose Object > Live Paint > Merge. Just note that for Live Paint groups that consist of many complex paths, the Gap Detection feature impedes performance. You may experience better performance by splitting very large Live Paint groups into several smaller ones or by turning off Gap Detection.

Using Live Paint to Edit Paths

If you think about it, Live Paint allows you to apply attributes—such as fills and strokes—to paths based on their appearance as opposed to their actual makeup. It would be even nicer if you could actually edit your paths based on appearance as well, don't you think? Adobe was apparently reading your mind (a scary thought) and added another tool to the mix—the Live Paint Selection tool—that enables you to select portions of objects based on their appearance.

Let's take a look at an example. Use the Line Segment tool to draw two perpendicular lines, creating an *X*. Select both paths, and press Command-Option-X (Control-Alt-X) or choose Object > Live Paint > Make to convert the two paths into a Live Paint group. Now, select the Live Paint Selection tool, and click one of paths. You'll notice that you can select each segment of the line individually. What were two paths before are now four line segments (**Figure 4.58**). With one segment selected, press the Delete key to remove that segment from the path. Select another segment, and change its Stroke attribute (**Figure 4.59**). You can also click one segment and then drag to select other segments in one step.

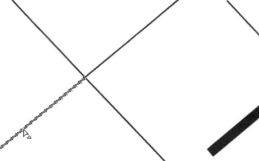

Figure 4.58 Using the Live Paint Selection tool, you can select visual segments of a path.

Figure 4.59 In a Live Paint group, you can easily apply different Stroke attributes to the segments of a path.

The Live Paint Selection tool can also select the fills of Live Paint areas. If you have two overlapping shapes in a Live Paint group, you can select the overlap and delete it (**Figure 4.60**). You can also double-click to select continuous areas of similar attributes and triple-click to select similar attributes across the entire Live Paint group.

At the end of the day, Live Paint adds a more flexible way to color and edit paths, and it also adds more value to the Pencil tool, because complete closed paths aren't required. The important point to remember is that a Live Paint group is a group, and anything you can do with a group in Illustrator you can do with Live Paint groups as well. For example, you can add attributes such as strokes to the Live Paint group for interesting effects (**Figure 4.61**). Experimenting with the Live Paint feature certainly helps you when you're editing paths, and the good news is that it's a fun feature to use.

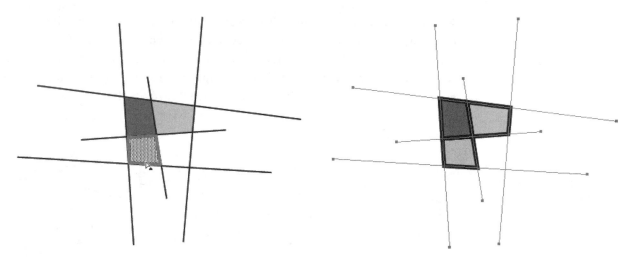

Figure 4.60 The Live Paint Selection tool enables you to select any area of a Live Paint group.

Figure 4.61 Adding a stroke to a Live Paint group at the group level makes it possible to apply strokes that appear only around areas that are filled.

EXPLORING THE PATHFINDER PANEL

In Chapter 2, *Vectors 101*, you learned about using the basic drawing tools such as the Rectangle tool and the Ellipse tool. Those tools are great on their own, but you'll often need to create shapes that are a bit more complex. Although you can use a variety of the tools we've mentioned so far in this chapter to create and edit paths of any shape, many times it's far easier to combine simple shapes to create more complex ones. It can also be easier to edit existing shapes using other shapes rather than trying to adjust the anchor points of individual paths.

Illustrator's Pathfinder panel, which you can open by choosing Window > Pathfinder, contains a wellspring of functions that you can perform with at least two selected paths.

Combining Shapes with Shape Modes

The top row of the Pathfinder panel contains four functions, called *shape modes*, which are used to combine multiple selected shapes in different ways. Once a shape mode is applied, the resulting shape is referred to as a *compound shape*.

When you create a compound shape from multiple selected objects, the resulting shape appears as a single object and takes on the attributes of the topmost object (**Figure 4.62**). Using the Direct Selection tool, you can select the individual objects in the compound shape and edit them. See the sidebar "Illustrator Shape Modes and Photoshop Shape Layers" for additional functionality that you can take advantage of when using compound shapes.

Figure 4.62 Here are some examples of the different possible shape modes you can apply.

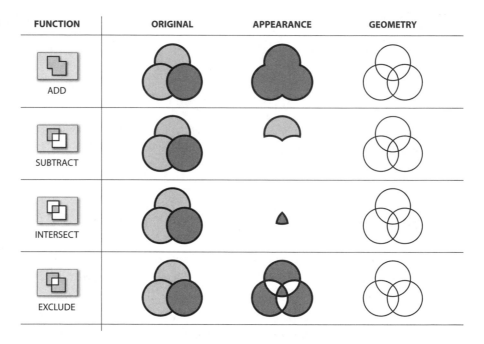

The following are the four shape modes you can choose from in the Pathfinder panel:

- **Add.** The Add shape mode combines all the selected shapes and gives the appearance as if they were all joined together. This function replaces the Unite pathfinder, which you can find in older versions of Illustrator.

- **Subtract.** The Subtract shape mode combines all the selected shapes and takes the top objects and removes them from the bottommost object. This function replaces the Minus Front pathfinder, which was found in older versions of Illustrator.

- **Intersect.** The Intersect shape mode combines all the selected shapes and displays only the areas in which all the objects overlap with each other.

- **Exclude.** The Exclude shape mode combines all the selected shapes and removes the areas in which the objects overlap with each other.

It is certainly useful to be able to select the individual objects of a compound shape, but many times you just want to create a new shape that combines all the selected shapes. To do so, you can expand a compound shape by clicking the Expand button in the Pathfinder panel. If, when you're creating a compound shape, you know that you want to expand it, you can hold the Option (Alt) key while clicking the Add, Subtract, Intersect, or Exclude button. This applies the function and expands the shape in one step.

In reality, using any of the Shape modes can give you similar results to creating compound paths. Compound shapes utilize Even-Odd File Rule.

Additionally, you can release a compound shape by choosing Release Compound Shape from the Pathfinder panel menu. Releasing compound shapes returns the objects to their individual states and appearances.

Illustrator Shape Modes and Photoshop Shape Layers

If you've used Photoshop before, you might be familiar with vector shape layers, which allow you to create vector-based masks. Although Photoshop is primarily a pixel-based program, these shape layers, as Photoshop refers to them, allow you to create vector shapes within your Photoshop document. Upon close inspection, you'll find that to help you create more complex shapes, you can create Photoshop's shape layers using a variety of modes, including Add, Subtract, Intersect, and Exclude—the same functions in Illustrator's Pathfinder panel.

These objects are interchangeable between the applications, and they retain their shape mode settings in the process as well. Create a compound shape in Illustrator, copy and paste it into Photoshop, and the compound shape becomes an editable vector shape layer. The same applies in reverse (**Figure 4.63**).

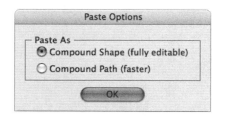

Figure 4.63 When you are pasting a shape layer from Photoshop, Illustrator asks whether you want to have it pasted as a compound shape.

Changing Paths with Pathfinders

The functions in the second row of the Pathfinder panel are called *pathfinders*, and unlike with compound shapes, when you use pathfinders, they do not retain their original objects. Once you apply a pathfinder function, the paths are changed permanently (**Figure 4.64**). The following are the six path-finder functions in the Pathfinder panel:

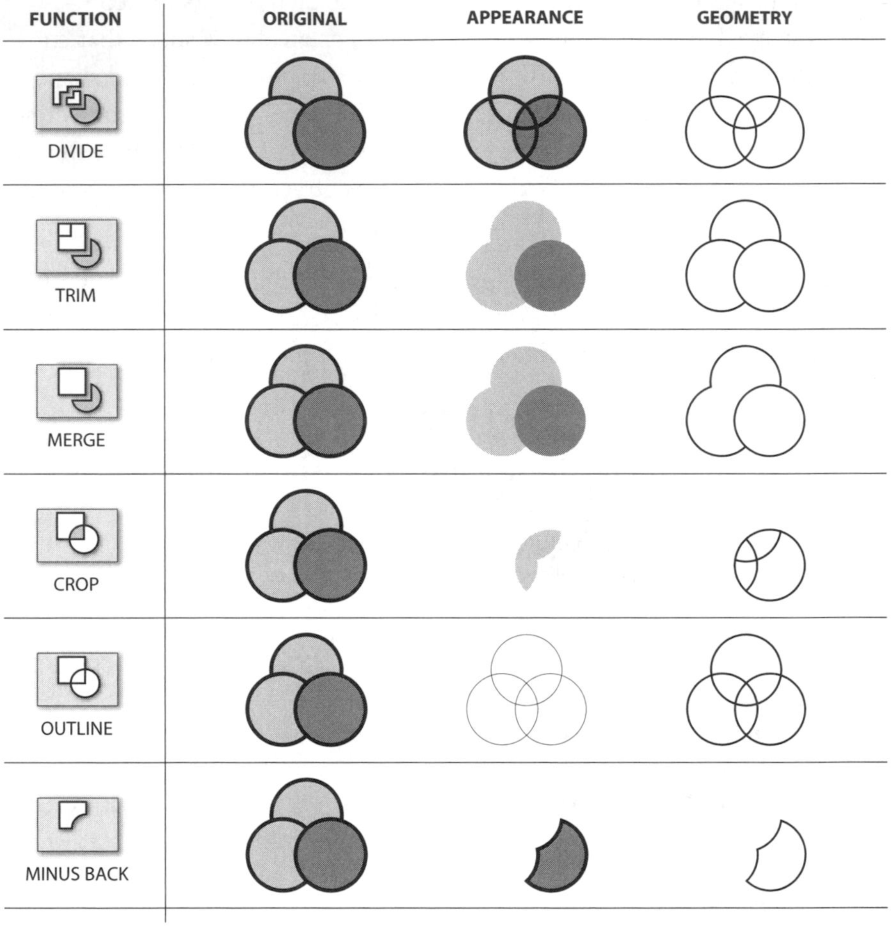

Figure 4.64 Here are some examples of the different possible pathfinder functions you can apply.

FUNCTION	ORIGINAL	APPEARANCE	GEOMETRY
DIVIDE			
TRIM			
MERGE			
CROP			
OUTLINE			
MINUS BACK			

- **Divide.** One of the most often-used pathfinders, Divide takes all selected objects and breaks them apart into individual shapes based on their overlapping parts. Open paths act like knives and slice paths that intersect with them.

- **Trim.** The Trim pathfinder removes all overlapping areas from the selected paths.

- **Merge.** The Merge pathfinder removes all overlapping areas from the selected paths and joins all areas of the same color.

- **Crop.** The Crop pathfinder takes the topmost selected object and removes all objects and areas beneath it that fall outside its path. Unfortunately, this pathfinder works on vector objects only, and you can't use it to crop a raster image (you'll need Photoshop for that). This function ignores strokes on objects, so it's best to perform an Outline Paths function before applying the Crop pathfinder.

- **Outline.** The Outline pathfinder converts the selected shapes to outlines and divides the lines where they intersect.

- **Minus Back.** The Minus Back pathfinder is similar to the Subtract shape mode, but instead of using the top object to define the subtracted area, the function uses the bottom object.

Once you've applied a pathfinder function, you can choose Repeat Pathfinder from the Pathfinder panel menu to apply the same effect again. In reality, it takes longer to access the panel menu than it does to just click the icon in the panel, but by having this function available, you can assign a keyboard shortcut to it in the Keyboard Shortcuts dialog if you find you use these functions often.

From the Pathfinder panel menu, you can also choose Pathfinder Options, where you can set the level of precision to use when applying pathfinder functions (lower numbers may result in more complex paths). You can also specify that Illustrator should remove redundant points (always a good idea) and unpainted artwork when performing Divide or Outline functions.

ALIGNING AND DISTRIBUTING OBJECTS

When working with a range of objects or anchor points, you will often want to align them evenly or distribute them across a specified distance. Rather than being forced to figure out the math on your own and then manually move each object, you can apply the variety of functions that Illustrator's Align panel contains to a range of objects in order to both align and distribute objects precisely. You can open the Align panel by choosing Window > Align.

To align a range of objects or anchor points, select them, and click one of the Align icons in the Align panel. Admittedly, these small icons can be hard to decipher, but if you move your pointer over them for a second, a tool tip pops up identifying the name of the function (**Figure 4.65**).

Figure 4.65 The icons in the Align panel can be a bit difficult to decipher, so it's a good idea to watch for the tool tips that pop up.

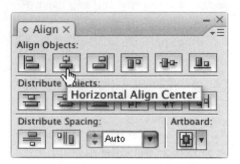

Aligning Objects to a Specific Object

You'll notice that when you align several objects, all of the objects move. However, sometimes you have the position of one object set perfectly, and you want to be able to align all of your selected objects to that specific object. You can do this by defining what Illustrator calls a *key object*.

To define a key object, select all the objects you want to align, and then, using the Selection tool, click the object to which you want all the other objects to align. When aligning individual anchor points, the last point you select becomes the key anchor point to which all other points are aligned.

Additionally, you can choose to align objects to the document artboard or to the current crop area. This can be helpful if you want to easily center objects on a page or to a defined crop area. You can turn this setting on and off in the Align panel (**Figure 4.66**) or in the Control panel.

Figure 4.66 You can choose to align objects to themselves, the artboard, or an active crop area.

The align functions consider a group of objects to be a single object, so performing an align function on a group won't do anything (you're basically aligning a single object to itself). However, you can select multiple groups and align them as if each group were a single object.

You can use the distribute functions that appear in the bottom half of the Align panel to space multiple objects evenly. Illustrator takes the objects at the two extremes of your selection and uses those as the boundaries of the distribution. All objects that appear between those two shapes are distributed evenly between them, based on the specific distribute function you choose (**Figure 4.67**).

By default, the align functions use the actual path of an object for calculating alignment. If you want Illustrator to factor in the actual appearance of the object (for example, stroke width), choose Use Preview Bounds from the Align panel flyout menu.

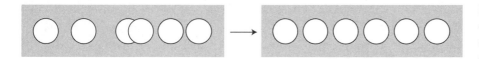

Figure 4.67 When you're distributing objects, the objects at the opposite extremes define the boundary, and all objects are distributed evenly between them.

If you choose Show Options from the Align panel menu, you can also perform distribute commands based on spacing. You can specify a numeric value and then distribute the selected objects vertically or horizontally. Specifying a Distribute Spacing value of 0 will distribute objects perfectly with no extra space between them (sometimes referred to as a *kiss fit*).

MAKING TRANSFORMATIONS

Drawing objects in Illustrator is only part of the design process. Once art is created, you can manipulate it in a multitude of ways. In Illustrator, the process of changing or manipulating a path is called a *transformation*, and transformations can include anything from simply moving an object to changing its size or rotation.

When you move a file, its x,y coordinates change, and Illustrator considers that a transformation. You can also move selected objects precisely by changing the x,y coordinates in the Control panel. Alternatively, double-click the Selection tool to open the Move dialog, where you can specify values numerically as well (**Figure 4.68**). Clicking the Copy button in the Move dialog leaves the original shape in place and moves a copy of it.

Figure 4.68 Double-clicking the Selection tool in the Toolbox opens the Move dialog where you can specify move functions numerically.

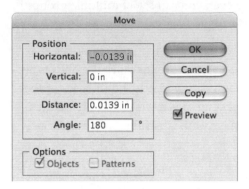

Of course, you can use the Selection tool to click and drag an object to reposition it manually. If you press and hold the Option (Alt) key while dragging, Illustrator creates a copy. Pressing and holding the tilde key moves pattern tiles within the fill of an object without moving the object.

Using the Bounding Box

The bounding box allows you to perform several common transform functions; you can do this by simply clicking an object and using just the Selection tool. Once you've made a selection, you can click an object to move it, or you can click any of the eight *handles* that appear on the perimeter of the bounding box to scale or resize the selection (**Figure 4.69**). Holding the Shift key while resizing constrains proportion. If you place your pointer just outside the edge of a handle, you can rotate your selection (**Figure 4.70**). If you hold the Shift key while you're rotating, you constrain rotation angles to increments of 45 degrees.

Figure 4.69 With the bounding box active, you can scale objects by dragging one of the eight handles.

Figure 4.70 Positioning your pointer just outside a handle, you can use the bounding box to rotate a selection.

By default, Illustrator has the bounding box setting turned on. To turn it off, choose View > Hide Bounding Box.

The bounding box appears only when you select objects with the Selection tool. Although the bounding box is certainly useful, it can get in the way as well. Illustrator has a feature called *snap to point*, where you can drag an object by an anchor point and easily align it to an anchor point in a different object. As your pointer approaches an anchor point, the object you are dragging snaps to it. When the bounding box is turned on, you can't always grab an object by the anchor point because doing so allows you to scale the object instead. Your alternative is to either turn off the bounding box or use the Direct Selection tool (which many Illustrator users do anyway). An easy way to access the Direct Selection tool is to press and hold the Command (Control) key when the regular Selection tool is active. Doing this will also make the bounding box temporarily disappear (until you release the Command key).

If you do turn off the bounding box function, you can still access similar functionality by using the Free Transform tool.

Living by the Numbers with the Transform Panel

The Transform panel, which you can access by choosing Window > Transform, is a production artist's best friend. In reality, it's a panel that can be helpful to anyone. The Transform panel provides numeric feedback on the exact specifications of a selection. This includes x,y coordinates, width and height measurements, and rotate and shear values. You can also use the panel to make numeric changes to selected objects.

You can enter values using any measurement system, and you can even specify math functions. For example, you can change the x coordinate of an object by adding a +.125 at the end of the value and pressing Enter or Tab. You can even mix different measurement systems, such as subtracting points from millimeters. Use the asterisk for multiplication functions and the slash for division. If you press the Option (Alt) key while pressing Enter for a value, a copy is created.

To lock the proportion of width and height values, click the link icon at the far right of the Transform panel. This allows you to specify just the height or the width of a selected object, and Illustrator scales the other value proportionally.

At the far left of the panel is a 9-point proxy that corresponds to the 8 points of an object's bounding box and its center (**Figure 4.71**). The point you click is extremely important—not only for the Transform panel, but for all transform functions. If you click the center point, the x,y coordinates you see in the Transform panel refer to the center point of your selection. Clicking a different point reveals the coordinates for that point of the selection. When specifying transformations such as width or height settings or rotation or skew values, the point you choose becomes the *origin point*—the point from which the transformation originates. Rotating an object from its lower-left corner yields very different results from that same rotation applied from its center point.

Figure 4.71 The 9-point proxy in the Transform panel enables you to set an origin point for a transformation. You can find the proxy in numerous transform dialogs and in the Control panel as well.

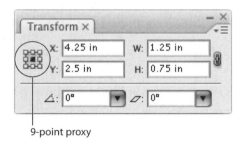

9-point proxy

In many cases, though, you'll also want to transform the strokes and effects. If this is the case, choose the Scale Strokes & Effects option from the Transform panel menu, which stays on until you turn it off. From the same panel menu, you can also choose to flip objects on their horizontal or vertical axis.

Using Preview Bounds

One of the benefits of using Illustrator is that you can be extremely precise when drawing objects. Illustrator's Control, Transform, and Info panels all provide exact feedback on coordinates, positioning, sizing, and more. By default, these panels use the actual vector path to determine these numbers, not the visual boundaries of the object. For example, you may have a shape that has a thick stroke or a scale effect applied to it that is not represented in the value you see in the Transform panel. When the Use Preview Bounds preference is activated in the General panel in Preferences, all panels use the visual boundary of a file as the value, not the underlying vector path.

Working with the Transformation Tools

Illustrator contains specific tools for performing scale, rotation, reflection (mirroring), and shearing (skewing). These specific tools allow you to perform transformation with precision and with more power than the bounding box or even the Control panel.

The four transformation tools—the Scale, Rotate, Reflect, and Shear tools—all work the same way. Here, we'll discuss the Rotate tool specifically; you can apply the same techniques to the other tools.

To rotate an object, select it, and choose the Rotate tool. Take a look at the selection on your screen, and you'll see a special icon that appears at its center. This icon, which looks like a small crosshairs, is your origin point (**Figure 4.72**). To perform a rotation, position your pointer a fair amount of space away from the origin point, and click and drag. You don't have to click the object itself to perform the rotation. If you click too close to the origin point, you'll find that it is difficult to control the rotation. The farther away you move your pointer from the origin point before dragging, the more leverage and control you have (**Figure 4.73**).

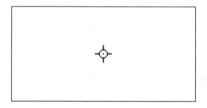

Figure 4.72 The crosshairs cursor indicates the precise location of the transformation origin point.

Figure 4.73 When using the Rotate tool, clicking away from the origin point gives you better leverage for rotating your selection.

While dragging with the Rotate tool, press the Shift key to constrain rotation to 45-degree increments, press the Option (Alt) key to create a copy, and press the tilde key if your object is filled with a pattern and you want to rotate just the pattern.

The powerful part of using a transformation tool is that you have control over the exact placement of the origin point. For example, if you select an object and then switch to the Rotate tool, you'll see the origin point, as we discussed earlier. At that time, you can click once anywhere on your screen to redefine that point elsewhere. If you then click and drag, Illustrator uses the repositioned origin point for the rotation. Alternatively, you can simply click and drag the origin point itself to any location on your screen.

The ability to reposition the origin point arbitrarily means you can specify an origin point that's outside the boundaries of your object. When using the Transform panel, you can choose from only one of the nine preset options using the 9-point proxy.

You can also specify transformations numerically with any of the four transformation tools listed here by making a selection and double-clicking the desired transformation tool. One of the powerful features of opening the dialog for a specific transformation tool is that when you enter a value, the next time you open the dialog, that same value remains. Additionally, the dialogs for each transformation tool record the last transformation you performed with the tool. For example, if you use the Scale tool to manually resize an object, you can then open the Scale tool dialog to see the exact percentage to which you scaled the object.

Transforming Multiple Objects at Once

When you select several objects, Illustrator performs all transformations based on a single origin point. This behavior is certainly fine for some needs, but sometimes you want to have transformations applied to a range of objects, and you want those transformations to be applied using individual origin points. For example, if you have several shapes selected and you want them each to rotate 45 degrees, you want each selected shape to rotate around its own center (**Figure 4.74**).

Figure 4.74 When you have several individual shapes (left), selecting them all and rotating them forces all objects to share a single origin point (center). With the Transform Each function, you can rotate multiple objects around their own individual origin points (right).

The Transform Each function was designed specifically for applying transformations across a range of objects, where each object maintains its own origin point. As an added bonus, the feature also contains something no other transformation tool has—a randomize function.

To use this feature, select a range of objects—even grouped objects—and choose Object > Transform > Transform Each to open the dialog. Selecting the Preview check box allows you to see the effects of the transformation before you apply it. Specify Scale, Move, Rotate, and Reflect settings, and if you'd like, click the Random button so that each object gets a slight variation of the settings you specify.

By far, the most important setting you need to specify in the Transform Each dialog is the origin point. Choose a point from the 9-point proxy to define the origin point for each selected object. Click OK to apply the transformations, or click the Copy button to create copies.

Even though the Transform Each function was created for applying transformations to multiple objects at once, it's a great tool to use on single objects as well. This is especially true since the Transform Each dialog allows you to specify multiple transformations in one step.

Exploring the Power of the Transform Again Feature

The Transform Again feature builds on the power of the transformation tools you've learned in this chapter. Illustrator always remembers the last transformation you applied, so choosing Object > Transform > Transform Again simply reapplies that transformation, even if you've selected a different object. The keyboard shortcut for this feature is Command-D (Control-D); it's a good idea to memorize it, because you'll use it often.

This example illustrates the power of this feature. Draw a rectangle on your artboard. Choose the Selection tool, and drag the rectangle to the right while holding the Option (Alt) key, which creates a copy of the rectangle beside the original. Now apply the Transform Again command. Illustrator now repeats the last transformation, leaving you with three rectangles, evenly spaced.

The Transform Each dialog allows you to apply multiple transformations in one step. Applying a Transform Again command after applying a Transform Each function simply duplicates those settings. The power to transform is now within you. Use it wisely.

CHAPTER FIVE

Brushes, Symbols, and Masks

Take a moment to think about the true strength of what a computer offers to a designer. Is it fancy drawing tools? Is it cool special effects? Is it the speed at which you can create art? Maybe. But that's all on the surface. In truth, you may find that a designer can draw something with a pencil and paper in half the time it would take to draw it using a computer. The real benefit of using a computer to a designer is that once they have created a design on a computer, they can edit it at will. When you're working with a deadline, it's far easier to make a small edit to a file than to have to redraw the whole design from scratch.

As you build files in Adobe Illustrator, you'll find you can accomplish a particular task in several ways. Your job is to find the most efficient way to create the art you need, which doesn't necessarily always mean the fastest way. You might be able to create two identical Illustrator files: in one, the file is huge, takes a long time to print, and is difficult to edit or update; the other is created using different features or techniques and results in a leaner, cleaner, and more editable file.

You already know about groups, layers, live effects, and graphic styles—all of which you can use to build more efficient objects. In this chapter, you'll learn to take advantage of other features such as brushes, symbols, and masks. By using these features, you will make your files more efficient and easier to update, which can mean the difference between being home in time for dinner with the family or pulling another all-nighter at the office when a deadline looms.

Unleashing the Power of Brushes

Each version of Illustrator brings new features and tools to the hands of designers. Some are cool effects, and some add useful functionality. And every once in a while, a feature is introduced that is so unique and powerful that it changes everything. The brushes in Illustrator are such a feature.

The concept is simple: Instead of drawing a predictable, boring line using the Pencil tool, the Paintbrush tool can create flourishes, lines with tapered ends, and artsy elements that mimic the strokes you can create with Speedball or calligraphy pens. More powerful than you might think, brushes support pressure-sensitive tablets and can even distribute art and patterns along a drawn path. By using brushes, you can streamline your work by creating complex artwork with just a few paths. Brushes are also easy to modify.

Under the hood, the Paintbrush tool functions exactly like the Pencil tool and allows you to click and drag to create a vector path. The difference is in the appearance of the path it creates. The Paintbrush tool applies predefined vector artwork to the paths you draw. When using a pressure-sensitive tablet, you can also control how the artwork is applied to the vector paths.

Stop! Before you start a new file or project, take a few moments to think about the art you will use and how you plan on creating the file. Taking a few minutes to plan allows you to understand the kinds of features you need to use, and this planning can save you a significant amount of time should you need to make changes to the file later.

Exploring Illustrator's Brush Quartet

Illustrator has four kinds of brushes; each offers a different kind of behavior in which art is applied to a path:

- **Calligraphic brush.** The Calligraphic brush allows you to define a *nib*, or tip, of a pen. The art that is drawn with a Calligraphic brush takes into account the angle and shape of the nib, resulting in natural thicks and thins and variable thickness (**Figure 5.1**).

Figure 5.1 With the help of a pressure-sensitive tablet, the Calligraphic brush can create strokes with natural thicks and thins to achieve a hand-drawn look and feel.

- **Scatter brush.** The Scatter brush allows you to define any vector art as a brush (except the ones listed in the sidebar "What's in a Brush?"). The art that is drawn with a Scatter brush consists of copies of the art, scattered across the vector path. You can control the way art is scattered in each brush's settings (**Figure 5.2**).

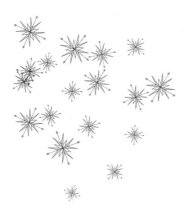

Figure 5.2 You can use a Scatter brush to create consistent borders or to quickly fill a page with what appears to be random art.

- **Art brush.** The Art brush allows you to define any vector art as a brush (except the ones listed in the sidebar "What's in a Brush?"). The art drawn with an Art brush is stretched across the entire length of the path, resulting in the controlled distortion of art along a vector path (**Figure 5.3**).

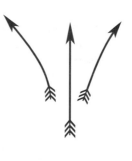

Figure 5.3 You can use an Art brush to apply artistic brush strokes or to create interesting variations of art.

- **Pattern brush.** The Pattern brush allows you to specify up to five already-defined patterns as a brush. The art that is drawn with a Pattern brush is distributed along a vector path based on the brush's settings, resulting in perfect corners and art that is contoured to the vector path (**Figure 5.4**).

Figure 5.4 A Pattern brush can bend art to match the curve of a path and can also contain a variety of settings that change based on the makeup of the path.

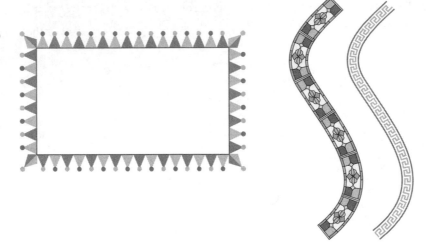

What's in a Brush?

When you're creating artwork that will be used to define a brush, be aware that brushes cannot understand all kinds of vector objects. Brushes cannot contain gradients, mesh objects, bitmap images, graphs, placed files, or masks. For Art and Pattern brushes specifically, the artwork also cannot contain editable type objects. If you want to include these kinds of objects, you either need to expand them or convert them to outlines first.

Applying Brush Strokes

To paint with a brush, choose the Paintbrush tool from the Toolbox, and then choose a brush from the Brushes panel. You create brush strokes the same way you create paths with the Pencil tool, so once you've selected a brush to use, click and drag on the artboard to define a path. When you release the mouse, Illustrator applies the brush stroke to the newly created vector path (**Figure 5.5**). Illustrator also indicates the applied brush stroke in the Appearance panel, making it easy to identify when a particular brush has been used (**Figure 5.6**).

Figure 5.5 When you create a brush stroke, a single vector path is defined, and the appearance of that path displays the brush.

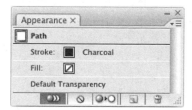

Figure 5.6 By identifying the brush applied to a path, the Appearance panel gives yet another reason for why it should always be opened on your screen.

You don't have to use the Paintbrush tool to apply a brush stroke to a vector path. Simply selecting a vector path and clicking a brush in the Brushes panel applies the brush to the selected path. The only benefit you gain by using the Paintbrush tool is the ability to define a brush shape using a pressure-sensitive tablet (see the sidebar "Can You Handle the Pressure?").

If you double-click the Paintbrush tool, you'll find that the preferences are identical to those of the Pencil tool.

Can You Handle the Pressure?

Illustrator has full support for pressure-sensitive pen tablets such as the line of Wacom tablets. You can set Calligraphic or Scatter brushes to use variable settings based on pressure, thus enabling you to easily draw lines of varying thickness or to apply different scatter settings.

The natural lines you can achieve with a Calligraphic brush and a Wacom tablet are perfect for sketching or drawing in Illustrator. It would seem that the next logical step after creating a sketch with the Paintbrush tool is to convert the art to a Live Paint group to quickly colorize the art. Unfortunately, the Live Paint feature doesn't support brushes, and converting a brushed path to a Live Paint group results in the loss of the appearance of the brush. Let's hope future versions of Illustrator will address this.

When using either the Calligraphic or Scatter brushes, Illustrator also supports Wacom's 6D Art pen. You can find a library of 6D Art pen brushes that is filled with 18 Calligraphic and 6 Scatter brushes in the Illustrator CS3 Goodies folder on the application installation CD. If you purchased Illustrator as a component of the Creative Suite, you'll find this library on the CS3 Standard Content CD.

Defining a Calligraphic Brush

To define a new Calligraphic brush, click the New Brush icon in the Brushes panel, or select New Brush from the Brushes panel menu. Choose New Calligraphic Brush from the New Brush dialog, and click OK to open the Calligraphic Brush Options dialog (**Figure 5.7**).

Figure 5.7 The Calligraphic Brush Options dialog allows you to click and drag the nib shape in the preview area to define its settings.

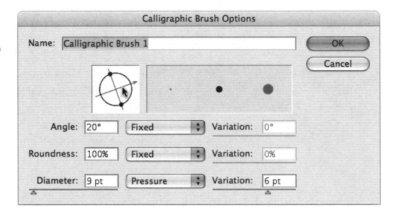

The Calligraphic Brush Options dialog allows you to specify the shape and behavior of the nib using three settings:

- **Angle.** You can set the angle of a Calligraphic brush to a fixed angle or to a random number. When the Roundness setting is to 100%, the Angle setting does not produce any noticeable change in the shape of the brush. With pressure-sensitive tablets, you can set the angle to change based on pressure, stylus wheel, tilt, bearing, or rotation. When you're not using the fixed option, the Variation slider allows you to specify a range that the angle can change, which you can also see in the preview area of the dialog.

- **Roundness.** You can set the roundness of a calligraphic brush to a fixed or random number. When the roundness is set closer to 100%, the tip of the nib becomes circular in shape (like a traditional ink pen). When the roundness is set closer to 0%, the tip of the nib becomes flat (like a traditional calligraphy pen). With pressure-sensitive tablets, you can set the roundness to change based on pressure, stylus wheel, tilt, bearing, or rotation. When you're not using the fixed option, the Variation slider allows you to specify a range that the roundness can change, which you can also see in the preview area of the dialog.

- **Diameter.** You can set the diameter, or size, of a Calligraphic brush to a fixed or random number. With pressure-sensitive tablets, you can set the diameter to change based on pressure, stylus wheel, tilt, bearing, or rotation. When you're not using the Fixed option, the Variation slider allows you to specify a range that the diameter can change, which you can also see in the preview area of the dialog.

> When you're using a pressure-sensitive tablet, giving the diameter setting a variation based on pressure enables you to create strokes that appear thicker as you press harder. If you have Wacom's 6D Art Pen, it makes sense to set the angle to the pen's Rotation attribute.

Defining a Scatter Brush

To define a new Scatter brush, start by creating the art for the brush on the artboard. Once it is complete, drag the artwork directly to the Brushes panel. Alternatively, you can select the art and click the New Brush icon in the Brushes panel or select New Brush from the Brushes panel menu. Choose New Scatter Brush from the New Brush dialog, and click OK to open the Scatter Brush Options dialog (**Figure 5.8**).

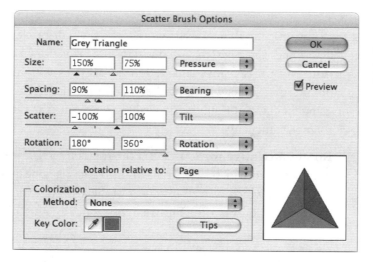

Figure 5.8 The Scatter Brush Options dialog presents a plethora of settings you can use to create a wide variety of results.

- **Size.** The Size setting can be a fixed or random number; this setting determines how big or small the art is drawn on the path, relative to the actual size of the art used to define the brush. For example, if you create a design that is 1 inch tall and use it to define a Scatter brush, a Size setting of 50% results in a Scatter brush that creates designs that are .5 inches tall. With pressure-sensitive tablets, you can set the size to change based on pressure, stylus wheel, tilt, bearing, or rotation. When you are not using the fixed option, the two values determine the range that the size can change.

- **Spacing.** The Spacing setting can be a fixed or random number and determines the amount of space that appears between each instance of art that is drawn on the path. Higher values add more space between each copy of the art, and lower values make the copies of art appear closer together. With pressure-sensitive tablets, you can set the spacing to change based on pressure, stylus wheel, tilt, bearing, or rotation. When you're not using the fixed option, the two values determine the range that the spacing can change.

- **Scatter.** The Scatter setting can be a fixed or random number and determines how far away each instance of art that is drawn deviates from the path. Negative values shift art lower and to the left of the path; positive values shift art higher and to the right of the path. With pressure-sensitive tablets, you can set the scatter to change based on pressure, stylus wheel, tilt, bearing, or rotation. When you're not using the fixed option, the two values determine the range that the scatter can change.

- **Rotation.** The Rotation setting can be a fixed or random number and determines the angle that each instance of art is drawn on the path. With pressure-sensitive tablets, you can set the rotation to change based on pressure, stylus wheel, tilt, bearing, or rotation. When you're not using the fixed option, the two values determine the range that the rotation can change.

- **Rotation relative to.** You can set the rotation so that it is relative either to the page, in which case all instances of the art appear consistent, or to the path, in which case all instances of the art rotate in accordance with the direction of the path (**Figure 5.9**).

Figure 5.9 Depending on your desired result, you can specify art to rotate in relation either to the page, where all the triangles are rotated in the same way (left), or to the path, where all the triangles are rotated to match the curved path (right).

- **Colorization.** The Colorization option lets you choose from one of four settings. If you choose the None setting, the Scatter brush creates art in the same color that is used to define it. If you choose the Tints setting, the Scatter brush creates art in varying tints of the current stroke color. If you choose the Tints and Shades setting, the Scatter brush creates art in varying tints of the current stroke color while preserving black-colored objects. If you choose the Hue Shift setting, the Scatter brush creates art and changes the key color of the art to the current stroke color. To define a key color, click the Eyedropper icon in the dialog, and click a part of the art in the preview area.

Defining an Art Brush

To define a new Art brush, start by creating the art for the brush on the artboard. Once it's complete, drag the artwork directly into the Brushes panel. Alternatively, you can select the art and click the New Brush icon in the Brushes panel or select New Brush from the Brushes panel menu. Choose New Art Brush from the New Brush dialog, and click OK to open the Art Brush Options dialog (**Figure 5.10**).

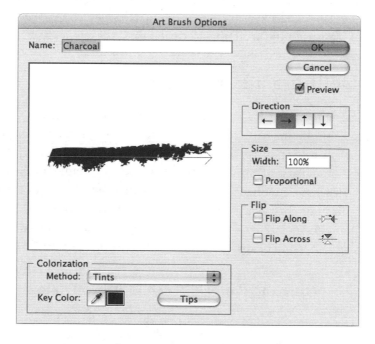

Figure 5.10 The Art Brush Options dialog gives you a visual preview of the direction that the art will appear in relation to the path.

- **Direction.** The Direction setting determines the orientation of the art with respect to the path to which the brush is applied. A blue arrow appears in the preview area, allowing you to visually understand how the art will be drawn on a path.

- **Size.** The Size setting determines how big or small the art is drawn on the path relative to the actual size of the art that was used to define the brush. For example, if you create a design that is 1 inch tall and use it to define an art brush, a Size setting of 50% results in an art brush that creates designs that are .5 inches tall. When specifying width values, you can also choose to keep the artwork scaled in proportion.

- **Flip.** The Flip Along and Flip Across settings enable you to reflect the artwork on both the horizontal and vertical axes.

- **Colorization.** The Colorization option lets you choose from one of four settings. When you choose the None setting, the art brush creates art in the same color that is used to define it. If you choose the Tints setting, the Art brush creates art in varying tints of the current stroke color. If you choose the Tints and Shades setting, the Art brush creates art in varying tints of the current stroke color while preserving black-colored objects. If you choose the Hue Shift setting, the Art brush creates art and changes the key color of the art to the current stroke color. To define a key color, click the Eyedropper icon in the dialog, and click a part of the art in the preview area.

Defining a Pattern Brush

To define a new Pattern brush, you first define the pattern swatches that will be used in the brush, using the methods you learned in Chapter 2, *Vectors 101*. A Pattern brush can contain up to five different pattern tiles, used for different parts of a path (see the "Pattern Tiles" bullet in the following list). Once you've defined the necessary pattern swatches, click the New Brush icon in the Brushes panel, or select New Brush from the Brushes panel menu. Choose New Pattern Brush from the New Brush dialog, and click OK to open the Pattern Brush Options dialog (**Figure 5.11**).

Dissecting the Pattern Brush Options Dialog

The various settings of the Pattern Brush Options dialog are as follows:

- **Pattern Tiles.** A Pattern brush can use up to five pattern tiles for the different parts of a drawn path. The side tile is used along the middle of the path, the outer and inner corner tiles are used whenever the path encounters a corner anchor point at 90 degrees, and the start and end tiles are used at the beginning and end of an open path. For detailed

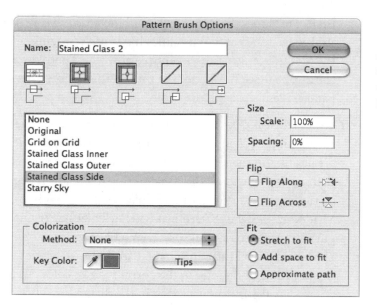

Figure 5.11 Though it might appear complicated at first, the Pattern Brush Options dialog makes it easy to define powerful Pattern brushes.

descriptions of each tile type, see "The Five Parts of a Pattern Brush" later in this chapter. To set a tile, click the preview box above each tile, and choose from the list of defined pattern swatches. Only pattern swatches from the current document appear in the list. It is not necessary to assign a pattern swatch to every tile in order to define a Pattern brush. For example, some Pattern brushes do not have start or end tiles defined.

- **Scale.** The Scale setting determines how big or small the pattern swatch is drawn on the path, relative to the actual size of the art that was used to define the pattern (by default, a Pattern brush applies art at the size the art was originally created). For example, if you create art that is 1 inch tall and use it to define a pattern swatch, a Scale setting of 50% results in a Pattern brush that creates tiles that are .5 inches tall.

- **Spacing.** The Spacing setting determines the amount of space that appears between each pattern tile that is drawn on the path. By default, all pattern tiles touch each other, and specifying higher values adds more space between them.

- **Flip.** The Flip Along and Flip Across settings enable you to reflect the pattern tiles on both the horizontal and vertical axis.

- **Fit.** The Fit setting, arguably one of most powerful settings among all the brushes, allows you to specify how pattern tiles are drawn on a path. The Stretch to Fit option modifies the brush's Scale setting to ensure a

To create a dashed line on a rectangle that will always have perfect corners, create two pattern swatches, one for a dash and one for a corner. Then create a pattern brush that uses the dash pattern as a side and the corner pattern as an outer corner tile, and choose the Add Space to Fit option.

perfect fit across the entire path, with no spaces between tiles. The Add Space to Fit option modifies the brush's Spacing setting to ensure the tiles fit evenly across an entire path. The Approximate Path option actually changes the size of the path so that it fits to the size of the pattern tiles.

- **Colorization.** The Colorization option lets you choose from one of four settings. When you choose the None setting, the Pattern brush creates tiles in the same color used when the pattern swatches are defined. If you choose the Tints setting, the Pattern brush creates tiles in varying tints of the current stroke color. If you choose the Tints and Shades setting, the Pattern brush creates tiles in varying tints of the current stroke color while preserving black-colored objects. When you choose the Hue Shift setting, the Pattern brush creates tiles and changes the key color of the tiles to the current stroke color. To define a key color, click the Eyedropper icon in the dialog, and click a part of the tile in the preview area (which is extremely difficult considering how small the previews for each tile are).

The Five Parts of a Pattern Brush

Most of the information about pattern brushes here comes from the genius mind of Teri Pettit, one of the engineers on the Illustrator team at Adobe. You can find more detailed information from Teri on a variety of topics at her Web site at http://tpettit.best.vwh.net/adobe/.

Pattern brushes comprise up to five different individual pattern tiles: side, outer corner, inner corner, start, and end. It's rare you would define a single pattern brush with all five of these types of tiles, though. This is because the corner tiles are mostly beneficial when creating borders, which are closed paths and therefore have no need for start or end tiles. Likewise, pattern brushes with start and end tiles are generally applied to open paths, which may not require corner tiles.

- **Side tiles.** The most common type of tile used, the side tile simply repeats itself along the path to which it is applied (**Figure 5.12**).

- **Outer Corner and Inner Corner tiles.** The terms *inner* corner and *outer* corner refer to the corners of a clockwise path, that is, one in which the top horizontal sections go left to right and the bottom horizontal sections go right to left. On such a path, the corners that point outward will use the outer corner tile, and the corners that point inward will use the inner corner tile. On counterclockwise paths, these roles will be reversed.

Figure 5.12 This is a pattern brush comprised of just a side tile (inset) to simulate stitching as it might appear on a baseball. The stitches follow the contour of the path and appear seamless.

If a rectangle is created by dragging it from top left to bottom right, or vice versa, the top of the rectangle runs from left to right, and all corners will use the outer corner tile. If the rectangle is drawn by dragging between the top-right and bottom-left corners, then the bottom of the rectangle runs from left to right. Thus, the brush pattern as displayed along the top of the rectangle will be upside down, and all corners will use the inner corner tile (**Figure 5.13**).

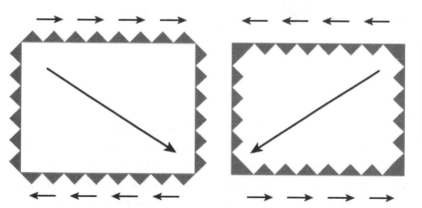

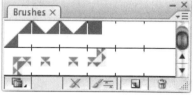

Figure 5.13 The arrows that appear within the rectangles indicate the direction in which they were drawn, while the arrows that appear along the outside of the rectangles indicate the direction the paths run in. The rectangle on the left runs clockwise and uses the outer corner tile, while the rectangle on the right runs counterclockwise and uses the inner corner tile.

- **Start and End tiles.** Start and end tiles appear, respectively, at the beginning and end of an open path. If a brush does not have start or end tiles defined, then the side tile will be used in their stead. Note that if a brush doesn't have inner or outer corner tiles defined, those sections of the path will appear blank.

A few things are somewhat confusing with regard to how Illustrator displays pattern tiles in the user interface. For example, the tiles appear in one particular order when listed in the Pattern Brush Options dialog (**Figure 5.14**), yet they appear listed in a completely different order when viewed in the Brushes panel (**Figure 5.15**). Although the order doesn't really make a difference, it's easy to get confused when you're assigning patterns to each tile.

Figure 5.14 The order in which pattern brush tiles appear within the Pattern Brush Options dialog. A diagonal line (slash) means there is no pattern associated with that tile.

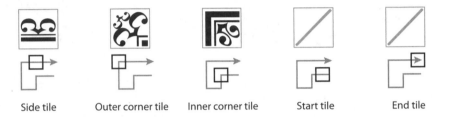

Side tile Outer corner tile Inner corner tile Start tile End tile

Figure 5.15 The order in which pattern brush tiles appear within the Brushes panel.

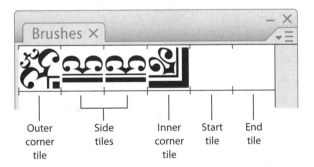

Outer corner tile Side tiles Inner corner tile Start tile End tile

In addition, because of the way inner corner tiles are drawn along paths, they are flipped (or reflected) negative 45 degrees, which means you need to compensate for that when defining the artwork for such tiles. It gets confusing because the Brushes panel shows a preview of the tile as though it appears correct, but the same tile appears reflected when viewed in the Pattern Brush Options dialog box (**Figure 5.16**). So that you remain sane, it's best to draw your pattern art normally and simply reflect it 45 degrees before defining it as a pattern.

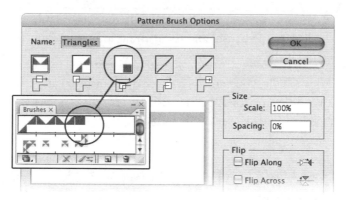

Figure 5.16 In the Pattern Brush Options dialog, the inner corner tile appears flipped, compared to the same tile that appears in the Brushes panel (inset).

Modifying Brush Strokes

Double-click any brush in the Brushes panel to specify or change its settings. Alternatively, you can hold the Option (Alt) key while dragging vector art from the artboard onto an existing Art or Scatter brush to modify or replace the brush. When you do, a thick black line appears around the brush icon indicating that you are about to modify it.

When you're about to modify a brush, Illustrator checks to see whether the existing brush has already been applied to objects in your document. If it finds such objects, Illustrator asks whether you want the existing paths to now take on the appearance of the modified brush or whether you want to leave them intact (**Figure 5.17**). If you want to leave them intact, Illustrator makes a copy of the modified brush rather than replacing the existing one.

Figure 5.17 Always watching what you're doing, Illustrator alerts you if your edits will affect objects that have already been drawn.

You can delete brushes from a document by dragging them to the trash icon in the Brushes panel.

Expanding Brush Art

When you apply a brush stroke to a path, only the vector path itself is editable. The art that makes up the brush stroke cannot be edited or otherwise tinkered with. However, you can easily reduce any brush stroke to editable

Like swatches, brushes travel with a file, so you don't need to expand a brush just because you're sending the file to someone else. When you define and use brushes, those brushes are saved in the file and are there until you manually delete them.

vector art by choosing Object > Expand Appearance. Doing so removes the link to the brush, and the path no longer updates if the brush swatch is updated.

Additionally, you can always access the original art that was used to create an Art, Scatter, or Pattern brush by dragging the brush from the Brushes panel to a blank area on the artboard.

SAVING SPACE AND TIME WITH SYMBOLS

Sometimes, a project calls for a range of repeating design elements. For example, when creating a map of a park, you might use icons to indicate restrooms or picnic areas. And when designing an item of clothing, you might draw the same button in several places. Illustrator has a feature that was created specifically to manage repeating graphics in a document, called *symbols*.

You can think of a symbol as a master art item, which is defined once per Illustrator document. Once created, you can place multiple *instances* of a symbol within a document. Each instance is simply an alias or a placeholder that points to the original defined symbol. Using symbols in a document offers several benefits. First, if you edit or modify a symbol, all instances of that symbol are automatically updated as well. Second, because Illustrator stores only a single copy of a symbol per document, you can take advantage of smaller file sizes. Smaller file sizes translate to faster open and save times, faster print times, and faster server transfer times.

Designers who create certain kinds of Web graphics can also take advantage of using symbols. In Chapter 11, *Web and Mobile Design*, we'll discuss how you can use symbols to generate smaller file sizes when creating SWF (Flash) and SVG files.

Working with Symbols and Instances

Defining a symbol is quick and easy. Select any artwork on your artboard, and drag it into the Symbols panel. Even faster, select your artwork, and press the F8 key. The Symbol Options dialog appears, giving you the opportunity to name the symbol (**Figure 5.18**). Ignore all the other settings in the

Symbol Options dialog, because they apply only to those symbols that will eventually be brought into Adobe Flash CS3 Professional (we cover these Flash-specific settings in detail in Chapter 11, *Web and Mobile Design*).

Figure 5.18 The Symbol Options dialog box gives you the ability to name your symbol as you create it, making it easier to reference later.

Unlike brushes, which are limited in the kinds of artwork they can contain, you can use any kind of artwork to define a symbol with the exception of place-linked images (for more information on linked images, see Chapter 9, *Mixing It Up: Working with Vectors and Pixels*). Embedded images, objects with live effects applied, and even editable text can be stored inside a symbol in Illustrator. Once you've defined a symbol, your artwork is stored in the Symbols panel, and a symbol instance is placed on your artboard in its stead. Like brushes, symbols belong to the Illustrator document and travel with it, meaning anyone who opens your document will always see it listed in the Symbols panel. Copying an instance from one document to another automatically copies the symbol as well.

You can drag additional instances from the Symbols panel right to your artboard, or you can select a symbol in the panel and click the Place Symbol Instance icon to add an instance to the center of your screen (**Figure 5.19**). Once on the artboard, you'll notice that a symbol instance doesn't give you access to the actual artwork because it is simply a placeholder (**Figure 5.20** on the following page). However, you can use any of Illustrator's transformation tools and functions with symbol instances. For example, you can scale or rotate a symbol instance as necessary. Additionally, you can specify transparency features and even apply live effects to symbol instances. You can place as many symbol instances in a document as you desire, and each instance can be scaled or transformed differently.

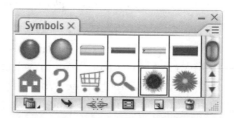

Figure 5.19 You can use the Place Symbol Instance icon to place symbols on the center of your screen.

 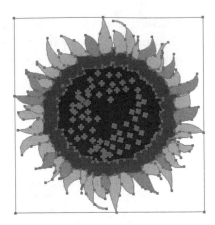

Figure 5.20 Even though a symbol may consist of many individual objects, it is treated as a single object on the artboard.

Figure 5.21 Once you break the link between the symbol and an instance, you can edit the artwork freely, although the art no longer has any association with the symbol.

At any time, you can select a symbol instance on the artboard and click the Break Link button that appears in the Control panel. Alternatively, you can click the Break Link to Symbol button in the Symbols panel. This action "expands" the symbol instance on the artboard, allowing you to access and edit each of the individual components (**Figure 5.21**). However, the artwork is no longer an instance, and it loses any connection with the symbol that is defined in the Symbols panel. The symbol itself remains untouched, and any other instances that exist on your artboard still reference the original symbol as well.

Replacing Symbols

If you think about it, a symbol instance is really just a container that references real artwork that resides in the Symbols panel. With this fundamental understanding, it should be possible to take a symbol instance that references one symbol and change it so it references a different symbol that you've defined. In Illustrator, the ability to switch an instance to point to a different symbol is called *replacing symbols*.

To replace a symbol instance, select it on the artboard, and then choose another symbol from the Replace Instance with Symbol pop-up in the Control panel. Alternatively, you can select the symbol instance on the artboard and click the symbol in the Symbols panel that you want to replace it with. With both the symbol instance on your artboard and the new symbol in the

Although you can't include linked images in a symbol, you can include embedded images. Because you can use symbols many times in a document with no adverse effect on file size, it makes sense to think about creating symbols from an embedded image if you need to use them often in a file.

Symbols panel selected, click the Replace Symbol icon in the Symbols panel, or choose Replace Symbol from the Symbols panel menu. The selected symbol instance updates accordingly. When replacing symbol instances, any transformations or effects that you've applied to any individual instances will remain intact.

Modifying Symbols and Instances

Illustrator CS3 introduces a wonderful way to edit symbols. But before you edit a symbol, it's important to understand an important concept: editing a symbol will cause any instances of that symbol that appear in your document to update. The easiest way to edit a symbol is to simply double-click it, which will isolate the symbol (similar to an isolated group). You'll experience a different behavior depending on whether you double-click a symbol instance on the artboard or a symbol in the Symbols panel. Let's take a look at the difference:

- **Double-clicking a symbol instance on the artboard.** When you double-click a symbol instance on the artboard, Illustrator dims out all other artwork in your file, and you can edit your symbol in the context of your entire document (**Figure 5.22**).

Figure 5.22 Double-clicking a symbol instance on the artboard tells Illustrator you want to edit your symbol art in the context of the other art on your page. As you edit your symbol, you'll see the other art in the background.

- **Double-clicking a symbol in the Symbols panel.** When you double-click a symbol in the Symbols panel, Illustrator hides all other artwork in your file and displays just the symbol artwork, in the middle of your document window (**Figure 5.23**).

Figure 5.23 Double-clicking on a symbol in the Symbols panel tells Illustrator that you want to edit the symbol without anything else getting in the way. All other art will disappear, allowing you to focus just on the symbol artwork.

You can nest symbols, meaning you can place one symbol inside another symbol. To edit nested symbols, keep double-clicking each symbol to drill down further within the symbol.

When a symbol is redefined, all instances on the artboard that reference the symbol are updated to reflect the change. Any attributes or transformations that were applied to the instances are preserved.

Using Symbols in Different Ways

When you take a moment to think about your project before you start working on it, you might be able to determine whether using symbols would benefit you. Here is a list of several ways symbols can help build better files:

- Although Illustrator doesn't use master pages, symbols can act like miniature "master art elements" in a file. For example, when creating several different ideas for a packaging concept, use symbols as the base for each design (that is, ingredients, nutrition information, weight, and so on). Updating a symbol then instantly updates all the design comps in the file at once.

- Create symbol libraries to store commonly used logos and icons. (You'll learn how to create custom libraries in Chapter 6, *Working with Color*.)

- Create symbol libraries to store collections of fashion elements, such as buttons, zippers, or labels, or to store other specific art elements, such as architectural elements or cartography symbols.

- The use of symbols is required in order to perform certain features in Illustrator, including creating custom 3D bevels and artwork mapped onto the surfaces of 3D objects. Chapter 8, *3D and Other Live Effects*, covers this functionality.

Of course, you can use symbols in Illustrator in plenty of other ways. The next section deals with some special tools created specifically for working with symbols: the Symbolism tools.

Having Fun with the Symbolism Tools

So, you've been reading along and totally get the benefits of using symbols where possible to create more efficient files. Say, for example, you are going to create a night sky for an illustration and need to fill the sky with stars. You create a symbol of a nice star with a cool glow effect and define it as a symbol. One by one, you drag out symbol instances and scale and rotate each star to achieve a more natural look (**Figure 5.24**). As you drag out yet another symbol instance, you think, there's got to be a better way to do this. The good news is, there is. The great news is, the better way is extremely fun!

Figure 5.24 Dragging out and editing individual symbol instances can be tedious.

In the Tools panel, you'll find the Symbol Sprayer tool. Hidden beneath it, you'll find seven more tools; together, these tools are referred to as the Symbolism tools (**Figure 5.25**). The reason for the name is that these tools all work using symbols, and not by any coincidence, the tools all begin with the letter *s*. (See? Adobe actually *does* pay attention to detail.)

Figure 5.25 The Symbolism tools all appear grouped in the Toolbox with the Symbol Sprayer tool.

Creating a Symbol Set

The Symbol Sprayer tool lets you easily add multiple symbol instances to a document. Select the Symbol Sprayer tool from the Toolbox, and then click any symbol in the Symbols panel. Because the Symbol Sprayer tool works only with symbols, it's important to first select a symbol to work with—otherwise the Symbol Sprayer won't work. Click and drag on the artboard, and you'll begin to see the Symbol Sprayer adding symbols to your page (**Figure 5.26**). When you release the mouse, a single outline appears around the perimeter of the symbols. What you have actually created is a *symbol set*, which is a collection of symbol instances (**Figure 5.27**). If you switch to the Selection tool, you'll find that you can't select the individual symbol instances, but you can move the entire symbol set as a whole.

Although it may seem silly that you can't select individual instances within a symbol set, that notion quickly changes when you realize that the Symbol Sprayer tool is interactive. Select the symbol set, and switch back to the Symbol Sprayer tool. If you click and drag, the Symbol Sprayer tool adds more symbol instances to the set. If you press the Option (Alt) key while dragging, you remove symbols from the set. In addition, the Symbol Sprayer tool has support for pressure-sensitive tablets, so the harder you press, the faster the instances appear.

It's certainly fun to spray symbols all over your document, but there is a way you can control the individual symbols that appear inside a symbol set. To do this, you need to employ the Symbolism tools.

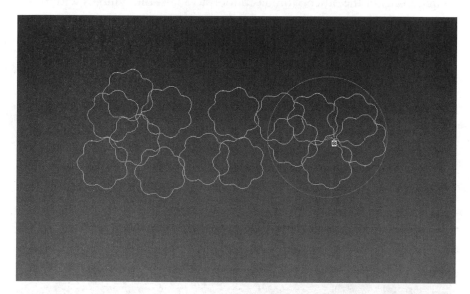

Figure 5.26 As you click and drag with the Symbol Sprayer tool, instances appear to flow onto your artboard.

Figure 5.27 Once you release the mouse, the symbol instances appear united in a single symbol set.

Using the Specialized Symbolism Tools

You can add different symbols to the same symbol set. Once you've created a symbol set using one symbol, choose another symbol from the Symbols panel, and add more symbols to your symbol set. You can add as many different kinds of symbols as you want to a symbol set.

Once you've created a symbol set with the Symbol Sprayer tool, you can switch to any of the other Symbolism tools to adjust the symbols within the set. It's important to realize that symbol sets are intended to create a natural collection of symbol instances. You'll find that you can't position symbol instances precisely with the Symbolism tools. On the contrary, the Symbolism tools are meant to offer Illustrator users a more free-flowing style, and it almost feels as if you are suggesting a particular movement or behavior to symbol instances rather than performing a definitive action to them. As you try each of these tools, you'll get a better feel for how they function and for how you might be able to use them for your projects.

For each of these tools, you'll notice that a circle appears, which indicates the diameter of the tool's area of influence (**Figure 5.28**). You can make this area larger or smaller by pressing the bracket keys ([ ]) on your keyboard (similar to Photoshop's keyboard shortcut for changing brush size).

Figure 5.28 You can resize the circle area, which indicates the tool's area of influence, to be bigger or smaller.

Although the Symbolism tools aren't meant to work on just one symbol instance at a time, you can make your area of influence small enough that you can affect a much smaller area or even individual symbols.

- **Symbol Shifter tool.** The Symbol Shifter tool moves symbol instances around. Clicking and dragging this tool pushes symbols in the direction of your cursor. If you hold the Shift key while dragging, Illustrator brings the symbol instances from the back of the symbol set's stacking order to the front.

- **Symbol Scruncher tool.** The Symbol Scruncher tool moves symbol instances closer together, making the appearance more dense. Clicking and dragging with the Symbol Scruncher tool causes instances to become attracted to your cursor and to slowly gravitate toward it. If you hold the Option (Alt) key while dragging, the reverse effect applies, and instances move farther away from your cursor.

- **Symbol Sizer tool.** The Symbol Sizer tool scales symbol instances within a symbol set. Clicking and dragging with the Symbol Sizer tool causes instances to become larger. If you hold the Option (Alt) key while dragging, the reverse effect applies, and instances become smaller (**Figure 5.29**).

Figure 5.29 The Symbol Sizer tool allows you to interactively scale the symbol instances within a symbol set.

- **Symbol Spinner tool.** The Symbol Spinner tool rotates symbol instances. Clicking and dragging with the Symbol Sizer tool causes instances to rotate toward the direction of your cursor. As you drag, arrows appear that indicate the direction in which the instances will rotate (**Figure 5.30** on the following page). Instances that appear closer to the center of the area of influence rotate at a lesser rate than objects toward the edges of the area of influence.

Figure 5.30 When dragging with the Symbol Spinner tool, arrows appear, helping you get an idea of how the instances will rotate.

- **Symbol Stainer tool.** The Symbol Stainer tool applies color tints to symbol instances. To use the Symbol Stainer tool, you must first select a color from either the Control, Swatches, or Color panel. Once a color is selected, clicking and dragging with the Symbol Stainer tool gradually tints the symbol instances. If you hold the Option (Alt) key while dragging, the reverse effect applies, and the instances will gradually return to their original colors.

- **Symbol Screener tool.** The Symbol Screener tool applies opacity to symbol instances. Clicking and dragging with the Symbol Screener tool causes instances to become transparent. If you hold the Option (Alt) key while dragging, the reverse effect applies, and instances become more opaque.

- **Symbol Styler tool.** The Symbol Styler tool applies graphic styles to symbol instances. To use the Symbol Styler tool, you must first select a graphic style from the Graphic Styles panel. Once you've selected a style, click and drag with the Symbol Styler tool to gradually add appearances from the style to the symbol instances. If you hold the Option (Alt) key while dragging, the reverse effect applies, and the instances gradually return to their original appearances. Note that using this particular tool can result in extremely slow performance, especially with complex symbols.

Switching Symbolism tools

When using the Symbolism tools, you'll often find yourself jumping from one Symbolism tool to another. You can either tear off all the Symbolism tools to access them easier, or you can use a special context-sensitive menu. If you're on a Mac, with any of the Symbolism tools selected, press Control-Option, and click. If you're on Windows, press Alt, and right-click to access a circular contextual menu that contains all the Symbolism tools (**Figure 5.31**). Move your cursor over the tool you want, and release the keys to switch to the Symbolism tool you have chosen.

Figure 5.31 The Symbolism contextual menu makes it easy to switch between the tools.

Double-click any of the Symbolism tools to see the options for the entire Symbolism toolset (**Figure 5.32**). The Intensity setting controls how quickly the Symbolism tools work, and choosing Pressure for the Intensity setting if you have a pressure-sensitive tablet makes it easier to control the flow of symbols and the edits you make to them.

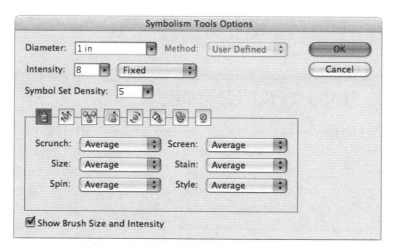

Figure 5.32 In one dialog, you can set the behavior and view options for all the Symbolism tools.

Expanding a Symbol Set

You can reduce a symbol set to a group of individual symbol instances by selecting the symbol set and choosing Object > Expand. Although the Symbol Sprayer works only with symbol sets, the remaining Symbolism

If you add multiple symbols to a single symbol set, using any of the Symbolism tools affects only the symbol that is currently selected in the Symbols panel. If no symbols are selected in the Symbols panel, the tools will work on all symbols.

tools work on individual symbol instances. You can also select several symbol instances and use a Symbolism tool to adjust them all at once. Still, you'll find that most times, you'll be using the regular Scale and Rotate tools to adjust individual symbol instances, and you'll be using the Symbolism tools for when you're working with symbol sets.

 Featured Matchup: Scatter Brush vs. Symbol Sprayer Tool

You may be wondering why there's a Symbol Sprayer tool in Illustrator, since you know that earlier in the chapter, we discussed the Scatter brush, which allows you to distribute graphics along a path.

Although the concept of creating multiple copies of art is common between the two, the differences end there. A Scatter brush is limited by what can be defined as a brush, whereas you have far fewer limitations when you are defining symbols. Additionally, using a Scatter brush to add many shapes to a file increases file size and adds complexity to the file. The Symbol Sprayer tool can spray hundreds of symbols onto a page without you having to worry about files getting too big.

Of course, you can adjust symbol sets that are created with the Symbol Sprayer tool using a range of Symbolism tools. This allows you to tweak a design until you're happy with the results. In contrast, when using a Scatter brush, you've already specified the settings of the brush before you've created the path. However, a Scatter brush can follow a specific path, whereas the Symbol Sprayer tool is harder to control if you need art placed at specific intervals.

USING GRADIENT MESH

As you learned in Chapter 2, *Vectors 101*, gradients allow you to fill an object with gradations of color that blend into each other. Although these gradients are certainly useful, they are limited from a creative standpoint because they can be used only in linear or radial forms. In Illustrator 8, Adobe introduced a radical new feature called Gradient Mesh, an incredible tool that allows you to create gradients in any shape. The results are painterly effects that look as if they had come right from Photoshop—yet they are all in vector form using the Gradient Mesh feature. And if you can achieve the appearance you're looking for while keeping your file in vector form, you can keep your art completely scalable and editable throughout the design process. For example, changing one color in a gradient mesh is far easier than trying to replace a color that's used in a Photoshop file.

However, the Gradient Mesh tool isn't the easiest feature to understand. Many people would like to use the feature, but they can't figure out any consistent way to explain its behavior. This section will help you understand what a gradient mesh is and how it works.

Before you learn how to apply a gradient mesh, let's talk about what a mesh is. A *mesh* is a grid consisting of multiple *mesh points* that act much like smooth anchor points (**Figure 5.33**). You can adjust each of these points (and their control handles) to control the shape of the mesh. A mesh is really a special kind of construct or object in Illustrator, and it does not act like a regular path does. Mesh objects do not have normal Fill or Stroke attributes and can't display certain kinds of live effects. Rather, you use mesh objects to contain two kinds of attributes in Illustrator: gradients and envelopes. We'll talk more about envelopes in Chapter 10, *Graphs, Distortion, and Blends*. When you're using a mesh to define a gradient, each mesh point determines a color stop (just like a regular gradient), and the control handles determine the way in which that color blends into other nearby colors.

Mesh points

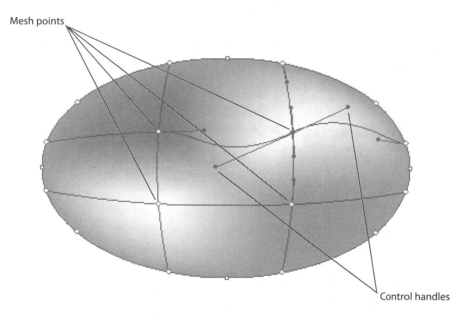

Figure 5.33 A mesh is a grid that consists of mesh points and control handles.

Control handles

You can create a Gradient Mesh object in Illustrator in two basic ways, and in both cases, you start by first drawing a regular vector object. You don't draw Gradient Mesh objects from scratch in Illustrator; you convert existing vector shapes to mesh objects. With a vector object selected, do one of the following:

- Choose Object > Create Gradient Mesh. This opens the Create Gradient Mesh dialog, giving you the ability to specify the number of rows and columns in your mesh (**Figure 5.34**). If your original object already has a color applied to it, you can use the Appearance and Highlight options to shade the object with white.

Figure 5.34 Choosing the number of rows and columns determines the number of mesh points in your mesh. You can always add or remove mesh points later.

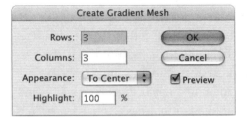

- Select the Mesh tool from the Toolbox, and click anywhere within your vector path. Each click with the Mesh tool adds mesh points to the mesh object. You'll also notice that as you add mesh points to an object, the paths connecting the mesh points match the contours of the object (**Figure 5.35**).

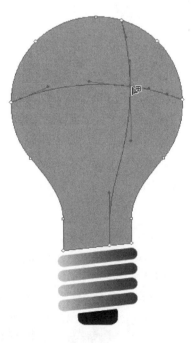

Figure 5.35 In this example of a lightbulb, notice how the mesh points and curves that are added aren't straight but match the contour of the object.

Once you have mesh points defined, you can switch to the Direct Selection tool and select each individual mesh point to adjust its position and its direction handles. With a mesh point selected, you can choose a color from the Control, Swatches, or Color panel to define the color for that point (**Figure 5.36**). As needed, you can switch back to the Mesh tool and click to add mesh points. To remove a mesh point from a mesh object, hold the Option (Alt) while clicking a point with the Mesh tool. In Illustrator CS3, you can use both process and spot colors in a gradient mesh, and the file will separate correctly when printed.

If you converted a path to a mesh object and then want to get the path back, you can select the mesh object and use the Offset Path function with a setting of 0. This creates a new path that you can edit and color as you want.

Figure 5.36 The control handles and paths that connect the mesh points define how colors blend and define the shapes and contours of the gradient.

For inspirational examples of what you can do with gradient mesh, check out *The Illustrator CS3 Wow! Book* by Sharon Steuer (Peachpit Press).

LOOKING BEHIND THE MASK

When we refer to masks, we're not talking about the kind you wear to Mardi Gras. *Masking* in Illustrator is a way to define parts of your artwork as being hidden from view. Rather than having to delete unwanted parts of your art, you can use a vector shape to define an area that acts like a window: Anything that appears within the borders of the shape is visible, and anything that falls outside its boundaries is not visible. The main benefit derived from using masks is that you aren't deleting anything from your file, and once a mask is created, it's possible to change the mask or the artwork behind it, as well as reposition the mask to show or hide different parts of your artwork.

When you use masks in a file and are required to make changes, you'll never have to re-create art that you've already deleted. Instead, everything you create is always in the file, and you simply choose what is or isn't visible. Additionally, a mask allows you to instantly clip parts of an image or an object. By using a mask, you can do with one click what might take tens of clicks if you use pathfinder functions to chop up and delete parts of objects. Of course, you can't remove parts of some kinds of objects at all, such as placed images, in which case masking is required anyway.

You can create three kinds of masks in Illustrator, each with its own benefits. A *clipping mask* allows you to specify a certain vector shape as a mask for other individual or grouped objects. A *layer clipping mask* allows you to specify a certain vector shape as a mask for all the objects within the same layer. An *opacity mask* allows you to use the luminance value of any object to create a mask for other individual or grouped objects. As you will see, this last type of mask—one of the most well-hidden features of Illustrator—is also the most powerful.

Creating Clipping Masks

A common use of clipping masks is showing only a portion of a placed image. For example, page layout applications such as Adobe InDesign allow you to place images into a frame. By resizing the frame and positioning the image within the frame, you can "crop" an image so that only a portion is visible. Being that Illustrator allows you to place images directly on the artboard (without requiring a frame), you must use a mask to achieve the effect of cropping an image in Illustrator.

Illustrator CS3 makes the process of cropping images in this way a tad bit easier by helping you create and edit the mask via the Control panel. Once you've placed an image into your document, click it to select it. You'll notice that there's a button labeled Mask in the Control panel. When you click this button, it first appears as if nothing has happened, but in reality, Illustrator has created a mask using a rectangle that matches the size of the image (**Figure 5.37**). Using the Selection tool (with the View > Bounding Box option turned on), you can simply resize the mask to reveal only the parts of the image that are important for your design (**Figure 5.38**).

Figure 5.37 With any image selected in Illustrator, you can use the Mask button in the Control panel to create a mask.

Figure 5.38 Once you've created a mask for the image, you can quickly "crop" the photo by adjusting the mask.

Once you've created your mask, you may want to reposition the image within the mask. You can easily do this by clicking the Edit Contents button that appears in the Control panel (**Figure 5.39**). When you first create a mask, Illustrator automatically assumes you want to edit the mask, so the Edit Clipping Path option is active. However, once the mask is already created and you've deselected it, the behavior is different in the following ways:

Figure 5.39 Choosing Edit Contents in the Control panel makes it easy to edit or adjust the art that appears within the mask.

- When Illustrator creates a clipping mask, it automatically creates a rectangle that matches the size of the image and then groups the two objects together. When you select the mask, you will be selecting the group, and both the image and mask will be editable.

- Clicking the Edit Clipping Path icon in the Control panel will enable you to edit the mask itself, without touching the contents within the mask (which in this case is the image).

- Clicking the Edit Contents icon in the Control panel will enable you to edit the image itself, without touching the mask (which in this case

Of course, you can always use the Direct Selection tool to select and edit a mask or its contents individually.

is the rectangle). Note that since the clipping mask function automatically created a group, you can also edit the contents of a mask simply by double-clicking it, which will isolate the group, essentially allowing you to edit the image.

In reality, a clipping mask can consist of any vector object, including editable text. To manually create a clipping mask, you first move the object that will become the mask to the top of the object stacking order. Then, you select *both* the path that will be the mask and the art you want to appear inside the mask (which will become the contents of the mask). Choose Object > Clipping Mask > Make, and only the art that falls within the boundaries of the mask object will remain visible. You can then follow the three mask behaviors listed previously to edit the mask and its contents.

In truth, because masked art is still selectable even outside the boundary of the mask, it can make life difficult when you have a lot of masks in a file, because you can easily select masked artwork when you don't intend to do so. Getting into the habit of using the Layers panel to lock the art that you aren't working with for a particular task helps avoid this.

A clipping mask uses the vector path as the boundary for the mask, even if the object has an appearance applied to it. If you want the appearance to become the mask, you'll need an Opacity mask, covered later in this chapter.

Organized Masking with Layer Clipping Masks

A layer clipping mask is similar to a clipping mask, with one main difference: instead of using a shape to mask other selected objects or group of objects, it uses one shape to mask an entire layer. In reality, layer clipping masks are far easier to control and work with because you aren't constantly selecting and deselecting objects to define what is or what isn't in a particular mask. Instead, you use the Layers panel, which you use to organize your artwork anyway, to create these kinds of masks. In fact, when creating a clipping mask, you don't have to have any art selected on your artboard at all, because the mask is an attribute of the layer.

To create a layer clipping mask, place the vector object that will be your mask at the top of the layer's stacking order. Click the layer name in the Layers panel once, which selects the layer (you don't want to target the layer; just select it in the panel). Then, click the Make/Release Clipping Mask icon at the bottom of the Layers panel (**Figure 5.40**). The topmost object in your layer now becomes a mask for all objects in that layer. The mask appears listed in the Layers panel with an underline, giving you a visual indication of its behavior (**Figure 5.41**).

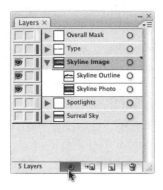

Figure 5.40 To create a layer clipping mask, select the layer first, and then define the mask.

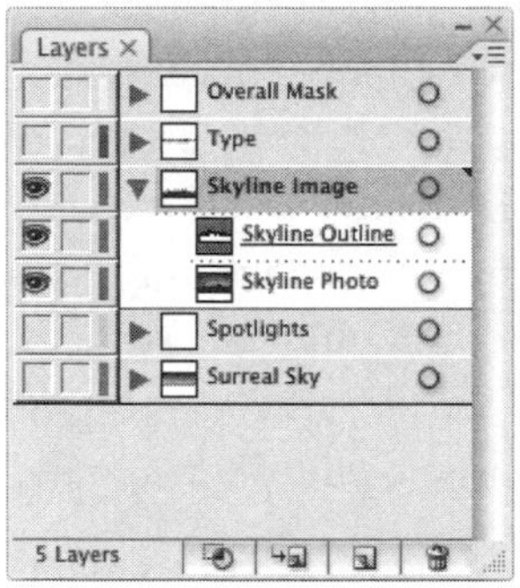

Figure 5.41 If you see something listed in the Layers panel with an under-line, you know that object is a clipping mask.

With layer clipping masks, you can easily drag items into a masked layer to have them affected by the mask, and vice versa. To release a layer clipping mask, select the layer, and click the Make/Release Clipping Mask button.

Because of a bug, releasing a layer clipping mask from the Layers panel will also release all layer clipping masks within any sublayers, forcing you to reapply the masks. Let's hope Adobe will address and fix this issue.

Retaining Layer Hierarchy with Layer Masks

Working with layer masks has an added benefit. As we mentioned earlier, when you create a regular clipping mask, Illustrator automatically creates a group that contains the mask and art within it. Back in Chapter 3, you also learned that a group in Illustrator is like a container, that stores all the objects within it. Because of this behavior, objects that reside within a group must always live within the same layer. That means if you have artwork that appears across several layers and you choose to mask that artwork with a clipping mask, you will lose all your layers. That's because in order to create the group with the mask, Illustrator has to bring all the artwork to the topmost layer.

When using layer masks, however, you can organize nested layers to easily mask the artwork you want, while preserving your entire layer structure in your file. The following is an example in which I use a variety of layers and masks to highlight this obvious benefit of layer masks:

1. The example consists of an Illustrator file with a placed image of a city skyline. First, I'd like to add a different sky and also throw in some effects such as spotlights in the sky. To do so, I've drawn a vector path that I will use to clip the buildings from the sky. You can see the path sitting above the image in the Layers panel (**Figure 5.42**).

Figure 5.42 The image appears at the bottom of the layer, while the path appears above it.

2. Highlighting the Skyline Image layer (remember that layers always have gray backgrounds in the Layers panel; objects have white backgrounds), I activate the layer mask by clicking the icon in the lower left of the Layers panel. This makes the topmost object in that layer a mask, effectively clipping the sky out of the illustration. It affects only the image on this layer, and the path appears with an underline in the Layers panel, indicating it is now a mask for the contents of its layer (**Figure 5.43**).

Figure 5.43 The layer mask affects artwork only within its own layer.

3. Now that the image is masked, I can turn on some other layers that I've created in the file, notably a gradient for the sky, some spotlights criss-crossing in the night, and some descriptive text (**Figure 5.44**).

Figure 5.44 By placing some artwork on layers that appear beneath the image (such as the spotlights and the sky), the entire artwork starts to take shape.

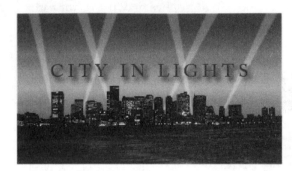

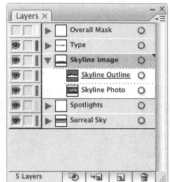

4. Now comes the tricky part. I like to create a rounded-corner appearance for all my artwork. To do that, I need to make an overall shape to use as a mask (**Figure 5.45**). However, if I try to create a clipping mask, all the items in my document will be brought up into the topmost layer, resulting in the loss of all my layers. To prevent this from happening, I select the bottom four layers in my Layers panel and drag them so that they become nested within the top layer (**Figure 5.46**). These sublayers sit beneath the path that will eventually be used as a mask for the overall mask layer.

Figure 5.45 The final artwork needs to fit within the area of this rounded-corner rectangle.

Figure 5.46 Rather than try to move artwork on the artboard, it's far easier to drag entire layers within the Layers panel.

5. Finally, I highlight the Overall Mask layer—the top layer in my document—and turn on the layer mask for that layer. This clips all the artwork in the file, yet the layer structure remains intact, even the masks that already exist in the nested layers (**Figure 5.47**). All elements are completely editable and are easily accessible in the Layers panel.

Figure 5.47 The final masked result presents the desired appearance and maintains all layers in the file.

Seeing Through Objects with Opacity Masks

When you're creating clipping and layer clipping masks, the vector path of the mask is what defines the boundary of what is visible and what is not. Additionally, anything that falls inside the mask area is completely visible, and anything that falls outside that area is completely hidden. Opacity masks bring a whole new level of functionality to Illustrator because in addition to using the vector path itself as the mask, the visual appearance of the mask is what defines what is shown and what is hidden.

If you've used Photoshop before, you're familiar with something called an *alpha channel*. In reality, an alpha channel in Photoshop is just like a mask, where the color black represents areas of the image that are visible and the color white represents areas of the image that are hidden. With an alpha channel, however, you can also specify a color of gray, which translates to part of an image that's partially visible. In fact, alpha channels support up to 256 levels of gray, which translate to up to 256 levels of visibility in such a mask. Because of this functionality, users can specify masks with soft edges and fades when they use Photoshop. Each pixel of the mask can represent a different opacity value. Opacity masks in Illustrator can take advantage of that same functionality.

When you use an object as an opacity mask, the vector path is not the only thing that determines what it shown and what is hidden—the visual makeup of the object is what determines the mask as well. Opacity masks support 256 levels of gray, meaning you can create a soft-edged mask in Illustrator. Let's see how this works by using a gradient as an opacity mask.

Creating an Opacity Mask

For this exercise, imagine you want to create a pattern that fades from 100-percent color to none. Begin by creating a rectangle and filling it with a pattern. Next, select the rectangle and copy it by pressing Command-C (Control-C). Now paste it in front of the first rectangle by pressing Command-F (Control-F). Fill the second rectangle with a regular black-to-white linear gradient. You now have two objects, stacked on top of each other, with the gradient visible on top (**Figure 5.48**).

Use the Selection tool to select both objects and open your Transparency panel. To create an Opacity mask, you have to expand the panel to show all its options, so click the triangles to the left of the Panel tab or choose Show Options from the panel menu. You will see a thumbnail of your selection in the Transparency panel (**Figure 5.49**). Finally, choose Make Opacity Mask from the Transparency panel menu. The result is a mask that uses the values of the gradient to define what parts of the object are visible below it—an object that effectively fades from a pattern to transparent (feel free to create an object that appears beneath the rectangle with the pattern if you don't believe me).

Figure 5.48 Two rectangles stacked on top of each other, and only the one filled with the gradient is visible.

Figure 5.49 A thumbnail of your selected art is visible in the Transparency panel.

Editing an Opacity Mask

Once you've created the opacity mask, you can use the thumbnails in the Transparency panel to work with both the mask and the artwork beneath it. Instead of one thumbnail as you saw before, there are now two thumbnails: the one on the left is the artwork, and the one on the right is the mask. To edit the artwork, click the left thumbnail. If you look at your Appearance panel, you'll notice that the object you have selected is a normal path that has a solid fill attributed to it. The name of the path displays with a dashed underline in both the Appearance panel and the Layers panel, indicating that

Shift-click the mask icon to temporarily disable the opacity mask. Option (Alt) click to display just the contents of the mask.

it has an opacity mask applied (**Figure 5.50**). At this point, the mask itself is not editable, and it can't even be selected.

Figure 5.50 A target with a dashed underline quickly identifies an object that has an opacity mask applied to it.

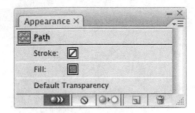

Clicking the Invert Mask button reverses a mask, and rather than having the color black appear as transparent, the color black represents areas that are opaque. The Transparency panel menu also has an option to set all new masks to be created so that they are inverted.

Clicking the right thumbnail selects the mask, allowing you to edit its attributes (**Figure 5.51**). Take a look at the Layers panel; doing so reveals something very interesting. Instead of displaying all the layers and objects in your file, when you click the mask thumbnail, the Layers panel switches to display just the opacity mask (**Figure 5.52**). The title bar of your document also indicates you are editing the opacity mask and not the art. These visual indications help you easily identify when you are editing art and when you are editing an opacity mask. To return to artwork editing mode, simply click the left thumbnail icon again.

Figure 5.51 Clicking a thumbnail in the Transparency panel tells Illustrator what you want to edit. A black outline around the thumbnail indicates which one is selected.

Figure 5.52 The Layers panel offers a visual cue to indicate when you are editing an opacity mask.

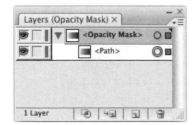

When you are editing either the artwork or the opacity mask, using the Selection tool to move items will result in both the artwork and the mask moving together. The reason for this is that by default, a mask and its artwork are linked with each other, indicated in the Transparency panel by a link icon that appears between the two thumbnail icons (**Figure 5.53**). Clicking the link icon allows you to move the mask and artwork independently of each other, and clicking between the thumbnails toggles the link behavior.

Figure 5.53 Clicking the link icon between the thumbnails allows you to move the art and the mask independently.

 Featured Matchup: Clipping Masks vs. Opacity Masks

When do you use an opacity mask instead of a clipping mask? One certainly doesn't replace the other, because each mask has specific benefits. A clipping mask uses the actual path of the vector object to define the clipping area. This means a clipping mask always has a hard vector edge. In contrast, an opacity mask uses the actual appearance of a shape as the mask, meaning you can create masks with soft edges or different levels of opacity. Additionally, opacity masks are controlled via the Transparency panel, making it easier to choose when you want to work with the mask or the artwork behind the mask. Of course, using an opacity mask means you're using transparency in your file, which requires flattening. When you're creating files for certain workflows that become complicated when you use transparency effects, using a clipping mask is beneficial. For more information about transparency and flattening, see Chapter 12, *Prepress and Printing*.

Taking Opacity Masks to the Next Level

Because opacity masks are "hidden" deep within the Transparency panel, they don't get much publicity. However, they are really one of the most sophisticated features you'll find; they offer a wide range of functionality. If you truly understand that opacity masks are just levels of gray that determine visibility, you can use these to achieve effects that you once thought were possible only in Photoshop.

Take photographs, for example. By using a vector object with a Feather live effect applied to it, you can create a soft-edged vignette for a placed photograph right in Illustrator (Chapter 8, *3D and Other Live Effects*, covers the Feather live effect). Additionally, you can use placed images themselves as opacity masks, which opens the door to creating Photoshop effects such as mezzotints and halos (**Figure 5.54**).

Figure 5.54 In this example, a mezzotint effect was applied to an object that was then used as an opacity mask for some type. The result is fully editable type that has a roughened appearance.

CHAPTER SIX

Working with Color

At one time, Adobe Illustrator (back in version 1.1) was black and white only. Then, Illustrator 88 introduced color features. Of course, back then, few designers could even afford to buy a color monitor. Technology eventually caught up, and color plays a huge role in a graphic designer's life today. The ability to add color and manipulate it, view it accurately on a monitor, and give life to artwork with color are abilities we take for granted now; however, the challenges of working with color are still present.

In this chapter, you'll learn about creating color in Illustrator and applying it to your artwork, as well as a variety of ways to edit or modify colors. Illustrator CS3 now comes with a collection of powerful inspirational tools that you can use to develop color harmonies and custom color palettes; you'll explore them in this chapter. Finally, you'll discover how to trust the color that appears on your computer screen and learn to use various settings to simulate different color viewing environments.

CREATING AND USING COLOR IN ILLUSTRATOR

Whether you are working with graphics that are to be printed (which use a combination of cyan, magenta, yellow, and black, also known as the CMYK color model) or those that are to be displayed on computer screens, televisions, or monitors (which use red, green, and blue, otherwise known as the RGB color model), you will always be specifying color as a combination of primary colors. When working in Illustrator, you'll find that, likewise, you define colors by mixing values of CMYK or RGB.

Of course, you can define and apply colors in plenty of ways. Some ways are more efficient than others, and some offer specific benefits. More so, some color features in Illustrator apply specifically to certain kinds of workflows and may even be irrelevant to some users. For example, using spot colors (solid, colored inks) serves no real purpose in the world of Web design, while Web-safe colors don't interest print designers in the least. But no matter what you're using your colors for, you'll find that, for the most part, you'll be creating and applying them via the Color panel and the Swatches panel (both available via the Window menu).

Using the Color Panel

The Color panel contains sliders that allow you to mix primary colors to create just about any custom color and apply it to your artwork. In fact, some graphics programs (such as FreeHand, for example) refer to this kind of panel as the Mixer. Think of it as a fine arts artist's palette that contains the primary colors. By mixing these colors, you can achieve any of your color needs. The Color panel doesn't store colors, so you can't use it as a repository for frequently used colors (that purpose is relegated to the Swatches panel, which we'll talk about shortly). However, anytime you select an object, the Color panel will display the color values of that object. So, you can use it either to apply color or to modify an existing color (**Figure 6.1**).

You can use the Color panel to specify colors using any of five sets of sliders: Grayscale, RGB (Red, Green, Blue), HSB (Hue, Saturation, Brightness),

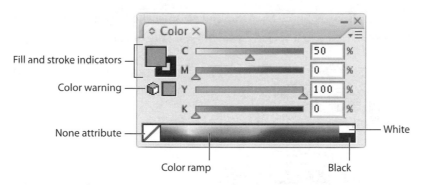

Fill and stroke indicators

Color warning

None attribute

White

Color ramp

Black

Figure 6.1 By adjusting the sliders in the Color panel, you can mix any color you need.

CMYK (Cyan, Magenta, Yellow, Black), and Web Safe RGB (216 colors that won't dither on a VGA computer screen). To switch between these, either choose one manually from the Color panel flyout menu or Shift-click the color ramp that appears toward the bottom of the Color panel.

The Color panel features fill and stroke indicators in the upper-left corner (similar to those found in the Tools panel). Clicking the fill indicator will allow you to specify a color for the Fill attribute of a selection, and clicking the stroke indicator does the same for the Stroke attribute. To save time, pressing the X key on your keyboard will toggle between the two attributes.

Although the Color panel doesn't store colors, you'll find that the color ramp at the bottom of the panel contains one-click shortcuts to the none, black, and white attributes. The keyboard shortcut for the none attribute is the slash (/). The Color panel will also display a color warning in the shape of a small 3D cube beneath the fill and stroke indicators when the chosen color is not a Web-safe color. Clicking the cube will set your current color to the closest Web-safe color match. For more information on Web-safe colors, refer to Chapter 11, *Web and Mobile Design*.

Pressing Shift-X will swap your fill and stroke colors, and pressing D will set your colors to the default white fill and black stroke.

Using the Swatches Panel

The Swatches panel stores a collection of predefined colors, making it easy to apply specific colors to your document quickly. Think of the Swatches panel as a box of crayons. You just choose the color you need and use it. In fact, the Swatches panel stores more than just solid colors; it also stores the two other types of fills that Illustrator supports: gradients and patterns. If the Swatches panel seems a bit cluttered with all these types of swatches,

See Chapter 2, *Vectors 101*, for more information on gradient and pattern fills.

you can click the Show Swatch Kinds icon at the bottom of the panel to limit the display to a specific swatch type (**Figure 6.2**).

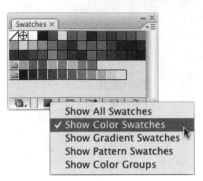

Figure 6.2 You can set the Swatches panel to display all kinds of swatches or just solid colors.

You can create a new color swatch in Illustrator in several ways:

• Click the New Swatch icon in the Swatches panel.

• Choose New Swatch from the Swatches panel flyout menu.

• Choose Create New Swatch from the Color panel flyout menu.

• Drag a color from the fill and stroke indicators in the Color panel to the Swatches panel.

• Drag a color from the Color Guide panel (the Color Guide panel is covered in detail later in this chapter).

Double-clicking a swatch opens the Swatch Options dialog and lets you edit the swatch (**Figure 6.3**). By default, swatches are names by their color values; however, you can name your swatches as you like. You can specify a color type for your swatch (refer to the "Hitting the Color Swatch Trifecta" section for explanations of these types) and a color mode as well.

Figure 6.3 The Swatch Options dialog lets you quickly edit your swatch settings.

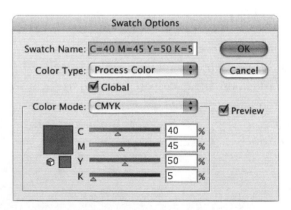

You can also automatically create swatches from the existing artwork in your file. With no objects selected, choose Add Used Colors from the Swatches panel flyout menu. If you want to add colors from a specific area in your document, select the objects desired, and choose Add Selected Color from the Swatches panel flyout menu. All new colors that are added will appear as global process colors, which are described in the next section.

You can also customize the view of your Swatches panel. By default, the swatches appear as little squares called *thumbnails*. But if you prefer, you can also have your swatches display in List view, which displays a little square beside the name of the swatch (**Figure 6.4**). You can choose from a variety of thumbnail and list sizes by selecting an option from the Swatches panel flyout menu.

The Swatches panel is always accessible via the Control panel, and it pops up when specifying a Fill or Stroke attribute. Holding the Shift key while clicking the Fill or Stroke icon will display the Color panel instead of the Swatches panel.

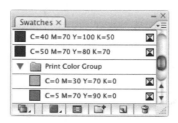

Figure 6.4 In List view, swatches appear listed by name.

Hitting the Color Swatch Trifecta

It would be simple if Illustrator offered only one type of solid color swatch, but, alas, it actually offers three: process color, global process color, and spot color swatches. Each of these serves a specific purpose, and it's important to understand when each should be used.

Process colors. A *process color* is one that is defined by a mixture of primary values. For color print work that is separated and printed using a four-color process (CMYK), for output to a color printer, or for Web design and video work, you want to define your swatches as process color swatches. Creating process color swatches allows you to easily apply set colors to art that you create in your document, but updating colors on existing objects is difficult. As you'll see shortly, you'll often want to look into using global process colors instead.

Global process colors. A *global process color* is the same as a process color with one main difference: the swatch is global in that if you ever update the swatch, all objects in the document that have that swatch applied update as well. Most production artists request that designers use global swatches because they are easier to manage in an entire document. To create a global process color swatch, check the Global option in the New Swatch dialog or Swatch Options dialog. In the Swatches panel, global process colors display with a small white triangle in their lower-right corners (**Figure 6.5**).

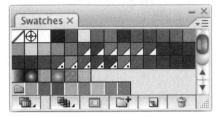

Figure 6.5 It's easy to identify a swatch by its appearance. Solid squares are process colors, squares with white corners are global process colors, and squares with white corners and dots are spot colors.

Spot colors. A *spot color* is a named color that appears on a custom plate during the color separation process. Instead of a printer breaking a color into cyan, magenta, yellow, or black, a spot color is a specific custom color ink that the printer creates for your print job. You might have a variety of reasons for using a spot color in a document:

- **Specific color.** Not every color can be reproduced using CMYK, which in reality has a small gamut. A custom color can be a bright fluorescent color, a color with a metallic sheen, or even one that involves specialized inks, such as the magnetic inks used on bank checks.

- **Consistent color.** Because process colors consist of a mixture of other colors, they can shift and appear differently, even on the same print job. When you're dealing with a company's corporate colors, you want to make sure color is consistent across all print jobs.

- **Solid color.** Process colors are formed by mixing inks in various percentages. Not only does this require perfect registration on a printing press (where all plates hit the same place on each sheet of paper), the process can also reveal odd patterns in reproduction in some cases (called *moiré patterns*). Spot color inks don't exhibit these issues and present a solid, clean appearance.

- **Cheaper color.** When you are performing a process color job, you're printing with four different color inks. But if you are creating a business card with black text and a red logo, it's cheaper to print using black ink and a single red spot color instead. Sometimes working with two or three spot colors gives your design the color it needs while keeping the printing costs down.

- **Something other than a color.** Print designs can be extremely creative, using processes such as foil stamping, die cutting, spot varnishing, or embossing. Even though these special effects don't print in ink, they still need to be specified to a printer. Spot colors allow you to easily define areas of color that will ultimately be regions of a gloss varnish effect, a die stamp, and so on.

You can define your own custom color (by choosing the Spot Color option in the Color Type pop-up menu), or you can choose a spot color from an existing library. Pantone libraries are the most common examples; they were created to help printers and designers standardize on colors by using a numbering system. To apply a color from a Pantone library, see "Working with Libraries" later in this chapter.

 ## Featured Matchup: Process vs. Global Process

At first glance, it may seem difficult to understand what the difference is between a process color and a global process color. But once you understand what each has to offer, it's easy to figure out when you should use each type of color swatch.

A process color swatch is simply a way to "memorize" the values for a particular color. The swatch contains the color breakdown (the individual values of each primary color), saving you from having to reapply multiple values to each object that you want to color in your document. To use it, you can select an object and then click a swatch to apply the chosen color to the object.

A global process swatch does the same thing but adds two main benefits in the way of productivity and creativity. First, when you select an object and then you choose a global process color swatch, an invisible "link" is created between the object and the swatch. This means if you ever modify the swatch (that is, edit its values), any objects in your document that you've already colored with that swatch will update as well. Second, global process colors show up in the Color panel with a tint slider, making it easy to specify different shades of your color.

So when defining your swatches, be sure to check the Global box in order to get the benefits of working with global process color swatches, including the ability to specify tint values.

Working with Groups of Color

As a designer, you may find it easier to organize your swatches into groups (**Figure 6.6**). In this way, you can find the colors you need quickly. More important, however, organizing colors into groups makes it easy to establish relationships between colors, which can be helpful when recoloring artwork using the Live Color feature (covered later in this chapter) or when using the Live Paint Bucket tool (covered in Chapter 4, *Advanced Vectors*).

Figure 6.6 Grouping swatches makes it easy to organize colors.

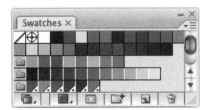

As with swatches, you can create a new group of swatches in several ways:

Swatch groups can contain only color swatches (process, global process, and spot) and not gradients or patterns.

• With nothing selected, click the New Color Group icon at the bottom of the Swatches panel to create an empty color group. Drag existing swatches from the Swatches panel directly to the group.

• Select multiple swatches in the Swatches panel using the Shift or Command (Control) key, and click the New Color Group icon at the bottom of the Swatches panel. The New Color Group dialog appears so you can name your group. Click OK to create the group.

• Select multiple swatches in the Color Guide panel using the Shift or Command (Control) key, and click the Save Color Group to Swatch Panel icon at the bottom of the Color Guide panel.

• With artwork selected on the artboard, click the New Color Group icon at the bottom of the Swatches panel. You can automatically convert all process colors to global process colors, as well as include specific swatches for tints of colors (**Figure 6.7**).

Figure 6.7 With a single click, you can easily create a new group of swatches from colors that appear in a selection.

You can edit any single swatch within a group simply by double-clicking it. However, if you want to edit a group (and all the colors within it), you can either double-click the group's folder icon that appears in the Swatches panel or select the group and click the Edit Color Group icon at the bottom of the Swatches panel. It's best to edit color groups when no artwork is selected, or any changes you make will be applied to your selection.

You edit groups on the Edit tab of the Live Color dialog (**Figure 6.8**). Saved color groups appear listed along the right side of the dialog (you can click the disclosure triangles to reveal the individual colors within them). Clicking a color group maps the colors within the group onto the color wheel, and clicking a specific color within the group highlights that color on the wheel. You can make adjustments to your colors on the wheel (refer to "Modifying Color" later in this chapter for detailed information on how to do this), and then you can save your changes or create entire new color

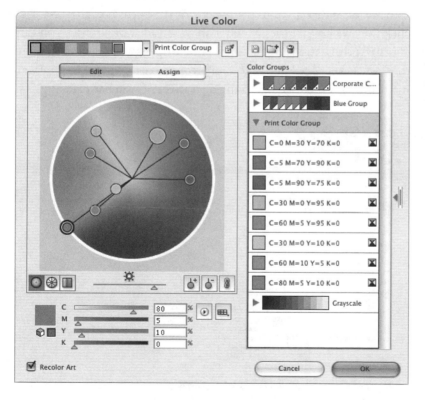

Figure 6.8 You can use the Edit tab of the Live Color dialog to adjust colors within groups. Existing color groups appear on the right side of the dialog.

groups using the icons at the top right of the Live Color dialog (**Figure 6.9**). Click OK to exit the Live Color dialog and return to your document.

Figure 6.9 You can modify, create, and delete groups easily within the Live Color dialog.

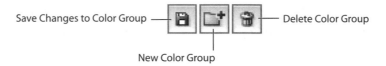

Save Changes to Color Group —   — Delete Color Group

New Color Group

Working with Libraries

Illustrator files can contain all kinds of attributes including colors, gradients, patterns, symbols, brushes, and graphic styles. You can save each of these attributes as libraries so that you can share them between Illustrator documents.

Illustrator makes the process of managing libraries easy by incorporating some features directly into the panels. At the bottom of the Swatches panel, click the Swatch Libraries Menu icon to see a list of libraries you can use (**Figure 6.10**). Choosing a swatch library opens a new panel containing those swatches. Applying any colors from a custom swatch library automatically adds those colors to the document's Swatches panel.

Figure 6.10 You can load swatch libraries right from the Swatches panel. Libraries appear in hierarchical format according to how they're organized within the Adobe Illustrator CS3/Presets/Swatches folder.

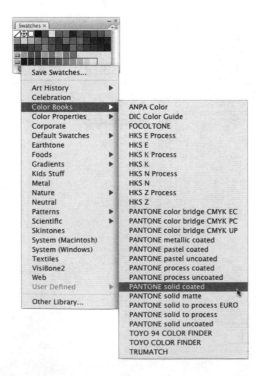

You can create your own custom library files by adding swatches to the Swatches panel and deleting any swatches you don't want (choosing Select All Unused from the Swatches panel flyout menu can help in that process). Then choose Save Swatch Library as AI, and name your library. Once saved, you can access your custom library by clicking the Swatch Libraries Menu icon. If you want to use your swatch library in Adobe Photoshop and Adobe InDesign as well, choose Save Swatch Library as ASE instead. ASE stands for Adobe Swatch Exchange, and you can import those colors into Photoshop or InDesign CS2 and newer (**Figure 6.11**). Adobe Swatch Exchange currently supports only solid-color swatches, not gradients or patterns.

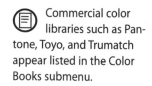 Commercial color libraries such as Pantone, Toyo, and Trumatch appear listed in the Color Books submenu.

Figure 6.11 You can open an Adobe Swatch Exchange file with Illustrator, Photoshop, or InDesign.

If you want a custom library to always appear on your screen each time you launch Illustrator, open the library, and choose Persistent from that library's panel menu (**Figure 6.12**).

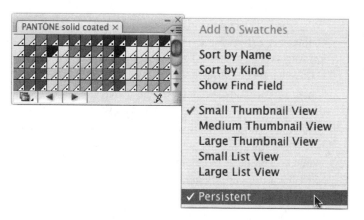

Figure 6.12 Making a custom library persistent will ensure it is always available on your screen.

Finding Your Pantone Number

When you load a Pantone color library, you'll find that the library contains hundreds if not thousands of colors. So, how do you find just the number of the color you need? From the library's panel flyout menu, choose Show Find Field. You can then type your Pantone number in the field to jump directly to your number (**Figure 6.13**).

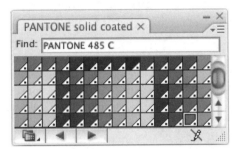

Figure 6.13 Once you choose Show Find Field, you can type a number to quickly find it.

But you may also find that, at times, it seems impossible to type your number. For example, if you try entering **485** for Pantone 485, you'll find that instead Illustrator will take you directly to Pantone 1485. To get Pantone 485, you will have to type a space before the numbers 485. Why? That's a great question. I'm glad you asked.

Teri Pettit, an engineer on the Illustrator team at Adobe, offers the following explanation:

"What the search command does is first look for a swatch starting with the characters you type. For example, if you type *lo*, it will first look for colors starting with *lo*, such as Loden Green. But if it finds none, it will then look for the first swatch name containing *lo* and will match Yellow.

"Characters are concatenated into the search string if they occur within the double-click time. Otherwise, it starts over with a new string.

"Since the Pantone libraries are not sorted in numerical order but semialphabetically, if you are searching for something like 613, it will find the substring match in Pantone 2613 before it will find the one in Pantone 613. By typing ' **613**' (there's a space before the 6), you prevent a match in 2613, and so on."

GETTING INSPIRED WITH COLOR

When you're working on creative projects, sometimes you are told which colors to use by the client directly (in the case of established corporate colors), a creative director, or maybe even a fashion designer in Paris. Other times, you are totally free to dream up any color you'd like to use. Although freedom is nice in this regard, it also offers challenges. How do you choose from so many colors? How do you ensure that the colors you have chosen work well with each other? How can you quickly generate numerous color variations to play with and choose from?

Traditionally, designers could garner such inspiration by perusing magazines or annuals or just by going for a walk and observing the outside world. Illustrator offers its own set of inspirational tools to help you choose the perfect colors for the task at hand through the Color Guide panel and something called *kuler* (pronounced like *cooler*).

Using the Color Guide Panel

Accessible via the Window menu, the Color Guide panel looks rather simple at first glance. However, it's a robust (and fun!) tool to use when you want to generate variations of colors as you work on your design (**Figure 6.14**). As you are about to find out, the Color Guide panel offers color suggestions that fit your exacting needs.

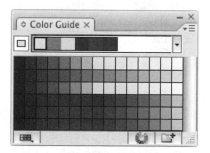

Figure 6.14 The Color Guide panel helps you quickly find harmonious colors.

To use the Color Guide panel, start by choosing a color harmony rule from the pop-up menu at the top of the panel (**Figure 6.15** on the following page). Don't worry if you aren't familiar with any of the harmony rules or

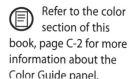

Refer to the color section of this book, page C-2 for more information about the Color Guide panel.

Refer to the color section of this book, page C-4, for more information about color harmonies.

their names. It really doesn't matter. Each one is just a different method for how colors are generated and how they relate to each other (covered in more detail in the color section of this book). There's no such thing as a right or wrong harmony rule—if you aren't happy with the colors you're seeing, just switch to a different rule.

Figure 6.15 You can choose from any of the 23 color harmony rules in the Color Guide panel.

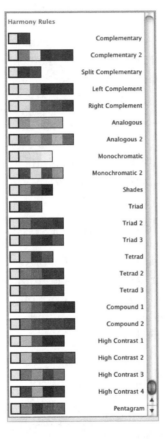

Once you've selected a rule, click any swatch color in the Swatches panel, or mix a color using the Color panel. Alternatively, you can select an object and click the Set Base Color to the Current Color icon in the Color Guide panel. Instantly, the Color Guide panel will generate variations of color for you. If you like any colors you see, you can drag them right to your Swatches panel or even to an object on your artboard. Alternatively, you can select several colors and click the Save Color Group to Swatch Panel icon at the bottom of the Color Guide panel.

By default, the Color Guide panel offers tint/shade variations of your colors. However, you can view warm/cool or vivid/muted variations instead, if you prefer. To do so, choose the desired option from the Color Guide panel flyout menu (**Figure 6.16**). And for specific control over how variations are created, choose Color Guide Options from the Color Guide panel flyout menu. This in turn opens the Variation Options dialog (we know, it should be named the Color Guide Options dialog, right?). The Steps setting determines how many variations of color the Color Guide panel displays in each direction of your color (**Figure 6.17**). For example, if you have the Tints/Shades option selected, a value of 7 steps will generate 7 tints and 7 shades for a total of 14 variations of your color. You can specify as few as 3 steps and as many as 20. In addition, you can adjust the Variation slider to control how much of a difference there is between each color that is generated.

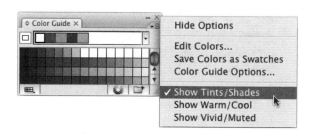

Figure 6.16 The Color Guide panel offers three different methods for generating color variations.

Figure 6.17 You can adjust the number of steps and the amount of difference between generated variations of color in the Variation Options dialog.

Limiting the Color Guide Panel

When expressing your creativity with color in Illustrator, the last thing you probably want to hear is how to impose limits. But on the contrary, carefully limiting the Color Guide panel can reap huge rewards. Let me explain: By default, the Color Guide panel offers suggestions of colors from a huge spectrum of color. But sometimes we're forced to work within specific guidelines or we need to work within a certain range of color. For example, a Web designer may want to see only those color suggestions that are Web-safe colors. A package designer working in a spot color workflow may want the Color Guide panel to offer suggestions from a Pantone library. Or a fashion designer may be limited to using only those colors available for a specific season or year.

The good news is that custom-fitting the Color Guide panel to your exact needs is not only possible but it's also incredibly easy to do. Let's take the example of a Web designer who wants to work within the Web-safe color library. At the bottom-left corner of the Color Guide panel is an icon that allows you to limit the color group to colors that appear within a specific library (**Figure 6.18**). Click the icon, and choose the Web library. You'll notice that the name of the chosen library now appears at the bottom of the Color Guide panel, indicating that the colors being suggested in the panel come from that library (**Figure 6.19**). Now, as you choose colors, the Color Guide panel can offer only those color suggestions that are Web-safe colors.

Figure 6.18 You can limit the Color Guide panel to any custom library—even those you create on your own.

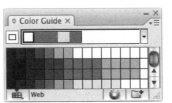

Figure 6.19 A quick look at the Color Guide panel reveals the library of colors to which it is limited.

Use the same method to limit the Color Guide panel to a Pantone swatch library, and the Color Guide panel will be able to list only variations of color that are in the chosen Pantone library (**Figure 6.20**). This can be helpful if you're working on a design that will be printed as a one- or two-color job. To release the limit, click the icon, and choose None from the top of the list.

Figure 6.20 Limiting the Color Guide panel to a Pantone library makes it easier to choose the right spot color for the job.

Tapping Into a Community Around Color with kuler

As we all know, color is subjective. What looks great to one designer may look awful to another. Likewise, some people might be really good at working with color, while others may be severely color-challenged. What would be wonderful for everyone would be some set of tools that designers could use to quickly generate palettes of color that look great while, at the same time, offer some way for designers to share their skills with others. The good news is that Adobe set out to deliver just that by creating a community of users who share a rather cool set of color tools, called *kuler*.

To use kuler, you must have an Internet connection.

Before we dive into kuler, it's important to understand where kuler comes from. Adobe Labs is a group at Adobe that develops experimental technology (*knowhow*, the interactive help panel within Illustrator CS3, is a project of Adobe Labs). Sometimes, Adobe Labs will release beta versions of their ideas so that users can play with them and offer helpful feedback. Adobe Labs also maintains a public Web site that everyone can access (http://labs.adobe.com), and they sometimes post beta versions of Adobe products as well. kuler (yes, always spelled with a lowercase *k*) is a project of Adobe Labs.

Refer to the color section of this book, page C-6, for more information on kuler.

The kuler Web Site

To access the kuler Web site, point your favorite Web browser to http://kuler.adobe.com. Adobe actually refers to kuler as a *Rich Internet Application* (RIA), and you need to have Flash Player 9 or newer in order to use it (the site will redirect you if you need to download a newer version of the Flash

Player). Although you can use parts of kuler without logging in, you'll get the full functionality by entering your Adobe ID. If you don't already have one, an Adobe ID is free and allows you to post to the Adobe User-to-User Forums, access free content from the Adobe Design Center, and purchase items through the online Adobe Store. If you've recently registered any Adobe software, you probably already have an Adobe ID. If not, click Register at the top right of the kuler Web site.

Once logged into kuler, you can choose from seven pages to visit, all of which appear listed on the left side of the Web site:

- **Create.** Creating a color theme in kuler is fun and easy. Start by choosing a rule, which defines the relationship between the colors you will create. Basically, you choose a base color, and the other four colors in the theme are generated automatically by kuler according to the rule you choose (**Figure 6.21**). Kuler offers six rules to choose from (refer to the color section of this book for more information on color rules), or you can choose Custom, which allows you to specify all five colors independently.

Figure 6.21 The Create page on the kuler Web site lets you generate harmonious color themes.

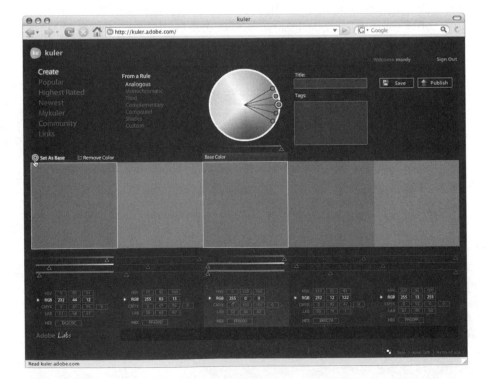

To adjust the colors, click and drag any of the circles around on the color wheel. Dragging in a circular motion adjusts the hue; dragging toward or away from the center of the circle decreases or increases saturation, respectively; and using the slider that appears directly beneath the wheel adjusts brightness. You can also adjust each swatch color by dragging the sliders that appear underneath them. Likewise, you can view color values in HSV, RGB, CMYK, LAB, and HEX. You can even specify values manually or copy and paste them. Double-click any color swatch to set it as the base color. You can delete color swatches to get fewer than five colors in your theme, but kuler currently supports a maximum of five colors per theme.

Name your theme by giving it a title, and then add as many descriptive tags as you can come up with (separating each tag with a comma). Tags make searching through color themes that much more powerful. Once you've created your theme, you're ready to save it. Click Save to save your color theme to your own private Mykuler page (see "Mykuler" in this list). Doing so means that the color theme is available only to you, and no one else will be able to view that theme. Alternatively, click Publish to save your color theme so you can access it from your Mykuler page and so others who are logged into kuler can view it, rate it, comment on it, and use it as well.

- **Popular, Highest Rated, Newest.** The Popular, Highest Rated, and Newest pages are where you can peruse color themes that other designers around the world have created and published with kuler (**Figure 6.22** on the following page). These pages are actually RSS feeds (you can subscribe to them if you'd like), and you can also use the Search field to find specific themes. As you mouse over each theme, the theme expands so you can better see the colors. In fact, to see even larger color swatches, click the large color swatches that appear at the top of the page. Click the swatches again to continue browsing color themes. Star ratings appear just to the right of each theme, and you can click the stars to log your own rating for each theme. Some themes have tags, which you can click to find other similarly tagged color themes. You can also add your own comments to any theme. If you like any particular theme, you can download it as an Adobe Swatch Exchange (ASE) file, or you can edit it directly in kuler.

Figure 6.22 A true community-driven site, kuler allows users to rate color themes and comment on them.

- **Mykuler, Community, Links.** Mykuler is a private page that only you can access. The page lists all the kuler themes you've created and gives you the ability to delete, download, or edit them. The Community page offers interesting profiles on designers who use kuler. The Links page offers a wealth of information about how kuler is used, along with links to articles and Web sites that deal with color and color theory.

The kuler Panel in Illustrator

Although the kuler Web site is nice and all, you still have to leave your design environment and use your Web browser to find your colors. That's why Adobe Labs took the next step and brought kuler directly into Illustrator. Choose Window > Adobe Labs > kuler to open the kuler panel (**Figure 6.23**), which is actually a Flash-based panel running inside Illustrator (cool, no?).

Figure 6.23 Similar to the knowhow panel we mentioned back in Chapter 1, *The Illustrator Environment*, the kuler panel, which looks like any other panel in Illustrator, is actually Flash running inside Illustrator.

Click the pop-up menu at the top of the panel to switch between Higher Rated, Newest, or Popular RSS feeds. You can also choose Edit Custom Feeds to subscribe to your own feeds. Enter any keyword in the Search field to find kuler themes that fit your exact needs. If you find a theme you like, then select it, and click the Add to Swatches icon at the bottom of the panel. Illustrator will automatically add the selected theme to your Swatches panel as a color group. Alternatively, you can click the triangle to the far right of any theme to open it in kuler directly (Illustrator will launch your default Web browser to do so).

The kuler panel is also a two-way street, meaning that if you develop some colors you like while using Illustrator, create a group in your Swatches panel (of five colors or less), and then click the Upload button in the kuler panel, Illustrator will take you to the kuler Web site, where you can then publish your theme.

The kuler Widget and kuler Desktop

After learning about kuler, it's easy to see how much fun it can be to use, and more important, it's easy to see how such an online community can be a valuable resource to every designer. In an effort to make kuler even more accessible (and to help show off some cool technology), Adobe Labs has also created a kuler widget (**Figure 6.24** on the following page) that can be used with the Dashboard feature of Mac OS X, as well as a cross-platform stand-alone kuler Desktop module (**Figure 6.25** on the following page) running on Adobe Integrated Runtime (AIR), formerly known as code name Apollo.

Figure 6.24 The kuler widget runs within Dashboard on Mac OS X. Clicking the lowercase *i* in the upper-right corner flips the widget over, allowing you to search by tag.

Figure 6.25 The kuler Desktop module is cross-platform and requires that you first install Adobe Integrated Runtime (formerly known as Apollo), also available from the Adobe Labs Web site.

You can download both of these freely from the Adobe Labs Web site; they offer the ability to search, view RSS feeds, and copy color values to your Adobe design applications.

MODIFYING COLOR

When you're faced with making changes to the color in your existing artwork, you may find that it is extremely time-consuming to do so. But the new Live Color feature, introduced in Illustrator CS3, makes it easy to modify the colors in your document in a plethora of ways.

It's important to realize that there really isn't a tool, function, or button in Illustrator that's called Live Color (it's more of a marketing term). Just about all the color editing you do will involve the Edit Colors button or the Recolor Artwork button. However, both of these buttons open a dialog named Live Color. The Live Color dialog is split into two specific tabs: You use the Edit tab to edit colors, and you use the Assign tab to recolor your artwork. We'll cover both tabs in detail, but before we get started, it helps to think of Live Color as an engine in Illustrator—a powerful engine that will allow you to take control over the modification of colors throughout your document.

Editing Color with Live Color

The Edit tab in the Live Color dialog is most useful for modifying colors within groups and for tweaking existing colors in a selection.

Refer to the color section of this book, page C-8, for more information on the Live Color dialog.

- To modify colors within an existing group, deselect any artwork on the artboard, highlight a color group by clicking the folder icon in the Swatches panel, and choose Edit Color Group from the bottom of the Swatches panel (**Figure 6.26**), or just double-click the folder icon of the group. Alternatively, if you want to work with colors from the Color Guide panel (instead of a group from the Swatches panel), click the Edit Colors icon at the bottom of the Color Guide panel. The Live Color dialog opens to the Edit tab, and you're ready to begin editing.

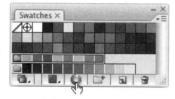

Figure 6.26 With a color group highlighted, you can choose Edit Color Group to edit the colors in the Live Color dialog.

- To tweak existing colors in a selection, select your artwork, and click the Edit or Apply Colors icon at the bottom of the Color Guide panel. The Live Color dialog opens to the Edit tab, but your artwork will be recolored using colors from the Color Guide panel. Click Get Colors from Selected Art to load the colors from your selected artwork into the Live Color dialog, and you're ready to begin tweaking (**Figure 6.27**).

Figure 6.27 The Get Colors from Selected Art button loads all colors from the selected artwork into the Live Color dialog.

At the center of the Edit tab in the Live Color dialog is a color wheel. Each color in your group, or in your selected artwork, appears mapped to the

At any time when using the Live Color dialog, you can reload the original colors from your selected artwork by clicking Get Colors from Selected Art.

color wheel as a circle (**Figure 6.28**). One of the circles will be slightly larger and represents the base color.

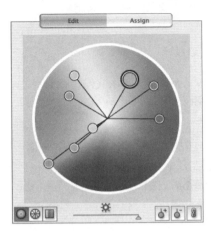

Figure 6.28 The color wheel is the center of the Live Color feature. Colors appear mapped as circles on the color wheel.

The relationships between all the mapped colors are indicated by lines, which all connect to each other through the center of the color wheel. Solid connector lines indicate that the colors are locked to each other, meaning that adjusting one color will adjust all others (while maintaining their relationship). Dashed connector lines indicate that the colors are independent, meaning they can be moved individually without affecting the others (**Figure 6.29**). You can toggle between locked and unlocked colors by clicking the Link/Unlink Harmony Colors icon. To add colors to your existing color group, click the color wheel anywhere with the Add Color tool. To remove a color, click its circle with the Remove Color tool.

Figure 6.29 Dashed connector lines indicate colors that can be adjusted independently.

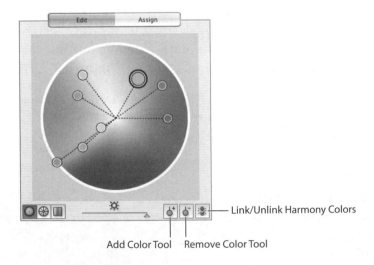

The color wheel is based on the HSB color model, which is more easily understood as a wheel, compared to other models such as CMYK or RGB (**Figure 6.30**). In the HSB color model, the H value represents *hue,* or the actual color itself; the S value represents *saturation,* or the amount of color; and the B value represents *brightness,* or the lightness/darkness of the color (also referred to as the *value* of the color). You can adjust the mapped circles on the color wheel in Live Color for various results:

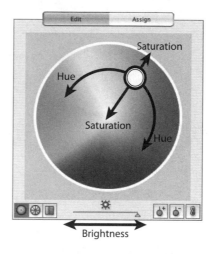

Figure 6.30 The HSB color model is displayed as 360 degrees of color.

- Moving a circle in a clockwise or counterclockwise direction, around the center of the color wheel, adjusts the hue of that color.

- Moving a circle toward or away from the center of the color wheel adjusts the saturation of that color.

- Dragging the slider that appears directly underneath the color wheel adjusts the brightness of the entire wheel.

- Control-click (right-click) a color circle to edit the saturation and brightness values of that color without changing its hue.

- Double-click a color circle to open the Color Picker.

By default, Live Color displays a smooth color wheel, but you may prefer a segmented color wheel, showing clear distinctions of hue and saturation. Alternatively, you can view your selected colors as vertical color bars

Clicking the little sun icon that appears above the brightness slider swaps the brightness and saturation settings, allowing you to use the slider to control saturation and the color circles to adjust brightness.

(**Figure 6.31**). These options are accessible via the three icons that appear to the lower left of the color wheel.

Figure 6.31 The Edit tab shown with a segmented color wheel (left) and vertical color bars (right).

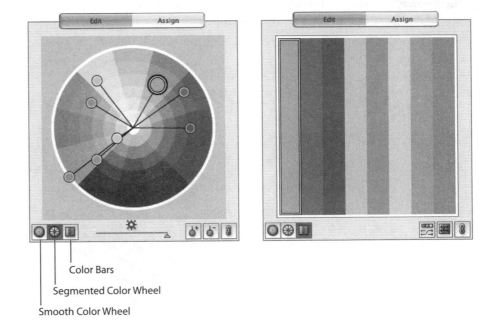

Color Bars

Segmented Color Wheel

Smooth Color Wheel

Although you can certainly have lots of fun dragging color circles all over the color wheel, it doesn't make for the precise kinds of adjustments you may be used to doing in Illustrator. To achieve a higher level of precision, you'll want to edit colors numerically. Click a color circle to select it, and then use the sliders and values that appear beneath the color wheel. These sliders are identical to those in the Color panel. You can switch between the RGB, HSB, CMYK, Web-safe RGB, Tint (for global process and spot colors), and Lab sliders. In addition, you can also choose a setting called Global Adjust, which allows you to edit all colors using the Saturation, Brightness, Temperature, and Luminosity sliders (**Figure 6.32**).

Figure 6.32 The Global Adjust sliders allow you to modify colors similarly to how you might adjust colors in Photoshop.

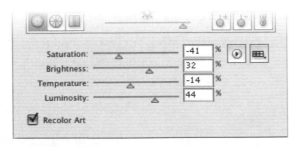

As with the Color Guide panel, you can also limit the Live Color dialog to a specific library of colors. This extremely powerful feature makes it possible to remap entire artwork or entire groups of color to a specific library of color…instantly. When you've completed editing your colors to your liking, click OK to return to your artboard.

Understanding the Recolor Art Check Box

People often mistake the Recolor Art check box that appears at the lower-left corner of the Live Color dialog as a preview option. But that isn't the case at all. The Recolor Art check box does exactly what its name represents—it recolors any artwork you have selected (it's grayed out if you launch the Live Color dialog without any art selected). So, why is this setting useful? Because you can turn it off. For example, you may want to start tweaking the color of an illustration only to realize that you want to leave the color as it was before you started editing it. But at the same time, you like the color variations you created and want to save those colors as a new color group. By unchecking the Recolor Art box, the selected artwork remains untouched on your artboard, but you can still access and work with those colors in the Live Color dialog.

Recoloring Artwork with Live Color

The Assign tab in the Live Color dialog is most useful for recoloring or remapping colors in your selected artwork, so you'll find the feature is available only when you have first made a selection in your document. However, depending on which location you launch the Live Color feature from, Illustrator will assume you're trying to perform different tasks and will act accordingly:

- **Recoloring artwork with the selected color group.** If you select some artwork, highlight a color group in the Swatches panel, and then click the Edit or Apply Color Group icon at the bottom of the Swatches panel, you're indicating you want to recolor your selected artwork with the selected color group. The Live Color dialog will launch to the Edit tab with your colors already remapped. You can click the Assign tab to continue recoloring your artwork.

Refer to the color section of this book, page C-10, for more information about the Assign tab.

- **Recoloring artwork with the colors from the Color Guide panel.**
  If you select some artwork and click the Edit or Apply Colors icon at the
  bottom of the Color Guide panel, you're indicating you want to recolor
  your selected artwork with the colors present in the Color Guide panel.
  The Live Color dialog will launch to the Edit tab with your colors
  already remapped. You can click the Assign tab to continue recoloring
  your artwork.

- **Picking your own color.** If you select some artwork and click the
  Recolor Artwork icon in the Control panel or choose Edit > Edit Colors > Recolor Artwork, you're indicating you want to pick the colors
  with which you want to recolor your artwork. The Live Color dialog
  will launch to the Assign tab with the current appearance of the colors
  preserved (**Figure 6.33**). You can then begin to recolor your artwork.

Figure 6.33 The Assign tab of the Live Color dialog seems a bit complex at first glance, but it will quickly become your friend. The main section in the middle lists all the colors from the selected artwork on the left (wide bars) and all the colors they are being remapped to on the right (narrow bars).

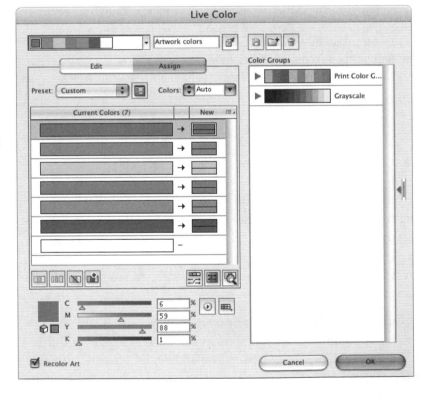

The quickest way to recolor your artwork is to select any of the color groups listed on the far right side of the Live Color dialog. This is why it makes sense to define color groups in the Swatches panel before you open the Live Color dialog, if your workflow allows it.

The main part of the Assign tab in the Live Color dialog is the list of current (or old) and new colors. Colors that exist within your selected artwork appear as wide bars along the left side, while the colors you are using to recolor your artwork appear in shorter bars along the right side. Each bar sits in a color row, and if you follow the direction of the arrow, you're indicating that the color appearing in the wide bar becomes the color that appears in the short bar. In fact, the arrow controls the recoloring behavior, and clicking the arrow in a color row toggles the recoloring on and off for that color row (**Figure 6.34**). For example, you'll notice that, by default, Live Color preserves black and white colors in your artwork (meaning they aren't recolored), so those colors will appear listed in color rows with the arrows turned off.

Creating color groups in advance also allows you to recolor artwork with a combination of spot and process colors quickly.

Current Color   Arrow   New Color

Color Row

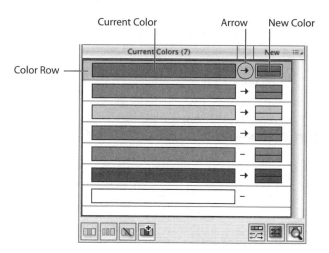

Figure 6.34 Color rows help you easily recolor your artwork.

At the top of the Assign tab is a pop-up menu that contains recoloring presets, a field where you can specify the number of colors you want to end up with, and an icon between the two to open the Recolor Options dialog (see the "Recolor Options" sidebar for information on the settings contained within that dialog).

Recolor Options

Clicking the Color Reduction Options icon on the Assign tab of the Live Color dialog opens the Recolor Options dialog (**Figure 6.35**). The presets that appear in the pop-up menu at the top of the dialog offer quick shortcuts to reducing artwork to one-, two-, or three-color jobs and to limiting the colors to a specific library of color. The Color Harmony preset sets the Colors value to Auto and results in the number of current colors listed in the Assign tab of the Live Color dialog to match the number of active colors in the chosen color harmony rule. This allows you to easily experiment with different color harmonies, because each time you choose one, the number of current colors will automatically adjust to match the harmony.

- **Colors.** You can manually set the number of colors to which you want to reduce your artwork.

- **Limit to Library.** You can limit new colors to a specific color library.

- **Sort.** You can choose to sort colors in the Assign tab using any of four different settings, or you can set it to none (where you can manually sort the colors yourself).

- **Colorize Method.** When reducing many colors to a single color, you must instruct Live Color how to handle different shades of colors. The differences between the five available options (Exact, Preserve Tints, Scale Tints, Tints and Shades, and Hue Shift) are illustrated in detail in the color section of this book. You can also choose to combine tints.

- **Preserve.** You can check these options to preserve (leave untouched) artwork that is colored white, black, and/or gray.

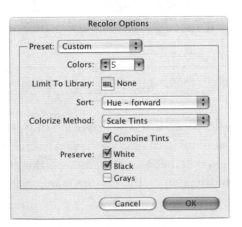

Figure 6.35 The Recolor Options dialog gives you control over how your artwork is recolored.

To identify where a specific color appears in your artwork, highlight a color row, and then click the magnifying glass icon (**Figure 6.36**) at the lower right of the Assign tab in the Live Color dialog. This will reduce the opacity of all colors except for the selected color, making it easy to identify where the color is used.

Figure 6.36 Use the magnifying glass to quickly identify where colors appear in your artwork.

You can manually reduce colors by dragging the wide color bars from one row to another. Combining two or more colors in a single wide color bar instructs Live Color to reduce those colors to one new color (**Figure 6.37**). You can double-click a small color bar to access the Color Picker. You can also choose a colorize method by clicking the far right edge of a small color bar (**Figure 6.38**). Unchecking the Apply To All box will allow you to specify different colorize methods for each new color.

Refer to the color section of this book, page C-1, for more information on colorization methods.

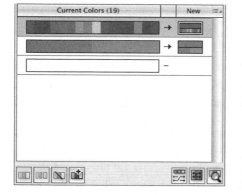

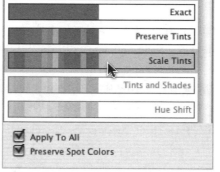

Refer to the color section of this book, page C-12, for more information on reducing and assigning colors.

Figure 6.37 You can drag as many colors as you like to a color row to convert all those colors to one new color.

Figure 6.38 Specifying an appropriate colorize method can help ensure satisfactory results when performing color reductions.

Icons that appear beneath the color bars allow you to randomly change color order and the saturation and brightness settings, as well as manage color rows. When you've recolored your artwork, click OK to apply the settings and return to the artboard.

Converting Art to Grayscale

Refer to the color section of this book, page C-14, for more information on color to grayscale conversions.

You may be tasked with converting color artwork to shades of gray. Traditionally, such a task in Illustrator has always been difficult because colors can be present in symbols, patterns, gradients, gradient meshes, and so on. Editing all the colors in these separate places can take quite some time. With the new Live Color feature in Illustrator CS3, converting artwork to grayscale is really easy—and really powerful.

It's important to realize that changing artwork from color into shades of gray isn't necessarily automatic. In other words, you can take different roads to perform such a conversion, and depending on the artwork at hand, you may choose a particular method in order to achieve a desirable result. For example, if you've used Photoshop to convert color images into grayscale, you know you can simply change your color mode from RGB or CMYK to Grayscale but that the result may not look that great. Seasoned users know they can use functions such as Photoshop's Channel Mixer or the new Black and White function that was added in CS3 to garner more pleasing grayscale conversions. Advanced users could probably rattle off several other methods as well.

In Illustrator CS3, we've found four ways to convert artwork from color into grayscale. These methods all take advantage of the Live Color engine, so they work on any artwork within your Illustrator document with the exception of linked or embedded raster images (see the sidebar "Converting Raster Content to Grayscale" for more information on that).

- **Use the Convert to Grayscale command.** Select your color artwork, and choose Edit > Edit Colors > Convert to Grayscale (**Figure 6.39**). Using this method is obviously the fastest method, but the results aren't always pretty. Different colors may convert to similar shades of gray, and often you'll find that this setting gives low-contrast results.

- **Desaturate the art.** Select your artwork, and click the Recolor Artwork button in the Control panel. At the bottom of the dialog, change the mode of the color adjustment sliders to Global Adjust. Drag the Saturation slider all the way to far left (the setting should read -100). This method requires an extra click or two, but by desaturating the color in this way, your result will have more contrast.

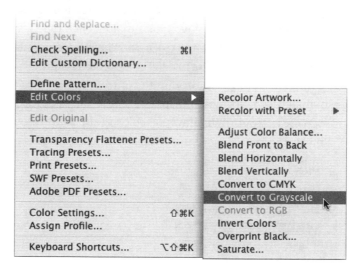

Figure 6.39 The newly
rewired Convert to Grayscale
function now works on all
objects with the exception
of placed images.

- **Use Adjust Color Balance.** Select your artwork, and choose Edit >
  Edit Colors > Adjust Color Balance. In the Adjust Colors dialog,
  choose Grayscale from the Color Mode pop-up menu, and check the
  Convert box. Adjust the Black slider until you get the desired result.
  This method is rather straightforward and gives you the freedom to
  adjust the density of the black values (**Figure 6.40**).

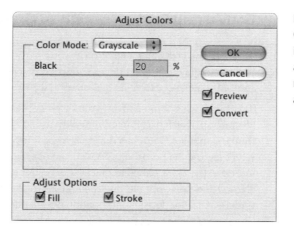

Figure 6.40 The Adjust
Color Balance function
is great for making color
adjustments, as well as
making black-and-white
adjustments.

- **Recolor the art using a Grayscale color group.** When you create
  a new print document, you'll notice that the Swatches panel already
  contains a color group labeled Grayscale, which contains 10 shades of

gray. Select your artwork, and click the Recolor Artwork button in the Control panel. In the Live Color dialog, click the Grayscale color group. This forces Illustrator to remap your existing colors to those colors of the selected group (**Figure 6.41**). Use the Assign tab in the Live Color dialog to move colors around to control exactly what shade of gray to which each color will remap. For an even greater level of control, you can create your own Grayscale color group with values you specify. This method requires more interaction than the previous ones but yields the most control over the conversion.

Figure 6.41 By recoloring your artwork with a gray-scale color group, you have complete control over the color conversion.

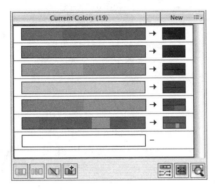

Converting Raster Content to Grayscale

Although the Live Color feature gives you plenty of options for converting color artwork to grayscale, what do you do when you also need to convert rasterized content—such as placed images—to grayscale?

If possible, you should convert your raster content to grayscale using Photoshop, which excels in editing bitmapped artwork. Don't fool yourself into thinking that Illustrator can do it all. For best results, use the new Black and White feature in Photoshop CS3. You can use Illustrator's Edit Original feature (found in the Links panel) to quickly open your image in Photoshop, make the change and save your file, and then return to Illustrator where the image will update itself. For detailed information on the Edit Original workflow, refer to Chapter 9, *Mixing It Up: Working with Vectors and Pixels*.

If you absolutely must convert pixels from color to grayscale directly in Illustrator, select the image, and choose Object > Rasterize. From the Color Model pop-up menu, choose Grayscale. Make sure you specify an appropriate resolution, and click OK. As an alternative, you can choose Effect > Rasterize to apply the conversion in a reversible way.

Colorization Methods

When simply recoloring art, Illustrator replaces one color with another. When reducing colors, however, you're often asking Illustrator to represent many different colors using a single color. The colorization method you choose determines how Illustrator will use a single color to represent all of the colors in a selected row. In these examples, a color illustration of a flower is reduced to one color (PANTONE Reflex Blue). Note the variety of results achieved when different colorization methods are chosen. You can find the Flower.ai file in the Adobe Illustrator CS3/ Cool Extras/Sample Files/Sample Art folder.

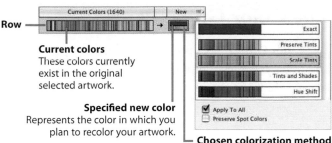

Row

Current colors
These colors currently exist in the original selected artwork.

Specified new color
Represents the color in which you plan to recolor your artwork.

Chosen colorization method
The bottom half of the icon displays a preview of the specified colorization method.

Recolor Options dialog
The Colorization Method options are also available in the Colorize Method popup menu in the Recolor Options dialog.

Original art

Exact
Exactly replaces each current color with the specified new color.

Preserve Tints
Useful for spot or global colors, this option applies the current color's tint to the new color, and is best used when all the current colors in the row are tints of the same or similar global color.

Scale Tints (default option)
Replaces the darkest current color in the row with the specified new color. Other current colors in the row are replaced with a proportionally lighter tint.

Tints and Shades
Replaces the current color with the average lightness and darkness of the specified new color. Lighter than average colors become proportionally lighter. Black is added to darker than average colors.

Hue Shift
Sets the most typical color in the Current Colors row as a key color and exactly replaces the key color with the new color. Other colors are replaced with varying amounts of brightness, saturation, and hue.

The Color Guide Panel

The Color Guide panel provides inspiration by generating variations of colors and offering color suggestions from a specific library of colors.

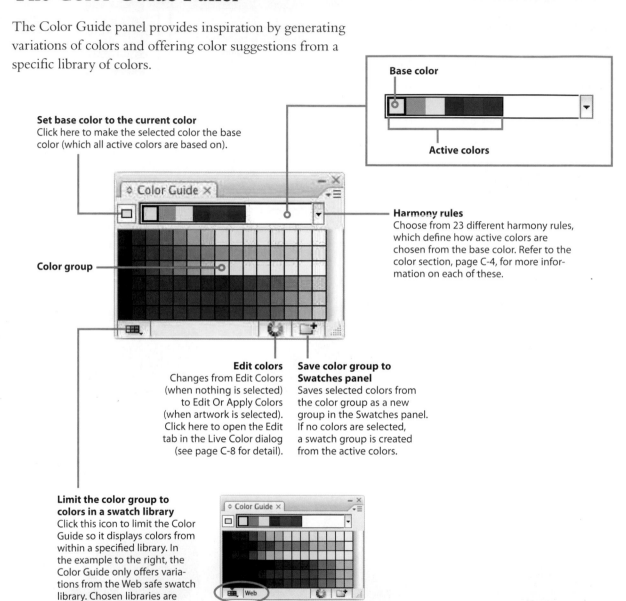

Base color

Active colors

Set base color to the current color
Click here to make the selected color the base color (which all active colors are based on).

Color group

Harmony rules
Choose from 23 different harmony rules, which define how active colors are chosen from the base color. Refer to the color section, page C-4, for more information on each of these.

Edit colors
Changes from Edit Colors (when nothing is selected) to Edit Or Apply Colors (when artwork is selected). Click here to open the Edit tab in the Live Color dialog (see page C-8 for detail).

Save color group to Swatches panel
Saves selected colors from the color group as a new group in the Swatches panel. If no colors are selected, a swatch group is created from the active colors.

Limit the color group to colors in a swatch library
Click this icon to limit the Color Guide so it displays colors from within a specified library. In the example to the right, the Color Guide only offers variations from the Web safe swatch library. Chosen libraries are displayed at the bottom of the Color Guide panel.

The color group has been limited to the Web swatch library.

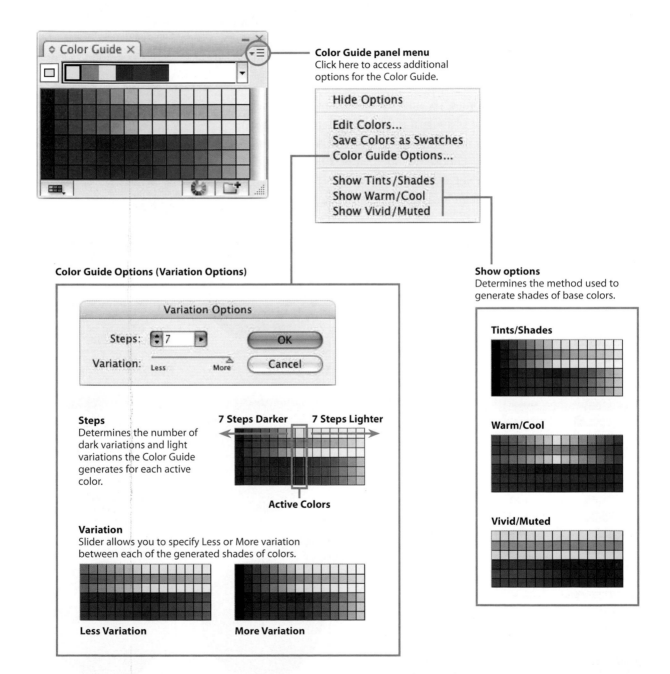

Color Guide panel menu
Click here to access additional options for the Color Guide.

Hide Options

Edit Colors...
Save Colors as Swatches
Color Guide Options...

Show Tints/Shades
Show Warm/Cool
Show Vivid/Muted

Color Guide Options (Variation Options)

Variation Options

Steps: 7   OK

Variation: Less   More   Cancel

Steps
Determines the number of dark variations and light variations the Color Guide generates for each active color.

7 Steps Darker   7 Steps Lighter

Active Colors

Variation
Slider allows you to specify Less or More variation between each of the generated shades of colors.

Less Variation   **More Variation**

Show options
Determines the method used to generate shades of base colors.

Tints/Shades

Warm/Cool

Vivid/Muted

Color Harmonies

A color harmony (also referred to as a color rule) is a set relationship between colors. For example, the Complementary color harmony defines two colors that appear exactly opposite each other on the color wheel. Illustrator features 23 different color harmonies (kuler features 6 of them) that you can choose from, each containing between 2 and 6 colors.

When choosing color harmonies, try not to focus too much on their names. Instead, use this page as a visual reference to better understand what each one represents on the color wheel. There's no such thing as a "good" or a "bad" harmony—choose the one that best fits the needs for a particular job or task. Better yet, experiment with a few until you find what you're looking for.

Color harmonies can be chosen from the Color Guide panel, the Live Color dialog, and from kuler's Create page.

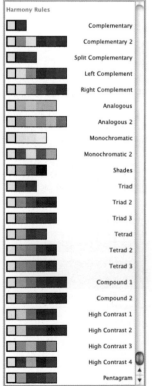

Choosing a harmony rule
Choose color harmony rules from the popup menu (left) that appears in the Color Guide panel, the Live Color dialog, or the Create page in kuler. Each harmony rule defines a specific color relationship on the color wheel (right).

Complementary*

Analogous*

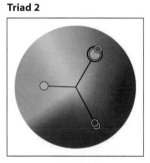

Analogous 2

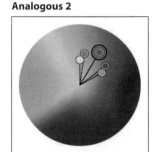

Triad 2

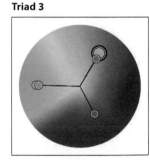

Triad 3

Compound 2

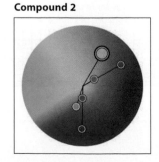

High Contrast 1

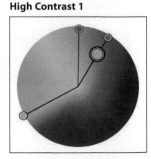

Complementary 2

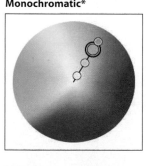

Split Complementary

Left Complement

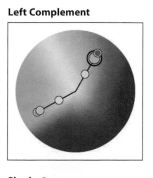

Right Complement

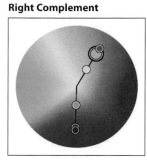

Monochromatic*

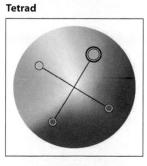

Monochromatic 2

Shades*

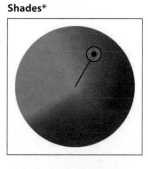

Triad*

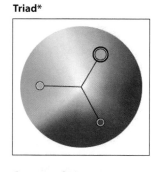

Tetrad

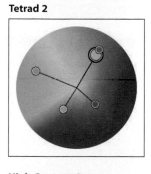

Tetrad 2

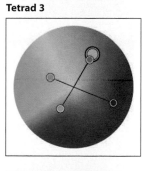

Tetrad 3

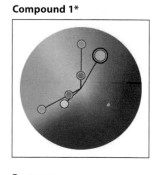

Compound 1*

High Contrast 2

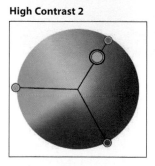

High Contrast 3

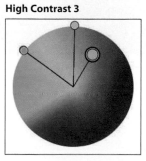

High Contrast 4

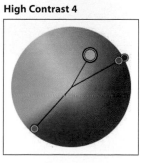

Pentagram

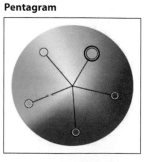

*Available in kuler

kuler

Adobe took a part of Illustrator's Live Color technology and made it available online, via kuler, the freely available online community built around color (http://kuler.adobe.com). You can also access colors from kuler using the kuler panel from within Illustrator, from the Mac OS X kuler Widget, and from the cross-platform kuler desktop which runs on Adobe AIR (Adobe's Integrated Runtime framework).

Step 1. Choose a color harmony rule
Choose from six different harmony rules, or create your own. Refer to the color insert, page C-4, for details on these rules.

Step 2. Spin the color wheel
Drag the color circles that appear on the color wheel to explore different color variations based on the base color. To change a base color, double-click one of the swatches below the wheel.

Step 3. Give your color theme a name
Add a title and assign as many tags as you can. The more tags you add, the easier it will be to find.

Step 4. Save or publish your color theme
Choose Save to store your theme on your private Mykuler page. Choose Publish to make your theme available to all other users in the kuler community.

Brightness
Adjust the brightness of the color wheel using this slider.

Base color
Colors that are generated by kuler are based on the color harmony rule that you choose and on the base color.

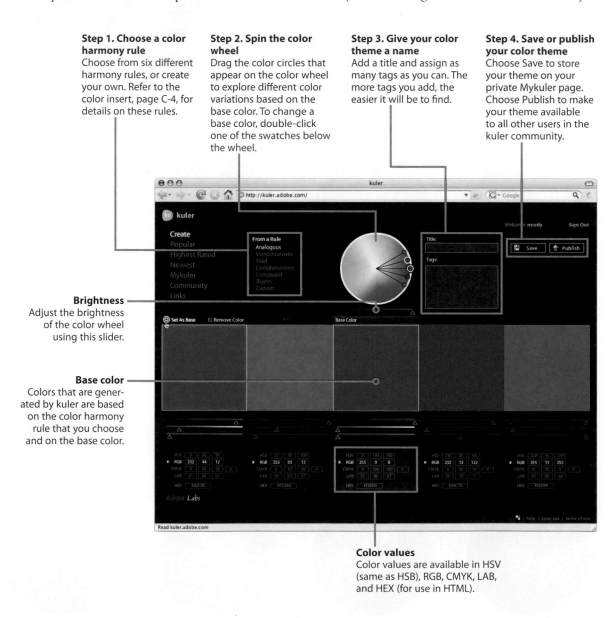

Color values
Color values are available in HSV (same as HSB), RGB, CMYK, LAB, and HEX (for use in HTML).

Download a color theme
Click here to download a color theme as an ASE (Adobe Swatch Exchange) file, which you can load into Illustrator, Photoshop, or InDesign.

Edit a color theme
Click here to load a theme into the Create page, where you can tweak it.

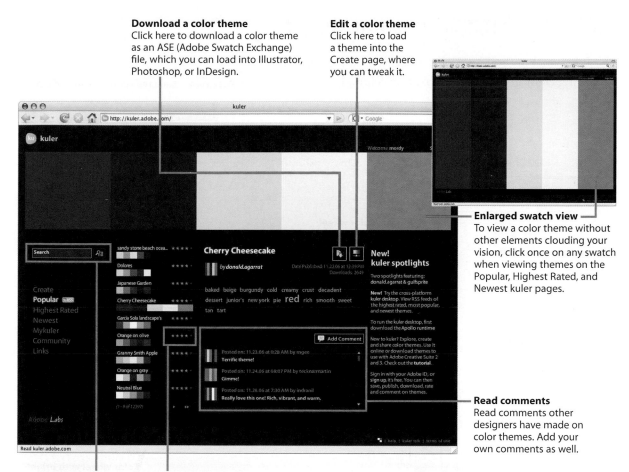

Enlarged swatch view
To view a color theme without other elements clouding your vision, click once on any swatch when viewing themes on the Popular, Highest Rated, and Newest kuler pages.

Read comments
Read comments other designers have made on color themes. Add your own comments as well.

Search themes
You can search for tags, names of themes, or even by designer names.

Rate color themes
As you peruse color themes created by other designers, you can rate them on a scale of 1 to 5.

kuler Widget
For Mac OS X users, the kuler Widget makes it possible to access color themes from Dashboard.

kuler Desktop
Running on Adobe AIR (Adobe Integrated Runtime), kuler Desktop is cross-platform.

Live Color Dialog: The Edit Panel

The Edit panel of the Live Color dialog is used most often for editing color groups and for making color adjustments.

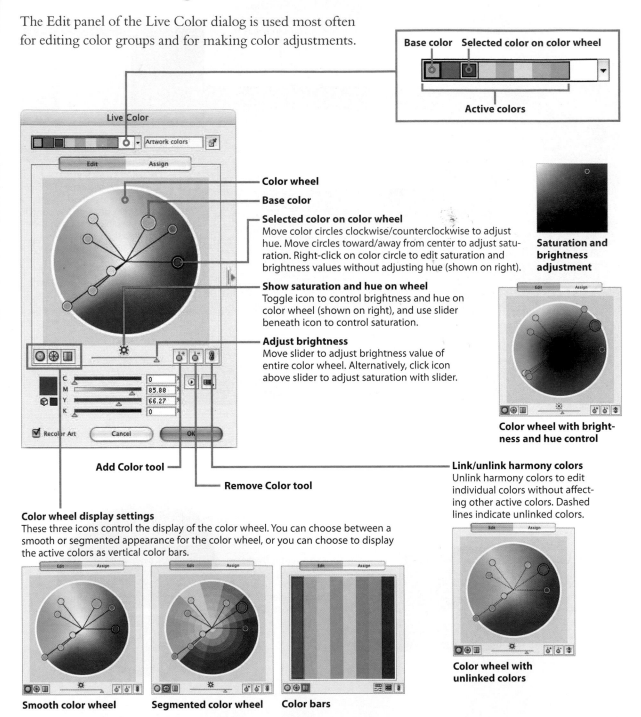

Base color   **Selected color on color wheel**

Active colors

Color wheel

Base color

Selected color on color wheel
Move color circles clockwise/counterclockwise to adjust hue. Move circles toward/away from center to adjust saturation. Right-click on color circle to edit saturation and brightness values without adjusting hue (shown on right).

Saturation and brightness adjustment

Show saturation and hue on wheel
Toggle icon to control brightness and hue on color wheel (shown on right), and use slider beneath icon to control saturation.

Adjust brightness
Move slider to adjust brightness value of entire color wheel. Alternatively, click icon above slider to adjust saturation with slider.

Color wheel with brightness and hue control

Add Color tool

Remove Color tool

Link/unlink harmony colors
Unlink harmony colors to edit individual colors without affecting other active colors. Dashed lines indicate unlinked colors.

Color wheel display settings
These three icons control the display of the color wheel. You can choose between a smooth or segmented appearance for the color wheel, or you can choose to display the active colors as vertical color bars.

Color wheel with unlinked colors

Smooth color wheel   **Segmented color wheel**   **Color bars**

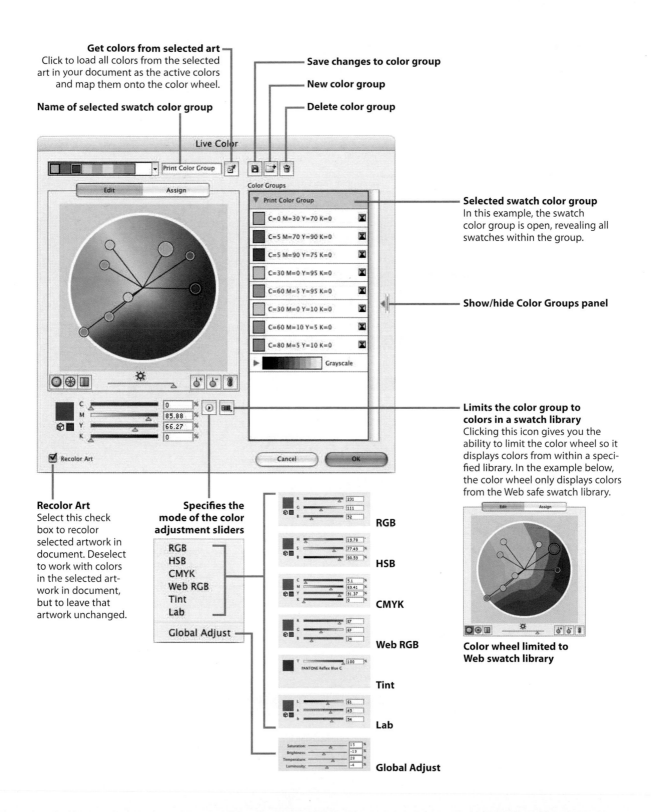

Get colors from selected art — Click to load all colors from the selected art in your document as the active colors and map them onto the color wheel.

Name of selected swatch color group

Save changes to color group

New color group

Delete color group

Live Color

Print Color Group

Edit   Assign

Color Groups

▼ Print Color Group

C=0 M=30 Y=70 K=0

C=5 M=70 Y=90 K=0

C=5 M=90 Y=75 K=0

C=30 M=0 Y=95 K=0

C=60 M=5 Y=95 K=0

C=30 M=0 Y=10 K=0

C=60 M=10 Y=5 K=0

C=80 M=5 Y=10 K=0

► Grayscale

C   0   %
M   85.88   %
Y   66.27   %
K   0   %

☑ Recolor Art

Cancel   OK

Selected swatch color group
In this example, the swatch color group is open, revealing all swatches within the group.

Show/hide Color Groups panel

Limits the color group to colors in a swatch library
Clicking this icon gives you the ability to limit the color wheel so it displays colors from within a specified library. In the example below, the color wheel only displays colors from the Web safe swatch library.

Recolor Art
Select this check box to recolor selected artwork in document. Deselect to work with colors in the selected artwork in document, but to leave that artwork unchanged.

Specifies the mode of the color adjustment sliders

RGB
HSB
CMYK
Web RGB
Tint
Lab

Global Adjust

R   231
G   111
B   52

RGB

H   19.78
S   77.49
B   90.59

HSB

C   5.1
M   69.41
Y   91.37
K   0

CMYK

R   E7
G   6F
B   34

Web RGB

T   100
PANTONE Reflex Blue C

Tint

L   61
a   43
b   54

Lab

Saturation: 15   %
Brightness: -19   %
Temperature: 28   %
Luminosity: -4   %

Global Adjust

Edit   Assign

Color wheel limited to Web swatch library

Live Color Dialog: The Assign Panel

The Assign panel of the Live Color dialog is used most often to recolor artwork.

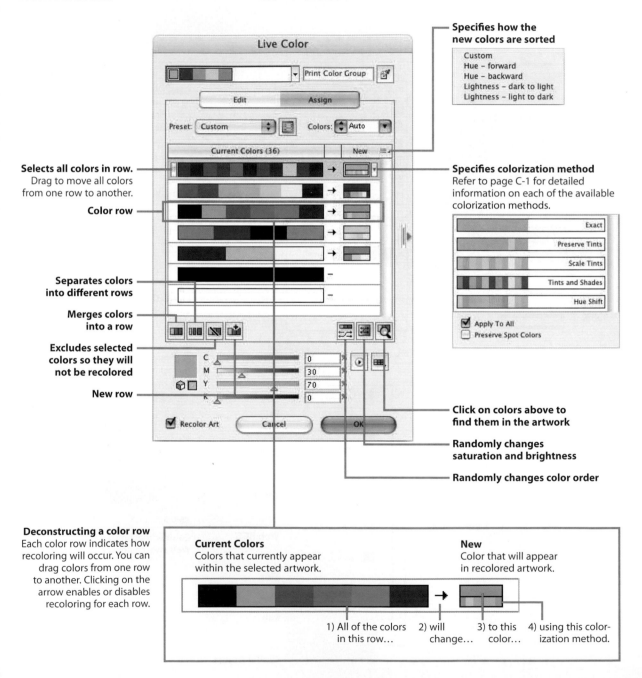

Specifies how the new colors are sorted

Custom
Hue – forward
Hue – backward
Lightness – dark to light
Lightness – light to dark

Selects all colors in row.
Drag to move all colors from one row to another.

Color row

Separates colors into different rows

Merges colors into a row

Excludes selected colors so they will not be recolored

New row

Specifies colorization method
Refer to page C-1 for detailed information on each of the available colorization methods.

Exact
Preserve Tints
Scale Tints
Tints and Shades
Hue Shift

Apply To All
Preserve Spot Colors

Click on colors above to find them in the artwork

Randomly changes saturation and brightness

Randomly changes color order

Deconstructing a color row
Each color row indicates how recoloring will occur. You can drag colors from one row to another. Clicking on the arrow enables or disables recoloring for each row.

Current Colors
Colors that currently appear within the selected artwork.

New
Color that will appear in recolored artwork.

1) All of the colors in this row…   2) will change…   3) to this color…   4) using this color-ization method.

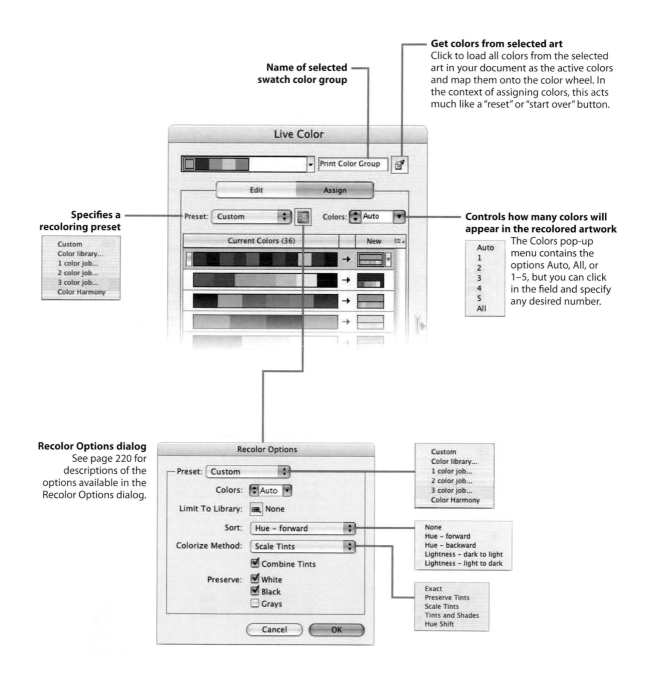

Get colors from selected art
Click to load all colors from the selected art in your document as the active colors and map them onto the color wheel. In the context of assigning colors, this acts much like a "reset" or "start over" button.

Name of selected swatch color group

Live Color

Print Color Group

Edit   Assign

Specifies a recoloring preset

Preset: Custom

Custom
Color library...
1 color job...
2 color job...
3 color job...
Color Harmony

Colors: Auto

Current Colors (36)   New

Controls how many colors will appear in the recolored artwork
The Colors pop-up menu contains the options Auto, All, or 1–5, but you can click in the field and specify any desired number.

Auto
1
2
3
4
5
All

Recolor Options dialog
See page 220 for descriptions of the options available in the Recolor Options dialog.

Recolor Options

Preset: Custom

Colors: Auto

Limit To Library: None

Sort: Hue – forward

Colorize Method: Scale Tints

☑ Combine Tints

Preserve: ☑ White
☑ Black
☐ Grays

Cancel   OK

Custom
Color library...
1 color job...
2 color job...
3 color job...
Color Harmony

None
Hue – forward
Hue – backward
Lightness – dark to light
Lightness – light to dark

Exact
Preserve Tints
Scale Tints
Tints and Shades
Hue Shift

Reducing Colors and Assigning New Colors

When you have full color artwork you want to recolor using just two colors, you can achieve better results by reducing the artwork to several colors initially and then manually reducing to two. In this example, we'll begin with full color artwork containing well over 1,000 colors and reduce it to just two spot colors.

---

1. Add swatches to document and create swatch groups
Creating a color group now that contains the final colors will make it much easier to recolor the artwork in Live Color later. Create a group called "2 Color Flower." Open the PANTONE Solid Coated library and drag PANTONE 440C (for the stem and leaves) and PANTONE Violet C (for the petals) into the group. In the illustration shown here, the Swatches panel is shown with Small List View.

2. Select artwork and open the Live Color dialog
Select the art in the file and choose Edit > Edit Colors > Recolor Artwork. This opens the Live Color dialog with the Assign tab highlighted. All the colors in the selection are loaded into the Current Colors list (there are 1640 colors in this example). Illustrator automatically remaps each color to itself, which you can see listed in the New list of colors.

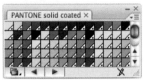

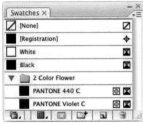

---

3. Reduce the artwork to two colors
To reduce the file to two spot colors, you must first exclude any black in the file. Click the Color Reduction Options icon to open the Recolor Options dialog. Deselect the Preserve Black and White options, set the number of colors to 2, and click OK to accept the settings.

4. Examine the reduced colors
Upon inspection of the color reduction, you'll find the results are not what you expected. All of the greens and the purples have been mapped to the same color row because Illustrator found some neutral shades of color in the artwork and kept those separate, while lumping all of the colors together. If you were to recolor the artwork with your group of two spot colors, both the petals and the stems + leaves of the artwork would be colored with the same color. You can see this more clearly by clicking the Edit tab to view the mapped colors on the color wheel. Notice the two colors the artwork is reduced to.

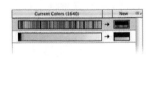

5. Reduce the artwork to five colors

Rather than jump directly to two colors, a more gradual reduction in colors gives you more options to work with. Select the Assign tab and specify 5 in the Colors field. By choosing five colors, the Live Color feature will still identify the neutral colors, but it will also separate the petals from the stems and the leaves. A quick look at the color wheel in the Edit tab makes it easy to see the five distinct color areas that Live Color has identified in the artwork.

6. Identify the colors in the artwork

You still need to reduce the number of colors from five down to two, but first, you can use Live Color to identify where the colors exist in your artwork. This makes it easier to make manual adjustments. Click the magnifying glass icon in the Assign tab and then click a color row to highlight those colors in your document. To select all of the colors in a row, click to the far left of the color row (an icon will appear when you mouse over that area). Highlight each row and identify the areas of color.

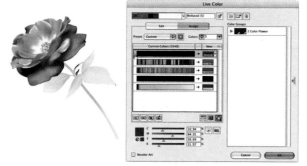

7. Manually reduce the artwork to two colors

The first row contains all of the colors used in the petals of the flower, which is perfect. But the remaining colors are spread across four rows. Select all of the colors in the second row by clicking at the far left of the row. Holding the Shift key, select the remaining three rows that appear beneath it and click the Merge Colors Into A Row icon to combine all those colors into a single row. The artwork has now been reduced to two colors, and the separation of the colors is also correct—one color for the petals and one color for the rest of the artwork.

8. Recolor the artwork with the desired color group

Now that the color mapping is correct, click once on the color group to select it. This remaps the artwork to use the two PANTONE colors that you specified earlier. If the colors appear in the wrong order, simply drag one icon in the New color list over the other to swap the colors. The result is a flower that will print correctly with two spot colors.

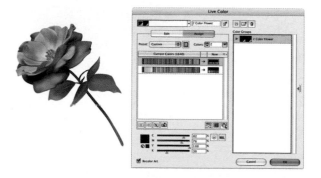

Convert to Grayscale

With the addition of Live Color in Illustrator CS3, there are now several ways to convert colored art to grayscale. Each offers different results, and some give the option to customize the conversion for the best result.

Original color artwork
The artwork featured in this example is a sample file included with Illustrator CS3. You can try these techniques yourself by opening the file Modern Dog Poster.ai in the Adobe Illustrator CS3/Cool Extras/Sample Files/Sample Art folder.

Desaturate
Select your artwork and choose Edit > Edit Colors > Recolor Artwork. Set Live Color to use Global Adjust and move the Saturation slider all the way to the left (–100). The result can't be adjusted.

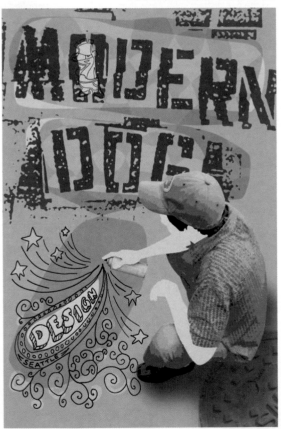

Adjust color balance
Select your artwork and choose Edit > Edit Colors > Adjust Color Balance. Set Color Mode to Grayscale and select the Preview and Convert check boxes. Use the Black slider to adjust to your liking (15% was used in this example).

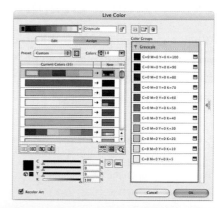

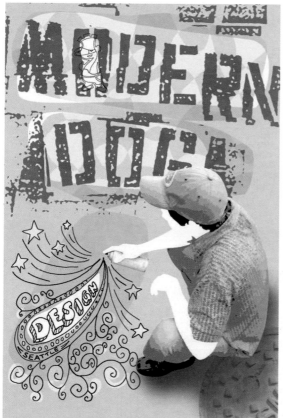

Convert to grayscale

Select your artwork and choose Edit > Edit Colors > Convert to Grayscale. The results can't be adjusted.

Recolor artwork

Load the Default > Print swatch library and add the Grayscale color group to your document by dragging its folder into the Swatches panel. Select your artwork and Choose Edit > Edit Colors > Recolor Artwork, select the Grayscale color group and adjust to your liking. In this example, I remapped the magenta color for the text headline to black, adding strong contrast to the overall conversion.

Colorizing a Graph

When generating graphs in Illustrator, each series of data is displayed as varying shades of gray by default. While gray charts don't make for very exciting presentations, it's easy to use the color features in Illustrator to quickly apply visually appealing colors to your graphs.

1. Create your graph

Follow the instructions in Chapter 10, *Graphs, Distortion, and Blends* to create a chart with your data. If you already have a graph created, open the file.

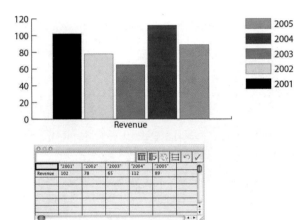

2. Create groups of colors

Recoloring artwork is a lot easier when you use color groups. You can either load existing color groups from the color libraries that ship with Illustrator, or you can create your own using the Color Guide or kuler. Add each new color group to your Swatches panel. Refer to Chapter 6, *Working with Color,* for more information on creating color groups, accessing libraries, and using the Color Guide panel or kuler.

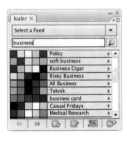

3. Recolor your graph.

Select the graph in your document and choose Edit > Edit Colors > Recolor Artwork. Then, click any of the color groups that appear on the right side of the Live Color dialog. Click different color groups to see what they look like. If you want to recolor the black elements in your graph as well, deselect Preserve Black in the Recolor Options dialog. Click OK when you've found the colors that work best for your graph.

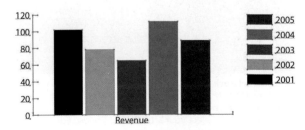

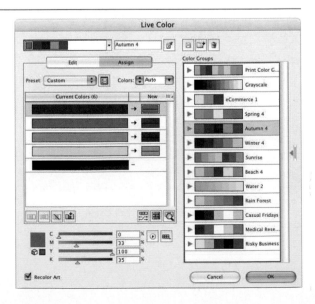

Performing One-Click Color Fixes

Although the Live Color dialog is certainly powerful, sometimes you might need to make a quick adjustment. If you select some artwork, you'll find a collection of functions available in the Edit > Edit Colors menu. These settings have actually been available in Illustrator for many versions now, but they were limited in that they worked only on certain basic vector objects (excluding gradients, patterns, symbols, gradient meshes, and so on). The functions you'll find here have all been retooled to use the Live Color engine and will work on everything with the exception of linked raster images. The functions (listed in the order in which they appear) are as follows: Adjust Color Balance, Blend Front to Back, Blend Horizontally, Blend Vertically, Convert to CMYK, Convert to Grayscale, Convert to RGB, Invert Colors, Overprint Black, and Saturate.

Viewing Color on the Screen

There was a time when we were all trained never to trust the color we saw on our computer screens. The myth has always been that although color management exists, it doesn't work. Some users even try to turn off color management (not something we suggest, even if it were possible, which it isn't). The reality is that these days the color we see on our screens is generally better than it has been in the past. Color management settings that were once inconsistent (even among Adobe applications) are now in sync with each other. The result is a more reliable viewing experience.

This section of the chapter in no way, shape, or form attempts to explain how color management works. Likewise, it doesn't explain how to ensure that your ink-jet printer and your computer screen look exactly the same. The topic of color management really requires an entire book of its own. In fact, if you really want to learn everything there is to know about color management, you should check out *Real World Color Management, Second Edition,* by Bruce Fraser, Chris Murphy, and Fred Bunting (Peachpit Press, 2005). For the scope of this book, we'll learn where to access your color management settings and how you can use some of Illustrator's color management features to simulate your artwork as it might appear on other specific devices.

Controlling Color Management Settings

You can control Illustrator's color management settings by choosing Edit > Color Settings. This opens the Color Settings dialog, and if you installed Adobe Illustrator CS3 as a part of Adobe Creative Suite 3, an icon and a message at the top of the dialog will indicate whether your settings are in sync with other Adobe Creative Suite 3 applications (**Figure 6.42**).

Figure 6.42 Illustrator's Color Settings dialog informs you whether your color settings are in sync with other Adobe Creative Suite applications.

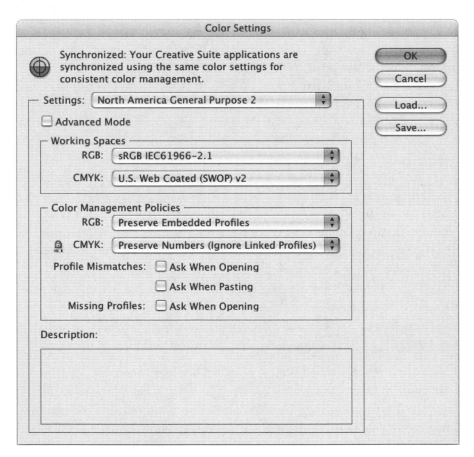

Checking the Advanced Mode option in the Color Settings dialog populates the Settings color with many additional color management settings.

Out of the box, Adobe has set all CS2 and CS3 applications to use the North America General Purpose 2 color setting. This is actually a generic "middle of the road" setting, meant to be used by those who are cross-media designers, meaning those who often work with both RGB and CMYK documents. However, if you work specifically in the print field or if you primarily work with video or the Web, you might be better off using North

America Prepress 2 or North America Web/Internet. If you aren't sure, leave it set to the default setting.

Proofing Colors

One of the most powerful functions of color management is the ability to simulate the viewing of your artwork on other devices. If you have the profile of another device, Illustrator can show you what your file will look like when it's displayed (or printed) on that device. Don't worry about hunting down device profiles either—your system already contains many useful ones. Let's take a closer look.

Choose View > Proof Setup > Customize to open the Proof Setup dialog. From the Device to Simulate pop-up menu, choose a profile. For example, you might use the Uncoated FOGRA29 profile to simulate what your art might look like when printed in a newspaper (**Figure 6.43**). Check the Preview box to see your artwork change in appearance as you select different profiles.

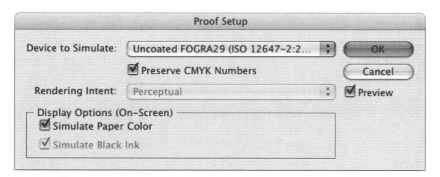

Figure 6.43 The Proof Setup dialog gives you the ability to specify what kind of device you want to simulate when proofing your artwork on your screen.

When your document is CMYK and you're choosing a CMYK profile, no color conversion occurs, and you can choose the Preserve CMYK Numbers option. Likewise, when viewing an RGB document and choosing an RGB profile, you can choose Preserve RGB Numbers. The option is obviously not available when proofing with a device profile that uses a different color model than the document (in such cases, a color conversion must take place, and there's no way to preserve the numbers).

When proofing artwork on devices with smaller color gamuts, you must also choose a rendering intent. The most commonly used method, Relative Colorimetric, moves out-of-gamut colors to the closest possible color that will print on the device. It also adjusts other colors so that colors appear to be accurate. The Absolute Colorimetric setting adjusts only out-of-gamut colors and may result in *posterization*, where many shades of similar colors are used. The Perceptual method shifts colors so they appear correct relative to each other, but it may not represent colors as being the most accurate match to the original values. The Saturation method enhances colors and makes them more vibrant and most suitable for business presentations where bright colors are more important than accurate colors.

To actually assign a different color profile to your document (instead of just proofing it on your screen), choose Edit > Assign Profile.

For an accurate onscreen representation of your artwork, you can choose to simulate paper color (avoiding the problem of viewing too bright of a white screen) and black ink (if you find the preview of black is too rich). Once you've specified your proof settings, you can quickly preview your artwork on your screen by choosing the View > Proof Colors setting.

Matching Spot Colors Across Applications

Although consistent color management settings will help ensure that your colors look the same across your different applications (Photoshop, Illustrator, InDesign, Acrobat, and so on), you may still experience colors that don't match up correctly. This is usually something that happens when spot colors appear in your file, but the good news is that it's easy to fix.

The problem is that, by default, Photoshop displays spot colors using LAB values (which are bright, vibrant, and match their printed color better). The default setting for Illustrator and InDesign is to use CMYK values instead, which often results in muted colors, especially when compared to Photoshop. The thing is, both Illustrator and InDesign support the ability to use LAB values when displaying spot colors, so it's simply a matter of turning it on. Before you do that, however, you need to understand something called *Book Color.*

Book Color is a setting that first appeared in Adobe CS2 applications and is present in CS3 applications as well. You may notice that when double-clicking a spot color swatch to view its settings, you'll see that the color mode for the swatch is set to Book Color (**Figure 6.44**).

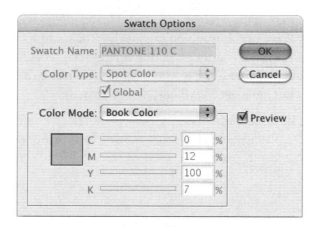

One of the reasons why designers use spot colors is simply because some colors aren't reproducible in CMYK. Bright blues, purples, greens, and oranges are perfect examples. Pantone delivers an entire Microsoft Excel spreadsheet to Adobe that lists each Pantone color, along with their LAB color equivalents. Obviously, the LAB color values match closer to the real color. However, many designers specify Pantone colors, even though they will be printing their file on press in a four-color process. Pantone also delivers a Solid to Process library that specifies the CMYK values of Pantone colors. Obviously, the latter is far less accurate and results in color shifts.

Since you now know that Photoshop uses LAB values to display spot colors on your screen and that Illustrator and InDesign use CMYK values for the same, you can begin to understand why spot colors viewed in Photoshop look different.

So, what does all this have to do with Book Color? Ordinarily, you can define a color swatch in Illustrator using CMYK values or LAB values, but not both. But a Book Color is special and *can* contain both CMYK and LAB information within it. By definition, a Book Color swatch contains both the CMYK and LAB values specified by Pantone. The question is, how does Illustrator determine when to preview the colors using the LAB values instead of the CMYK ones?

The answer is an odd one, only because of the name of the feature you need to use: Overprint Preview. If you choose View > Overprint Preview in Illustrator (or in InDesign or Acrobat, for that matter), the LAB values generate the onscreen preview. The regular preview settings use the CMYK values. In this way, you can preview the more vibrant LAB values on your screen, but if you ever decide later in your workflow to convert your Pantone color to CMYK, you'll get the exact CMYK values you expect (otherwise you'll get a LAB-to-CMYK version).

Likewise, if you'd like more accurate colors when printing composite proofs from Illustrator, check the Simulate Overprint box in the Print dialog.

CHAPTER SEVEN

Typography

Adobe Illustrator is a top-notch illustration tool, but it is also capable of setting professional-level type—its typography features are on par with those found in the award-winning Adobe InDesign.

In truth, prior to Illustrator CS, setting type in Illustrator was something you did only if you really had to do it. Tasks such as setting columns of type, creating lists with tab leaders, and creating text wraps were either impossible or extremely difficult to do and control. With the release of Illustrator CS, however, Adobe replaced an aging text engine with a modern, powerful one that offers features such as paragraph style sheets, optical kerning, and OpenType support. Even more important, this new text engine brings a level of global technology to Illustrator that enables seamless integration across multiple systems and languages.

In this chapter, we'll explore some of these important technologies, such as Unicode compliance, as well as some of the newer typography features found in Illustrator. Toward the end of the chapter, we'll discuss a very important side effect of all this new technology—backward compatibility with previous versions of Illustrator.

Getting Global Text Support with Unicode

For more information on the Unicode standard, visit www.unicode.org.

When you use your keyboard to type words on your computer, each character that you type is stored on your computer by a number. Every font also has a number assigned to each of its characters. This method of mapping characters to numbers is called *character encoding*. The idea is that when you type an *a*, your computer matches up its code with the code in the selected font, and an *a* shows up on your screen. Simple, right?

Besides Unicode support, Illustrator also has fantastic support for Asian languages and type features such as Mojikumi, Kinsoku, and composite fonts. To activate these extended features in the English-language version of Illustrator, turn on Show Asian Options in the Type panel in Preferences.

The problem is that not every computer uses the same encoding system. For example, Mac and Windows use different character encodings. Operating systems in different languages and countries around the world also use a variety of encodings. Conflicts also exist in that one system may encode a certain character with a number, whereas another system may have a completely different character encoded for that same number. Because there are so many different ways of encoding characters, you can run into a situation where you create a file on one computer, and simply opening that same file on a different computer results in words not appearing correctly. If you've ever typed something on Windows and transferred it to a Mac and noticed that certain characters appear as question marks, appear as weird boxes, or disappear completely, you can now understand why that happened.

In 1991, a standard was formed called Unicode, which, as its name implies, is a single encoding that can be used to describe every single character, in any language, on any computer platform. The new text engine that was introduced in Illustrator CS uses Unicode, and if you use Unicode-compliant fonts to create your documents, you can pass your documents across the world and have them display correctly on any computer.

Understanding the Way of the Font

Have you heard about the latest reality show? Ten designers have to create a logo, but first they have to get their fonts to work on their computers. Seriously though, you'd think that in a day and age where we can put people on the moon and do just about anything wirelessly, we would have figured out the whole font thing by now. As you will soon learn, different font formats are available, and each offers different capabilities. In addition,

Illustrator is specifically sensitive to corrupt fonts, and although a bad font may work in other applications, it can still cause problems in Illustrator. Several font management utilities are available, including Suitcase, Font Reserve, FontExplorer, and Font Agent, and each of these has components to help you identify and repair problematic fonts.

More importantly, different font formats are available. As a designer, you may be familiar with PostScript Type 1 fonts, TrueType fonts, or Multiple Master fonts. Adobe reduced support for Multiple Master fonts with the release of Illustrator CS, and although those fonts might still work in Illustrator today, there's no way to take advantage of the extended technology that they were meant to bring. TrueType fonts aren't used as much in print workflows because when they were first introduced, they weren't as reliable as PostScript Type 1 fonts (although nowadays, those problems no longer exist). Because of this, PostScript Type 1 fonts have always been perceived as being higher-quality fonts.

If you find that Illustrator is crashing frequently, the cause might be a corrupt font. By turning off all fonts and activating them one by one, you can help troubleshoot these issues and locate a problematic font.

Another font type, called OpenType, has introduced a new era in working with fonts, bringing extended functionality and even higher quality to the desktop.

What's Your Type?

We once had a bumper sticker that declared, "Whoever dies with the most fonts wins." There's nothing a designer loves more than a unique font that no one else has. At the same time, with so many fonts out there, you want to make sure you're using high-quality fonts. These days, fonts come in several formats:

- **PostScript Type 1.** Originally developed by Adobe, PostScript Type 1 fonts consist of a printer or outline font, a screen or bitmap font, and usually a font metrics file (an .afm file). Type 1 fonts have been considered the high-quality standard over the years, although OpenType is changing that.

- **TrueType.** Originally developed by Apple and Microsoft, the intent of TrueType was to overtake the Type 1 font standard. A TrueType font consists of a single file. TrueType fonts have traditionally been prevalent on Windows computers.

- **Multiple Master.** Originally developed by Adobe, Multiple Master fonts were intended to give the designer creative freedom to scale fonts to custom widths and weights. They are actually a flavor of Type 1 fonts. Some Multiple Master fonts also allow designers to scale serifs as well. Adobe has since dropped development and support for this format.

- **OpenType.** Originally developed by Adobe and Microsoft, the intent of OpenType is to create a universal font format that includes the benefits of Type 1 and TrueType font technologies. In fact, an OpenType font can contain either Type 1 or TrueType outlines. An OpenType font is Unicode compliant, is cross-platform, and consists of a single font file.

Introducing OpenType

At one time, Adobe offered certain fonts in "expert" collections; these were created because the type designer wanted to create additional glyphs and characters but ran out of space. Creating an expert version of the font gave the designer another 256 glyphs to work with.

Although PostScript Type 1 fonts are great, they have some issues and limitations, which make them difficult to use. For one, Type 1 fonts are not Unicode compliant. Second, Type 1 fonts are platform dependent, which means that if you have the Mac version of a font, you can use that font only on a Mac. You need to purchase a Windows version of a Type 1 font to use it on a Windows computer. Additionally, a Type 1 font consists of two files: a screen font and a printer font, both of which you must have to correctly print a file. If you forget to send either of these files to a printer, the file won't print. Finally, a Type 1 font is limited to 256 glyphs per font. A *glyph* is a specific graphical representation of a character. For a given character, there may be a default glyph and then alternates. For example, a *ligature* is a glyph that represents multiple characters. Although the English language doesn't usually require that many glyphs, some languages, such as Chinese, Japanese, and Korean, are severely affected by this limitation.

OpenType fonts address all of these limitations and offer extended functionality. OpenType fonts are Unicode compliant, are platform independent (you can use the same font file on both Windows and Mac), and consist of a single font file (both printer and screen fonts are embedded into a single file). In addition, OpenType can contain more than 65,000 glyphs in a single font. With the 256-glyph limit gone, type designers can create fonts with extended character sets that include real small caps, fractions, swash characters, and anything else they dream up.

OpenType fonts work with applications that don't support OpenType, but those applications see only the first 256 glyphs in that font.

The good news is that you already have OpenType fonts! Illustrator (whether you bought it separately or as part of the Adobe Creative Suite) automatically installs 100 OpenType fonts on your computer. You can quickly identify OpenType fonts in two ways: a green *O* icon appears to the left of their font names when you're scrolling through the font menu (**Figure 7.1**), and they end in the letters *Std* (standard) or *Pro*. OpenType Pro fonts contain extended character sets.

OpenType + Illustrator = Intelligent Fonts

Although the technological benefits of OpenType fonts are nice, they are just half the story. From a design perspective, OpenType fonts also offer superior typographical functionality through something called *automatic glyph replacement*.

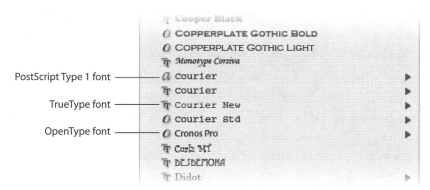

PostScript Type 1 font

TrueType font

OpenType font

Figure 7.1 Illustrator's WYSIWYG font menu not only displays a preview of the font but also displays icons to identify the font type—this is especially helpful when you have multiple versions of a font.

To best describe what automatic glyph replacement is, we'll use ligatures as an example. A ligature is a special combination of characters that don't ordinarily look that great when they appear together. For example, common ligatures include *fi* or *fl* where the lowercase *f* collides with or overlaps the following *i* or *l* character. So type designers create a new glyph, called a *ligature*, which somehow connects the two letters and makes them aesthetically pleasing (**Figure 7.2**).

finish finish

Figure 7.2 An *f* and an *i* character as they appear together in a word (left) and appearing combined as a ligature in the same word (right).

The way ligatures are traditionally applied, a designer locates two characters that appear together, and if the font has a ligature for that character pair, the designer manually deletes the two characters and replaces them with the ligature character. Besides the extra time it takes to make this switch, this method has two issues. First, a spelling checker will find errors when ligatures are used, because the spelling checker sees a ligature and not two separate letters. Second, if you change the font of your text to a typeface that doesn't have a ligature, you end up with a garbage character where the ligature was.

Automatic glyph replacement is when Illustrator automatically inserts a ligature for you, as you type, when you're using an OpenType font. Illustrator watches as you enter text, and if it finds a ligature in the font you are using for the characters you type, it automatically swaps the individual characters for the ligature. But that isn't even the cool part. Even though the ligature appears on your screen and prints, Illustrator still sees it as two separate characters (you can even place your cursor between the two characters).

That means if you run the spelling checker, you won't get a spelling error, and you won't run into issues if you change fonts. If the font you switch to doesn't have a ligature, the individual characters are displayed.

What's astounding is that if you take into account that each OpenType font can contain up to 65,000 glyphs, you'll realize that this functionality goes way beyond simple ligatures. Many OpenType fonts can also automatically replace fractions, ordinals, swash characters, real small caps, discretionary ligatures, contextual alternates, and more. Of course, the beauty of this functionality is that it happens automatically, so you don't have to even search through a font to find these special characters.

Using the OpenType Panel

OpenType sets perfect fractions because each typeface can contain all ten numbers at normal, numerator, and denominator sizes.

Although automatic glyph replacement is nice, giving a computer program total control over how your text appears is something that should exist only in the movies. In real life, a designer has complete control over a project. Choose Window > Type > OpenType to bring up the OpenType panel where you can specify exactly where and how Illustrator replaces glyphs. When you select text that is styled with an OpenType font, you can use the eight icons at the bottom of the panel to turn on and off the automatic glyph replacement for each kind of feature (**Figure 7.3**). If icons appear grayed out, that indicates the font you have selected doesn't contain those kinds of glyphs.

Figure 7.3 With text selected, clicking the different icons in the OpenType panel gives you instant feedback about the different glyphs available in a particular OpenType font.

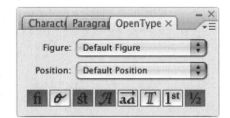

OpenType features can also be set within paragraph and character styles, which are covered later in this chapter.

The nice aspect of using the OpenType panel is that you can experiment with different type treatments simply by toggling a few of the panel icons. You can still use Type 1 and TrueType fonts with Illustrator, of course, and you can even mix them within the same document, but the OpenType panel works with OpenType fonts only.

Finding Glyphs and Fonts

If you are trying to find a specific glyph in a font, it is usually a tiresome game of trying to find the right keystroke combination. If you've ever run your fingers across the keyboard, typing every key just to find where the square box is in the Zapf Dingbats typeface (it's the lowercase *n*, by the way), you know what we mean.

The reality is, because a font can have up to 65,000 glyphs, it can be almost impossible to find the glyph you need. More to the point, how do you even know what glyphs are in a font to begin with? The answer is that you use the Glyphs panel.

You can see a graphic representation of all the glyphs in any font installed on your computer by opening the Glyphs panel (choose Type > Glyphs).

You can resize the Glyphs panel by dragging from the lower-right corner. By clicking the two icons at the bottom-right side of the panel, you can make the previews bigger and smaller. You can choose any font (even non-OpenType ones) from the pop-up at the bottom of the panel, and you can use the pop-up menu at the top of the panel to show only specific kinds of characters in a chosen font. If your cursor is in a text object on your artboard, double-clicking any icon in the Glyphs panel places that glyph within your text. If an icon contains a small black arrow in its lower-right corner, that indicates alternate glyphs for that character (**Figure 7.4**).

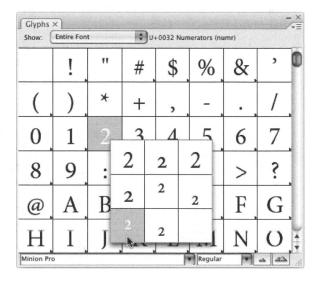

Figure 7.4 OpenType fonts can contain a variety of glyphs for each character, including small caps, old style, numerator, and denominator versions.

Using the Find Font Dialog

Knowing what fonts are used in your document is important when you're sending files out for others to use, especially printers. Sometimes it might be necessary to switch fonts, either when you want to replace a Type 1 font with an OpenType version or when you are missing fonts and want to substitute them for ones you have installed on your computer.

Choose Type > Find Font to open the Find Font dialog where you can see a list of all fonts used in an open document. An icon at the far right of each listing identifies the type of font. Fonts in this list don't appear in alphabetical order. Rather, they appear according to where they appear first in the document's object stacking order.

The bottom portion of the dialog allows you to replace fonts with those that already exist in the document or with those that are installed on your computer (**Figure 7.5**). You can also use the check boxes to filter the kinds of fonts you want to see listed. If your system contains many fonts, unchecking some of the options that appear at the bottom of the dialog will limit the results you see in the Find Font dialog, making it easier to make font choices and changes.

Figure 7.5 The Find Font dialog is great for replacing fonts, but it's even better for quickly seeing all the fonts used in a document.

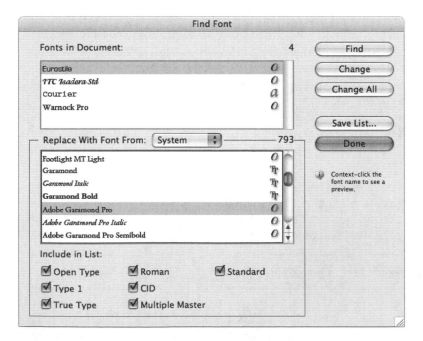

Earlier in the chapter, we defined OpenType, Type 1, and TrueType fonts. Here's a description of the remaining options found in the Find Font dialog:

- **Roman.** *Roman* doesn't mean "not italic," as in the face. *Roman* here instead refers to the language or character set. Fonts that use alphanumeric characters are roman fonts.

- **CID.** CID fonts are basically the opposite of roman fonts. CID is short for *Character IDentifier.* CID fonts were developed for Asian markets and languages such as Chinese, Japanese, and Korean (what Adobe often refers to as *CJK*). CID fonts are usually several fonts "sewn" together because many Asian fonts contain far more than 256 glyphs (the limit with PostScript Type 1 fonts). The use of OpenType fonts and something called *composite fonts* (available only when using Asian fonts in Illustrator) have replaced much of the need for CID fonts these days.

- **Multiple Master.** Multiple Master fonts are a special flavor of Type 1 PostScript and were originally developed to allow designers to interactively scale fonts on horizontal and vertical axes. This would give a great amount of control to designers to customize a font as needed, but the need for this kind of control never really materialized. The features available in OpenType fonts are far more important to designers. Adobe has not made Multiple Master fonts for some time now.

- **Standard.** Standard fonts are fonts that are installed and used by the operating system.

SPECIFYING CHARACTER AND PARAGRAPH OPTIONS

Just about all of the text settings you would expect to find in a page layout program are present in Illustrator. You can find these settings in the Control panel when you select the Type tool or in the Character and Paragraph panels, both of which you can find in the Window > Type menu.

Using the Character Panel

The Character panel allows you to specify the font family and font style (italic, bold, and so on) as well as the settings for type size and leading (pronounced *ledding*, which controls the vertical distance from one baseline to the next). You can also specify *kerning*, which is the amount of space that appears between individual text characters (see the sidebar "Optical Kerning"), and the *tracking*, which is the amount of space that appears between characters over a range of text (entire words, paragraphs, and so on).

Horizontal and vertical scaling can make type appear narrower or wider, although most designers avoid these settings because they can distort text. Use the condensed or extended versions of fonts instead, if they are available. You can apply the baseline shift setting to individual characters and use it to adjust where the selected text sits relative to the baseline of the type object. The character rotation setting allows you to rotate individual characters within a text string, although you should be aware that you'll most likely need to perform manual kerning when you use this setting. You can specify whether you want selected text underlined or crossed out (the strikethrough feature), and you can also choose from the Language pop-up menu to indicate to Illustrator what language the selected text is (**Figure 7.6**). This is helpful for hyphenation and spelling dictionaries (discussed later in this chapter).

Figure 7.6 When creating multilingual documents, choosing a language for text tells Illustrator which spelling and hyphenation dictionaries to use.

Optical Kerning

Getting just the right kerning is critical when you're working with logos and headlines; it can often mean the difference between text that is easy to read and text that is difficult to understand. Kerning is usually set in a typeface automatically and described in a metrics file that identifies the amount of space each letter has. Some font designers also include kerning pairs, which are letters that have natural white space between them when set side by side (the letters *V* and *A* are the most commonly used example of this).

Illustrator has a setting in the Kerning field of the Character panel called Optical, which performs kerning automatically. Rather than using metrics tables to define the space between letters, Illustrator looks at the actual glyph shapes and kerns the characters as they appear to the eye (**Figure 7.7**). Using optical kerning has two immediate benefits.

Figure 7.7 The word on the top is set to Auto kerning and is using metrics to determine kerning. Notice the open space between the *m* and the *u* and how the *u* almost touches the base of the *s*. The word on the bottom is set to Optical kerning. Notice how the letters appear evenly spaced.

mustard
mustard

First, you can apply optical kerning to any text in your file—even body copy or the 4-point legal text that appears at the bottom of an advertisement. Although designers spend time kerning logos and headlines, it's too time-consuming to kern all of the text in your file. With optical kerning, you can kern all of the text in your document with a single click. You can even specify optical kerning in a character or paragraph style.

Second, kerning applied by hand is good only for the typeface you've chosen. Once you change your text to use a different typeface, you need to redo the kerning. When using optical kerning, Illustrator automatically makes adjustments because it is always using the visual appearance of the text to do the kerning.

Of course, you can always override or make additional adjustments to optically kerned text. Once you've specified optical kerning to text, you can kern that text as you would normally. Generally, for well-designed fonts, metrics kerning is superior to optical. But optical kerning is very useful for poorly made fonts (almost every shareware font, for instance). It's also handy for specific pairs that the type designer might have missed.

In one case, optical kerning can work against you, and that's when you're using the underscore character to create fields when you're designing forms. With optical kerning turned on, the underscore characters won't touch each other; the result is what appears to be a dashed line. However, you can select the underscore characters and change the kerning to the Auto setting to get the appearance of a solid line (**Figure 7.8**).

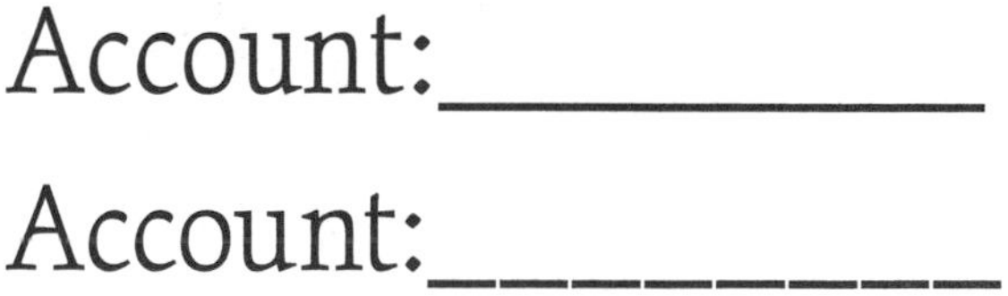

Figure 7.8 The word on top is set to Auto kerning, and the underscore characters appear as one line. The word on the bottom is set to Optical kerning, and the underscores appear as a dashed line.

Account:_____
Account:_____

Using the Paragraph Panel

The Paragraph panel allows you to choose between seven different ways to align your text. You can also specify left, right, and first-line indents and add space before or after paragraphs. There's also a check box to enable/disable hyphenation for the selected paragraph(s).

Through the Paragraph panel flyout menu, you can also choose to use the Adobe Single-line Composer or the Adobe Every-line Composer to determine how line breaks are specified in a paragraph of text (see the "Featured Matchup" sidebar).

Setting Tabs

To create tab settings in Illustrator, select a Path Type or Area Type object, and choose Window > Type > Tabs. Clicking the magnet icon at the far right of the panel aligns the panel with your selected text. Choose between one of the four kinds of tabs (left, center, right, and decimal), and click the ruler to add a tab. As you drag a tab on the ruler, a vertical line appears onscreen to help you visualize where the tab stop will be (**Figure 7.9**). You can add up to 99 tabs on a single line (if you can find a page big enough), and to delete a tab, you simply drag it off the ruler. Clicking a tab selects it, and you can specify an exact coordinate for it if you don't have a steady hand. Additionally, you can specify any character as a leader; doing so fills up the space between tabs with the specified character.

Figure 7.9 Setting tabs in previous versions of Illustrator was never fun. Now, it's easy to align tabs perfectly.

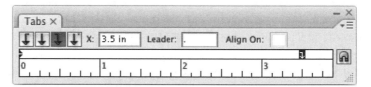

Featured Matchup: Adobe Single-Line Composer vs. Adobe Every-Line Composer

When good designers talk about setting a nice paragraph of text, they refer to the *color of the type*. In this case, they aren't referring to black, blue, or yellow. Rather, they are talking about how readable the text is, which is heavily influenced by the spacing that appears between letters and words, and how text is broken from line to line. It is especially common to see *rivers* in justified text, which are areas of white space that seem to connect from line to line so that your eyes see them when you are looking at the paragraph.

Using a technology that first appeared in InDesign, Illustrator offers two "engines" that you can use to compose a paragraph of text. The Adobe Single-line Composer looks at each line as it flows text into an Area Type object. Based on hyphenation and justification settings, as well as on font and point size, the Single-line Composer determines how many words can fit on each line. It does so by looking at the first line, flowing the text, then moving on to the next line, and so on. Once a line of text has been set, it's as if Illustrator isn't even aware of its existence. Sometimes, the result is a line that doesn't fit right. As a designer, you might look at such a line and manually break it differently by adding a forced line break somewhere in the paragraph in an attempt to create better spacing.

In contrast, the Adobe Every-line Composer looks at the entire paragraph as it flows text into an Area Type object. As it composes type, Illustrator analyzes the previous lines and sees whether it can get better spacing, fewer hyphens, and so on. The result is a paragraph of text that has superior color and that requires less manual work from the designer (**Figure 7.10**).

Keep in mind that with the Every-line Composer, adding a manual line break might result in text reflowing above your cursor, not just after it. This happens because Illustrator is relentless in trying to set the perfect paragraph of text; by making a forced line break, you've changed the layout of the paragraph. If you are manually breaking lines in a paragraph of text, you should consider using the Adobe Single-line Composer.

Figure 7.10 The paragraph on the left was set using the Single-line Composer, and the paragraph on the right, which has fewer spacing problems and a more even look, was set using the Every-line Composer.

At its Worldwide Developer Conference today, Apple® announced plans to deliver models of its Macintosh® computers using Intel® microprocessors by this time next year, and to transition all of its Macs to using Intel microprocessors by the end of 2007. Apple previewed a version of its critically acclaimed operating system, Mac OS® X Tiger, running on an Intel-based Mac® to the over 3,800 developers attending CEO Steve Jobs' keynote address. Apple also announced the availability of a Developer Transition Kit, consisting of an Intel-based Mac development system along with preview versions of Apple's software, which will allow developers to prepare versions of their applications which will run on both PowerPC and Intel-based Macs.

At its Worldwide Developer Conference today, Apple® announced plans to deliver models of its Macintosh® computers using Intel® microprocessors by this time next year, and to transition all of its Macs to using Intel microprocessors by the end of 2007. Apple previewed a version of its critically acclaimed operating system, Mac OS® X Tiger, running on an Intel-based Mac® to the over 3,800 developers attending CEO Steve Jobs' keynote address. Apple also announced the availability of a Developer Transition Kit, consisting of an Intel-based Mac development system along with preview versions of Apple's software, which will allow developers to prepare versions of their applications which will run on both PowerPC and Intel-based Macs.

Defining Text Styles

Some people who use page layout programs refer to paragraph styles as *text style sheets*.

Sure, there are lots of text settings, and having to constantly choose between them can make design work boring and time-consuming. Have no fear, though, paragraph and characters styles can get you back to having fun designing in no time. As with page layout applications, you can define a style that stores paragraph- and character-based settings, which you can apply to selected text with the click of a button. In Chapter 3, *Objects, Groups, and Layers*, you learned how to create graphic styles, which is similar in concept.

If a style appears with a plus sign after its name, that indicates the selected text contains an *override*, or a setting that doesn't match the style. Pressing the Option (Alt) button while clicking the style name clears the override.

To define a paragraph or character style, you can use one of two methods. The first is what some call the "show me" way, where you style text on your artboard in the usual way. Once you've got your text styled the way you want, you select the text and click the New Style button in either the Paragraph Styles or Characters Styles panel. This way is more visual and allows you to experiment with ideas before committing to creating a particular style. The second way is the "flying blind" method, where you create a new style and then double-click the style name in the panel to define the settings for that style (**Figure 7.11**). This way is useful when you already have a pretty good idea of what settings you want to define in the style.

Figure 7.11 When flying blind, you can quickly specify font style settings in the Paragraph Style Options dialog.

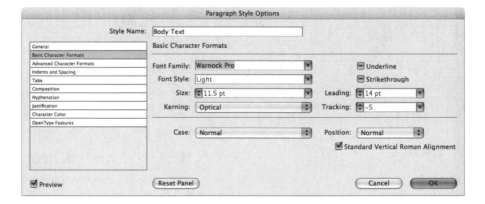

Everything that we've discussed in this chapter with regards to styling text can be stored as an attribute in a paragraph or character style. Once a style is defined, you can apply the style to selected text just by clicking the style name in the Character Styles or Paragraph Styles panel. To modify a style, double-click its name, and when you've made changes, any text that has that style applied in your document is updated with the changes.

WORKING WITH AREA TYPE

In Chapter 2, *Vectors 101*, you learned the differences between point type and area type (or point text and area text). Because area type has more structure than point type, you will find that area type has many features that you would expect to find in a page layout application. For example, an Area Type object can contain multiple columns of text within a single frame and can flow text from one frame to another, which is called *text threading*.

Creating and Editing Text Threads

Text that flows across multiple type objects is called a *text thread*. In previous versions of Illustrator, this was called *linking text boxes* and was difficult to work with. Taking a note from its sister application InDesign, Illustrator makes it possible to easily manage text threads.

An Area Type object always displays two boxes on its path, one located at the upper left of the object, called the *in port*, and one located at the lower right, referred to as the *out port* (**Figure 7.12**). Text flows into an Area Type object through the in port and exits the object via the out port. The ports themselves are also used to control text threads.

In Port ——

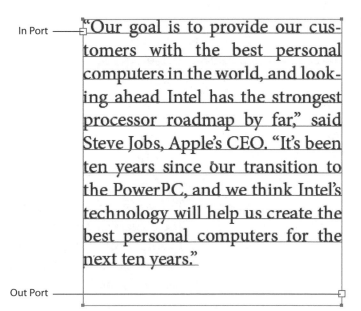

Out Port ——

Figure 7.12 Every Area Type object in Illustrator has an in port and an out port.

To create a new text thread, you must first have an existing text object to work with.

1. First, either use the Type tool to drag out an Area Type object or click any closed vector path with the Type tool to convert the shape to an Area Type object.

2. Switch to the Selection tool, and select the Area Type object.

   With the object selected, you'll see the in and out ports, of which both will be empty (colored white). An empty in port indicates the beginning of the story, and an empty out port indicates the end of a story.

3. Using the Selection tool, click the Area Type object's out port, and you'll notice your cursor changes to the place text icon.

4. At this point, you can either click an existing closed vector path or click and drag an empty area on the artboard to create a second Area Type object. The two objects are now linked together.

You can see that the objects are linked because the out port of the first object and the in port of the second object are filled with a blue arrow. A line connects the two ports so that you can easily identify the direction of a thread when the Area Type objects are selected (**Figure 7.13**). To turn this preview off, choose View > Hide Text Threads.

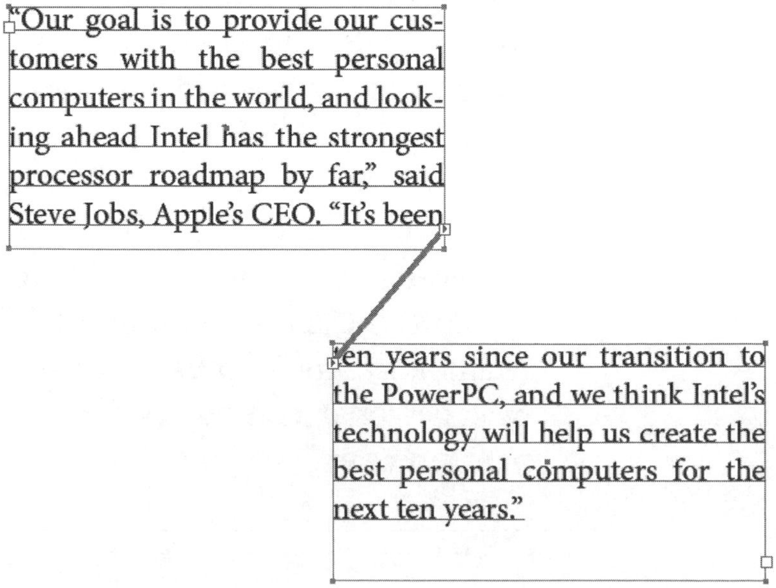

Figure 7.13 A blue arrow and a connecting line help identify the direction of a text thread.

"Our goal is to provide our customers with the best personal computers in the world, and looking ahead Intel has the strongest processor roadmap by far," said Steve Jobs, Apple's CEO. "It's been

ten years since our transition to the PowerPC, and we think Intel's technology will help us create the best personal computers for the next ten years."

You can add as many objects to a text thread as you'd like. To remove an object from a text thread, simply select it, and press the Delete key on your keyboard. Illustrator automatically updates the thread with the remaining objects for you. To add a new Area Type object in the middle of an existing thread, you can always click the out port (even though it has a blue arrow in it) and drag out a new text object, which will be inserted into the thread.

Because Area Type objects are enclosed areas, a finite amount of text can fit within them. *Overset text* is what happens when you have an Area Type object that has more text than it can handle and doesn't have another text object to link to. An object's out port displays a red plus sign to indicate where overset text exists (**Figure 7.14**). When working with objects that contain overset text, you can either edit the text so that there are fewer words, enlarge the Area Type object to allow for more text, or create a thread and link the object with other text objects.

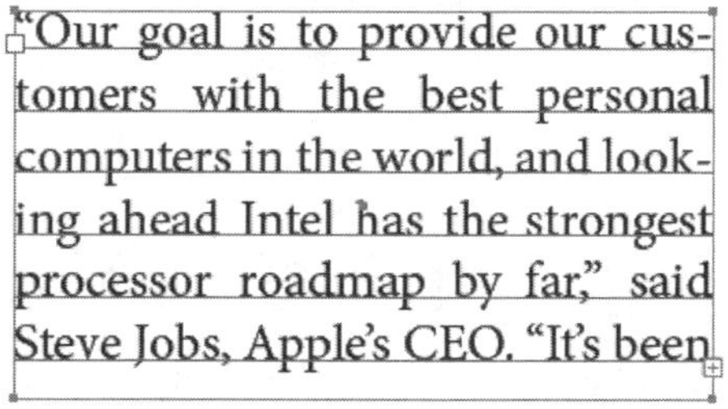

➡ You can also extend a text thread from the beginning of a story by clicking the empty in port and then drawing a new Area Type object.

"Our goal is to provide our customers with the best personal computers in the world, and looking ahead Intel has the strongest processor roadmap by far," said Steve Jobs, Apple's CEO. "It's been

Figure 7.14 A production artist never wants to see one of these. The plus sign in the out port indicates that there is overset text, and it could mean text reflow has occurred.

Transforming Type

When you have the bounding box option turned on (View > Show Bounding Box), you can use the Selection tool to resize text objects, but there's a difference between transforming Point Type and Area Type objects in this way. When you are working with a Point Type object, the bounding box that appears around the text gives the illusion of an Area Type object (sans in and out ports). When you use the Selection tool to scale the Point Type object by dragging any of the eight handles, the text scales in size as well. If you don't hold the Shift key while scaling, the text will not scale in proportion.

In contrast, when you select an Area Type object with the Selection tool, you can click and drag any of the eight handles to resize the text frame, but the text that resides inside the Area Type object will not be scaled. Of course, you can always use the Scale tool to apply the transform to the text as well.

Setting Area Type Options

One of the benefits of working with area type is that you can easily define the area in which the text will be contained. You can also specify many different settings as to how text will fill this defined area, which you can access by selecting an Area Type object and choosing Type > Area Type Options.

In the Area Type Options dialog, you can adjust the overall width and height of the Area Type object, as well as specify both rows and columns. The *Gutter value* determines the amount of space that appears between each row or column. The *Inset Spacing setting* determines the amount of space that appears between the border of the actual Area Type object and where the text begins. You can think of it like margins that are specific to this Area Type object. You can also choose from a variety of settings to determine where the first baseline is calculated. By specifying a text flow, you can also control whether text flows from column to column or from row to row. Click the Preview button so that you can preview the changes you make before you apply them.

Achieving Perfect Alignment

As designers, we are extremely particular about the appearance of the art we create. Setting type can present a designer with a variety of challenges because each character of each font is different. Even though a column of text is set to be justified, that doesn't mean that, from a visual perspective, it will appear so. Punctuation and special characters can present optical illusions and make text appear as though it is set incorrectly, even though mathematically it is set correctly. Because of these issues, a designer might struggle to align text so that punctuation marks sit just outside the actual margin of text to ensure a clear line that the human eye can follow.

However, this sort of struggling is no longer necessary because Illustrator has two features that take care of these optical issues. With an Area Type object selected, you can choose Type > Optical Margin Alignment to have Illustrator make sure that margins on both sides of an Area Type object are visually straight from a design perspective (not a mathematical one). Additionally, you can select an Area Type object and choose Window > Type > Paragraph to open the Paragraph panel. Then, choose Roman Hanging Punctuation from the Paragraph panel menu to force all punctuation marks such as commas, periods, and quote marks to appear outside the margin of the text at the beginning and end of a line (**Figure 7.15**).

"Our goal is to provide our customers with the best personal computers in the world, and looking ahead Intel has the strongest processor roadmap by far," said Steve Jobs, Apple's CEO. "It's been ten years since our transition to the PowerPC, and we think Intel's technology will help us create the best personal computers for the next ten years."

Figure 7.15 The Roman Hanging Punctuation setting makes setting great-looking text almost too easy.

PUTTING TYPE ON A PATH

Having text follow along a path is nothing new to Illustrator users. However, if you've used Illustrator before, you'll find that since Illustrator CS, type on a path is implemented quite differently than in previous versions—to the point where it might even seem like a new feature.

To make it easier to learn how to use this feature, you will start by creating type on an open path. After you've done this, you will understand how to perform the same function on a closed path.

1. Using your tool of choice, create an open path, or you can select an open path that already exists on your artboard.

2. Choose the Type tool, and move your cursor so that it touches the path and changes to the Type on a Path tool icon, with a line through the icon.

3. Click the path to create a Path Type object.

    This action removes any stroke attributes from the path, but you can apply them to the path again later if you want. At this point, you'll see the blinking text insertion icon, and you can enter or copy text onto the path.

4. Now switch to the Selection tool, and select the path with the text on it (you can click either the path or the text).

Everything you're learning about type on a path here can be applied to InDesign as well, because the functionality is identical to Illustrator.

As you look at the selection, you'll notice a vertical line with a small white box on the left, a line at the center, and a small white box and a line on the far right (**Figure 7.16**).

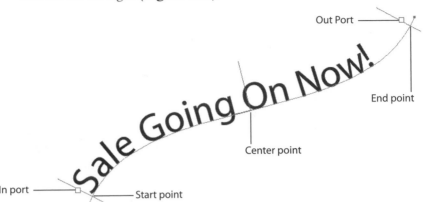

Figure 7.16 A Path Type object is similar to an Area Type object in many ways.

The small boxes should look familiar to you—they are in and out ports. The ports are there because Illustrator treats type on a path like area type. The two vertical lines that appear on either end define the boundary, or the start and end points, of the text. The line in the center determines the center point between the start and end points and allows you to specify which side of the path the text sits on.

Prior to Illustrator CS, Type on a Path objects behaved similarly to Point Type objects.

You can use the in and out ports to thread text across multiple Path Type objects, and you can even create a thread of text that includes both Path Type and Area Type objects (très cool). By dragging the start and end points, you can define the area of the path that can contain text. For example, you can have a long path but have text appear on just a small portion of that path (**Figure 7.17**). If you think about it, adjusting the start and end points on a Path Type object is akin to adjusting the width of an Area Type object. You can also drag the middle line to either side of the path to flip the text.

Figure 7.17 By moving the position of the start and end points, you can control the portion of the path that can contain text.

Working with Path Type with Closed Paths

Now that you understand how path type works, you're ready to learn how to work with path type on a closed path. When you convert a path to a Path Type object, the point at which you click the path becomes the start point. On an open path, you can easily see the start and end points because they are on opposite sides of the path. However, when you are working with a closed path, the point you click becomes the start point *and* the end point (a closed path is continuous).

If, for example, you want to place text on a circle, click the top of the circle to create the start point and the end point; if you center your text, it actually aligns to the bottom of the path (**Figure 7.18**). To get text to align to the top center of a circle, either click at the bottom of the circle when you're creating the Path Type object or adjust the start and end points so that the center of the text rests at the top of the circle (**Figure 7.19**).

To convert a closed path to a Path Type object, you have to hold the Option (Alt) key while clicking the path with the Type tool. Or you can simply use the Type on a Path tool.

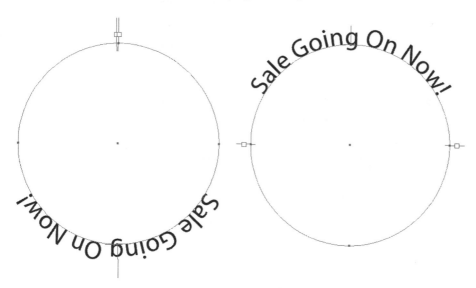

Figure 7.18 At first placing text on a circle seems nonintuitive—clicking at the top of a circle centers your text at the bottom of the circle.

Figure 7.19 Changing the position of the start and end points can make it easier to center text at the top curve of a circle.

Setting Path Text Options

Positioning text on a path—especially a curved path—can be difficult because the spacing can look irregular. However, you can adjust these and other settings by selecting the Path Type object and choosing Type > Type on a Path > Type on a Path Options. The following settings are available in the Type on a Path Options dialog:

- **Effect.** The Effect setting controls the orientation of the text relative to the path. Prior to Illustrator CS, all Type on Path objects used the Rainbow setting, which rotated each character to be tangent to the path. Illustrator now allows you to also choose from Skew, 3D Ribbon, Stair Step, and Gravity (**Figure 7.20**).

- **Align to Path.** The Align to Path setting determines which part of the text actually lines up with and touches the path. You can choose from Baseline (the default), Ascender, Descender, and Center (**Figure 7.21**).

- **Spacing.** You can use the Spacing setting to help get consistent spacing between characters on curved paths (the setting doesn't do much on straight paths). Where paths make sharp curves, the spacing between characters could appear at odd angles or with inconsistent spacing. Specifying a higher spacing value brings characters closer to each other and corrects the spacing issues.

- **Flip.** The Flip setting allows you to control the side of the path on which the text appears.

Figure 7.20 Listed here are the five effect settings you can use with path type.

Rainbow

Skew

3D Ribbon

Stair Step

Gravity

Figure 7.21 Listed here are the four align settings you can use with path type.

If you want to apply an appearance to the path itself on a Path Type object, click just the path with the Direct Selection tool (it might be easier to do this while you are in the Outline view mode). You can then apply attributes to the path as you would normally. To offset text from the path itself, use the Baseline Shift setting; however, if you're working with wavy or curved paths, using one of the Align to Path settings offers better results because it takes advantage of the Spacing setting.

WRAPPING TEXT AROUND OBJECTS

Graphic layouts sometimes call for text wrapping around the perimeter of other objects. Because the wrap is an attribute of the object, not the text, you'll find the text wrap feature listed under the Object menu. You can specify text wraps for individual objects or for groups. Similar to what you learned about groups in Chapter 3, *Objects, Groups, and Layers*, applying a text wrap to an entire group allows you to specify one text wrap setting for the entire group. Choosing several objects and then applying a text wrap simply applies an individual text wrap to each selected object. Once you've made a selection, choose Object > Text Wrap > Make.

Older versions of Illustrator required that you apply a text wrap by selecting both the text and the object. Doing this in Illustrator CS2 creates a wrap around both the text and the object, so make sure you have just the object selected.

A text wrap's boundary is defined by the object's appearance, not its vector path. If you have live effects applied to an object, a text wrap that is applied to that object will follow the appearance.

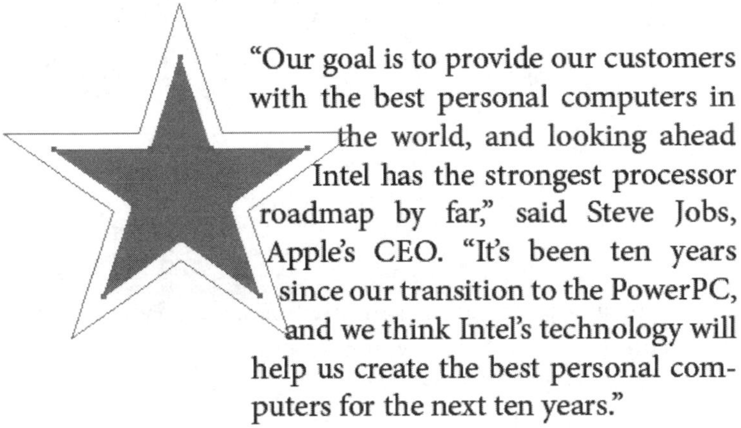

Figure 7.22 Illustrator offers a simple text wrap feature. For more sophisticated text wraps, InDesign is a good alternative.

Unlike layout applications such as InDesign, Illustrator's text wrap feature doesn't allow you to edit the text wrap in the form of a path. You can specify only the offset value, which you can access by selecting the object with the wrap and choosing Object > Text Wrap > Text Wrap Options.

Once a text wrap has been applied to an object, any area text that appears below it in the stacking order will wrap around the object (**Figure 7.22**). Point type is not affected at all by text wraps. To remove a text wrap, select an object that has an existing text wrap already applied, and choose Object > Text Wrap > Release.

"Our goal is to provide our customers with the best personal computers in the world, and looking ahead Intel has the strongest processor roadmap by far," said Steve Jobs, Apple's CEO. "It's been ten years since our transition to the PowerPC, and we think Intel's technology will help us create the best personal computers for the next ten years."

EDITING TEXT

There's a saying that goes, "The written word is forever," but obviously that saying was meant to be applied *after* the client had already reviewed the job. As a designer, making text edits is a part of life. Illustrator does have several features that make AAs (author's alterations) a bit easier to digest, including a powerful find-and-replace function and a spectacular spelling checker.

Using Find and Replace

Illustrator may be a single-page-per-document application, but a find-and-replace feature can still be helpful when you're making specific edits across large amounts of text. Choose Edit > Find and Replace to search across all text within a single Illustrator document. The arrows at the end of both the Find and Replace With fields allow you to specify special characters including tab characters and nonbreaking hyphens (**Figure 7.23**).

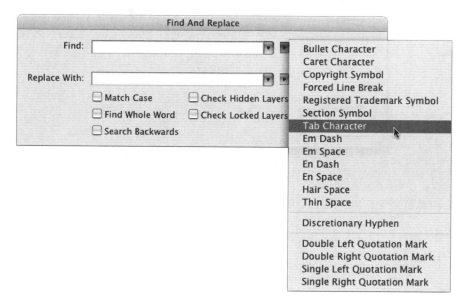

Figure 7.23 You don't have to remember special codes to find special characters. Illustrator provides you with a list of common characters for search-and-replace functions.

Displaying Invisible Characters

When performing text edits, it can be helpful to identify where nonvisible characters appear. You can make spaces, tabs, soft and hard returns, and end-of-story markers visible by choosing Type > Show Hidden Characters. When visible, these characters display in blue icons.

Checking Spelling

We're sure that you've never sent a job off for print or uploaded a Web page with a typo in it. But just in case, it never hurts to learn how to check your spelling, especially since Illustrator's spelling checker is quite the linguist— it speaks many languages.

You can specify what language a selected string of text is by choosing from the pop-up menu that appears at the bottom of the Character panel. You can also specify the language within a character or a paragraph style sheet.

When Illustrator's spelling checker encounters text that is specified as Spanish, it uses its Spanish dictionary to check the spelling, and it does the same for any other language that you've specified.

To run the spelling checker on your document, choose Edit > Check Spelling, and click the Start button. Illustrator starts suggesting corrections for misspelled words; you can also choose to ignore them or add a word to Illustrator's dictionary (**Figure 7.24**).

Figure 7.24 The spelling checker in Illustrator can prove to be helpful, even for documents that contain a small amount of text.

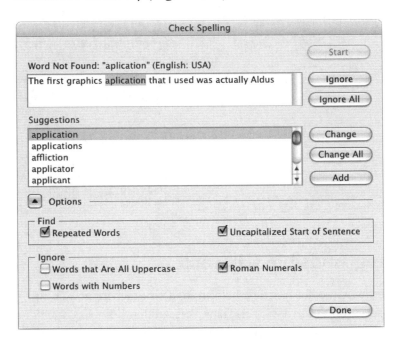

Working with Legacy Text and Backward Compatibility

After reading this chapter, you'll probably agree it's obvious that the text features that appear in Illustrator's next-generation text engine are a powerful set of tools that brings a professional level of typography into the hands of users such as yourself. Beyond that, the advanced technology that enables Unicode and OpenType support and features such as optical kerning means you can rely on consistent type today and in the future.

All of this functionality comes at a price, though, when you consider backward compatibility with versions of Illustrator that use the older text engine.

At the end of the day, the text engine that appeared in Illustrator CS wasn't just an enhancement—it was a new feature.

When you have a particular feature in a new version—say symbols in Illustrator 10—you can use this feature in that version, but you can't export that file to an older version and expect to edit it, right? For example, you can't create a symbol in Illustrator 10, save the file as an Illustrator 8 file, open it in Illustrator 8, and expect to edit the symbol. This is because the symbol feature doesn't exist in version 8. The visual appearance is correct, but the art isn't editable as a symbol anymore.

Because of the huge advancement in technology of the new text engine in Illustrator CS, text isn't compatible with previous versions of Illustrator. You can think of this as a line drawn in the sand, with Illustrator CS3, CS2, and CS on one side and all older versions (Adobe calls these *legacy* versions) on the other.

Opening Legacy Illustrator Files in Illustrator CS3

Let's take a common design scenario. You launch Illustrator CS3 and open a file that contains text that was created in a legacy version of Illustrator (say Illustrator 10). When you open the file, you're presented with a warning dialog that states the following: "This file contains text that was created in a previous version of Illustrator. This Legacy text must be updated before you can edit it." The dialog presents you with three options:

- **Update.** Clicking the Update button converts all the legacy text in your file so it is compatible with the new text engine. This process may result in some of your text reflowing and displaying different line breaks and kerning. However, sometimes no reflow occurs at all. Because this happens as you open the file, you won't see the reflow or kerning changes happen if they do, and so if text placement is critical, you should avoid choosing this option (you'll see how you can update the text manually later). The only time it makes sense to choose Update is when you know you will be changing or deleting the text anyway.

- **Cancel.** In essence, clicking Cancel is like saying, "I always wanted to be a welder anyway." Cancel simply closes the file, and Illustrator forgets this little incident ever happened.

- **OK.** If you click OK, the file opens, and none of the legacy text is affected at all—the file opens just as it did in Illustrator 10. The catch is, you can't edit the legacy text, which appears in the document much like a placed file—in a box with an X through it. You can print the file perfectly and make edits to other art in the file, but Illustrator treats the text as a *foreign object*, which cannot be edited. However, you can convert individual legacy text objects to the new text engine as you need to, as you will soon learn.

Basically, if you are opening a file where you know you will be changing or deleting the text, choosing Update is the best way to go because you don't care whether the text reflows. If, however, you just want to open a file so that you can print it, or if text placement is important (which it usually is), choosing the OK option is the smart choice.

Updating Legacy Text in an Open Document

If you choose to open a legacy Illustrator file by clicking OK, the file opens, but each text object is not editable until you convert it to the new text engine (**Figure 7.25**). You can do so on an object-by-object basis by selecting the Type tool and clicking a legacy text object, at which time Illustrator presents you with another dialog that offers three options (**Figure 7.26**):

Figure 7.25 A legacy text object is not editable, and it appears much like an image does.

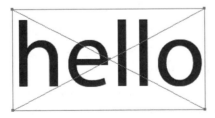

Figure 7.26 Trying to edit legacy text with the Type tool results in another dialog.

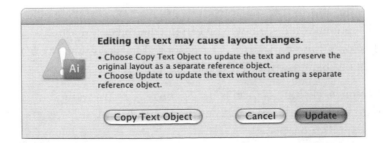

- **Copy Text Object.** Choosing the Copy Text Object option converts the legacy type to the new text engine, and therefore the text is editable. Some reflow may occur in the conversion, but Illustrator creates a copy of the legacy text on a locked and dimmed layer beneath the new converted text. If the new text does actually reflow, you can see the difference between the new text and old text, which is on the layer beneath it. You can then adjust the new text to perfectly match the legacy text.

- **Cancel.** Choosing Cancel leaves the legacy text as a foreign object—it can be printed but not edited.

- **Update.** Choosing Update converts the text to the new text engine so that you can edit it. However, a copy of the legacy text is not created, so if the text does reflow, you might not be able to tell.

For converting tag lines, logotype, and other sensitive type treatments, choosing the Copy Text Object option is obviously the best. However, if you have a lot of text objects to convert, it can take a long time to ensure that all of the text matches the legacy document (although depending on the task, you might not have a choice). The Update option can be useful if you want to make an edit to just a few lines of text and the reflow there won't make a difference anyway.

You may find that when you're updating text, no significant reflow occurs. If, after updating several text objects, you decide to convert all the legacy text at once, you can choose Type > Legacy Text > Update All Legacy Text. Additionally, you can select several legacy text objects on your artboard and choose Type > Legacy Text > Update Selected Legacy Text. Both of these options perform the same function as choosing the Update option, but they apply to multiple legacy text objects at once.

If you do choose the Copy Text Object option so that you can see whether there is text reflow, remember that the copy of the legacy text that was created will still print. Once you have matched the new text to the legacy text, you must delete the legacy text copy either by removing it manually from the Layers panel or by choosing Type > Legacy Text > Delete Copies.

When opening files that were created in previous versions of Illustrator (what Illustrator refers to as *legacy* files), you might have to adjust text objects. To prevent you from accidentally overwriting your original files, Illustrator tacks on the word *[converted]* to your file name when it opens legacy files. You can disable this behavior in Illustrator's General Preferences, although we don't suggest it.

Saving Illustrator CS3 Files to Illustrator Legacy Versions

It's said that sticking your hand into a thornbush isn't painful because the thorns are shaped facing in toward the center of the bush. It's pulling your hand out of the thorn bush that causes the wound. With Illustrator, moving text from legacy versions to the CS versions is a straightforward transition. However, trying to move text from the CS versions of Illustrator so that it is compatible with legacy versions can be painful.

Based on a preference in your Document Setup dialog, either the text is broken up into individual Point Type objects (the default setting) or the text is converted to outlines. You can change this setting by choosing File > Document Setup, navigating to the Type panel, and choosing Preserve Text Editability or Preserve Text Appearance, respectively. In Chapter 13, *Saving and Exporting Files*, you will learn how to create files that are compatible with legacy versions of Illustrator.

Basically, you can't do much to avoid this issue. Some scripts (such as Rick Johnson's excellent Concat Text script, which you can find at http://rj-graffix.com/software/scripts.html) allow you to select broken-up text and combine it into a single string of editable text. Although these scripts will help, they certainly aren't a solution. If you're creating a file that must have editable text that you can use in a legacy version of Illustrator, you might consider creating your file in Illustrator CS3 but saving it in Illustrator 10 format and adding the text using version 10.

CHAPTER EIGHT
3D and Other Live Effects

So far, we've only scratched the surface with the kinds of effects Adobe Illustrator has to offer. Soft drop shadows (such as those we discussed in Chapter 3, *Objects, Groups, and Layers*) are certainly cool, but they are only a small sampling of Illustrator's live effects, which include 3D effects, warp distortions, and a wide range of pixel-based Adobe Photoshop effects. In fact, the 3D effects in Illustrator are quite significant, as you will see later in this chapter.

As you read this chapter, remember that you can apply live effects to fills and strokes individually, as well as to objects, groups, and layers. You apply all live effects via the Effect menu, and once applied, they appear in the Appearance panel and can be edited or deleted at any time. Additionally, you can apply multiple live effects to a single target.

It's also important to realize you can apply live effects to type without needing to convert to outlines. As you make changes to the text, the applied effect updates. This makes it easy to apply warp and 3D effects to text, and more important, it allows you to work with editable text.

COMBINING FEATURES AND EFFECTS

New features aren't added haphazardly in Illustrator. Rather, each new feature is carefully thought out in regard to how it might interact with other existing features in Illustrator. One of the most powerful tasks that you can do with live effects in Illustrator is apply several of them to a single object or, even better, use effects in combination with other features, such as transparency and blends (**Figure 8.1**).

Figure 8.1 You don't have to be a high roller to see the benefits of combining features in Illustrator. This example uses the 3D effect with artwork mapping, transparency, and blends.

When using Illustrator, you should always be asking yourself "what if" questions. For example, you know that you can apply transparency to objects in Illustrator, so what if you applied transparency to a 3D effect? Would you be able to see through the 3D object? (We'll discuss how to do this later in the chapter.) Experimenting in Illustrator is a great way to discover new techniques and creative ideas. The worst that can happen is you get something that doesn't look that great; the Undo function serves nicely at this point.

The effects are listed in this chapter in the order in which they appear in Illustrator's Effect menu.

Throughout this chapter, we ask "what if" questions and explore the ways that live effects integrate with other Illustrator features. These questions are answered with advice on how to get the most out of Illustrator. More important, the "what if" scenarios will open your eyes to the power of Illustrator's live effects.

DECONSTRUCTING THE EFFECT MENU

The Effect menu is basically split into four main sections. At the very top are two settings: Apply Last Effect and Last Effect. The former allows you to duplicate the last effect you applied, including all its settings; the latter opens the dialog for the last effect you applied so you can choose different settings. The next section of the Effect menu is something called Document

Raster Effects Resolution, which we'll get to in a moment. The remaining two sections are Illustrator Effects and Photoshop Effects; each section contains a collection of effects in those two categories. For the most part, Illustrator effects are Illustrator-specific features, whereas Photoshop effects are a collection of filters taken from Photoshop (see "Featured Matchup: Illustrator Effects vs. Photoshop Effects" later in this chapter).

Is It Vector, or Is It Raster?

You already know that a live effect is simply an appearance that is added to an object, meaning the underlying vector object exists in your document in its original state. As you change the underlying object, the appearance updates to reflect that change. If you want to lock in an appearance, you need to choose Object > Expand Appearance to alter the actual vector paths, at which point the effect is no longer live and can't be edited.

Some effects, such as Drop Shadow, are raster-based. Even though this effect appears grouped in the Illustrator Effects section, when the appearance is expanded, the drop shadow becomes a raster image (**Figure 8.2**). The same applies when you print a file, because all effects are expanded when they are sent to the printer (your file remains in an unexpanded state, however, allowing further editing).

Refer to Chapter 12, *Prepress and Printing*, for more information on what happens when you print Illustrator files.

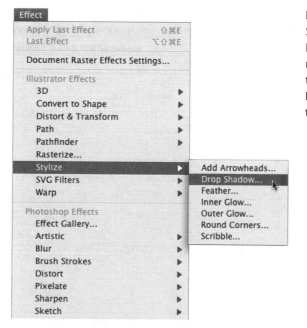

Figure 8.2 Many of the Stylize effects, including Drop Shadow, produce raster-based results, even though they are listed in the Illustrator Effects section of the Effect menu.

The following is a list of features that appear in the Illustrator Effects section of the Effect menu; these produce raster images when output or expanded:

- 3D Extrude & Bevel and 3D Revolve, when raster images or gradients are present in mapped artwork (see "Specifying Mapped Artwork" later in this chapter)

- Rasterize

- Stylize > Drop Shadow

- Stylize > Feather

- Stylize > Inner Glow

- Stylize > Outer Glow

Each of these is covered in detail later in this chapter.

Massaging Pixels in Illustrator

When you choose to save a file as EPS, all effects are expanded, and any raster-based effects are rasterized. This means Illustrator EPS files can contain raster content and can't be scaled infinitely when placed in other applications. See Chapter 13, *Saving and Exporting Files,* for information.

If it is true that some effects in Illustrator produce a rasterized result, who determines the resolution of those rasters? When you work in Photoshop, you can't even create a new file without first defining its resolution. But with Illustrator, which is vector-based, you don't think much about resolution. So the question is, what determines the resolution of these raster-based effects? To find the answer, choose Effect > Document Raster Effects Settings.

The Document Raster Effects Settings dialog is where you can specify the resolution for raster-based effects. In fact, the dialog offers all the necessary settings for determining how raster-based effects eventually print (**Figure 8.3**).

- **Color Model.** Depending on the document's Color Model setting to which your file is set, you'll either see CMYK, Grayscale, and Bitmap listed here or see RGB, Grayscale, and Bitmap. This is because a document cannot contain both CMYK and RGB elements. This setting can be extremely useful, because it allows you to change the color model of an object (even an image) as a live effect, which can always be edited. For example, you can turn a colored object into grayscale as an effect.

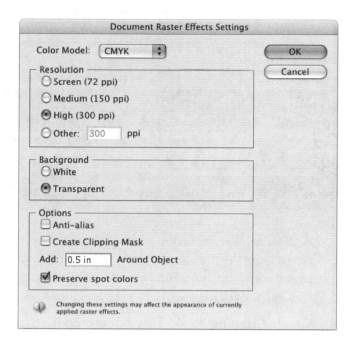

Figure 8.3 When using live effects, choosing the right settings in the Document Raster Effects Settings dialog is key to achieving the best results from your files.

- **Resolution.** This setting determines the resolution at which raster-based effects (both the Illustrator effects mentioned earlier and the Photoshop effects) are rendered. You can also specify this resolution setting in the Raster Effects pop-up menu (under Advanced) when you create a document using a new document profile. Illustrator's default resolution setting is 300 ppi for print documents and 72 ppi for Web, mobile, and video documents. The Resolution setting has a direct bearing on the performance of Illustrator, and just as in Photoshop, working at higher resolutions means more number crunching for your computer and more time for you to stare at your screen watching the progress bars slowly creep along. This is an extremely important setting and should not be overlooked. See the sidebar "Featured Matchup: Illustrator Effects vs. Photoshop Effects" later in this chapter for details on whether you need to change this setting before or after you create your file.

- **Background.** You can choose whether the resulting raster has a transparent background or a white background. If your effect overlaps other objects, you probably want to use the Transparent setting

(**Figure 8.4**), although remember that the file still needs to be flattened (see Chapter 12, *Prepress and Printing*, for more information on transparency flattening).

Figure 8.4 In this example, the artwork on the left used the White Background setting, whereas the artwork on the right used the Transparent Background setting.

- **Anti-alias.** You can define whether the raster image is antialiased. Antialiasing slightly blurs color boundaries to avoid the appearance of jagged edges. For more information on antialiasing, refer to Chapter 11, *Web and Mobile Design*.

- **Create Clipping Mask.** This setting creates a clipping mask around the area of a shape so you can have it blend into a background (raster images are always rectangular and may block out objects that appear behind them). This setting won't work well for objects that have Drop Shadow, Feather, or Glow effects applied, because clipping masks have hard edges. You don't need this setting if you specify the Transparent option for the background.

- **Add Space Around Object.** This is a very important setting. When certain effects, such as Feather or Gaussian Blur, are applied, the resulting raster image has a soft edge. To ensure that this soft edge fades into the background correctly, you must make the bounding box of the raster image larger than the actual object. If you don't, the fade stops abruptly, and you see a visible line where it ends. By default, Illustrator adds 36 points (.5 inch) of space around an object, but if you have a large blur setting, you may need to increase this amount (**Figure 8.5**).

- **Preserve spot colors.** If your artwork contains spot colors and you want to prevent those from being converted to process colors, this setting instructs Illustrator to preserve those spot colors, employing overprinting where necessary. Refer to Chapter 12, *Prepress and Printing*, for more information on overprinting.

Figure 8.5. On the left is a circle with a 60-pixel Gaussian Blur effect applied. With the default Add .5 in Around Object setting, the blur is visibly clipped. On the right, that same blur appears correctly with the Add *Space* Around Object setting increased to 1.5 inches.

Any live effects you apply in your document will use the settings in the Document Raster Effects Settings dialog, and you can't have different settings for different effects. Well, you can, sort of—just not in any way that Adobe intended, though. All live effects update when you make a change in the Document Raster Effects Settings dialog, but once you expand a live effect, that object no longer updates when you change the settings. So if you need to use different settings for different objects, then apply an effect to one object, use the Object > Expand Appearance function to expand the effect, lock in the document raster effects settings for that effect, and finally apply a different setting to another object. Of course, once you expand an effect, you have no way to go back and perform edits to it.

3D: ENTERING A WHOLE NEW WORLD

Few features in Illustrator are as fun to use as the 3D effect. You might want to clear your calendar for a few days so you have time to explore all the cool functionality you're about to discover.

However, before you tie a bungee cord to your ankles and jump into the spectacular world of 3D, it's important to realize just what the 3D effect in Illustrator is capable of and what its limitations are. In this way, you'll get a better idea of what you can realistically expect from the 3D effect:

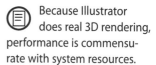 Because Illustrator does real 3D rendering, performance is commensurate with system resources.

- **The 3D effect in Illustrator is real 3D.** Unlike 3D plugins or other vector-based applications that have 3D features (such as Macromedia FreeHand or CorelDRAW), the 3D effect in Illustrator isn't some cheesy feature. Rather, Illustrator does real 3D rendering in a true 3D environment. Although the artwork that appears on the artboard is 2D, within the Effect dialog, the artwork exists in a 3D space where you can rotate and view it from any angle (**Figure 8.6**).

Figure 8.6 Once you've applied a 3D effect to a shape, you can choose to view it from any angle.

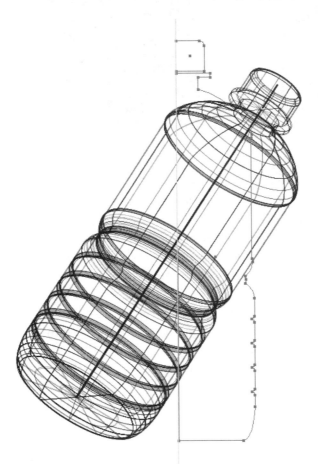

- **The 3D effect in Illustrator is vector-based.** Illustrator applies 3D effects to vector objects, and the result is a vector object. Lighting and shading take place through the use of blends (more detail on this later). Illustrator does not use ray tracing—a pixel-based rendering technique that can create shading and lighting with reflections and refractions.

- **The 3D effect in Illustrator supports artwork mapping.** Illustrator's 3D effect has the ability to map 2D artwork onto the surface of 3D objects. Artwork that will be mapped onto a 3D surface must first be defined as an Illustrator symbol.

- **The 3D effect in Illustrator is self-contained.** Because 3D in Illustrator is an effect, it applies to particular objects you have selected. Each object is treated as a separate entity and lives in its own individual 3D world. This means separate 3D objects cannot interact with or intersect each other (for example, a rod that pierces a sphere). Additionally, each object maintains its own vanishing point. This limitation makes it difficult to create 3D compositions in which multiple objects share the same vanishing point (although using groups can make a difference).

- **The 3D effect in Illustrator is proprietary.** The 3D effect is an internal feature and is applicable only within the Illustrator application. You cannot export 3D geometry from Illustrator (although you can export the 2D representation of that artwork), and you cannot import 3D geometry from CAD or 3D modeling applications (such as Maya or Strata). This also means the 3D support in Photoshop CS3 Extended doesn't work with 3D art made from Illustrator.

- **The 3D effect in Illustrator is a live effect.** As a live effect, the 3D features in Illustrator abide by the same rules as other effects. This means you can apply 3D effects to groups (which is important, as you'll see later), you can save them as graphic styles, you can edit them easily, and you can expand them.

Many different uses come to mind when we think about using the 3D effect in Illustrator. Drawing boxes and bottles for product packaging concepts and mock-ups, as well as text headlines or logos with added dimension, are some examples. However, as you will see, the 3D effect in Illustrator can also serve in an extremely creative fashion. As you explore the different capabilities of the 3D effects, try to envision how you might use them to create illustrations or design elements. We will help by offering examples along the way, providing a spark for your creativity.

Looking Inside the 3D Effect

The 3D feature in Illustrator is extremely deep and comprises four components, each serving a different purpose:

- **Extrude & Bevel.** The Extrude effect adds dimension to an object by extending it and giving it depth. Although 2D objects have an X axis and a Y axis, an extruded object also adds a Z axis. A simple example is a square with just one side (front) that becomes a cube (**Figure 8.7**) with six sides (front, back, top, bottom, left, and right). A *bevel* is a chiseled effect you can add to the surface of an extruded object (**Figure 8.8**).

Figure 8.7 When you start with a regular square (left), adding an Extrude effect results in a six-sided cube (right).

Figure 8.8 Bevels can add a chiseled appearance to an extruded object.

- **Revolve.** The Revolve effect adds dimension to an object by defining an axis and then revolving the shape around that axis. A simple example is a rectangle with just one side (front) that becomes a cylinder (**Figure 8.9**) with three surfaces (side, top, and bottom).

Figure 8.9 When you start with a regular rectangle (left), adding a Revolve effect results in a three-sided cylinder (right).

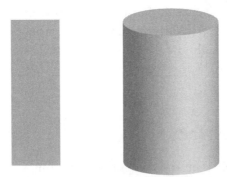

- **Rotate.** The Rotate effect doesn't add dimension at all but simply allows you to rotate your object in 3D space (basically an extrude without the depth added). This allows you to apply perspective to an object using a 3D reference (**Figure 8.10**).

Figure 8.10 When you start with a regular square (left), adding a Rotate effect results in a shape that appears to have the perspective of 3D (right).

- **Artwork Mapping.** Artwork mapping is a feature used to render 2D artwork onto the surface of a 3D object (**Figure 8.11**).

Figure 8.11 Once you've created regular artwork (left), you can map it onto the surface of a 3D object (right).

Naturally, each of these four components is a full-blown feature and requires its own detailed instructions. However, before we get to that, you need to learn some general information about how the 3D effect in Illustrator works.

Illustrator allows artwork mapping only on objects with the 3D Extrude & Bevel or 3D Revolve effect applied. The 3D Rotate effect does not support artwork mapping.

Fills and Strokes and the 3D Effect

To harness the depth of the 3D effect in Illustrator, you have to learn what makes the effect tick. The way in which you create and edit your vector shape has an effect on how the 3D settings are applied to that shape. For example, take two identical shapes: One has a stroke applied, and the second has the stroke set to None (**Figure 8.12**). When the same 3D Extrude effect is applied to both objects, each assumes a different appearance (**Figure 8.13**).

Figure 8.12 These shapes are identical with the exception of the 1-point stroke applied to the one on the left.

Figure 8.13 The extruded area of the shape on the left takes on the appearance of the object's stroke attribute, whereas the shape on the right uses the appearance of the fill.

Here's what happens: right before Illustrator applies 3D to an object, the effect breaks apart the elements internally and applies the 3D effect to each of the elements. When you have an object that has just a fill applied, the fill itself is extruded, and the extruded areas are shaded in the same color as the fill. However, if a stroke is applied to the object as well, Illustrator extrudes the fill and the stroke, and the appearance of the extruded areas shows the stroke color, not the fill color.

In fact, when you have a stroke applied, Illustrator is really extruding two separate objects—the fill and the stroke around it (**Figure 8.14**). If you change the Fill setting to None, you'll be able to see right through the middle of the object, because then Illustrator is extruding only a stroke, not a fill (**Figure 8.15**).

There's another side effect to applying a 3D effect to an object with a stroke applied that pertains to artwork mapping. You already know that artwork mapping allows you to apply 2D art to the surface of any 3D object. We'll discuss exactly how artwork mapping is applied later in the chapter, but one of the main tasks you'll need to do with artwork mapping is choose on which surface of a 3D object you want your mapped artwork to appear (you can apply artwork to multiple surfaces, as you will learn later).

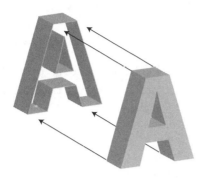

Figure 8.14 When an object with a fill and a stroke is extruded, you can think of the stroke as a slipcase for the fill.

Figure 8.15 When no fill is present, Illustrator extrudes only the stroke, resulting in a hollow shape.

When you apply an Extrude effect to a rectangle with just a fill, the result is a 3D object that has six surfaces. However, if you apply a stroke to that rectangle, the result is a 3D object with 24 surfaces. This is because Illustrator counts all the surfaces generated by the fill as well as those generated by the stroke (the surfaces that appear along the inside of the stroke, even though they are not visible, are still counted as surfaces). Because of this, it can be difficult to choose from the numerous surfaces to figure out which one you want the artwork mapped onto.

Of course, sometimes you will want to apply a stroke to an object with a 3D effect, such as with extruded text. By adding a stroke to your text object, you can create text that is filled with one color but that is extruded using a different color (**Figure 8.16**). Chances are you won't be mapping artwork onto your text, so this example is a good use of a stroke on a 3D object.

Figure 8.16 When extruding text, adding a stroke allows you to create a powerful contrast to the extruded effect.

In review, feel free to use strokes on your objects if you need them to achieve the look you want. However, be aware that adding strokes slows performance and makes artwork mapping a confusing process because of all the extra surfaces.

Editing a 3D Effect

Because 3D is a live effect in Illustrator, you can make edits to the original vector shape on the artboard, and the 3D effect updates accordingly. You can also change the color of the object, and the 3D effect automatically updates as well, including the shading of the object.

You know that you can double-click an effect listed in the Appearance panel to edit 3D effects that have already been applied to artwork. However, it's important to remember that the artwork that appears on your artboard after you've applied a 3D effect is 2D. If you want to rotate a 3D object, don't do it on the artboard using the usual transformation tools. Rather, double-click the 3D effect in the Appearance panel, and rotate the object in the 3D Options dialog. Changing the artwork on the artboard produces undesirable results (**Figure 8.17**). For more information on transforming artwork that has live effects applied, see the sidebar "Transforming Objects with Effects" later in this chapter.

Figure 8.17 What started as a water bottle (left) may not appear the same when you rotate it on the artboard (right). To rotate the bottle in 3D, you have to edit the 3D effect.

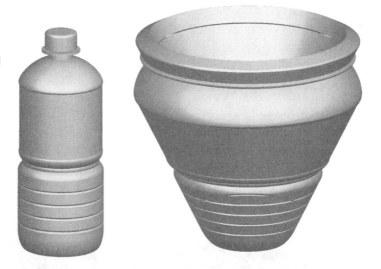

Applying the 3D Extrude & Bevel Effect

Now that you generally understand how the 3D effect works in Illustrator, you will learn how to apply the effect, determine all its settings, and, perhaps most important, study a few practical examples of how you might use such an effect.

As we defined earlier, the Extrude & Bevel effect adds depth to an object. To apply this effect, select a vector object on the artboard, and choose Effect > 3D > Extrude & Bevel to open the 3D Extrude & Bevel Options dialog. First, select the Preview box in the dialog so you can see what the 3D effect looks like as you adjust the settings. If you don't have a large screen, it helps to position your artwork on one side of the screen before you apply the effect and to move the 3D Extrude & Bevel Options dialog (when it opens) to the other side so you can see the preview on the artboard (**Figure 8.18**).

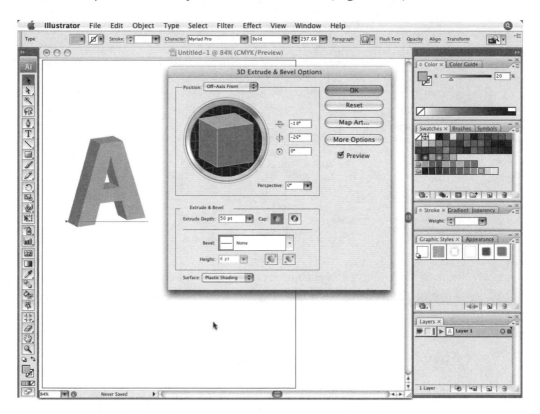

Figure 8.18 Especially on smaller screens, it helps to keep your art positioned on the left side of the screen so you have room to preview the art while you make adjustments in the 3D Extrude & Bevel Options dialog.

At this point, you are ready to begin experimenting with the settings in the dialog. To make the feature more approachable, Adobe splits the dialog into two parts. By default, only half the settings appear in the dialog. By clicking the More Options button, you can expand the dialog to show all the settings we will be talking about here (**Figure 8.19** on the following page).

You'll always have to select the Preview box when you open the dialog. Adobe chose this behavior for performance reasons.

Figure 8.19 By clicking the More Options button, you can expand the 3D Extrude & Bevel Options dialog to see all the available settings.

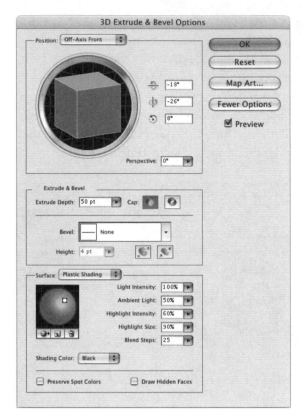

The 3D Extrude & Bevel Options dialog is divided into three sections—Position, Extrude & Bevel, and Surface—each covering a different aspect of 3D.

Specifying the Position Settings

The Position section of the 3D Extrude & Bevel Options dialog allows you to rotate your object within 3D space (on its X, Y, and Z axes) in order to control the view of your object. In 3D applications, the term *camera* is used to define the view of the object (as if you were seeing the object through the lens of a camera; **Figure 8.20**).

The most distinctive element in the 3D Extrude & Bevel Options dialog is what Adobe engineers affectionately call the *track cube*—a visual representation of the position of your 3D object. The track cube acts much like a trackball, only it isn't round (and hence it's called the track *cube*). To adjust the position of your 3D object, simply click and drag the track cube. As you

Most 3D applications allow you change the position of the objects and the camera in a scene. Because each 3D effect lives within its own 3D world, Illustrator's camera is always stationary, and you are adjusting the position of the object only.

adjust the position, a wireframe preview appears on your screen, indicating how the object will appear (**Figure 8.21**). When you release the mouse, a full preview, with shading, appears.

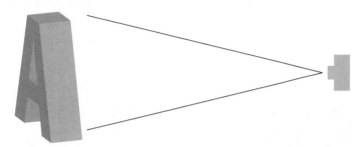

Figure 8.20 The Position setting allows you to rotate the view of an object, as if you were looking at the object through the lens of a camera.

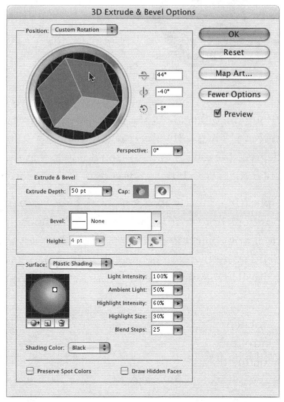

Figure 8.21 As you adjust the track cube, a wireframe preview shows you what your art will look like.

The track cube is more than just fun to play with—it also has some pretty cool functionality. The sides of the cube are shaded in different colors to help you easily identify the position of your object: The front side is blue, the back is a dark gray, the top and bottom are light gray, and the left and right sides are a neutral gray.

Illustrator utilizes a track cube instead of a trackball because It Is difficult to differentiate between the multiple sides (front, back, and so on) of the 3D object using a sphere as a reference.

While the 3D Extrude & Bevel Options dialog is open, press the Option (Alt) key, and the Cancel button turns into a Reset button. Clicking the Reset button resets the values in the dialog so you can start fresh.

In addition, as you move your pointer over the edges of each side, you'll notice the edges highlight in red, green, and blue (**Figure 8.22**). Clicking and dragging these highlighted edges constrains the object to rotate along only one axis, making it easier to control the position of your object. Holding the Shift key while dragging the track cube simulates a rotation of the floor beneath the object, and dragging the outer ring of the track cube constrains the rotation in the other direction.

Figure 8.22 Moving your pointer over the edges of the track cube allows you to adjust one axis at a time.

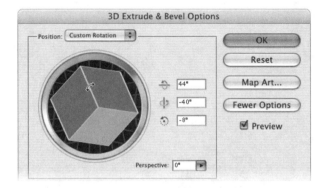

Along the right side of the track cube are three values representing the three axes that a 3D object needs. Each axis can have a value of –180 to 180 degrees (for a total of 360). You'll notice that the highlighted, colored track cube edges match the color shown for the icon in each of these three axes.

Appearing directly above the track cube is a pop-up menu that lists preset positions from which you can choose. Choosing one of these presets positions your object in a variety of different views. Unfortunately, you cannot define your own presets here, but these presets can make it easy to apply consistent views throughout your artwork (**Figure 8.23**).

Figure 8.23 Choosing one of Illustrator's preset position settings can make it easy to position several objects with the same view, such as when you are creating isometric art.

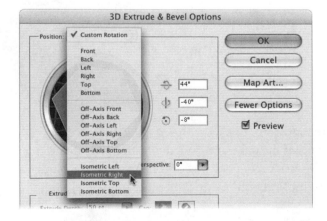

Last, you can add perspective to your object by dragging the Perspective slider. This setting mimics the natural lens distortion that occurs if you move your object closer to the lens of the camera (**Figure 8.24**). If you hold the Shift key while adjusting the slider, you will see your preview update in real time (system performance permitting). Using the Shift key to generate real-time previews actually works when using any slider in the 3D dialog.

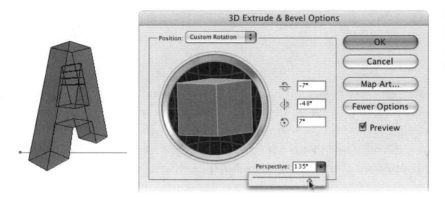

Figure 8.24 Adjusting the Perspective slider can add natural distortion to your object.

You will notice that as you increase the Perspective value, your 3D object becomes darker. Think about it: As you move an object closer to the lens of a camera, less light is available to reflect off the object, and the object becomes darker. Soon we'll talk about surface and lighting options, which you can use to adjust the lighting of the object.

Specifying the Extrude & Bevel Settings

The Extrude & Bevel section of the 3D Extrude & Bevel Options dialog allows you to define the depth of your object as well as how the edges of your 3D object appear, also known as the *bevel*.

To adjust the depth of your object, enter a numeric value, click and drag the Extrude Depth slider, or enter a value in the field. If you hold the Shift key while adjusting the slider, you can preview the Extrude Depth setting in real time. The values used for the Extrude Depth settings are shown in points, although you can specify values in inches or any other format, and Illustrator will do the conversion for you. You can specify an extrude depth up to 2,000 points (a tad more than 27.75 inches). Speaking of measurements, when you're trying to create package mock-ups, it's always a good idea to work at actual size or in scale to ensure that your 3D object is proportioned correctly.

By default, Illustrator creates closed extruded objects from filled paths. However, you can also specify the extrude setting you want to use so it shows only the extrusion and not the actual face or back of the shape. Toggling between the two Cap settings allows you to control whether your objects have a solid or hollow appearance (**Figure 8.25**).

Figure 8.25 The Cap setting appears as two icons. The shaded icon indicates the selected setting.

When you extrude an object, you can almost think of copying your object, offsetting the copy from the original, and then connecting the two with straight lines (**Figure 8.26**). A bevel is defined when you connect the two shapes with a line that is not straight, and therefore, the extrusion follows the direction of the line (**Figure 8.27**).

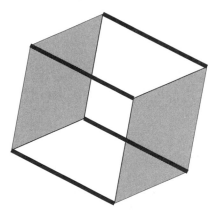 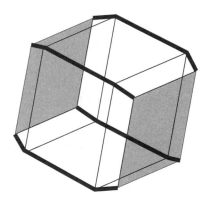

Figure 8.26 A normal extrude is created by connecting the front and back faces of an object with a straight line.

Figure 8.27 An extrude with a bevel is created by connecting the front and back faces of an object with a line that is not straight.

Illustrator provides ten bevels, which you can choose from the Bevel pop-up menu (see the sidebar "Defining Your Own Bevels"). The Height setting controls the size of the bevel. You can also choose whether you want the bevel to be subtracted from the size of the original shape or whether you want it added to the shape (**Figure 8.28**).

Figure 8.28 Toggling between the Bevel Extent In and Bevel Extent Out options can affect the overall size of your object.

When you specify a bevel, sometimes you might see rendering errors caused by self-intersecting paths. You can usually alleviate the problem by specifying a smaller bevel size, using a less complex bevel, or adjusting the position or perspective settings.

Defining Your Own Bevels

Illustrator ships with a collection of ten bevel shapes—some simple and straightforward, others more complex. However, you may find you want to create your own bevel shapes. The good news is that you can create just about any bevel you can dream up. The not-so-good news is that it takes a few steps to create a custom bevel, and you'll need to quit and restart Illustrator before you can use your bevel.

Bevels are actually regular open-ended paths defined as symbols. These symbols live in a file called Bevels.ai, which you will find in your Illustrator Plug-ins folder. Simply open the file, and follow the directions that appear on the artboard of the file (the directions are clear and straightforward).

Be careful not to delete any of the existing bevels in the file, or you'll lose them forever. It might be a good idea to create a backup of your Bevels.ai file before you modify it on your own. If the file is locked, you may need administrator rights to edit it.

Specifying the Surface Settings

The first two settings, Position and Extrude & Bevel, define the actual geometry of the shape. The Surface section of the 3D Extrude & Bevel Options dialog enables you to control the appearance of the surface of your object. This includes the type of shading used, and it indicates how light will interact with the object. If you talk to a photographer, he will tell you that, above all, lighting is of utmost importance. As you'll find out, the same is true with 3D.

You may have noticed that when you first selected the Preview box to see what your 3D effect looks like on the artboard, the object changed somewhat in color. For example, if your original object was filled with a bright yellow color, the object might now show a darker, muddy yellow color instead. By default, 3D objects in Illustrator are rendered with a single light source from the upper right and are shaded by adding black to the original fill color, giving that darker appearance.

Using the Surface pop-up menu, you can choose from one of four options to specify the type of surface you want your 3D object to have. The surface type you choose also defines what other surface settings are available for your object and ultimately how you see the final 3D object (**Figure 8.29**). The four surface settings are as follows:

Figure 8.29 From left to right, this art demonstrates examples of Plastic Shading, Diffuse Shading, No Shading, and Wireframe.

- **Plastic Shading.** You use the Plastic Shading setting when you want your object to have a highly reflective surface, such as like glass or metal. This shading option enables you to adjust and control a lighting highlight on the object.

- **Diffuse Shading.** You use the Diffuse Shading setting when you want your object to have a matte surface, such as like paper or wood. This shading option does not have a highlight setting.

- **No Shading.** The No Shading option disables shading completely and renders each side of your object using the solid color defined for the object. Granted, this option doesn't leave your object with a 3D appearance, but if your intent is to expand the 3D effect so that you can edit the geometry of the shape, this setting could be helpful.

- **Wireframe.** The Wireframe surface setting removes all filled areas, or *walls*, from your object and displays the object's 3D wireframes. The result is technical and rather cool, and it is useful for creating design elements. The rules that make up the wireframe are set to .25 point in width and cannot be changed without first expanding the 3D effect.

On the left side of the Surface section of the dialog is a lighting sphere, which is used to control how light is directed at your 3D object. A small white circle indicates the light source, and you can drag it to control the direction of the light (**Figure 8.30**). As you move the light source, you can hold the Shift key to see the shading preview in real time. To add lights (you can add up to 30 of them), click the New Light icon that appears directly beneath the sphere, and to delete a selected light, click the Delete Light icon. You can also send lights behind an object by clicking the Move Selected Light to Back of Object icon.

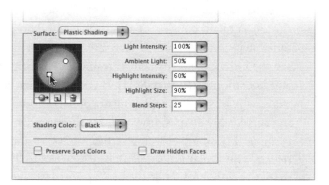

Figure 8.30 You can drag lights across the sphere to adjust the shading of the 3D object.

To the right of the lighting sphere are five settings that define how the surface and the lighting interact with each other. Depending on the surface option you select, you may see all or only some of these options:

- **Light Intensity.** The Light Intensity setting controls the strength, or brightness, of the selected light. Think of this setting as a dimmer switch—the closer the value is to 100, the brighter the light; the closer the value is to 0, the dimmer the light. You can use this setting to apply different intensity values for each selected light.

- **Ambient Light.** The Ambient Light setting is a general lighting setting that affects the entire surface of the object. By default, this is set to 50%, which is a neutral setting. Think of this setting as a global lightness/darkness setting for the object itself, not for the individual lights.

- **Highlight Intensity.** The Highlight Intensity setting controls the contrast or transition between the surface and the highlight. Higher values produce sharper highlights, indicating a more reflective surface, like glass. This highlight setting is applied globally to all highlights on the object (you can't set this differently for different lights). This setting is available only when you choose the Plastic Shading option.

- **Highlight Size.** The Highlight Size setting controls the size of the highlights on a 3D object. This highlight setting is applied globally to all highlights on the object (you can't set this differently for different lights). This setting is available only when you choose the Plastic Shading option.

- **Blend Steps.** The Blend Steps setting is an extremely important setting, and therefore, it's difficult to understand why it appears listed at the bottom of the dialog, grouped with other lighting settings and seemingly hidden. Illustrator uses blends to create shading, not gradients (blends are covered in depth in Chapter 10, *Graphs, Distortions, and Blends*). A blend consists of a start object and an end object, with multiple "steps" in between. If there are too few steps in a blend, you can see the individual steps, which results in shading that appears posterized and not smooth (**Figure 8.31**). By default, Illustrator specifies 25 blend steps, which is fine for viewing art on a computer screen or for printing smaller 3D shapes; however, for the best results in a high-resolution print workflow, a blend step setting of 200 or more is necessary. The reason why Illustrator's default setting is set to 25 is strictly for performance reasons. A higher Blend Steps setting results in much slower 3D performance, so it's a good idea to work with the default setting and then increase it right before you send your final file to the printer.

Figure 8.31 Without enough steps in a blend, you can see "stair-stepping" side effects (referred to as *banding*) rather than a smooth transition of color.

Illustrator also offers a pop-up menu from which you can choose a shading color. By default, Illustrator adds black to your object to simulate shading; however, you can choose Other and pick any color from the color picker or from existing swatches in your document to use as a shading color instead. If you use colors other than black for shading, the result will be as if you were casting a colored light on your object.

Using Spot Colors in 3D Objects

If your object is filled with a spot color and if you use black or a spot color as your shade color, choosing the Preserve Spot Colors option causes the overprint function to be utilized when you're creating blends for shading. The result is an object that prints and separates correctly using the spot colors. You may have to view your file with Overprint Preview turned on if you want to preview the art correctly on your screen.

Illustrator and 3D Geometry

Although it's true that the 3D feature in Illustrator is doing real 3D rendering in a 3D world, that's true only while a 3D effect dialog is open on your screen. Once you click OK, Illustrator creates a 2D representation of that graphic and displays it on your artboard (Illustrator's artboard is only 2D). If you want to view your object differently, you can always edit the effect by double-clicking it in the Appearance panel, at which time the dialog opens. At this point, you're in the 3D world again, where you can rotate the object in space and then click OK to create the 2D representation that is displayed on the artboard.

Because Illustrator knows that the end result will be a 2D drawing, it saves processing time by calculating and drawing only the visible sides of an object. For example, if you were to create a rectangle and extrude it to create a cube, at any one time you would be able to view only three of the six surfaces. You can see this for yourself by following a few quick steps to expand the appearance of a 3D object:

1. Using the Rectangle tool, draw a 2-inch square.

2. Give the square a fill of 25K and a stroke of None.

3. Choose Effect > 3D > Extrude & Bevel.

If you want to use gradients to do your own shading (which decreases file size when you're exporting art to Flash), choose the No Shading option, expand the appearance of the object, and then manually fill the shapes with gradients.

4. Leave the position set to Off-Axis Front, set the Extrude Depth to 2 inches, and click OK to apply the effect.

5. Choose Object > Expand Appearance to expand the 3D effect.

6. Deselect the object so nothing is selected.

7. Switch to the Direct Selection tool, and move each panel of the cube. You'll see that only the visible surfaces of the cube are there (**Figure 8.32**).

Figure 8.32 A regular square (left), with an Extrude effect applied (center), and then expanded, and then with the front face removed (right).

Sometimes, however, you might want the full geometry of the 3D object rendered. For example, if you wanted to expand the cube you created to modify the 3D object on your own, you might want all the surfaces to be available. For this reason, Illustrator includes the Draw Hidden Faces option, which forces Illustrator to render the entire object, even the surfaces that aren't visible. Again, you can easily see the difference by following a few short steps using the Draw Hidden Faces option:

1. Using the Rectangle tool, draw a 2-inch square.

2. Give the square a fill of 25K and a stroke of None.

3. Choose Effect > 3D > Extrude & Bevel.

4. Leave Position set to Off-Axis Front, and set Extrude Depth to 2 inches.

5. Click the More Options button in the 3D Extrude & Bevel Options dialog, and select the Draw Hidden Faces box.

6. Click OK to apply the 3D effect.

7. Choose Object > Expand Appearance to expand the 3D effect.

8. Deselect the object so nothing is selected.

9. Switch to the Direct Selection tool, and move each panel of the cube. You'll see that all the surfaces of the cube are there, even those hidden from view (**Figure 8.33**).

 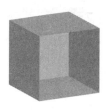

Figure 8.33 A regular square (left), a regular square with an Extrude effect applied with Draw Hidden Faces turned on (center), and then expanded, and with the front face removed (right).

As you learn more about the 3D effect, you'll find the Draw Hidden Faces option has other uses as well.

Creating a Photorealistic Button

Now that you've learned the different settings for the 3D Extrude & Bevel effect, it's time to put that knowledge to good use. In this exercise, you will create a realistic button (the kind you would find sewn to a shirt), but don't worry—you don't need to know how to draw. Illustrator's 3D effect allows you to create this button easily by drawing simple shapes.

1. Using the Ellipse tool, create a .25-inch circle.

2. Give the circle a fill of 25K and a stroke of None.

3. With the circle selected, double-click the Selection tool in the Toolbox to open the Move dialog.

4. Specify a Horizontal value of .375 inch and a Vertical value of 0, and click the Copy button. This gives you two buttons.

5. Now, select both circles, and double-click the Selection tool to open the Move dialog again.

6. This time, specify a Horizontal value of 0 and a Vertical value of .375 inch, and click the Copy button. You now have four circles (**Figure 8.34**).

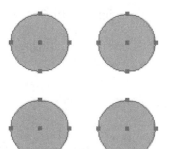

Figure 8.34 Once you've created the duplicates, you should see four stacked circles.

7. Select all four circles, and click the Add to Shape Area button in the Pathfinder panel. This combines the four circles into a single compound shape.

8. Using the Ellipse tool, create a 2-inch circle.

9. Give the circle a fill of 25K and a stroke of None.

10. With the circle selected, choose Object > Arrange > Send to Back.

11. Using the Selection tool, select all five circles, and open the Align panel.

12. Click the Horizontal Align Center button once and the Vertical Align Center button once. Because you combined the four smaller circles with the Add to Shape Area function, they are centered nicely within the larger circle (**Figure 8.35**).

13. With all five circles still selected, open the Pathfinder panel, and click the Subtract from Shape Area button. This "cuts" the smaller circles out from the larger one, allowing you to see through the button. This action also combines all five circles into a single object, allowing you to apply a single 3D effect to all the circles at once (**Figure 8.36**).

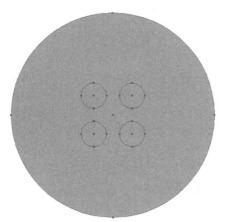

Figure 8.35 All the circles, centered, now make up the shape of a button.

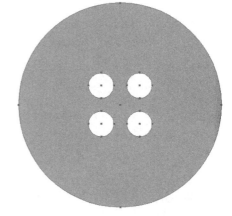

Figure 8.36 Once you've subtracted the smaller circles from the larger one, you're left with the art that you will use to create a button.

14. With the button selected, choose Effect > 3D > Extrude & Bevel, and check the Preview box.

15. Set Extrude Depth to .25 inches, and set the bevel to Rounded.

16. Adjust the position to your liking, and click OK to apply the effect (**Figure 8.37**).

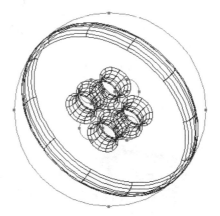

Figure 8.37 A wireframe preview allows you to position your 3D object with precision.

Because 3D is applied as a live effect, you can change the color of the button simply by applying a different fill color to the shape. Additionally, you can double-click the effect in the Appearance panel to edit the effect and change the position of the button so you can view it from virtually any angle (**Figure 8.38**). This is a great example of how you can use the 3D Extrude & Bevel effect in a creative way, allowing you to easily create design elements that might otherwise be difficult to draw.

Figure 8.38 Once you've created the button in 3D, you can change its position so you can view it from any angle.

Applying the 3D Revolve Effect

As we briefly discussed earlier, the Revolve effect adds dimension to an object by rotating a 2D shape around an axis. To apply this effect, select a vector object on the artboard, and choose Effect > 3D > Revolve to open the 3D Revolve Options dialog. First, check the Preview box in the dialog so you can see what the 3D effect looks like as you adjust the settings. If you don't have a large screen, it helps to position your artwork on one side of the screen before you apply the effect and to position the 3D Revolve

Options dialog, when it opens, to the other side so you can see the preview on the artboard.

At this point, you are ready to begin experimenting with the different settings in the dialog. As with the 3D Extrude & Bevel Options dialog, the 3D Revolve Options dialog has a More Options button, which expands the dialog to reveal all the settings for the feature (**Figure 8.39**).

Figure 8.39 Similar to the 3D Extrude & Bevel Options dialog, you can expand the 3D Revolve Options dialog to reveal more options.

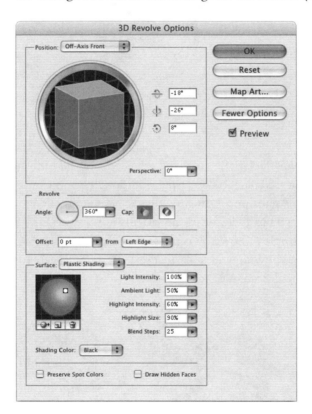

The fully expanded 3D Revolve Options dialog is divided into three sections: Position, Revolve, and Surface. The Position and Surface sections are identical to those in the 3D Extrude & Bevel Options dialog, so we will focus on just the Revolve section here.

Specifying the Revolve Settings

The Revolve section of the 3D Revolve Options dialog allows you to define exactly how your object will appear when revolved around an axis. Before we discuss the settings, it's important you first understand how the 3D

Revolve effect in Illustrator works. By default, the leftmost point of the selected object becomes a vertical axis for the effect. An object can have only one axis, and the axis is always vertical. Unfortunately, Illustrator doesn't preview or show you this axis onscreen, so think of it as an imaginary axis (**Figure 8.40**).

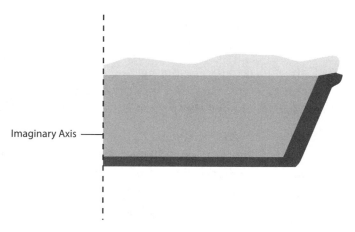

Imaginary Axis

Figure 8.40 By default, Illustrator's 3D Revolve effect uses the leftmost side of an object as the vertical axis.

Now that you understand how the 3D Revolve effect works, you can learn how to use the remaining settings in the Revolve section of the dialog:

• **Angle.** The Angle setting determines how far around the axis the artwork travels. By default, the angle is set to 360, which creates a shape that goes completely around the axis, resulting in a closed shape. Smaller values result in an object that seems to have a piece missing (**Figure 8.41**). You may find the Angle setting useful when you want to create a cutaway view to the inside of an object or when you want to display just a portion of an object, like a single slice of pie (**Figure 8.42** on the following page).

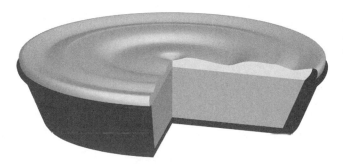

Figure 8.41 Using a large Angle setting can leave you with almost an entire pie ...

Figure 8.42 … or you can be left with just a small slice of pie with a small Angle setting.

- **Cap.** Similar to the Cap setting in the 3D Extrude & Bevel Options dialog, here you can toggle between objects that have either a solid appearance or a hollow appearance.

- **Offset.** The Offset setting is specific to the invisible axis. An Offset value repositions the axis and effectively allows you to revolve an object from a point other than its leftmost edge. The result is an object that is hollow (**Figure 8.43**). In addition, you can specify whether the axis is offset from the left or the right side of the object.

Figure 8.43 Adding an Offset value to the 3D pie results in a pie that resembles a Danish pastry with a hollow center.

Drawing a Sphere

Now that you've learned how the 3D Revolve effect works, you can learn how to create a simple object—a sphere (**Figure 8.44**).

Figure 8.44 From left to right: creating a circle, deleting an anchor point to create a semicircle, and applying a 3D Revolve effect to create a sphere.

1. Using the Ellipse tool, draw a 2-inch circle.

2. Give the circle a fill of 25K and a stroke of None.

3. Select the Direct Selection tool, and deselect the circle.

4. Then select just the left anchor point of the circle by clicking it once.

5. Once the anchor point is selected, press the Delete key on your keyboard to remove the selected anchor point and the paths connected to it. You will be left with half a circle.

6. With the semicircle selected, choose Effect > 3D > Revolve. The default settings are fine for this exercise.

7. Click OK to apply the effect.

The most important part of this exercise was deleting half the circle. As we mentioned earlier, the left side of the object is what defines the invisible axis on which the object revolves. If you were to apply a 3D Revolve effect to a full circle, the result would be quite different (**Figure 8.45**). In fact, applying the 3D Revolve effect with an offset value specified would produce a doughnut shape, which is nice but not what you intended (**Figure 8.46** on thc following page). Getting hungry?

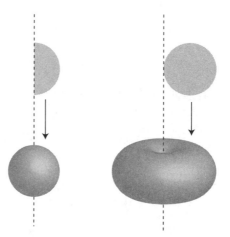

Figure 8.45 It's important to pay attention to where the vertical axis is. With a semicircle (left), the vertical axis is positioned to create a sphere. With a full circle (right), though, the vertical axis is positioned to create a doughnut shape.

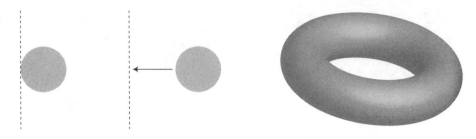

Figure 8.46 Starting with a full circle (left) and specifying an offset for the axis (center) results in a doughnut shape (right).

Drawing an Exercise Barbell

To get your mind off food for a while, here's a little mental exercise that uses the 3D Revolve effect and incorporates the use of groups—an extremely important aspect of creating complex 3D shapes (see sidebar "The Importance of Applying 3D Effects to Groups" later in this chapter). In this example, you will create a group of shapes that will result in a great-looking barbell. Again, you don't want to focus on drawing a barbell as much as trying to build the shapes that will eventually help Illustrator's 3D feature draw it for you (it's always preferable to let the computer do all the hard work while you relax and rack up the billable hours).

To create the barbell, perform the following steps:

1. Choose View > Show Rulers, and drag out a vertical guide (anywhere on your screen is fine).

    Although creating a guide isn't necessary, you will find that this vertical guide will help you visualize where the invisible axis will be. In addition, the guide will help you align the objects so they are all aligned to the same left edge.

    Remember when you used ordinary circles to create a button using the Extrude effect? Well, this time, you're going to use ordinary rectangles to create your barbell.

2. Use the Rectangle tool to create a rectangle with a width of .25 inches and a height of 3.25 inches.

3. Give the rectangle a fill of 60K and a stroke of None. This shape will be the handle for your barbell.

4. Position the rectangle so that its left edge touches the vertical guide you created in the previous step (**Figure 8.47**).

5. Create a second rectangle with a width of 1.25 inches and a height of .25 inches.

6. Give the rectangle a fill of 25K and a stroke of None. This shape will be one of the weights that appear on your barbell.

7. Choose the Selection tool, and select both rectangles.

8. Then, click the larger rectangle once, and open the Align panel.

9. Click the Horizontal Align Left button once and the Vertical Align Bottom button once.

10. Then select just the smaller rectangle, and double-click the Selection tool in the Toolbox to open the Move dialog.

11. Specify a value of 0 for Horizontal and .25 inch for Vertical, and click OK (**Figure 8.48**).

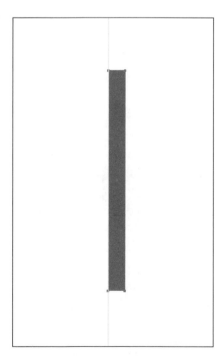

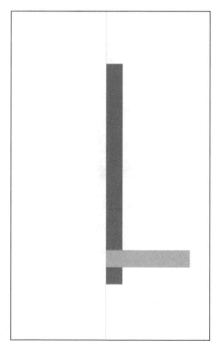

Figure 8.47 Aligning the rectangle to a guide will help you visualize where the vertical axis will be.

Figure 8.48 The first two rectangles are in position. Notice how they both are aligned to where the vertical axis will be.

12. Select the small rectangle, and double-click the Selection tool to open the Move dialog.

13. Specify a value of 0 for Horizontal and .375 inch for Vertical, and click the Copy button. You will now see two stacked rectangles. These will be the weights that appear on one side of the barbell.

14. To create the weights that will appear on the opposite side of the barbell, select both small rectangles, and open the Move dialog once again.

15. Enter a value of 0 for Horizontal and 2.125 inches for Vertical, and click the Copy button. You now have all the shapes necessary to create your 3D shape (**Figure 8.49**).

Figure 8.49 All the necessary shapes are now created and aligned correctly.

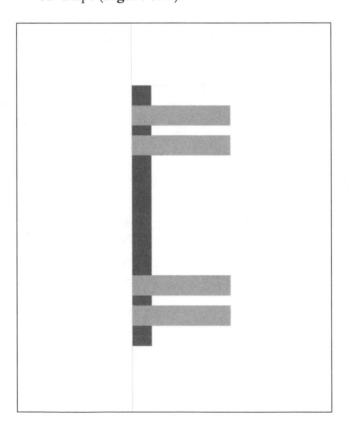

16. Use the Selection tool to select all the objects, and choose Object > Group. This will allow the 3D effect to treat all the objects as one unit so they all share a single vertical axis.

17. With the group selected, choose Effect > 3D > Revolve, and turn on the preview.

18. Edit the position of the object to your liking using the track cube, and then click OK to apply the effect (**Figure 8.50**).

Figure 8.50 Adding a Perspective setting can add a touch of realism to your barbell.

The most important part of this exercise is to try to visualize where the invisible axis is. When you think of a barbell, you may think of it as you normally see it—lying on the ground in a horizontal format. Because Illustrator's Revolve effect always uses a vertical axis, you had to think of the barbell as standing on its side. Once it's created, you can use the track cube to rotate it into any position or orientation you need.

The examples you've tried so far should help fuel your creativity and give you the information you need to create complex 3D objects on your own.

The Importance of Applying 3D Effects to Groups

When applying any 3D effect, it's important to understand its limitations so you can figure out how to make it do what you want. Previously in this chapter, we stated that Illustrator's 3D effects have two main limitations: 3D objects cannot intersect each other, and each 3D object lives in its own 3D world. Hence, each object maintains its own individual vanishing point or invisible axis. Basically, multiple objects in your document cannot share a single vanishing point, share the same perspective, or revolve around the same axis.

If you were paying attention in Chapter 3, *Objects, Groups, and Layers*, you remember that effects produce a different appearance when applied at the group or layer level instead of at the object level. Because 3D is a live effect, the same rules for how groups work apply here as well. If you apply a 3D effect at the group level, all objects inside that group can share the same vanishing point or perspective.

In the example of the barbell you just created, you were able to create a single axis that all the objects shared by grouping all the objects together before applying the 3D effect. Had you selected the objects in the file and applied the 3D Revolve effect without first creating a group, the result would be different and not what you would expect (**Figure 8.51**).

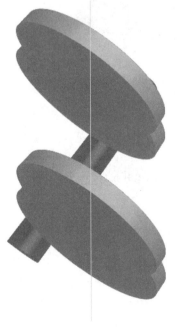

Figure 8.51 If you take the same barbell example but skip the step that collects all the shapes within a single group, the result is quite different.

Applying the 3D Rotate Effect

The Revolve effect doesn't add dimension to an object. Rather, the effect allows you to position a 2D object in a 3D space. Basically, the 3D Rotate effect does the same as the 3D Extrude effect without adding any depth. To apply this effect, select a vector object on the artboard, and choose Effect > 3D Rotate to open the 3D Rotate Options dialog. The settings for this 3D effect are identical to those we've already discussed, although take note that the 3D Rotate effect is limited to far fewer options (**Figure 8.52**). Most notably, you can specify only the Diffuse Shading or No Shading option, there are no bevels, and there is no support for artwork mapping (which we'll cover next).

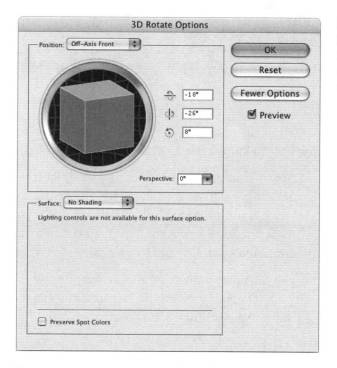

Figure 8.52 Although there is a More Options button in the 3D Rotate Options dialog, you'll find it doesn't really offer that much.

The 3D Rotate effect can be useful for applying distortion to artwork, such as making artwork look as if it's mounted on a billboard. It also enables you to add perspective to your artwork as well.

Mapping Artwork to 3D Surfaces

One of the features that really sets Illustrator's 3D effect apart from the 3D effects in other vector applications is the ability to map 2D artwork onto the surface of a 3D object. This method of combining 2D and 3D graphics is called *artwork mapping*.

So that you understand what artwork mapping really is, let's take a closer look at a 3D cube. As we discussed earlier in the chapter, a 3D cube has six surfaces. Each of these surfaces is treated as a separate entity, and artwork mapping is the process of placing artwork on these surfaces (**Figure 8.53**).

Figure 8.53 Starting with a normal square, a 3D Extrude effect produces a cube with six surfaces. When 2D artwork is placed onto these surfaces, the result is a 3D object with artwork mapping.

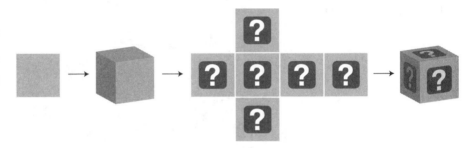

You have to know a few facts before you get started with artwork mapping:

- Artwork must first be defined as a symbol before it can be mapped to a 3D surface. This is actually pretty cool because as you modify a symbol, you will see it automatically update on any 3D surfaces. Refer to Chapter 5, *Brushes, Symbols, and Masks*, for detailed information on how to create and modify symbols.

- You can't map a single symbol across multiple surfaces of a 3D object. If your 3D object has multiple surfaces, you can map symbols to each side individually (**Figure 8.54**).

Figure 8.54 To create the appearance of artwork that wraps around multiple sides of an object, you have to create multiple symbols and map each section separately.

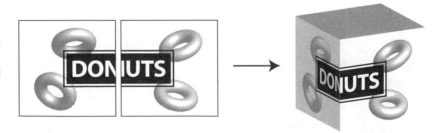

- When rendering a 3D object, Illustrator uses corner anchor points to define a new surface. Smooth anchor points will not define a new surface. When drawing your art, carefully specifying where corner or smooth anchor points appear on your path gives you greater control over how many surfaces are created and where they appear (**Figure 8.55**).

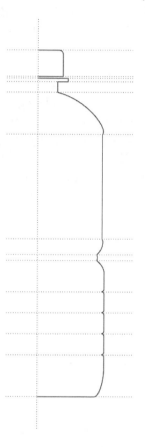

Figure 8.55 By using corner anchor points at certain points on the path of this profile of a water bottle, you can specify several surface areas to which you can map art.

- Stroked objects make things more complicated. As you learned earlier in the chapter, objects with fills and strokes applied result in an object that has many more surfaces, which makes it difficult to work with. When you're creating a 3D object that will have artwork mapped to it, it's best to avoid using stroked paths.

- Although the 3D effect in Illustrator produces vector results, sometimes the 3D effect has to rasterize mapped artwork. If your mapped artwork contains gradients or raster images (such as those placed from

Photoshop), Illustrator renders them at the resolution that is set in the Document Raster Effects Settings dialog. Even if your mapped art contains a high-resolution Photoshop file, Illustrator resamples it to match the resolution set in the Document Raster Effects Settings dialog. For best results, make sure the resolution setting in this dialog is high enough for your output needs. Refer to the beginning of this chapter for more information about the settings in this dialog.

Specifying Mapped Artwork

To map artwork onto the surface of a 3D object, you must first apply a 3D effect to an object. Then, from either the 3D Extrude & Bevel Options dialog or the 3D Revolve Options dialog, click the Map Art button to open the Map Art dialog (**Figure 8.56**). If the Preview option in the resulting Map Art dialog isn't checked, turn it on so that you can see what your mapped artwork will look like as you make adjustments to it.

Figure 8.56 The Map Art button appears directly below the Cancel button in the 3D Revolve Options or 3D Extrude & Bevel Options dialog.

Before you can map art onto your object, you have to choose onto which surface of the object you want to place your artwork. At the top of the Map Art dialog, the buttons with arrows allow you to navigate or step through each of the surfaces of your object. As you step through each surface, Illustrator displays the selected surface in the center of the Map Art dialog. In addition, Illustrator tries to help you identify the selected surface by highlighting it with a red outline on the artboard (**Figure 8.57**). Depending on the color of your object, this red outline could be helpful, or it could be barely visible.

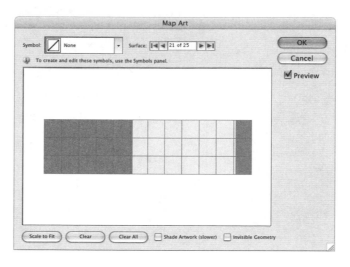

Figure 8.57 Illustrator tries to help you identify each of the surfaces, although the alignment of the red outlines isn't always perfect on the artboard.

The surface that appears in the Map Art dialog is shaped as if it is laid flat. You'll notice as you step through the different surfaces on your object that some show a light gray background whereas others show a dark gray background. Some surfaces may even show a background that is dark gray only in certain areas. This is Illustrator's way of letting you know which surfaces, or which parts of a surface, are not visible or are hidden from view (**Figure 8.58**). As you would expect, if you choose to use the track cube to view your object from a different perspective, the shaded surface areas in the Map Art dialog update accordingly.

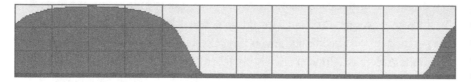

Figure 8.58 This surface, which is the section that connects the body and neck of the water bottle, has both shaded and nonshaded sections.

Once you've chosen the surface you want to map art onto, use the Symbol pop-up menu to choose a symbol. The selected symbol appears on the surface area in the Map Art dialog with a bounding box. You can drag the symbol to position it to your liking on the surface, and you can also drag the handles to resize it (**Figure 8.59**). As you adjust the position of the symbol, you will see the preview update on the actual 3D object on the artboard. Alternatively, you can use the Scale to Fit button at the bottom of the Map Art dialog to have Illustrator resize your symbol to fit to the surface, although it does so nonproportionally.

Figure 8.59 You can move and rotate a symbol so that it appears as you need it to on the surface of the object.

It's easier if you create your symbols at the correct size before you map them to a surface; this way, you won't have to worry about getting just the right size or position in the Map Art dialog.

A surface can contain only one symbol. If you want multiple art items to appear on a single surface, you have to define a single symbol with all the elements in it.

Once you're happy with the size and position of your symbol on the selected surface, use the arrows at the top of the dialog to navigate to another side to map additional symbols, as needed. At any time, you can click the Clear button to remove a symbol from a selected surface, or you can click the Clear All button to remove symbols from all surfaces at once.

By default, Illustrator calculates shading and lighting only for the actual surface of a 3D object, not artwork that is mapped to a 3D surface. Illustrator does this purely for performance reasons. We mentioned earlier that Illustrator uses blends to calculate shading, and breaking down intricately mapped artwork and shading each element with blends takes quite a bit of processing. However, to get a realistic appearance, most likely you will want your mapped artwork to be shaded, even if it takes a bit longer to do so. Selecting the Shade Artwork (slower) check box forces Illustrator to shade both the surface of your object and the mapped artwork. This setting applies to the entire object, and you don't need to turn it on for each individual surface.

The last setting in the Map Art dialog is a check box labeled Invisible Geometry, which is a slightly technical term. When this option is turned on, Illustrator hides the actual 3D object on your artboard and displays just the mapped artwork. The result is a symbol that appears to float in space. A good example of when this setting might be useful is when you want to make text appear as if it were wrapped around a sphere (**Figure 8.60**).

Figure 8.60 You can map artwork around a sphere (left), and by using the Invisible Geometry option in the Map Art dialog, you can hide the sphere leaving just the artwork (right).

When you're happy with your artwork mapping settings, click OK to accept the settings in the Map Art dialog, and then click OK to close the 3D dialog.

What If ... You Add Transparency to 3D?

Throughout this entire book, you've seen how transparency is integrated into Illustrator's feature set with features such as soft drop shadows and opacity masks. You might ask yourself, "What if I added transparency to a 3D object?" After all, wouldn't it be cool to make a 3D object that was also transparent so that you could see right through to the back of the object?

Have no fear—as if the 3D effect wasn't cool enough, you can also create transparent 3D objects—but you'll have to follow these two steps in order to get transparency and 3D to work together:

1. As you learned earlier in the chapter, before Illustrator applies a 3D effect to an object, it breaks the object down into its components (fills and strokes). In that process, transparency attributes are tossed out, and just the appearance remains. For example, if you set an object to 50% opacity, the 3D effect sets the object to a 50% tint of that color, but you won't be able to see through to what's behind the object. The trick is that you have to sneak transparency into the 3D effect without letting the effect know about it. You can accomplish this in one of two ways. If you have a single object that you're working with, you can target just the fill of the object in the Appearance panel and then change the Opacity value (**Figure 8.61**). Alternatively, you can create a group (you can create a group of one object, if you'd like). If transparency is applied to any object within a group, that transparency makes it through the 3D effect unscathed.

If your symbol contains transparency or over-print settings, those will not interact with the 3D object itself. For example, if a symbol uses a blend mode and you mapped that symbol to a 3D object, you wouldn't see the symbol multiplying with the 3D shape, because the appearance is limited to the symbol itself.

Figure 8.61 When you're using the Appearance panel, targeting the fill allows you to apply transparency to just the fill and not the entire object.

2. Another useful nugget of information that we learned earlier was that by default, Illustrator renders only the parts of a 3D object that are visible. To speed up the rendering process, Illustrator doesn't bother drawing the sides of a 3D object that are hidden from view. Well, this presents a problem if you're creating an object that is transparent and you expect to see through the front of the object to the back side that's behind it. After all, if Illustrator isn't drawing the hidden side of an object, how does Illustrator know what the back side of the object looks like? The answer is that you have to force Illustrator to draw the hidden sides—you do this by turning on the Draw Hidden Faces option in the 3D Extrude & Bevel Options or 3D Revolve Options dialog.

Once you've addressed these two issues, you'll end up with a 3D object that is truly transparent (**Figure 8.62**). Adding transparency to 3D objects opens new doors to creativity, such as when creating transparent glass bottles and vases. And don't forget to throw some artwork mapping in there as well. If you map art to a transparent 3D object, you'll be able to see through to the art on the other side. Now you've got to admit, that's pretty freakin' cool, no?

Figure 8.62 This martini glass is transparent, allowing you to see what is inside.

What If . . . You Blend 3D Objects?

In Illustrator, you can select two objects and choose the Object > Blend > Make feature to morph one vector shape into another. This technique, as you'll discover in Chapter 10, *Graphs, Distortions, and Blends*, can be useful for a variety of tasks including shading, special effects, and object distribution. However, what if you created a blend using two 3D objects? Would the 3D effect morph as well, along with the blend?

The answer is, yes, it will! If you apply a 3D effect to an object and then duplicate that object (so you have two identical objects), you can create a blend between them. Because 3D is a live effect, you can edit the 3D effect of one of the objects and change the position so you're viewing the object from a completely different angle. The blend will then update—and generate the intermediate steps (**Figure 8.63**).

Figure 8.63 By creating a blend between spheres with mapped artwork, you can create the illusion of the sphere rotating.

Not impressed? Well, in Chapter 11, *Web and Mobile Design*, we'll learn how to use blends to create instant Flash animations that you can put on your Web site. That means you can create a box and have it rotate in space. Hey, wait—don't go running off to that chapter yet—we still have plenty of cool stuff to cover here.

What If . . . You Apply a 3D Effect to a Graph?

We haven't covered graphs yet (we'll get to that in Chapter 10, *Graphs, Distortions, and Blends*), but a graph consists of a group of objects. And because a 3D effect applied at the group level results in all the objects in that group sharing the same effect, what happens if you apply a 3D Extrude effect to a graph? The answer is that you get a powerful way to present numbers in an eye-catching manner (**Figure 8.64** on the following page). And if you add transparency to a 3D graph—well, you can see where that might lead.

Figure 8.64 Adding 3D effects to just about anything, such as graphs, for example, can turn something ordinary into something unique and attention-grabbing.

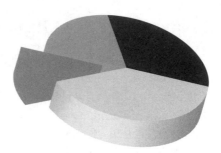

Can't Find Your Object? Get Smart (Guides)

When you apply a live effect to an object, the underlying object remains, and only the appearance changes. With effects such as 3D, there could be a large difference between how the object appears on your artboard and the actual shape. When you need to select the vector object to edit it, you might have a hard time trying to locate its exact position. Some users will tell you to switch to the Outline preview mode for such editing, but don't listen to them. Instead, turn on the Smart Guides feature by choosing View > Smart Guides. There are actually many different kinds of smart guides (all covered in Appendix B, *Application Preferences*), but one in particular—Object Highlighting—can make it easier to find the objects you want.

The Object Highlighting attribute of smart guides identifies the underlying original artwork when you move your pointer over artwork that has had effects or envelopes applied to it (**Figure 8.65**).

Figure 8.65 When moving the pointer over this 3D object, the Object Highlighting setting of Smart Guides identifies the vector artwork used to define the shape.

CONVERT TO SHAPE: CHANGING FOR THE BETTER

The Convert to Shape effect takes the fill of your targeted selection and converts it to a rectangle, a rounded rectangle, or an ellipse. When you first see this effect, you might scratch your head thoughtfully and ask yourself, "Well, if I had wanted a rectangle, wouldn't I have drawn the shape that way in the first place?" This is a good question if your object has only one fill, but if you've added multiple fills, you'll realize that you can apply the Convert to Shape effect on just one of them, which means you can have a single shape with fills that have different shapes. This effect is particularly useful for text objects and for groups and layers as well.

Applying the Convert to Shape Effect

To apply any of the three Convert to Shape effects, target the fill of an object, group, or layer, and choose Effect > Convert to Shape > Rectangle. Although you can choose between the Rectangle, Rounded Rectangle, and Ellipse options, it doesn't matter which one you choose because the ensuing Shape Options dialog allows you to easily switch between the three different shapes via a pop-up menu at the top of the dialog (**Figure 8.66**).

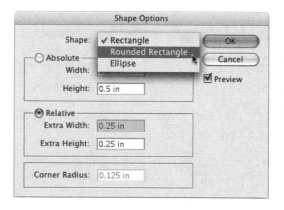

Figure 8.66 It doesn't make a difference which shape you choose from the Convert to Shape submenu, because you get a chance to change your mind in the Shape Options dialog.

The Shape Options dialog gives you two options for specifying the size of the targeted fill:

- **Absolute.** The Absolute setting allows you to define a specific width and height for the fill shape, which can be completely different from the size of the object's actual path.

- **Relative.** The Relative setting allows you to define a specific amount that is added to the object's actual size. For example, if the object's actual path is 4 x 4 inches and you use a relative setting with the Extra Width and Extra Height settings set to .5 inch, the shape effect produces a shape that is 4.5 x 4.5 inches. The Relative setting is useful when you want to create a shape that changes when the original object changes (see the following "What If … You Apply the Convert to Shape Effect to Text?" example).

When you choose the Rounded Rectangle setting from the Shape pop-up menu, you can also specify a corner radius for the fill shape.

What If … You Apply the Convert to Shape Effect to Text?

A practical use for the Convert to Shape effect is to create a background for an object that dynamically adjusts itself as you change the object. A good example is when you want to create a button that has text inside it. Using the Convert to Shape effect, you can have Illustrator automatically resize the button as you change the text within it. Here are the steps required to create this dynamic shape:

1. Choose the Type tool, and click a blank area on the artboard to create a Point Type object.

2. Using your keyboard, type **Dynamic**.

3. Set your text to 36-point Myriad Roman.

4. Switch to the Selection tool, and select the Type object.

5. Then, open the Appearance panel, and from the panel menu, choose Add New Fill.

6. In the Appearance panel, drag the fill you just created so it appears listed beneath the characters in your Type object (**Figure 8.67**).

Figure 8.67 Move the fill you created so it appears below the characters in the Type object.

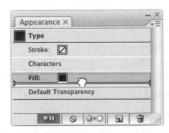

7. With the new fill highlighted in the Appearance panel, choose a color from either the Control panel, the Color panel, or the Swatches panel.

   At this stage, you won't see the color change into your text, because the fill you are coloring appears beneath the characters in the Type object.

8. With the colored fill still highlighted in the Appearance panel, choose Effect > Convert to Shape > Rounded Rectangle.

9. In the Shape Options dialog that appears, choose the Relative options, and specify .125 inch for both the Extra Width and Extra Height fields.

10. For the Corner Radius, specify a value of .25 inch, and click OK to apply the effect (**Figure 8.68**).

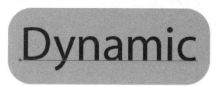

Figure 8.68 The second fill you created now acts like a background for the text.

11. Switch to the Type tool, and edit the text.

    You will notice that as you change the text, the colored background expands or contracts as necessary to match the text.

As always, a little bit of experimenting not only gets you more comfortable with these kinds of effects but also helps you think of ways you can get your work done faster and more efficiently (which is a good thing).

DISTORT & TRANSFORM: TRANSFORMING YOUR DESIGN

Throughout your design process, you are constantly making changes to your artwork. Sometimes, you need to alter paths by distorting them, and other times you need to transform them using functions such as Scale or Rotate. Illustrator features a variety of these functions as live effects, which makes it easy to go back and perform tweaks or changes to these settings as necessary.

Distortion Effects

Illustrator features six different distortion effects, each providing a different type of look and feel. Distortion effects in particular are useful when applied to strokes or fills individually, and this is especially so when you're building complex appearances that contain multiple fills and strokes. You can find each of the effects listed here by first choosing Effect > Distort & Transform and then choosing one of the following distortion effects:

- **Free Distort.** The Free Distort effect displays your art with a rectangular bounding box. You can drag any of the four corners to stretch or apply a distortion (**Figure 8.69**). This is useful if you want to add perspective to make art appear as if it has a vanishing point, although the 3D Rotate effect offers similar functionality in that regard.

Figure 8.69 The Free Distort effect lets you stretch artwork to apply perspective or distortion.

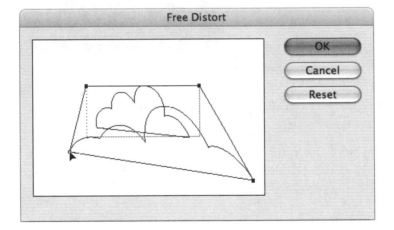

- **Pucker & Bloat.** The Pucker & Bloat effect offers a slider that applies distortion to your objects by spiking paths. When you're looking for a really funky shape, this distortion effect probably fits the bill.

- **Roughen.** The Roughen effect allows you to take straight paths and make them appear as if they just experienced an earthquake (**Figure 8.70**). The Roughen dialog offers the ability to adjust size and detail; you can also specify whether you want the result to have smooth (rounded) or corner (straight) path segments.

Figure 8.70 You can use the Roughen effect to create torn paper effects or simply to apply an uneven look to vector art.

- **Tweak.** At first, the Tweak effect appears to be similar to the Pucker & Bloat distortion, but the Tweak effect adjusts control points in addition to anchor points on paths. The result is a path that is far less predictable.

- **Twist.** The Twist effect allows you to twist art from its center using a specified angle.

- **Zig Zag.** The Zig Zag effect is similar to the Roughen effect, but it creates methodical zigzag patterns on selected objects.

Illustrator also has other distortion tools and effects. The Warp effect, covered later in this chapter, provides a way to stretch art using predefined warp styles. We cover other distortion features such as envelopes and the Liquify set of tools in Chapter 10, *Graphs, Distortion, and Blends*.

Transform Effect

If you want to rotate or scale an object on your artboard, using the Transform effect is overkill. Rather, the Transform effect is useful when you want to apply transformations to parts of an object. For example, you might scale two different fills within the same object so they are different sizes. To do so, apply the Transform effect by choosing Effect > Distort & Transform > Transform.

The Transform Effect dialog is actually identical to the one that appears when you use the Transform Each function (which we covered in Chapter 4, *Advanced Vectors*). However, the Transform Effect dialog has one huge addition—the ability to specify copies (**Figure 8.71** on the following page).

Figure 8.71 The Transform Effect dialog mimics the Transform Each dialog, and it includes the ability to set the number of copies you want transformed.

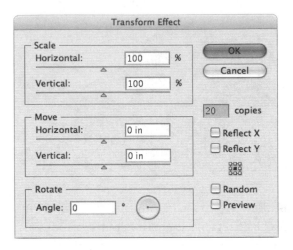

Transforming Objects with Effects

Because we're on the topic of transformations, we'll discuss a few concepts you should be aware of when performing standard transformations on the artboard—specifically when scaling or rotating objects that have live effects applied to them.

By default, when you scale an object on the artboard, Illustrator does not scale the values that you may have specified for any live effects applied to that object. For example, if you specify a 30-pixel Gaussian Blur effect and then scale that object 200 percent, the Gaussian Blur is still set to 30 pixels. To scale an object's live effect attributes, you must turn on the Scale Strokes & Effects setting, which you can find in Illustrator's General Preferences panel or by double-clicking the Scale tool in the Toolbox.

It's also important to realize that the values of certain effects have limits. For example, you can't set a Gaussian Blur to anything greater than 250 pixels. Even if you have Scale Strokes & Effects turned on, you can scale your artwork only up until the limit, at which point Illustrator just uses the maximum value it allows. If you need to scale objects to extremely large sizes (for creating signs or banners, for instance), you first have to expand the effect and then scale it as you would any object.

Finally, the values that are specified in the dialogs of live effects are relative to the rulers of your document. In many cases, modifying your object may cause unexpected results. For example, say you apply a drop shadow to an object and specify an offset that sets the shadow down and to the right. If you rotate the object 180 degrees on your artboard (effectively turning it upside down), the drop shadow still displays at the lower right of the object. To get the correct appearance, you need to edit the drop shadow effect and set the offset so that the drop shadow now falls up and to the left. Alternatively, you can expand the effect before you perform the rotation. This issue requires special attention from printers, who often compose files or create work and turn layouts for their presses. It should be noted that InDesign's drop shadows suffer from the same symptoms.

PATHS: DRAWING OUTSIDE THE LINES

At some point, editing vector paths is something that just about every Illustrator user has to come to terms with. However, sometimes performing some of these edits makes sense as a live effect, which allows the paths to be updated easily. Specifically, three path functions—Offset Path, Outline Object, and Outline Stroke—are available as live effects. You can find all these effects by choosing Effect > Path and then choosing the required function.

For the most part, these effects are useful when you apply them to Type objects. The Outline Object effect is particularly useful for using text in a way that normally requires the text to be outlined into vector paths. In addition, the Offset Path effect can be helpful when you're trying to create type effects in tandem with the Pathfinder effects, as described later in this chapter (see "What If … You Combine Offset Path and Pathfinder Effects on a Text Object?").

PATHFINDER: CREATING COMPLEX SHAPES

The Pathfinder effects are identical to those in the Pathfinder panel (covered in Chapter 4, *Advanced Vectors*), only here they are applied as live effects. Before you question the reason for making these available as live effects, remember that you can apply live effects to groups and layers. Applying these effects to type may also prove useful.

The following Pathfinder commands are available as live effects: Add, Intersect, Exclude, Subtract, Minus Back, Divide, Trim, Merge, Crop, Outline, Hard Mix, Soft Mix, and Trap. Refer to Chapter 4, *Advanced Vectors*, for details on each of these functions.

To apply any of the Pathfinder effects, make a selection, choose Effect > Pathfinder, and choose the Pathfinder function you need.

What If … You Combine Offset Path and Pathfinder Effects on a Text Object?

A design may sometimes call for a word or sentence of text to be outlined with a single line that encompasses all of the letters. The Offset Path filter is perfect for this, but the effect outlines each letter that appears in the text. The result is a mess of paths that overlap, making the text difficult—if not impossible—to read. If you were to expand the appearance of the overlapping paths, you might use the Pathfinder Add function to create a single unified shape, but if you do, the text can no longer be edited. This is where a Pathfinder effect can be really helpful.

Follow these steps to learn how you can apply both the Offset Path and Pathfinder effects to text:

1. Choose the Type tool, and click a blank area on the artboard to create a Point Type object.

2. Using your keyboard, type **Outline**.

3. Set your text to 36-point Myriad Bold.

4. Switch to the Selection tool, and select the Type object.

5. Then, open the Appearance panel, and from the panel menu, choose Add New Stroke.

6. With the new stroke highlighted in the Appearance panel, choose Effect > Path > Offset Path.

7. In the Offset Path dialog that appears, specify a value of .0625 inch for Offset, and click OK to apply the effect (**Figure 8.72**).

Figure 8.72 Adding an Offset Path effect to the new stroke you created adds an outline around the text.

8. With the new stroke still highlighted in the Appearance panel, choose Effect > Pathfinder > Add. The effect is applied immediately (**Figure 8.73**).

Figure 8.73 The Add function combines all the individual paths created with the Offset Path effect, resulting in a single combined outline.

9. Switch to the Type tool, and edit the text. You will notice that as you change the text, the outline updates accordingly.

RASTERIZE: CREATING VECTORS THAT ACT LIKE PIXELS

Illustrator has a Rasterize command in the Object menu that gives you the ability to rasterize any object in Illustrator. The Rasterize effect in the Effect menu gives you the same functionality—but as a live effect. When you think about it, the result of applying this effect is a bit of an oxymoron: The object is a vector, yet it appears and acts like a raster image.

To apply the Rasterize effect, select an object, and choose Effect > Rasterize. The options that appear in the Rasterize dialog are similar to those in the Document Raster Effects Settings dialog, and you can even choose to have the Rasterize dialog pick up the resolution settings from that dialog by selecting the Use Document Raster Effects Resolution radio button (**Figure 8.74**).

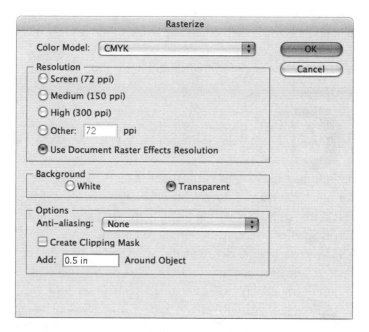

Figure 8.74 To ensure a consistent overall appearance, you might want to have the Rasterize effect share the same resolution setting as in the Document Raster Effects Settings dialog.

You might want to use the Rasterize effect for several reasons. For example, you might want to disable antialiasing on small text so that it appears easier to read when displayed on a Web site (you can find more information on this in Chapter 11, *Web and Mobile Design*). In addition, you can use the Rasterize effect to change the color model of selected artwork (see the following "What If … You Apply the Rasterize Effect to a Raster Image?" example).

What If … You Apply the Rasterize Effect to a Raster Image?

It doesn't take a whole lot to realize that the Rasterize effect can turn vector elements into raster elements, but have you ever thought about the possibility of applying the Rasterize effect to a placed raster image in Illustrator? Not only is it possible, but it's extremely useful as well. Besides the obvious ability to temporarily downsample high-resolution files to a lower resolution for faster processing, the Rasterize effect has the ability to change color modes. That means you can place a full-color photo into a layout but use the Rasterize effect to change the image to grayscale. Of course, since it's a live effect, you can always switch it back to color at any time.

In addition, you can use this method of converting images to grayscale for when you want to convert an entire file to grayscale—including both raster and vector objects. In such a case, you may find it easier to apply the Rasterize effect at the layer level, where all items on a layer can be converted to grayscale.

STYLIZE: NOW YOU'RE STYLIN'!

The group of Stylize live effects gets a bit more visibility than other effects for one main reason: the celebrity factor. Among the different effects you'll find in the Stylize submenu is the rock star of all live effects, the Drop Shadow effect. Although there's nothing that special about the Drop Shadow effect per se, it seems designers these days are trying to find untold ways to add drop shadows to their artwork. We don't discriminate between different live effects (we're an equal opportunity educator), and the reality is, plenty of other useful effects appear in the Stylize submenu, including Add Arrowheads, Feather, Inner and Outer Glow, Round Corners, and the sleeper live effect of the year—Scribble.

The Scribble effect looks simple at first glance, but refer to "What If … You Apply the Scribble Effect to Multiple Fills?" later in this chapter to see how powerful the effect can be.

We cover the Drop Shadow live effect in Chapter 3, *Objects, Groups, and Layers*.

The Add Arrowheads Effect

If you need to add arrowheads to the end of paths for creating diagrams or callouts, the Add Arrowheads live effect is just for you. With any path selected, choose Effect > Stylize > Add Arrowheads. In the Add Arrowheads dialog, you can specify 27 different types of arrowheads for both the start and end of your path (**Figure 8.75**). A helpful Preview check box makes it easy to see the results of the effect on your artboard as you experiment with different arrowhead styles.

Another way to add an arrowhead to a stroke is to define and use a custom Pattern brush. Refer to Chapter 5, *Brushes, Symbols, and Masks*, for more information on Pattern brushes.

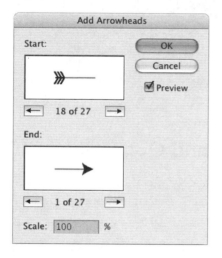

Figure 8.75 The Add Arrowheads dialog offers a variety of styles, although unfortunately, there's no way to define or create your own.

Illustrator uses the stroke width of your path to determine the size of the arrowhead, but you can adjust the size to perfection by using the Scale setting at the bottom of the dialog. You'll also notice that the arrowheads always match the orientation of the path, so if you adjust the path after you've added the effect, the arrowhead updates accordingly.

It's interesting to note that the Add Arrowheads effect works on both open and closed paths. The filter is also a great way to quickly figure out the direction of a path.

The Feather Effect

Vector paths are known for their clean, crisp edges, but at times, you want a softer edge to your objects. That's where the Feather effect can be of help. Choose Effect > Stylize > Feather, and specify an amount to determine

Try using a Feather on an object you're using as an opacity mask; this allows you to create a mask with soft edges.

how soft of an edge you want your shape to have. You can even apply a Feather effect directly to a placed photograph (**Figure 8.76**).

Figure 8.76 With a placed image selected, you can apply a Feather effect as you would to any vector object.

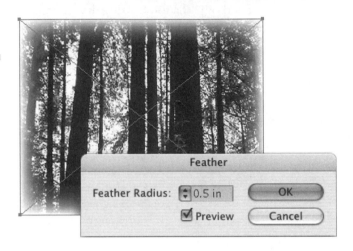

The Inner Glow and Outer Glow Effects

Glow effects can some-times appear too soft for your needs. To beef up a glow effect, try applying two or three glow effects to the same object.

As a variation to the Drop Shadow effect, Illustrator also offers an Inner Glow and an Outer Glow effect. You can find both of these effects in the Effect > Stylize submenu.

The Inner Glow effect adds a soft glow to the inside area of an object. From the Inner Glow dialog, you can choose the Center option, which starts the glow from the center of the object and extends it toward the edges, or you can choose the Edge option, which begins the glow in the opposite direc-tion—from the edge toward the center of the shape (**Figure 8.77**). The Outer Glow effect adds a soft glow to the outside edges of an object.

Figure 8.77 Depending on the desired effect, you can specify an Inner Glow effect to start from the center (left) or the edge (right).

The Round Corners Effect

Illustrator's Rounded Rectangle tool is so year 2000. Welcome to today's fast-paced world where you can add rounded corners to any object, no matter how many corners the object has (**Figure 8.78**). When you select an object and choose Effect > Stylize > Round Corners, you can use the Preview check box to experiment with different Radius settings until you get just the look you need. Of course, you can always change the Radius setting because it's a live effect.

Figure 8.78 The usefulness of the Round Corners effect becomes apparent when you apply it to objects with many corners.

Unfortunately, you can't specify which corners of your object will get rounded—the Round Corners effect rounds all corners. If you want only some corners to be rounded in your object, you need to apply the Round Corners effect and then expand the effect so that you can manually adjust each corner as necessary.

For an interesting effect, try applying the Round Corners effect to type.

The Scribble Effect

If there's one thing you can count on with vector graphics, it's clean, sharp edges. However, sometimes a design calls for something a little bit less technical and more natural. The Scribble effect in Illustrator is perfect for this task. And, as you will see, the power of the Scribble effect lies in its ability to randomize individual attributes, giving the effect a truly natural and hand-drawn appearance. One of the nicest aspects of the Scribble effect is its ability to draw outside the lines. In fact, what the Scribble effect really does is convert your object into one long stroke (**Figure 8.79**).

Figure 8.79 Here, using one of the many settings in the Scribble effect, we illustrate how the object's appearance is converted to one long stroke.

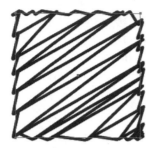

To apply the Scribble effect, select an object, and choose Effect > Stylize > Scribble to open the Scribble Options dialog. The dialog contains five main settings that control the overall appearance of the Scribble effect. Some of the settings also have a Variation slider, allowing the scribble appearance to vary throughout your object.

As you will quickly find out, making even small adjustments to the Scribble effect settings can have a large impact on the appearance of the object. Using a combination of different settings, you can also achieve a variety of different styles for your Scribble. To illustrate this, Adobe added a pop-up menu at the top of the dialog that contains different presets (**Figure 8.80**). Switch between the different presets to see the ways you might use the Scribble effect. Unfortunately, you cannot define your own presets. However, you can always save your Scribble setting as a graphic style once you've applied it to an object.

Figure 8.80 A variety of presets helps you quickly learn the different types of styles you can achieve with the Scribble effect.

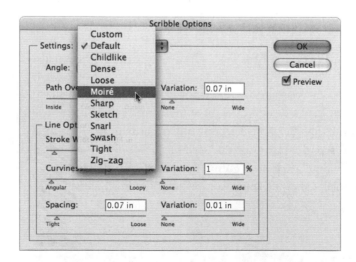

Although it may seem a bit daunting at first, the different settings in the Scribble Options dialog are rather straightforward:

• **Angle.** The Angle setting defines which direction the stroke will travel. Click and drag the dial to adjust the setting or enter a value manually in the field.

• **Path Overlap.** The Path Overlap setting defines how far the stroke overlaps the edge of the object's path. You can also set this to a negative value, which effectively defines how close the stroke can come to the edge of an object's path. You can also set a variation, which allows the Path Overlap setting to randomly change throughout the object within the value you define (**Figure 8.81**).

Figure 8.81 Adding a Variation to the Path Overlap setting allows the Scribble effect to draw outside the lines using a natural technique.

• **Stroke Width.** The Stroke Width setting defines the thickness of the stroke that Illustrator uses to create your Scribble effect. Unfortunately, this setting does not have a variation slider.

• **Curviness.** The Curviness setting defines how much a stroke loops when it changes direction. A very small number produces more of a straight zigzag effect with pointy ends, while a larger number produces loose changes in direction with loopy ends (**Figure 8.82**). You can also define a Variation value so that this setting appears differently throughout the object.

Figure 8.82 Smaller Curviness settings create sharp lines (left), while higher values create a more freestyle appearance (right).

- • **Spacing.** The Spacing setting defines how dense the strokes appear. Again, this setting has a Variation slider, which allows the Scribble effect to vary the spacing throughout the object.

What If … You Apply the Scribble Effect to Multiple Fills?

Adding a Scribble effect to an object can certainly give it a hand-drawn look and feel, but sometimes you need something more than just strokes traveling in the same direction. Combining multiple fills—each with a different Scribble effect setting—can produce cross-hatching effects that produce wonderful patterns, textures, and edges. Here's how it is done:

1. Using the Ellipse tool, draw a circle that is 4 inches in diameter.

2. Give the circle a fill of Black with a stroke of None.

3. With the circle selected, open the Appearance panel, and target the fill by clicking it.

4. Choose Effect > Stylize > Scribble to open the Scribble Options dialog.

5. Choose Default from the Setting pop-up menu, and make the following adjustments: set Stroke Width to .01 inches, set Curviness to 2%, and set Spacing to .03 inch.

6. Leave all the remaining settings, and click OK to apply the effect (**Figure 8.83**).

7. With the fill still highlighted in the Appearance panel, choose Duplicate Item from the panel menu to create a second fill with the same attributes as the first.

8. Double-click one of the Scribble effects listed in the Appearance panel (it doesn't matter which one) to edit the effect.

9. Change the Angle setting to 130 degrees, and click OK to apply the edit (**Figure 8.84**).

Figure 8.83 Applying the Scribble effect to the circle gives it an interesting appearance.

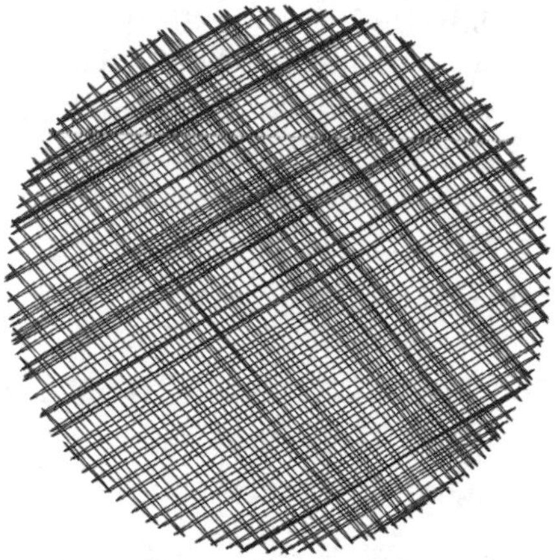

Figure 8.84 Adding a second fill with another Scribble effect gives the circle a lattice-like appearance. Notice the cross-hatch effects around the edges of the shape as well.

SVG FILTERS: APPLYING TECHNICAL EFFECTS

Scalable Vector Graphics (SVG) is a vector-based file format that can be used for displaying graphics on the Web and handheld devices. We discuss SVG graphics in detail in both Chapter 11, *Web and Mobile Design*, and Chapter 13, *Saving and Exporting Files*, but you can apply certain effects to graphics that are saved in the SVG format. These effects, called *SVG filter effects*, are really XML-based instructions that are applied when the SVG graphic is rendered in a Web browser or viewer. As a result, these effects are useful only when applied to graphics that will eventually be saved as SVG.

Illustrator ships with a collection of 18 SVG filter effects, although if you know how to code them yourself, you can also write your own. To apply an SVG filter effect, select an object, and choose Effect > SVG Filters > Apply SVG Filter. Once the Apply SVG Filter dialog is open, you can click a filter from the list and click OK. Alternatively, you can highlight a filter and click the Edit SVG Filter button to modify the selected filter effect, or you can click the New SVG Filter button to create a new SVG filter effect from scratch. Additionally, you can delete selected filters by using the trash can icon in the Apply SVG Filter dialog.

For information on how to create your own SVG filter effects (and download existing code), visit www.w3.org/TR/SVG/filters.html.

SVG Effects should be the last effects applied in the stacking order when multiple effects are being specified; otherwise, the SVG effect will end up being rasterized.

Illustrator can also import SVG filters. To do so, choose Effect > SVG Filters > Import SVG Filter. In the ensuing dialog, open an SVG file with a filter effect in it; when you do, Illustrator will import that filter into your current file.

WARP: CHOOSING YOUR DISTORTION

Refer to Chapter 10, *Graphs, Distortion, and Blends*, for detailed information on Illustrator's other distortion features, as well as a "Featured Matchup" sidebar of those features as they compare to the Warp effect.

The Warp effect is one of several distortion functions in Illustrator's arsenal. You can use Warp to apply any of 15 different preset distortions to any object, group, or layer.

To apply a Warp effect, make a selection, and choose Effect > Warp > Arc. Even though all 15 warp styles are listed in the submenu, you don't have to worry about choosing the right one just yet—the Warp Options dialog lets you choose from any of the preset warp styles.

When the Warp Options dialog appears, select the Preview check box so you can preview your warp on your artboard as you adjust the settings. Click the Style pop-up menu to choose from the list of warp styles, which comprise Arc, Arc Lower, Arc Upper, Arch, Bulge, Shell Lower, Shell Upper, Flag, Wave, Fish, Rise, Fisheye, Inflate, Squeeze, and Twist. Little icons appear to the left of each warp style to help you visualize what each one does, although trial and error works better in our opinion (**Figure 8.85**).

Figure 8.85 The little icons that appear to the left of each Warp effect help you understand what each option does.

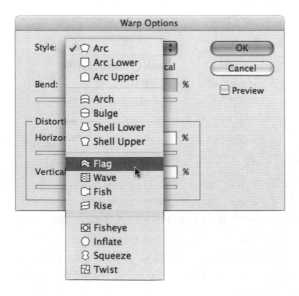

Once you've chosen a warp style, you can specify whether the warp is applied horizontally or vertically, and you can adjust how slight or extreme the warp is applied by adjusting the Bend slider. Additionally, you can use the Horizontal and Vertical Distortion sliders to apply additional distortion to your selection.

Warp effects are particularly useful when applied at the group or layer level, where you might often add or remove elements from the group. For example, you might apply a Warp effect to a logo to show movement or excitement. If you applied the Warp effect at the group level, adding new art to the group will automatically cause the new art to take on the same Warp effect.

What If ... You Apply the Warp Effect to 3D Text?

A powerful way to accentuate a logo or headline is to add a 3D Extrude effect to text. Because 3D is a live effect, there is no need to first convert text to outlines. Adding a Warp effect to 3D text can take things to the next level and open a world of possibilities. Try it:

1. Choose the Type tool, and click a blank area on the artboard to create a Point Type object.

2. Using your keyboard, type **SPECTACULAR**.

3. Set your text to 36-point Myriad Bold, and specify a fill of 25K and a stroke of 60K.

4. Using the Selection tool, select the text, and choose Effect > 3D > Extrude & Bevel.

5. The default settings are fine for this exercise, so click the OK button to apply the effect (**Figure 8.86**).

Figure 8.86 When you've applied the 3D effect, you'll notice that the extrude color is the darker stroke color you specified earlier.

6. With the text still selected, choose Effect > Warp > Arc.

7. Specify a Bend value of 30%, and click OK to apply the effect (**Figure 8.87**).

Figure 8.87 Applying a Warp effect to the 3D text combines the two effects for a truly spectacular result.

Of course, you can use the Type tool to edit the text as needed—both the 3D and the Warp effects update accordingly. Turning on the Smart Guides feature makes it easier to select the text on the artboard.

APPLYING PHOTOSHOP EFFECTS

The effects we have discussed to this point are considered Illustrator effects, and for the most part, they are vector in nature and make adjustments to vector paths (with the obvious exception of the Rasterize effect and most of the Stylize effects).

However, Illustrator also has the ability to apply a variety of purely pixel-based effects to any object, group, or layer. These effects are grouped in the Photoshop Effects section of the Effect menu. The same rules as to how effects are applied through the Effect menu and edited via the Appearance panel apply to these effects as well.

In truth, the Photoshop effects in the bottom portion of the Effect menu are really Photoshop filters. You can copy Photoshop filters and plugins into the Illustrator Plug-ins folder (found in the same folder in which the Illustrator application file appears), and they appear listed in the Effect menu as well.

At first, it may seem unnatural to find that you can apply a Gaussian Blur or an Unsharp Mask in Illustrator, but you'll quickly find that you can achieve wonderful designs and cool effects by employing Photoshop filters such as Crystallize and Mezzotint. Some of the graphic styles libraries that ship with Illustrator employ a variety of these effects, and by reverse-engineering them, you can learn how to use them.

Featured Matchup: Illustrator Effects vs. Photoshop Effects

At first glance, it may appear that the Illustrator effects are purely vector in nature and the Photoshop effects are raster-based ones, but this isn't true. Effects such as Feather and Drop Shadow, which appear in the Stylize submenu, are listed as Illustrator effects, and they produce raster content. So what then is the distinction between Illustrator and Photoshop effects?

The difference is relatively simple yet absolutely critical: resolution.

At the beginning of the chapter, you learned how the Document Raster Effects Settings dialog determines the resolution at which effects are rasterized when the document is either flattened or printed. But the setting is also important for determining the appearance of some effects. Let's take a look at an example:

1. Open the Document Raster Effects Settings dialog, set the resolution to 72 ppi, and click OK.

2. Draw two identical circles.

3. Apply a Feather effect to one circle (an Illustrator effect) and a Gaussian Blur effect to the other (a Photoshop effect), and then observe the results (**Figure 8.88**).

4. Now open the Document Raster Effects Settings dialog, change the resolution to 300 ppi, and click OK. Observe the results of the effects (**Figure 8.89**).

You'll notice that the appearance of the Gaussian Blur effect has changed, but the Feather effect remained the same. This happens because the Gaussian Blur effect (and all Photoshop effects, for that matter) uses absolute measurements to calculate the effect. You'll notice the Gaussian Blur effect dialog specifies the blur value in pixels (**Figure 8.90**). Changing the resolution—the number of pixels in your file—changes the appearance of your effect. In contrast, the Feather effect—and all Illustrator effects—uses relative units to calculate the effect (**Figure 8.91**). The Feather dialog specifies the feather value in inches (or whatever measurement system you've chosen in preferences), so when you change the resolution setting, Illustrator simply adjusts the number of pixels it uses in the effect, as needed.

Figure 8.88 Shown are a circle with a Feather effect applied (left) and a circle with a Gaussian Blur effect applied (right). You can see that both are similar.

Figure 8.89 The circle with the Feather (left) remains unchanged in appearance, but the circle with the Gaussian Blur (right) now displays differently than it did before the change in resolution.

continues on next page

Featured Matchup: Illustrator Effects vs. Photoshop Effects *(continued)*

Overall, we refer to Photoshop effects as *below-the-line* effects because they appear below the divider line in the Effect menu (**Figure 8.92**). When using below-the-line effects, it's best to ensure that your document raster effects settings are correct before you begin working on your design. Otherwise, the appearance of your artwork will change when you adjust it later (or if your printer adjusts it). If you use above-the-line effects (Illustrator effects), you can get better performance by leaving the document raster effects settings at a lower resolution until you are about to send the file out for high-end output.

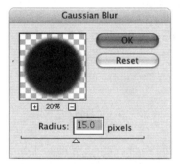

Figure 8.90 The Gaussian Blur effect uses pixels to calculate the effect.

Figure 8.91 The Feather effect uses relative units (in this case, inches) to calculate the effect.

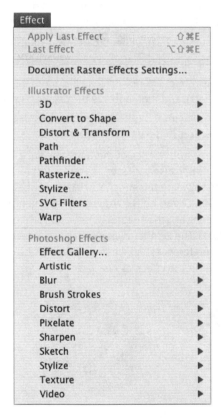

Figure 8.92 All effects that appear below the line are considered Photoshop effects and are resolution-dependent.

A Gallery of Effects

Going through each Photoshop effect listed in the Effect menu is beyond the scope of this book, but one feature that really makes it easy to experiment with a wide range of Photoshop effects is the Effects Gallery. If you're familiar with Photoshop's Filter Gallery feature, you'll find that the Effects Gallery is the same. Once you've targeted an object, group, or layer, choose Effect > Effects Gallery, which opens the Filter Gallery dialog. The dialog is split into three main sections: a preview on the left, a list of the different effects you can apply in the center, and the parameters for the selected effect on the right (**Figure 8.93**).

To preview different effects, click an effect in the center area (expand the folders to see the individual effects), and adjust the settings at the upper right of the dialog. Once you've found the effect you like, click the OK button to apply it.

Be aware that copying objects with below-the-line effects from one document to another may cause the appearance to change if the two files have different resolution settings.

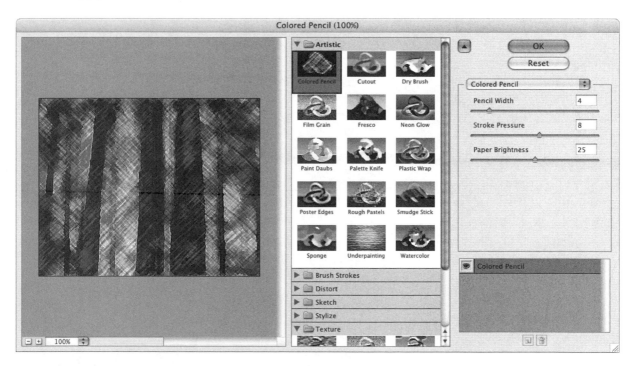

Figure 8.93 You can spend hours going through the effects in the Filter Gallery dialog.

CHAPTER NINE

Mixing It Up: Working with Vectors and Pixels

There's no velvet rope barring entry to Adobe Illustrator's exclusive vector graphics club. Pixels are always welcome inside. In fact, in the previous chapter, you learned how certain live effects use pixels to produce their appearance. In Illustrator, there is indeed a peaceful coexistence between vectors and pixels, and as we discussed in Chapter 2, *Vectors 101*, you can gain benefits by combining both vectors and pixels (such as adding a soft drop shadow to text). There's no reason why you should feel that you have to choose only one graphic type or the other.

Although Illustrator does have the ability to support pixels in some ways (as you'll see throughout this chapter), it in no way replaces the need for applications such as Adobe Photoshop. Quite the contrary, in this chapter you'll see how you can bring pixel-based images from Photoshop into Illustrator documents. You will also learn how both Photoshop and Illustrator can work together by enabling you to share editable content between them. You can then focus on producing the kinds of graphics you need by relying on the strengths of each of these powerful applications.

So turn up the music and feel the pulsing beat of vectors dancing with pixels, because this chapter will also cover Illustrator's ability to assimilate pixels and convert them into vector paths using a feature called Live Trace.

PLACING RASTER-BASED FILES

When creating designs and layouts in Illustrator, at times you will need to incorporate raster-based content, such as photographs. Naturally, these images are neither created nor edited in Illustrator—raster-based application programs such as Photoshop take care of doing that. However, you can *place* raster-based content into your Illustrator file. In fact, Illustrator works very much like a page layout application in this way.

When you place an image, Illustrator can incorporate that image in the file in two ways. In the first, Illustrator places a preview of the image on your artboard, but the image file itself is not incorporated into the Illustrator file. The image file exists as an external reference, separate from the Illustrator file. This technique is referred to as *place-linking* because the image file is linked to the Illustrator document. If you were to misplace the linked file, Illustrator would not be able to print the image.

In the second technique, Illustrator places the actual image file within the Illustrator document and incorporates the image into the Illustrator file. This is referred to as *place-embedding*, where the image becomes part of the Illustrator file.

You can choose which technique you want to use when you physically place the file. For a detailed explanation of the numerous benefits and caveats of using each technique, refer to the sidebar "Featured Matchup: Place-Linked Files vs. Place-Embedded Files."

Placing an Image

You can place a raster file into an Illustrator document using one of three methods. You can either place a file, open it directly, or drag it right onto your artboard. Each method has its own benefits; your task is to determine which one you will use.

Method One: Placing a File

When you already have a file open and you need to place an image into your document, this method offers the most options and is one of the most commonly used ways to place a file.

1. From an open document, choose File > Place, and navigate to a raster file on your hard drive or server.

2. At the bottom of the Place dialog are three check boxes (**Figure 9.1**). Check the Link box to place-link the file (unchecking the Link box place-embeds the file), check the Template box to have the image automatically placed on a template layer, and check the Replace box to have the image replace one that is already selected on the artboard.

   See "Manual Tracing with Template Layers" later in this chapter for more information on creating a template layer.

3. Once you've selected the file and checked the options you need, click the Place button to place the file into your document.

Figure 9.1 When placing a file, you can control whether an image is place-linked by checking the Link check box in the Place dialog.

Method Two: Opening a File

Choose File > Open, choose a raster file on your hard drive or server, and then click the Open button. Illustrator creates a new letter-sized document and places the image in the center of it. When you're opening a raster file in this way, the image is always place-embedded within your Illustrator document. The document takes on the color mode of the image.

Method Three: Dragging a File

From Adobe Bridge, from the Finder on Mac OS, or from any Windows Explorer window, drag a raster file right onto your Illustrator artboard. You can also select multiple files and place them all at once (**Figure 9.2**). Using this method, Illustrator place-links the files. To place-embed images while dragging them into your document, hold the Shift key while dragging the images.

It is notably easier to drag files into your document when Bridge is in Compact mode.

Figure 9.2 When you're dragging several images at once from Bridge, an icon indicates the placement of multiple files into your Illustrator document.

Featured Matchup: Place-Linked Files vs. Place-Embedded Files

When placing an image into Illustrator, you can choose to have the image linked to your document or embedded within it. Each method has its own benefits, and which you choose depends on your needs and your workflow.

When you place-link an image, a preview of the image appears in your layout, but the actual image exists in a completely separate file. At all times, Illustrator needs to know where this file is. Otherwise, Illustrator won't be able to print the file correctly. In fact, if you were to save your Illustrator file and send it off to someone else (such as a service provider, for example), you would have to send the external linked image along with the file. If you have several linked images in your document, you have to keep track of many files. In contrast, a place-embedded file exists within your Illustrator document, and therefore, the original external image that you placed is no longer required. When you send the document to another user, the image travels along with the single Illustrator file.

Images—especially high-resolution ones—feature hefty file sizes. When you choose to embed a placed image, the file size of the image is added to the size of your Illustrator file. For example, if your Illustrator file is 1 MB in size and you place-embed a 30 MB image into your document, the size of your Illustrator document grows to 31 MB. When you place-link an image, however, the file is never added to your document, so the Illustrator file stays at 1 MB.

Although managing multiple files and file size are issues that will affect your decision to link or embed image files, one of the main reasons you will choose to link a file rather than embed it is so you can easily update the image when necessary. When you place-link a file, the image you see in your layout is a preview of the file that really exists elsewhere. Anytime you make an adjustment to the original image (say, in Photoshop), the preview in your layout updates to reflect those changes. Illustrator even has a feature called Edit Original that assists in this process of updating linked images (see "Managing Placed Images" later in this chapter). However, if you place-embed an image, you can no longer update that image easily.

Placing Native Photoshop Files (PSD)

Typically, the interchange file formats for images that are used in print design layouts are TIFF or EPS, but Illustrator allows you to place native Photoshop files (PSD) as well.

PLACING RASTER-BASED FILES 337

Generally, placing a native Photoshop file isn't any different from placing any other file. Illustrator enjoys a wonderful relationship with Photoshop, however, and you can take advantage of extended functionality when placing Photoshop files.

If the PSD file you are placing contains Photoshop Layer Comps, Illustrator presents you with the Photoshop Import Options dialog, where you can choose which Layer Comp will be visible in the file from the Layer Comp pop-up menu (**Figure 9.3**). Check the Show Preview box to see what the Layer Comp looks like before you place the file. You can also choose whether Illustrator or Photoshop controls how layer visibility is updated by choosing from the When Updating Link pop-up menu. The Photoshop Import Options dialog offers additional options, which are covered later in this chapter in "Working with Adobe Photoshop."

The Layer Comps feature in Photoshop allows you to create named sets of visible layers. For more information on Layer Comps, refer to Photoshop's Online Help or *Real World Adobe Photoshop CS3,* by David Blatner, Conrad Chavez, and Bruce Fraser (Peachpit Press, 2007).

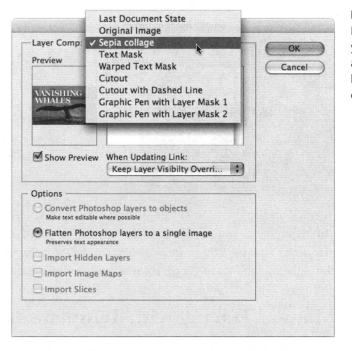

Figure 9.3 The Photoshop Import Options dialog allows you to control the appearance of your Photoshop file before you place it into your document.

Unfortunately, once you place an image into an Illustrator document, you don't have any way to access the Photoshop Import Options dialog to change to a different Layer Comp. To work around this apparent oversight, you can use the Relink function, which effectively places the file again and opens the dialog (see "Managing Placed Images" for information on relinking files).

For a detailed description of the different file formats and their benefits and roles in a design workflow, refer to Chapter 13, *Saving and Exporting Files.*

Working with Placed Images

Once you've placed an image into an Illustrator document, the image acts like a single rectangular shape that can be transformed (moved, scaled, rotated, sheared, and reflected). You can apply opacity and blend mode values from the Transparency panel, and you can also apply many different live effects to a placed image, including Feather and Drop Shadow.

Sometimes a design calls for showing only a portion of a placed image. Programs such as Photoshop (which can crop images) and page layout applications such as Adobe InDesign (which use picture frames) are able to display only portions of an image. Illustrator, however, has no such tool or functionality. To have only a portion of an image display on your artboard, you have to create a mask (**Figure 9.4**). (See Chapter 5, *Brushes, Symbols, and Masks*, for more information on creating masks).

Figure 9.4 Using a clipping mask, you can display just a portion of a placed image.

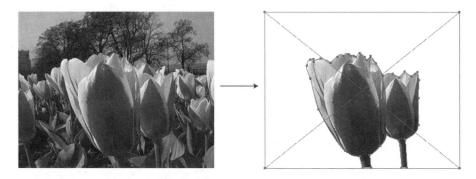

You can also apply color to certain kinds of placed images. Illustrator allows you to apply either a solid process or a spot color to a 1-bit TIFF image or to any image that uses the grayscale color model. Simply select the image on the artboard, and choose a fill color as you would for any vector object.

Manual Tracing with Template Layers

Template layers are not to be confused with Illustrator templates, which are actual Illustrator files that contain elements already inside of them. Illustrator templates are covered in Chapter 1, *The Illustrator Environment*.

Sometimes you may want to place an image into Illustrator—not as a design *element* but rather as a design *guide*. For example, you might sketch an idea for a design on paper and then scan that sketch into your computer. Then, you would place that scan into your Illustrator document as a guide for drawing final shapes with Illustrator's vector tools. Alternatively, you may place a map into Illustrator so that you can create your own customized directions to an event.

In these cases, you may not actually want to trace the scan exactly as it appears (using Illustrator's Live Trace feature, covered later in this chapter, might be a better choice for such a task), but rather, you may just want the image to act as a reference. To prevent the image from getting in the way of your design, you might want to adjust the opacity of the image (**Figure 9.5**). Additionally, you may want to lock the image so that you don't move it accidentally.

Figure 9.5 Drawing on top of an image at full strength may be difficult (left). Placing an image on a dimmed template layer allows you to trace over the image with ease (right).

Rather than going through the process of adjusting and locking images, Illustrator has a way to manage this process in a more dignified manner—using a template layer. Once a template layer has been created, the image on that layer automatically becomes locked, and the opacity level of the image is set to 50%. You can check the Template option at the bottom of the Place dialog when placing an image to have the image automatically appear on a template layer, or you can double-click any layer and check the Template option (**Figure 9.6**).

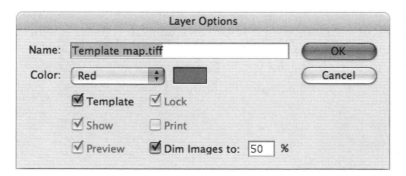

Figure 9.6 The Template option appears in the Layer Options dialog and applies to a single layer.

MANAGING PLACED IMAGES

Whether the images you place in a file are linked or embedded, it's important to be able to track where those images came from and to access additional information about the images. To manage all the placed images in your document, choose Window > Links to open the Links panel.

By default, the Links panel lists all the images in your document. However, from the Links panel menu, you can specify that the Links panel display only missing, modified, or embedded images (**Figure 9.7**). In addition, you can choose to have the Links panel list images sorted by name (file name), kind (file type), or status (up-to-date or modified).

Figure 9.7 Icons in the Layers panel indicate additional information about the images that are placed in your document. No icon indicates a place-linked file.

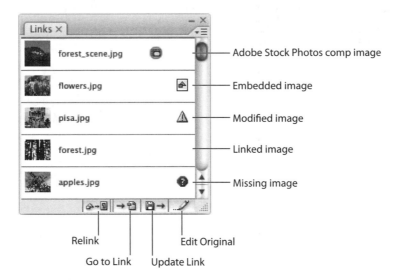

Double-clicking any file listed in the Links panel opens a Link Information dialog, offering additional information about the image. Besides listing the file size of the image, the Link Information dialog also gives you the location of the image (the file path) and detailed scaling and rotation information (**Figure 9.8**).

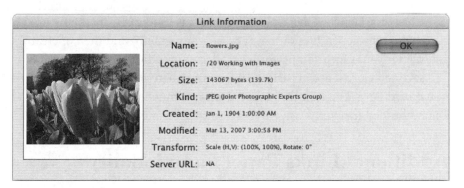

Figure 9.8 Double-clicking a listing in the Links panel opens Link Information, a dialog containing useful information.

Along the bottom of the Links panel are four buttons (refer to the earlier Figure 9.7) that allow you to perform certain functions with the images in your document. To use these functions, first highlight an image in the Links panel, and then click the desired button.

- **Relink.** The Relink button allows you to replace one image with a different one. When you click the Relink button, the Place dialog appears, allowing you to choose another file, which replaces the selected image. You can use Relink either to swap high-resolution files for low-resolution ones or to replace FPO (For Position Only) placeholder images with final copies. Additionally, you can use the Relink function and choose to replace your file with the same image (replacing it with itself), which allows you to access different Place settings or to replace an embedded image that was updated.

- **Go to Link.** The Go to Link button adjusts the view setting of your document window so that the highlighted image in the Links panel is centered on your screen. In addition, the image becomes selected. This makes it easy to quickly find an image, and it is especially useful in documents that contain many placed images.

- **Update Link.** The Update Link button allows you to update place-linked images when Illustrator detects that external files have been modified outside of Illustrator. Images that have been modified appear with a yellow warning icon in the Links panel. The Update Link button is dim when an embedded image is chosen.

- **Edit Original.** You can click the Edit Original button when you want to modify a place-linked image in the image's creator application. When you highlight an image in the Links panel and click Edit Original,

Refer to Appendix B, *Application Preferences,* for information on the Update Links setting in the File Handling & Clipboard panel in Preferences, which controls whether Illustrator updates modified files automatically or manually.

Illustrator launches the application that was used to create the file (or that is set to open files of that type on your system) and then opens the file for you. Once you perform any necessary edits on the file, simply save and close it and return to Illustrator, where the image updates accordingly. The Edit Original button is dim when you highlight an embedded image.

Additional Links Panel Functionality

In addition to the functions in the Links panel that we've already discussed, you can take advantage of several other important settings through the use of the Links panel, which you'll find listed in the panel menu (**Figure 9.9**).

Figure 9.9 The Links panel menu grants you access to additional features for working with placed images.

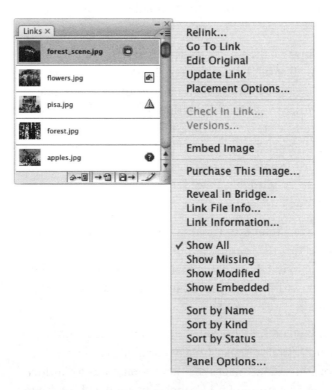

- **Placement Options.** When you relink or replace a file, you can use the Placement Options setting to define how an image appears once it has been placed into your document. By default, Illustrator preserves any transforms you've applied to the image that you're replacing, but you can also choose from four other settings. A helpful illustration

within the Placement Options dialog explains what each setting does
(**Figure 9.10**).

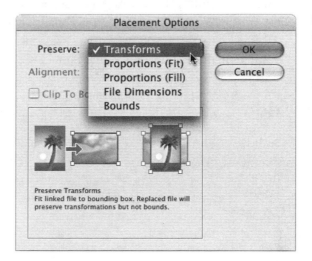

Figure 9.10 Each setting in the Placement Options dialog offers an illustration and a description for what it does.

- **Embed Image.** If you have a place-linked image in your document, you can select the image in the Links panel and choose the Embed Image option from the Links panel menu to embed that image in your file.

- **Purchase This Image.** When placing a comp that you've downloaded using the Adobe Stock Photos service, Illustrator displays a special icon that indicates the image is an Adobe Stock Photos comp image (you can find the Adobe Stock Photos service in Bridge). After the client approves the use of an image, you can choose the Purchase This Image option in the Links panel menu, at which point you are led through the process of purchasing the image through the Adobe Stock Photos service.

- **Link File Info.** Images and files can contain metadata (refer to Chapter 1, *The Illustrator Environment*, for more information), and at times, you may need to view the metadata of images you've placed into your document. For example, you may want to know whether you have the rights to reproduce the image or whom you need to credit for using an image. The Link File Info option in the Links panel menu allows you to view the placed image's metadata (you won't be able to edit it, however).

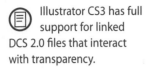 Illustrator CS3 has full support for linked DCS 2.0 files that interact with transparency.

- **Panel Options.** Always trying to accommodate, Illustrator allows you to customize the Links panel somewhat by choosing Panel Options from the Links panel menu. You can choose a thumbnail size, or if you prefer, you can eliminate thumbnails altogether (**Figure 9.11**; this is useful when you have many placed images in your document). Additionally, you can choose the Show DCS Transparency Interactions option to have Illustrator alert you when placed Desktop Color Separations (DCS) 1.0 files interact with transparency in your document. This setting results in slower performance, though.

Figure 9.11 With thumbnails turned off, the Links panel in Illustrator looks just like the one in InDesign.

Faster Access to Image Settings with the Control Panel

When you select an image on your artboard, a Mask button appears in the Control panel, making it easy to quickly apply a mask and crop the image. Refer to Chapter 5, *Brushes, Symbols, and Masks*, for more information on using masks.

Although the Links panel offers a single location from which to track information about your placed images, you can also use the Control panel to quickly access certain settings and features that pertain to a selected image. The Control panel displays the file name, the color mode, and the resolution of a selected image. In addition, for linked images, the Control panel offers options to embed or edit the file via the Edit Original feature, which was discussed earlier in the chapter. You can also click the image's file name in the Control panel to access additional features that are found in the Links panel (**Figure 9.12**).

Figure 9.12 Clicking the file name of a linked image in the Control panel offers a shortcut to several often-used functions.

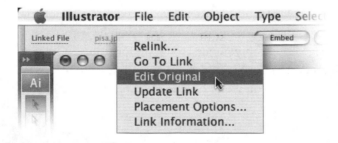

Using the Document Info Panel

The Links panel isn't the only place where you'll find information about place-linked and place-embedded images. You can choose Window > Document Info to open the Document Info panel, which offers information on a lot more than just images. In fact, the Document Info panel can prove quite useful for providing document information on a variety of attributes and settings (**Figure 9.13**).

By default, the Document Info panel shows information on only those objects that are selected on the artboard. To find out information about all the objects in a file, choose Select > All, or you can uncheck the Selection Only option in the Document Info panel menu.

To find out information about certain aspects of an Illustrator document, choose from one of these settings in the Document Info panel menu:

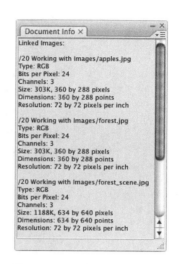

Figure 9.13 The Document Info panel provides detailed information on just about anything you could ask for about your file, including linked images.

- **Document.** The Document setting displays the color mode for your document, along with a listing of other important document settings such as text editability and color profile.

- **Objects.** This setting displays the total number of objects in your file, broken down by object type. This setting offers a quick way to find out how many linked or embedded images you have in your document, how many objects are colored with spot colors, or how many transparent objects there are.

- **Graphic Styles.** To see a list of all the graphic styles that are used in your document, as well as to how many objects each style is applied, choose this setting.

- **Brushes.** The Brushes option lists all the brushes used in your document.

- **Spot Color Objects.** This setting lists the spot colors used in your document.

- **Pattern Objects.** The Pattern Objects option lists all the patterns used in your document. This is especially helpful because it includes patterns that are used inside complex appearances and Pattern brushes.

- **Gradient Objects.** This setting lists all the gradients that are used in your document.

- **Fonts.** The Fonts option lists all the fonts used in your document.

- **Linked Images.** The Linked Images option lists all the linked images that appear in your document, along with information about each image.

- **Embedded Images.** The Embedded Images setting lists all the embedded images that appear in your document, along with information about each image.

- **Font Details.** The Font Details option lists information about the fonts used in your document. This is helpful when you want to quickly find out whether you are using OpenType, TrueType, or PostScript fonts in your document.

You can save all the information listed in the Document Info panel by choosing Save from the Document Info panel menu. A text file is created that contains the information for all the items just outlined.

CONVERTING RASTERS TO VECTORS USING LIVE TRACE

Certain Illustrator features, such as Pathfinder, are incredibly useful and, as a result, are used many times a day. Features such as 3D are also extremely cool, but they aren't used as often. Every once in a while, a feature comes along in Illustrator that is cool and fun to use but that is also practical enough that you use it on a regular basis. Illustrator's Live Trace is such a feature.

The concept is simple enough: take a raster-based image, and convert it into a vector-based image. You would want to do this to get around the limitations of a raster-based file. For example, if you want to scale artwork up in size or if you want to edit the artwork easily and use spot colors, you want to work with a vector-based file.

Separate applications (such as Adobe Streamline) and Illustrator plug-ins (such as Free Soft's Silhouette) have the ability to convert raster content into vectors, but Live Trace is a far step above and beyond what those tools are capable of doing. One of the main reasons for this is because of how Live Trace works.

Live Trace uses a two-step process when converting rasters to vectors. In the first step, Live Trace *conditions* the raster image for optimal tracing. This means Illustrator makes adjustments to the raster image, such as adjusting contrast or blurring jagged edges. In the second step, Live Trace draws vector paths, creating highly accurate vector art (**Figure 9.14**). Although the tracing is theoretically done at that point, Illustrator retains a link to the original raster image so you can adjust the tracing settings. As you update the different raster conditioning and vector tracing settings, you can preview the results immediately. This makes it easy to get just the right tracing result that suits your needs best.

ORIGINAL SCAN

ORIGINAL SCAN ENLARGED 300%

Figure 9.14 Illustrator's Live Trace feature starts with the original raster image (top), conditions the image (center), and then converts it to clean vectors (bottom). The first two examples in this three-page spread use the default (Simple Trace) setting for tracing, whereas the third shows the Grayscale tracing setting.

CONDITIONED IMAGE

CONDITIONED IMAGE ENLARGED 300%

TRACED RESULT

TRACED RESULT ENLARGED 300%

ORIGINAL SCAN

ORIGINAL SCAN ENLARGED 300%

CONDITIONED IMAGE

CONDITIONED IMAGE ENLARGED 300%

TRACED RESULT

TRACED RESULT ENLARGED 300%

ORIGINAL SCAN

ORIGINAL SCAN ENLARGED 300%

CONDITIONED IMAGE

CONDITIONED IMAGE ENLARGED 300%

TRACED RESULT

TRACED RESULT ENLARGED 300%

Tracing an Image

Tracing an image is simple. Select any raster image in your Illustrator document, and click the Live Trace button in the Control panel. Alternatively, you can choose Object > Live Trace > Make. This action traces the image using Illustrator's default trace preset. Illustrator ships with 14 tracing presets, each optimized for different kinds of images and desired result. Once the image is traced, it maintains a live link to the raster image, and you can customize the tracing settings. For example, once the image is traced, the Control panel changes to reflect different settings, including a Preset pop-up menu (**Figure 9.15**). Choose from any of Illustrator's different presets to see a different traced result on your screen.

Figure 9.15 The Preset pop-up menu in the Control panel lets you quickly experiment with different tracing presets.

If you know which tracing preset you want to use before you trace your image, you can select it directly by clicking the upside-down triangle that appears just to the right side of the Live Trace button and choosing it from the list that pops up (**Figure 9.16**).

Figure 9.16 It doesn't look like a pop-up menu, but it is. Clicking the upside-down triangle allows you to apply a specific tracing preset when you first choose to trace an image.

As long as Illustrator maintains a live link to the raster image, you won't be able to edit the actual vector paths that were created during the tracing process. In order to do so, you either have to expand the traced object or convert it to a Live Paint group. We discuss both of these options later, but for now, we'll focus on how to customize the tracing settings so that you can get the best results from the Live Trace feature.

If you're happy with the traced results, there's no need to expand the object. Illustrator can print the vector paths just fine (it expands the paths in the print stream).

Exploring the Live Trace Preview Options

Once you've traced an image, Illustrator displays the traced result on your artboard so you can see the results. However, Illustrator offers a variety of settings that you can use to control how both the raster image and the traced vector result appear on your artboard.

When a traced image is selected on the artboard, the Control panel updates to contain two icons that, at first glance, look like triangles. Upon closer inspection, you'll notice that one icon features a jagged edge; this icon is used to control how the raster image is previewed. The icon on the right, which has a smooth edge, is used to control how the traced vector result is previewed (**Figure 9.17**). Each of these settings is separate and can be chosen independently of the other.

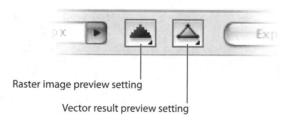

Raster image preview setting

Vector result preview setting

Figure 9.17 Once you've traced an image, you can use the two icons in the Control panel to control how the artwork appears on the artboard.

Previewing the Original Raster Image

In the Control panel, the jagged triangle on the left controls how the raster image is viewed. Click the icon once, and choose from one of the four available settings (**Figure 9.18** on the following page).

Figure 9.18 You can preview the raster image with the Original Image setting (left), the Adjusted Image setting (center), or the Transparent Image setting (right). The No Image option is not shown for obvious reasons.

ORIGINAL IMAGE

ADJUSTED IMAGE

TRANSPARENT IMAGE

ORIGINAL IMAGE

ADJUSTED IMAGE

TRANSPARENT IMAGE

ORIGINAL IMAGE

ADJUSTED IMAGE

TRANSPARENT IMAGE

- **No Image.** This setting completely hides the raster image from the screen (and is the default setting).

- **Original Image.** This setting displays the original raster image in your document, which can be useful when you're comparing the original image to the traced result.

- **Adjusted Image.** This setting displays the raster image as it appears after Live Trace has applied the raster conditioning adjustments. This preview mode is great for seeing how Live Trace works, and it makes it easier to preview any adjustments you make to the raster image settings.

- **Transparent Image.** This setting displays a dimmed preview of the bitmap image beneath the traced result, letting you see the traced results as compared to the original raster image.

Previewing the Traced Vector Result

In the Control panel, the smooth triangle on the right controls how the traced vector result is viewed. Click the icon once, and choose from one of the four available settings (**Figure 9.19**).

TRACING RESULT

OUTLINES

OUTLINES WITH TRACING

Figure 9.19 You can preview the vector result with the Tracing Result setting (left), the Outlines setting (center), and the Outlines with Tracing setting (right). The No Tracing Result option is not shown.

TRACING RESULT

OUTLINES

OUTLINES WITH TRACING

TRACING RESULT

OUTLINES

OUTLINES WITH TRACING

354 CHAPTER 9: MIXING IT UP: WORKING WITH VECTORS AND PIXELS

- **No Tracing Result.** This setting hides the traced vector objects from the screen.

- **Tracing Result.** This setting displays the vector result of the tracing (and is the default setting).

- **Outlines.** This setting highlights the actual Bézier paths that were created when the image was traced.

- **Outlines with Tracing.** This setting highlights the Bézier paths as semitransparent, enabling you to compare filled areas of the traced vector result with the original bitmap image. The color of the outlines will match the color specified for guides in the Guides & Grid panel in Preferences.

Tweaking to Get the Perfect Trace

What makes the Live Trace feature a joy to use is the ability to make adjustments to the settings while you see the results update on your screen. Aside from the presets you can apply, Illustrator contains a dialog chock-full of settings you can use to ensure that you get the results you need from the Live Trace feature.

To access these settings, select a Live Trace object, and click the Tracing Options dialog button in the Control panel. Alternatively, you can choose Object > Live Trace > Tracing Options. Once the Tracing Options dialog appears on your screen, you'll notice that it's split into several different sections (**Figure 9.20**).

First, a Preview check box appears on the far right of the dialog, which allows you to see results update as you make changes to the different settings. Next, directly underneath the Preview check box is a list of important details about your traced object. The values for the number of paths, anchor points, colors, distinct closed areas, and image resolution update as you adjust the settings in the dialog. Keeping an eye on these values helps you make decisions as you edit your trace settings. At the top of the dialog is a Preset pop-up menu, similar to what you see in the Control panel when you have a Live Trace object selected. Stepping through the different presets in the Tracing Options dialog allows you to see the settings for each of the presets.

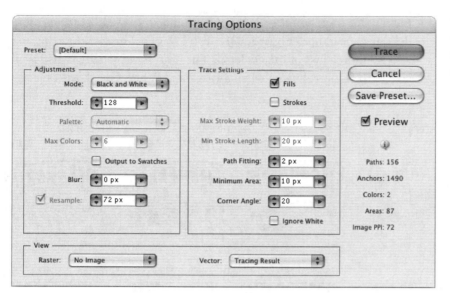

The rest of the Tracing Options dialog is separated into three sections called Adjustments, Trace Settings, and View. The View section allows you to specify how the traced object appears on your artboard, as discussed in the earlier "Exploring the Live Trace Preview Options" section.

The following "Modifying the Raster Adjustments" and "Adjusting the Vector Trace Settings" sections will help you clearly understand the two-step process that the Live Trace feature performs when converting raster images into vector form.

Modifying the Raster Adjustments

The Adjustments settings found on the left side of the Tracing Options dialog apply to the raster conditioning that occurs before the image is traced.

- **Mode.** Live Trace converts a bitmap image to either 1-bit black and white, 8-bit grayscale, or 8-bit color, which you can choose from the Mode pop-up menu.

- **Threshold.** The Threshold setting determines the boundaries between pixels when using the Black and White trace setting. For example, in a gray bitmap, a high Threshold setting results in more gray pixels becoming black vector objects and thus a heavier appearance. In that same image, a low Threshold setting results in more gray pixels ignored, making for more white-colored objects and an overall lighter or more delicate appearance (**Figure 9.21**). Too low of a Threshold setting may also result in a loss of image detail. The Threshold setting is also available in the Control panel when a Black and White Live Trace object is selected.

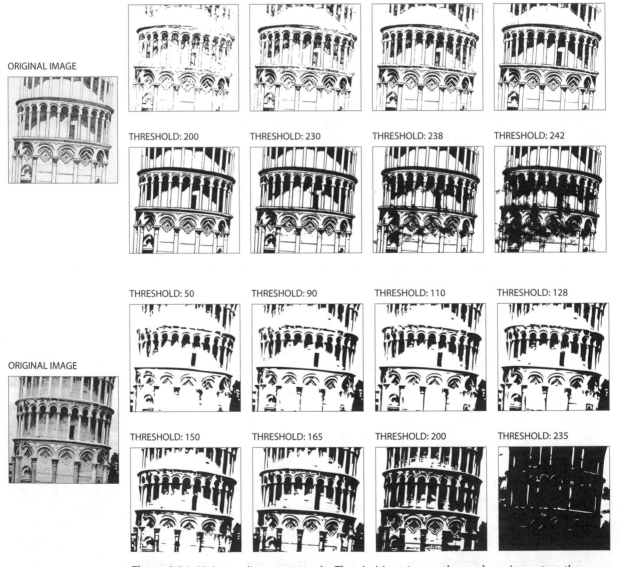

Figure 9.21 Making adjustments to the Threshold setting can have a large impact on the overall appearance of the traced result. Here are examples of an image with a variety of different Threshold settings.

- **Palette.** By default, Illustrator uses the selective color reduction method to choose the best colors to fit the image (based on the Max Colors value). However, you can choose specific colors that Illustrator should use when tracing your image. To do so, you must first load a custom swatch library (refer to Chapter 1, *The Illustrator Environment*, for instructions on how to define a custom swatch library). When a custom swatch library is opened in your document, the Palette pop-up menu displays all the loaded custom libraries (**Figure 9.22**). Live Trace then uses the colors that appear within the custom swatch library that you choose.

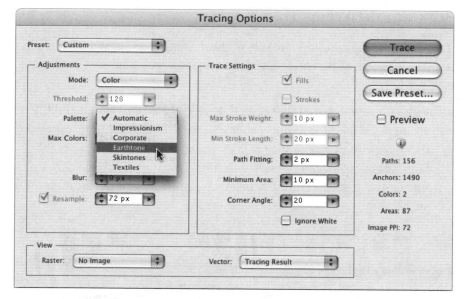

Figure 9.22 Loading several custom libraries allows you to quickly experiment with a variety of color schemes.

- **Max Colors.** The Max Colors setting determines the maximum number of colors that can be used in the final traced result. This setting is not available for the Black and White Mode setting or when you choose a custom color palette. Live Trace uses the selective color reduction method to reduce the number of colors in the raster image to match this setting during the conditioning process. The Max Colors setting is also available in the Control panel when a Grayscale or Color Live Trace object is selected.

Check the Output to Swatches option to have Illustrator add each color that is used during the tracing process as a global process color in your Swatches panel.

- **Blur.** The Blur setting applies a Gaussian Blur to the image, which helps remove noise from the raster image. This reduces the number of anchor points in the tracing result, especially when you are tracing photographic images.

- **Resample.** The Resample setting lets you change the resolution of the bitmap image to help obtain a better traced result. Resampling a high-resolution image to a lower resolution greatly enhances the speed performance of Live Trace.

Adjusting the Vector Trace Settings

The Trace Settings on the right side of the Tracing Options dialog apply to the actual tracing of the image and determine how the final vector paths are drawn.

- **Fills.** When you have Fills selected, Live Trace creates closed and filled vector paths for all resulting vector objects. Fill tracing produces results that more closely match the original image, including variable-width lines that are common in marker or ink renderings (**Figure 9.23**). Fill tracing also results in more complex vectors because it needs more anchor points.

Figure 9.23 When you choose the Fills setting, the traced paths appear with thick and thin edges, closely matching the original image.

- **Strokes.** With the Strokes setting selected, Live Trace creates stroked open paths for all areas that fall within the Max Stroke Weight setting. Areas that exceed this setting result in unfilled areas outlined with a 1-point stroke. Stroke tracing results in paths with fewer anchor points (**Figure 9.24**).

Figure 9.24 When you choose the Strokes setting, the traced paths appear consistent, which results in a less complex traced image overall.

- **Max Stroke Weight.** The Max Stroke Weight setting determines the heaviest stroke weight Live Trace can use when tracing the image. This setting is available only when you use the Strokes trace setting.

- **Min Stroke Length.** The Min Stroke Length setting determines the shortest path that Live Trace can use when tracing the image. This setting is available only when you use the Strokes trace setting.

- **Path Fitting.** Path Fitting determines how closely Live Trace follows the shape of the original raster image. A lower Path Fitting setting results in paths that closely match the original raster image yet might also reveal imperfections or irregular paths that aren't smooth. A higher setting produces smoother paths with fewer anchor points but might not match the raster image as closely (**Figure 9.25**).

Figure 9.25 This figure shows examples of a variety of Path Fitting settings for the same image. Notice how the paths get smoother as the number is increased but that the result doesn't match the original sketch as much.

ORIGINAL SCAN ENLARGED 300%

PATH FITTING: 1 pixel

PATH FITTING: 2 pixels

PATH FITTING: 4 pixels

PATH FITTING: 6 pixels

PATH FITTING: 8 pixels

- **Minimum Area.** The Minimum Area setting sets a threshold for how large a section of the raster image has to be in order to be traced into a vector object. By setting a minimum area, you can have the Live Trace feature trace only those areas of pixels that meet a minimum size. For example, if Minimum Area is set to 9 pixels, Live Trace ignores regions of pixels that are less than 3 by 3 pixels in size.

- **Corner Angle.** The Corner Angle setting defines the sharpness of the angles used in the resulting vector objects. This setting is measured in degrees, not pixels. If you think of 0 degrees as perfectly flat and 180 degrees as a hard corner (rather than a rounded one), anything sharper than the Corner Angle setting (the default is 20) is converted to a corner anchor point rather than a smooth anchor point.

- **Ignore White.** White areas in a trace are filled with the color white by default. This means that if you position your traced artwork over a background, the white areas will block out the background. If you'd like your trace to treat white areas as being filled with the none attribute, you can check the Ignore White setting. In this way, backgrounds will show through the nonblack areas of your traced artwork.

Editing Live Trace Paths

Once you've achieved a trace result that you're satisfied with, you might want to edit the Bézier paths, either to delete portions of the image or to apply your own colors, gradients, or patterns. To edit the vector paths of the traced object, you will need to either expand the trace or convert the traced object to a Live Paint group.

Expanding a Live Trace Object

With a Live Trace object selected, click the Expand button in the Control panel. Alternatively, you can choose Object > Live Trace > Expand. You can then use the Direct Selection tool to edit anchor points and Bézier

The Minimum Area setting is also available in the Control panel when you have a Live Trace object selected.

Once you've specified your settings in the Tracing Options dialog, you can click the Save Preset button to define your own tracing presets.

If you select both the Fills and Strokes options, Live Trace converts the raster to a vector using a combination of both stroked and filled paths.

paths (**Figure 9.26**). At this point, the traced object is no longer linked to the original raster image, and you can no longer adjust the traced result using any of the Live Trace options.

Figure 9.26 Once you've expanded a Live Trace object, you can edit the paths as you would with any vector object.

You can press Option (Alt) while clicking the Live Trace button or when choosing a Live Trace preset from the Control panel to both trace and expand an image in one step.

Converting Traced Images to Live Paint Groups

In Chapter 4, *Advanced Vectors,* you learned about Illustrator's Live Paint feature, which allows you to apply fill attributes to areas, even if they aren't fully enclosed shapes. If you've traced an image because you want to fill regions of the image with color, converting the Live Trace object to a Live Paint group makes a lot of sense.

With a Live Trace object selected on the artboard, click the Live Paint button that appears in the Control panel. This action expands the traced object and converts all of the resulting vector objects into a Live Paint group in a single step. You can then use the Live Paint Bucket tool to fill your art with color without any additional steps (**Figure 9.27**). For more information on Live Paint groups, refer to Chapter 4, *Advanced Vectors*.

For performance reasons, Gap Detection is turned off for Live Paint groups that are created directly from a Live Trace object. You can turn Gap Detection on manually, or you can create smaller Live Paint groups to get better performance.

Figure 9.27 What started out as a pencil sketch quickly turns into final art when you combine the Live Trace and Live Paint features in Illustrator.

TURNING VECTORS INTO RASTERS

It's easy to see the benefits of converting raster images into vector-based artwork to allow for better scaling and editing. Interestingly enough, Illustrator can also perform the transition in reverse—converting vector-based artwork into rasterized art. Sometimes this is done to achieve a special effect where you might want to see a pixelated image (**Figure 9.28**). Alternatively, you might start with a gradient mesh object, which you then rasterize and convert back to vectors using Live Trace to achieve a posterized graphic effect (**Figure 9.29**).

Figure 9.28 Rasterizing text at an extremely low resolution can add an interesting design element to your layout.

Figure 9.29 Once you've rasterized a gradient mesh object (left), performing a Live Trace can produce abstract design elements (right).

 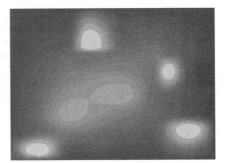

To convert vector artwork to pixels, select the art, and choose Object > Rasterize, which opens the Rasterize dialog. You'll find you can choose from a variety of settings when rasterizing artwork (**Figure 9.30**).

- **Color Model.** Depending on the document color mode setting to which your file is set, you'll see CMYK, Grayscale, and Bitmap listed here, or you'll see RGB, Grayscale, and Bitmap. This is because a document cannot contain both CMYK and RGB elements. This setting can be extremely useful because it allows you to change the color model of an object (even an image). For example, you can convert colored objects to grayscale.

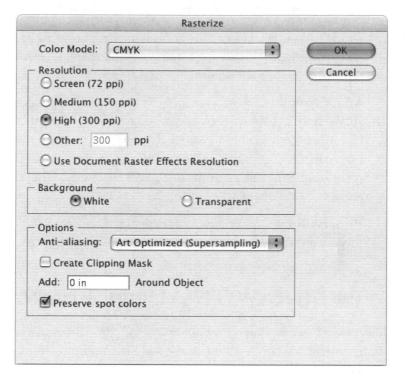

- **Resolution.** Here in the Rasterize dialog, the default resolution is set to 300 ppi, which is usually sufficient for print-related artwork. If you want all your artwork in your document to appear consistent, you can also specify that the resolution setting should match the setting found in the Document Raster Effects Settings dialog.

- **Background.** You can choose whether the resulting raster will have a transparent background or a white background. If your effect overlaps other objects, you probably want to use the transparent setting, although remember that the file still needs to be flattened (see Chapter 12, *Prepress and Printing*, for more information on transparency flattening).

- **Anti-aliasing.** You can define whether the raster image will be anti-aliased. Antialiasing slightly blurs color boundaries to avoid the appearance of jagged edges. For more information on antialiasing, refer to Chapter 11, *Web and Mobile Design*.

- **Create Clipping Mask.** Creates a clipping mask around the area of a shape so that you can have it blend into a background (raster images are always rectangular in shape and may block out objects that appear behind them). This setting won't work very well for objects that have Drop Shadow, Feather, or Glow effects applied, because clipping masks have hard edges. This setting is not necessary if you specify the Transparent option for the Background.

- **Add X Around Object.** Depending on the kind of artwork that you are rasterizing, you may experience some clipping when the artwork becomes rasterized. This is especially possible when rasterizing objects that have soft edges, such as Feather effects, applied. Specifying extra space around the object results in a larger raster image, but that incorporates all of the artwork.

- **Preserve Spot Colors.** If your artwork contains spot colors, checking this option will preserve the spot colors in the resulting raster image.

WORKING WITH ADOBE PHOTOSHOP

Illustrator's sister application is Photoshop, and throughout this entire book, we have discussed how both Illustrator and Photoshop are different. Yet, at the same time, they have a lot in common. For one, they are both Adobe products, and therefore, they share similar user interfaces and many of the same tools and panels. At a much deeper level, however, they share common technology. For example, both applications use the Adobe Color Engine, an Adobe shared component used for color management. Both Illustrator and Photoshop also use the Adobe Text Engine, which makes it possible for both applications to exchange text easily and share many of the same text features.

At the end of the day, a graphics professional can gain a tremendous amount of power from using both of these applications. Rather than trying to force one of these powerhouse applications to do everything, you can take advantage of the benefits that each application offers and use both to complete your work.

Whether you're starting in Illustrator and then bringing your art into Photoshop for finishing touches, or whether you're starting in Photoshop and then bringing your designs into Illustrator, both applications can work together in many ways. For the remainder of this chapter, we explore how you can use both Illustrator and Photoshop in your workflow.

Going from Illustrator to Photoshop

When you want to bring art from Illustrator into Photoshop, you can open an Illustrator file directly in Photoshop, but doing so results in a single flat image that isn't editable. Instead, consider exporting a native Photoshop file from Illustrator directly; this preserves certain elements in an editable form. Using the Export command in Illustrator results in a Photoshop file that you can edit far more easily when you open it in Photoshop.

To export a Photoshop file from Illustrator, choose File > Export, and choose Photoshop (.psd) for the file format.

When exporting a PSD file, you can choose between CMYK, RGB, and Grayscale color models, and you can specify a resolution for your file. If you choose to export a flat image, all Illustrator layers are flattened into a single nontransparent layer (what Photoshop calls the Background layer). Alternatively, you can choose the Write Layers option, which preserves Illustrator's layering where possible. You can also choose to preserve text and other native elements, as we discussed earlier.

The following is a list of the attributes that can be preserved when Illustrator exports a native Photoshop file; see "Exporting to the Adobe Photoshop (PSD) Format" in Chapter 13, *Saving and Exporting Files*, for additional details:

- **Layers.** Any layers that you've created, and the names of those layers, are preserved when you open the file in Photoshop. By carefully creating a layer structure in Illustrator, you can take advantage of greater editability when the file is opened in Photoshop.

- **Vectors.** If you used the shape modes in the Pathfinder panel to create compound shapes, these objects are converted to Photoshop shape layers, which are editable vectors in Photoshop. If you want a path to be preserved as a vector shape, you must apply a shape mode to it in order to preserve it as a vector in Photoshop. If you have a single shape that you want to preserve as a vector, select the shape, and choose Make Compound Shape from the Pathfinder panel menu.

- **Text.** Illustrator preserves text objects so that they are editable when the file containing them is opened in Photoshop.

- **Transparency.** If you've applied opacity values or blend modes from Illustrator's Transparency panel, those values are also preserved when the file is opened in Photoshop.

- **Masks.** If you create clipping masks in your file, those masks are preserved and show up in Photoshop as layer masks. Because masks allow you to work in a nondestructive fashion, you can create files that are more flexible in your workflow.

- **Slices.** If you create Web slices in your Illustrator file, those slices appear when the file is opened in Photoshop. Additionally, any optimization settings that you've applied to your slices, including settings that you've applied from the Save for Web dialog, are preserved and can be edited once the file is opened in Photoshop.

Often, layers are combined because overprint commands are applied to some objects on those layers. Targeting each layer and checking the Isolate Blending option in the Transparency panel can help keep the layers from merging on export.

Illustrator does its best to keep elements editable during the export process. However, if you find that certain elements are not being preserved, the cause may be that preserving editability would change the appearance of the artwork. Try rearranging the layers in Illustrator to avoid issues where artwork appearance is dependent upon the interaction of multiple layers.

Honoring Crop Marks in a File—Illustrator's Export Function

To ensure that you export a file using the exact dimensions that you require, or to ensure the proper positioning of your art, it's best to draw a rectangle of the size you need and position it on the page. Then, choose Object > Crop Area > Make to specify the crop area (**Figure 9.31**). Alternatively, you can use the Crop Area tool to define a crop area well. Refer to Chapter 1, *The Illustrator Environment*, for more information.

Figure 9.31 When you set crop marks before exporting your file, Illustrator sets the bounding box where you set the crop marks. If art extends beyond the crop area, that art is still preserved in the file, thus allowing you to reposition the artwork in Photoshop as needed.

Copying and Pasting Between Illustrator and Photoshop

Copying and pasting art between Illustrator and Photoshop works extremely well. You can copy text freely between the two applications, and when you paste art from Illustrator into Photoshop, you can paste the art as a Photoshop smart object, which preserves editability within Photoshop. In fact, when you paste art from Illustrator in Photoshop, you are presented with a dialog asking whether you want the art to be pasted as pixels, a path, a shape layer, or a smart object (**Figure 9.32**).

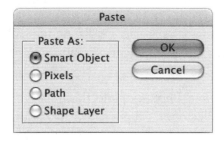

Figure 9.32 Photoshop offers you several options when pasting artwork from Illustrator. Pasting art as a smart object allows you to edit the pasted artwork in Illustrator if needed.

Going from Photoshop to Illustrator

When you open a native Photoshop file or place-embed one into an existing document, Illustrator prompts you with the Photoshop Import Options dialog, asking how you want the Photoshop file to be placed (refer to Figure 9.3, earlier in this chapter). You can choose the Flatten Photoshop Layers to a Single Image option, or you can choose the Convert Photoshop Layers to Objects option, in which case Illustrator tries to keep as many of the elements in the Photoshop file editable as possible.

The following are the attributes you can preserve when Illustrator embeds a native Photoshop file using the Convert Photoshop Layers to Objects option in the Photoshop Import Options dialog:

- **Layers.** Any layers you've created, and the names of those layers, are preserved when you open the file in Illustrator. If you've created groups of layers in Photoshop, those groups show up in Illustrator as sublayers, thus preserving the hierarchy of the file.

- **Vectors.** If you've created vector shape layers in Photoshop, those layers are converted into editable compound shapes when the file is opened in Illustrator.

- **Text.** Text objects that appear in the file are editable when the file is opened in Illustrator.

- **Transparency.** If you've applied opacity values or blend modes from the Layers panel, those values are preserved when you open the file in Illustrator as well. Because Photoshop applies these settings at the layer level, you may find that these transparency settings are applied to the layer that an object is on rather than to the object itself.

- **Masks.** If you create layer masks in your Photoshop file, those masks are preserved and show up in Illustrator as opacity masks. Additionally, the boundaries of the file become a layer-clipping mask, acting almost like crop marks.

- **Slices.** If you create Web slices in your Photoshop file, those slices appear when you open the file in Illustrator. Additionally, any optimization settings that you've applied to your slices, including settings that you've applied from the Save for Web dialog, are preserved and can be edited once the file is opened in Illustrator.

- **Image Maps.** If you've assigned a URL to a Web slice, that URL is also preserved when the file is opened in Illustrator.

Illustrator does its best to keep elements editable during the embedding process. For example, if you have a text object with a drop shadow that overlaps a background, Illustrator keeps the text editable and also places the drop shadow on a separate layer, allowing you to position the text and the drop shadow without affecting the background beneath it. If you find that certain elements are not being preserved, the cause may be that preserving editability would change the appearance of the artwork. Try rearranging the layers in Photoshop to avoid issues where appearance is dependent upon the interaction of multiple layers.

CHAPTER TEN

Graphs, Distortion, and Blends

In case you haven't figured it out by now, the underlying theme of this book is learning to combine the features in Adobe Illustrator with each other, rather than focusing on each feature just on its own. This chapter is certainly no exception.

You may be asking yourself what it is that graphs, distortions, and blends have in common so that they deserve to share space within the same chapter. The answer is that, for the most part, these seemingly disparate features firmly drive home the notion that using a combination of features can reap big rewards.

After all, graphs on their own can be pretty boring, but with a few live effects applied, such as 3D or Drop Shadow, you can end up with a graph that seemingly pops off the page and demands a reader's attention. Not only do tools and effects help make for more interesting-looking graphs, but they can also help make for more *effective* graphs. The Liquify distortion tools can turn a gradient mesh into something special, and the Envelope distortion features can add just the right look to text. As for blends, combining them with features such as symbols and SWF Export can turn static Web art into wonderful animations.

To finish the chapter on a bright note, we'll even talk about the innovative vector Flare tool for creating cool lens-flare effects.

PUTTING THE "ART" IN CHART

We are bombarded with information on a daily basis. Whether it is from newspapers, the Internet, BlackBerrys, magazines, outdoor advertising, television, or radio, we can absorb only a limited amount. At the same time, certain bits of information require a degree of focus and attention in order for us to process and really understand them.

Aware of the challenges, designers often turn to graphs or charts to present complicated information in a simpler manner. Also known as an *infographic,* a well-designed graph presents key data points in a visually stimulating way that quickly conveys a message to the reader (**Figure 10.1**). Graphs are often used in annual reports, business or sales presentations, and magazine or newspaper articles.

Figure 10.1 In today's fast-paced work, graphs help people visualize and digest numerical data. In this example, the percentage of teens interested in golf is highlighted. A salesperson for golf equipment might use this to bring attention to growth in that segment.

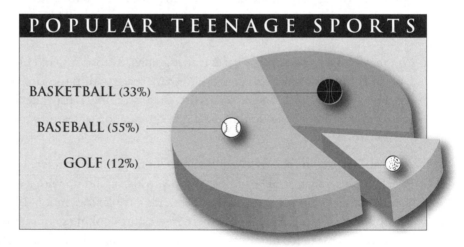

Graphs and *charts* are often used as inter-changeable terms. Throughout this chapter, however, we refer to the numerical elements as *charts* and the entire overall graphic as *graphs.*

Using graphs is a great way to communicate numeric information in a visual and graphical manner; when you use such a way to represent your data, you can turn a jumble of numbers into compelling data points. The important part is to remember that a graph is meant to communicate information. As you'll see in this chapter, Illustrator offers many ways to control a graph's appearance, and it can be easy to get caught up in making a graph look so pretty that the reader misses its entire point.

Exploring the Anatomy of a Graph

Before we get into the specifics of creating and editing graphs, let's first explore how Illustrator constructs them.

A graph can consist of several different elements, including the chart itself, a value and category axis, and a legend. These elements are each created as individual groups so that they can be managed easily. A graph in Illustrator is a special kind of parent group that comprises individual groups (**Figure 10.2**). Depending on the settings you use, a graph can have all or just some of these groups.

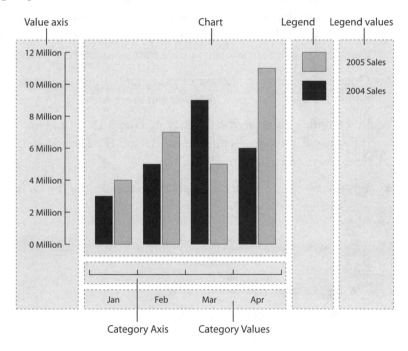

Figure 10.2 A graph in Illustrator consists of many different parts.

As long as the special parent group contains the elements, you can make edits to the graph data or the settings of the graph itself, and Illustrator updates the graph accordingly. However, if you remove the parent group (by choosing Object > Ungroup), the individual elements act like regular vector objects, and you can no longer edit the graph data. (See the section "Ungrouping a Graph" later in the chapter, where we discuss under which circumstances you would want to ungroup a graph.)

Because a graph is a group, all that you've learned so far about how groups work and how you can apply effects to groups applies to graphs as well.

Creating a Graph in Illustrator

Creating a graph in Illustrator involves specifying a size for your graph (much like drawing a rectangle), and the data for the graph.

1. To create a graph, choose one of the nine graph tools in the Toolbox (**Figure 10.3**), and click your artboard once. This opens the Graph dialog where you must first specify the size for the graph and then click OK. Alternatively, you can click and drag with the graph tool on the artboard to generate a size for the graph on the fly.

    The size you specify is the area that is enclosed within the value and the category axis (or the X and Y axis). This size won't necessarily be the final size of all the elements in the graph because items such as values and legends will appear outside the boundaries of the two axes.

2. Once you've specified the size of your graph, Illustrator opens the Graph Data window, in which you can enter the data for your graph.

    Refer to the options in the "Specifying Graph Data" section for detailed information about the settings in the Graph Data window and the different ways you can format your data.

3. When you're done, click the Apply button, and close the Graph Data window.

If you aren't sure which type of graph you want to use, you can choose any type in which to enter your data. You can always change between types after you've created the graph.

Figure 10.3 The nine different graph tools are grouped together in the Toolbox.

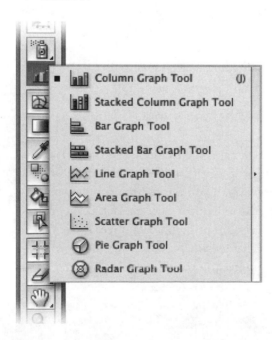

Choosing a Graph Type

Creating a graph in Illustrator is much like following a recipe. You take a few numbers here, take a few values there, and toss them together, and Illustrator produces a functional visual representation of your data. In the world of graphs, you can present data in many different ways. Illustrator has nine different ways; each of these is called a *graph type*. Refer to Table 10.1 for more specific examples of these graphs and how they compare.

- **Column graph.** A column graph presents a single group of data as a series of vertical columns. This common graph type is often used to compare a range of values.

- **Stacked column graph.** A stacked column graph presents multiple groups of data as a series of vertical columns. Multiple values are accumulated and stacked on top of each other. Stacked column graphs are used to compare a range of values and also to indicate how individual data points may have contributed to the overall totals.

- **Bar graph.** A bar graph presents a single group of data as a series of horizontal bars. The bar graph type is identical to the column graph type, but it is in a horizontal format.

- **Stacked bar graph.** A stacked bar graph presents multiple groups of data as a series of horizontal bars. Multiple values are cumulated and added to the ends of the bars. The stacked bar graph is identical to the bar graph type, but it is in a horizontal format.

- **Line graph.** A line graph presents multiple groups of data as a series of connected lines. Line graphs are often used to show continuous measurements or trends over time.

- **Area graph.** An area graph is similar to a line graph, but the areas created by the lines are filled in, thus offering a visual representation of volume. This presents a cumulative value of the areas as well.

- **Scatter graph.** A scatter graph maps multiple data points as individual dots, which makes it possible to chart trends and compare nonlinear data points.

- **Pie graph.** A pie graph presents a single group of data points as slices or wedges of a circle. Pie charts are generally used to show percentages or to show how a whole is broken up into individual parts.

By default, Illustrator creates graphs using different shades of gray, which isn't exactly exciting when it comes to making important presentations. Instead of trying to come up with colors that work well together, remember that you have Illustrator's Color Guide and Live Color feature at your disposal. Refer to Chapter 6, *Working with Color*, for more information on recoloring artwork.

- **Radar graph.** A radar graph, also called a *web* or *polar graph*, plots data points in a circular pattern, which reveals values with overlapping areas.

Table 10.1 Examples and Uses of Graph Types

Graph Type	Description	Example
Column graph	This column graph displays how many pitches of each kind were thrown in a baseball game.	
Stacked Column graph	This stacked column graph displays the same information as in the previous graph, but now you can also view how many pitches of each kind were thrown for a ball or a strike.	
Bar graph	This bar graph also displays how many pitches of each kind were thrown in a baseball game	
Stacked Bar graph	This stacked bar graph displays the same information as in the bar graph, but now you can also view how many pitches of each kind were thrown for a ball or a strike.	

Graph Type	Description	Example
Line graph	This line graph displays ticket sales across a range of several months. The graph shows growth in ticket sales over time, and the weekend games draw larger crowds.	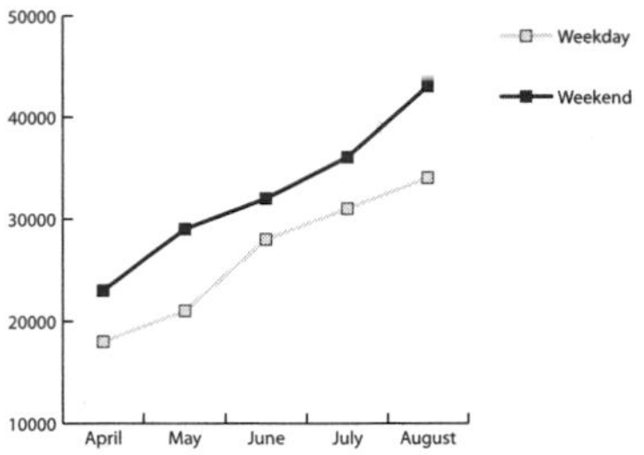
Area graph	This area graph displays the same data as in the previous line graph, but here you can see the total cumulative attendance of both weekday and weekend ticket sales.	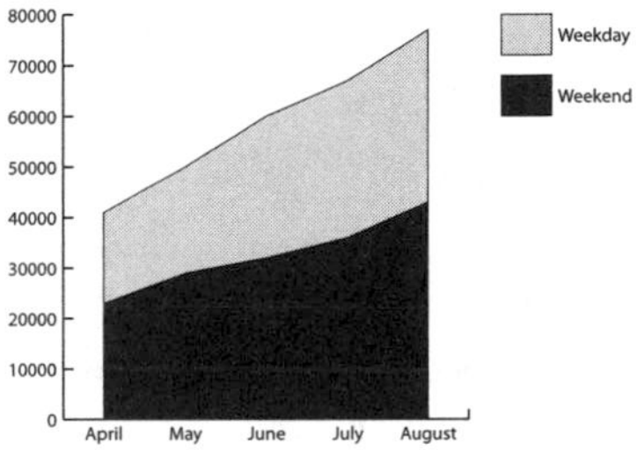
Scatter graph	This scatter graph compares the ages of hitters with the number of home runs they hit. The chart shows data for three different decades, and the data reveals a peak in home runs hit by hitters aged 30 to 35.	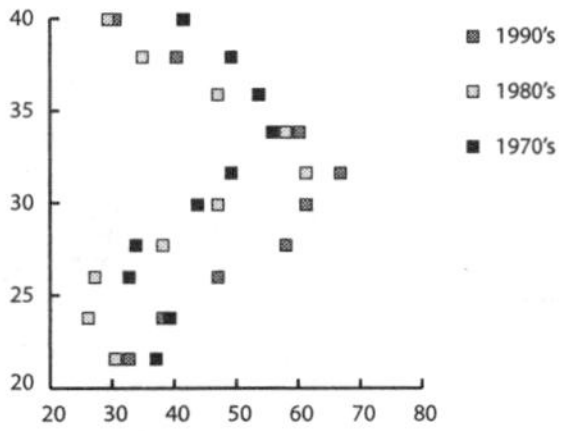
Pie graph	This pie graph breaks down the type of tickets sold at a baseball game. You can clearly see that the majority of tickets sold are from advanced sales.	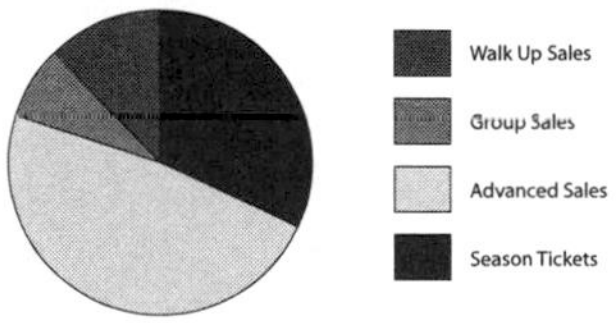
Radar graph	This radar graph compares the sales of beer and soda over the course of a nine-inning baseball game. The graph reveals that beer sales spike between the third and fifth innings, whereas soda sales peak between the seventh and ninth innings.	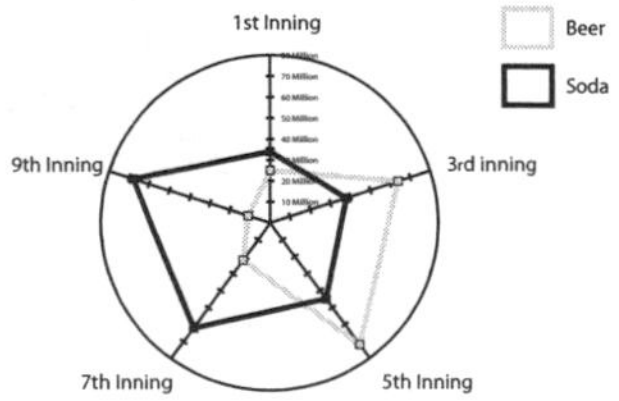

Specifying Graph Data

When you create a graph in Illustrator, you are presented with the Graph Data window, which is the life and soul of a graph (**Figure 10.4**). After all, without any data, Illustrator can't draw a meaningful graph. If you've ever seen a spreadsheet before (such as in Microsoft Excel), you'll recognize the vertical columns and horizontal rows of cells where you can specify data. You can click and drag the vertical lines to adjust the width of each row. This won't have any effect on the appearance of your graph, but it will allow you to view all your data if it extends beyond the boundary of each cell.

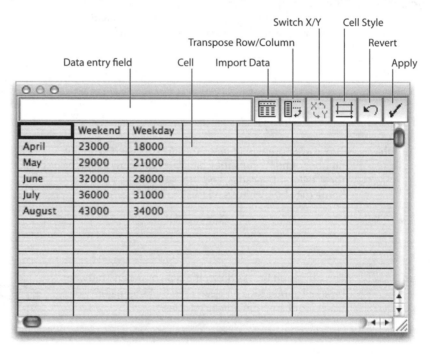

Figure 10.4 The Graph Data window contains the values that determine how a graph is drawn.

If you've already created a graph and you've closed the Graph Data window, you can always reopen this window for further data editing. To do so, with a graph selected on your artboard, just choose Object > Graph > Graph Data; the Graph Data window will appear.

Across the top of the Graph Data window are several items. A field where you can enter data for a selected cell (to select a cell, simply click it) appears along the entire top left side. Along the top right of the window are the following six icons, which offer additional functionality:

- **Import Data.** Illustrator allows you to import data from an external file by clicking the Import Data icon. Illustrator presents you with a system dialog box that allows you to choose a file to use. The file you choose must be a tab-delimited text (TXT) file. Unfortunately, Illustrator does not allow you to import Excel files directly. If you have data that already exists in an Excel file, you can save the Excel file as a tab-delimited text file, which you can then import into Illustrator. Alternatively, you can also copy and paste data from Excel right into the Graph Data window.

- **Transpose Row/Column.** When you click the Transpose Row/Column icon, the data that is already entered in the Graph Data window is swapped so that rows become columns and columns become rows. This is useful for when you either enter data incorrectly or want to experiment with a different graph result.

- **Switch X/Y.** When editing graph data for a scatter graph, the Switch X/Y icon allows you to swap the X and Y axes. The icon is disabled for all other graph types.

- **Cell Style.** By default, each cell in the Graph Data window is wide enough to display seven digits, and each value is shown with two decimal places. By clicking the Cell Style icon, you can change both the column width and the number of decimals. This setting applies to all the cells in the Graph Data window (you can't apply different settings to individual cells).

- **Revert.** Clicking the Revert icon returns the graph data to the values specified when you last clicked the Apply button.

- **Apply.** The Apply button takes the values specified in the Graph Data window and generates or updates your selected graph.

Formatting Data Within the Graph Data Window

Almost as important as the data itself is the way you actually enter it into the Graph Data window (**Figure 10.5** on the following page). The graph type you choose and the way in which you format the values within the cells of the Graph Data window are the two items that most impact how Illustrator draws your graph.

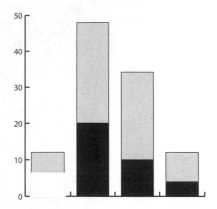

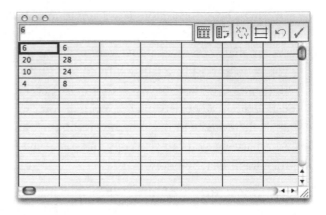

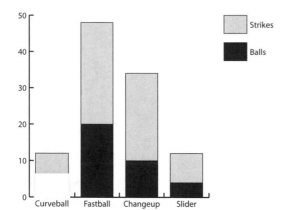

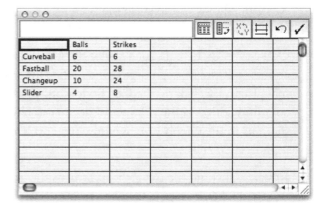

Figure 10.5 These two graphs represent the same data, but the bottom one has legend and category labels added to make the meaning of the graph immediately apparent.

For example, if you just specify numeric values in the Graph Data window, Illustrator draws the graph correctly, but people who read your graph may not understand its significance. For a graph to be effective, a reader needs to understand what the values mean. One way to help a reader make sense of a graph is by adding labels, which identify what a particular axis or data point represents.

In the Graph Data window, you can specify labels simply by entering the text of the labels within the cells. If Illustrator sees a value that contains letters instead of numbers, it assumes the cell contains a label, and not a numerical value that affects the graph itself (**Figure 10.5**). To specify a number as a label (for example, a year such as 2007), you must enclose it in quotation marks ("2007").

Customizing Graphs

Once you've created a graph, you can edit it and customize it to fit your needs. At any time, you can select a graph and open the Graph Data window where you can change the data. When you check the Apply button, your graph updates to reflect the new data.

However, there can be more to a graph than just the data itself. For example, a graph has a category axis, a value axis, a legend, and other elements. To make adjustments to these settings, select a graph on the artboard, and choose Object > Graph > Type to open the Graph Type dialog. Depending on the type of graph that you have chosen, the Graph Type dialog offers several panels with specific options (**Figure 10.6**).

Working with data and labels can get confusing at times, but don't get frustrated. Keep your Graph Data window open, and use the Apply button to quickly see the results of how Illustrator draws your graph. You can then make quick adjustments to the data as needed.

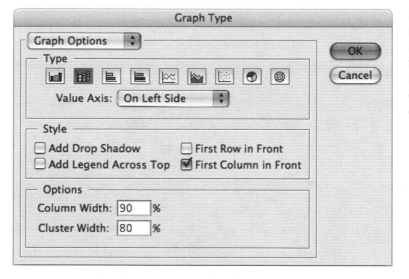

Figure 10.6 Illustrator offers additional settings for how graphs appear through the Graph Type dialog. Each graph type maintains options specific to its type of graph.

Utilizing Graph Designs

Purely from a numbers point of view, bars, lines, and squares get the point across when you're creating a graph. However, there's plenty of room for creativity when you're drawing graphs as well. Sometimes, a graphic can add a really nice touch to the overall appearance of a graph, and it can even make it easier to pick up on key data points.

There's also plenty of good information on creating graph designs in Illustrator's Help.

In Illustrator, custom art that is used instead of bars to display values in a graph is called a *graph design*. For the most part, graph designs behave much like patterns do. First you define a graph design. Once defined, you can apply the graph design to a graph in your document. Illustrator supports two kinds of graph designs: a Column graph design, which is used for drawing columns in column graphs, and a Marker graph design, which is used for drawing markers in line or scatter graphs.

Here are the steps you need to follow to create a graph design:

The Graph Data window must be closed in order to define or apply graph designs.

1. Select the art on your artboard you'd like to use as a graph design. You can use most Illustrator objects in a graph design, with the exception of editable text or placed images—although you can use symbols.

2. Choose Object > Graph > Design to open the Graph Design dialog.

3. Click the New Design button, and then click the Rename button so you can give your graph design a unique and recognizable name. Click OK (**Figure 10.7**).

Figure 10.7 Here we've defined a graph design using a baseball that we traced and expanded.

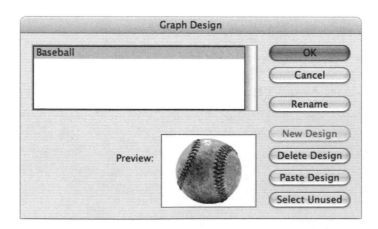

Now that you've created a graph design, here are the steps you need to follow in order to apply the graph style to your graph:

1. Select the graph object on the artboard.

2. If you're working with a column graph, choose Object > Graph > Column. From the Graph Column dialog, choose a column design and a column type (**Figure 10.8**).

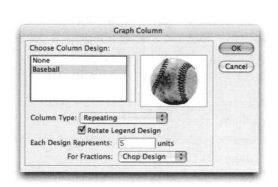
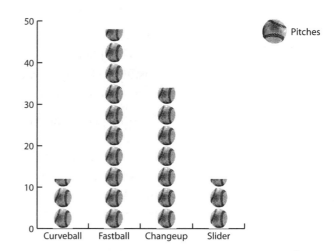

Figure 10.8 On the left is the Graph Column dialog where we used the Baseball design for the columns of the graph. On the right is the finished graph.

3. If you're working with a line or scatter graph, choose Object > Graph > Marker. From the Graph Marker dialog, choose a marker, and click OK.

Ungrouping a Graph

At any time, you can decide to ungroup your graph, although if you do so, the graph is reduced to regular vector objects and is no longer editable as a graph object. Designers may ungroup a graph once they know the numbers won't change anymore. Once ungrouped, a designer can edit the objects freely.

In the Adobe Illustrator CS3/Cool Extras/ Sample Files/Graph Designs folder, you'll find four files that contain predefined graph designs and samples of different graphs.

Raising the Bar with Graphs

You can take advantage of the graph feature in Illustrator in numerous ways. Once you've created a graph, you can use the Direct Selection tool to select individual parts of a graph and apply different fill or stroke attributes (by default, Illustrator generates graphs using different shades of gray). You can also apply other Illustrator features, such as live effects (like 3D or Scribble) or transparency. You can even use graph elements as masks for photographs.

In addition, you can use an Illustrator graph as a guide for more customized artwork. For example, you may want to create an intricate infographic using customized shapes. By creating a simple graph with real data, you can draw artwork in scale to depict numeric data in a visual way (**Figure 10.9**).

If bringing data into Illustrator isn't your cup of tea, you can use Excel to generate a graph, which you can then save as PDF from Excel (if you have Acrobat installed on your computer, you should have a utility called PDFMaker available from within Microsoft Office). Once you've created the PDF, open it in Illustrator, where you can customize it as needed (you won't be able to edit the graph data, however).

Figure 10.9 Graphs don't have to be boring. Use Illustrator's feature set and your creativity to create graphs that demand attention.

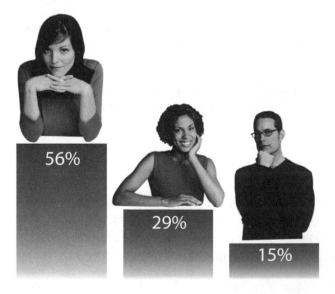

Graphs That Reset to Shades of Gray

Graphs seemingly have a tendency of defaulting their appearance to shades of gray when the graph data is updated. At times, you might customize the appearance of a graph by adjusting colors and the like, and those settings remain intact after you've updated the graph data. Yet, other times, the graph defaults to shades of gray. Why does this happen?

Believe it or not, there's a reason behind everything, and in this case, Teri Pettit, a developer on the Illustrator team who worked on the graph feature, was kind enough to provide the following explanation:

"Editing objects inside graphs is sort of like having action recording turned on, with the actions being stored with the graph instead of in a separate file. Whenever you change the graph data or graph attributes, Illustrator first creates a new default graph at the location that the graph was first created, as if you had just dragged out the graph tool and entered the data. Then all the 'graph actions' (edit history) that were recorded since the beginning of time (that is, since the creation of that graph, including any previous graph it was duplicated from) get played back, complete down to the transforms that moved that graph to where it is now.

"Just as not every edit you can do in Illustrator is recordable by actions, not every edit you can do in Illustrator is recordable by graphs. In fact, many fewer are recordable by graphs. So for the most part, if the edit is performed by a feature that was introduced after Illustrator 5, either it entirely ignores graphs or in some cases the edit is performed but is not recorded. This is because most of the features added since Illustrator 6 abide by different rules internally.

"Sometimes even when some changes are recordable, if other changes are made that are not recordable, the act of making the nonrecordable changes will make some of the recorded changes no longer work. (They are still remembered, but they fail to apply, like playing back an action that can't find the right kind of selection anymore.) When that happens, you can get your graphs reverting to default shades of gray.

"The safest way to make sure your edits to graphs 'stick' is to confine yourself to editing them using the parts of the application that were available in Illustrator 5. For example, scale objects with the Scale tool instead of the bounding box, the Transform panel, or the Transform Each command, and apply paint styles with the Swatches panel or the Color panel instead of dragging and dropping color onto objects.

"If you want to apply live effects to graph columns in a way that gets remembered, you have to make a named style and then apply that named style to the graph columns. (Graphic styles are covered in depth in Chapter 3, *Objects, Groups, and Layers*.)

"Another good tip to follow is to not try to keep making new graphs by duplicating the same old template graphs for years and years and modifying them. Since the edit history is forever, it can get pretty crafty after editing a graph hundreds of times. If all you are going to change is graph data, that's fine, since data changes aren't recorded as a graph edit. But if you are going to be setting up different column styles and text styles and graph style attributes and transformations, it is cleaner to start fresh than to make extensive edits to an old graph."

Thanks for the detailed explanation, Teri! You can find more wisdom from Teri on her Web site at http://tpettit.best.vwh.net/adobe/.

Combining Multiple Graph Types

When comparing data, it can be helpful to employ a combination of graph types to display different data points. For example, you might want to display one set of data as a Column graph but another set of data as a Line graph. To better compare the two data points, you might overlay the Line graph over the Column graph to attempt to discover a trend. You can do this easily in Illustrator, so let's explore the thinking behind it, as well as the steps it takes to create it.

The obvious theme in this chapter so far has been around baseball, so we'll continue with that example. It might be interesting to compare the number of home runs a player hits over the course of many seasons to the number of strikeouts that a player has had over the same period of time. Such an analysis may reveal a trend (for example, as home runs go up, perhaps strikeouts also go up, and so on), and we'll want an easy way to look at both the home run data and the strikeout data. As Barry Bonds of the San Francisco Giants chases home-run history, let's create a chart that displays his progress. Here are the steps we'll follow to create such a chart:

1. Select the Column Graph tool, and drag out a wide rectangle. This opens the Graph Data window, where you can entire the data.

2. Finding batting statistics for Barry Bonds isn't very difficult with the help of Google, or you can simply copy the values from **Figure 10.10**. Remember that to create the years as labels and not data, you must enclose the numbers that represent the years in quotation marks.

3. Click Apply in the Graph Data window. This applies the data and draws the graph (**Figure 10.11**). The graph doesn't look very charming at the moment, and because there are so many years, the labels across the bottom of the graph overlap each other, but don't worry. We'll make everything look fabulous soon enough. This, by the way, is one of the reasons why it's never a good idea to have a client sit with you while you work (you can just hear them saying, "But I don't want the chart to be colored gray...").

4. Now we'll specify a different type of graph to offset the different sets of data. Although the Column format works well for the number of strikeouts, the Line format would be better for displaying the home runs. Select the Group Selection tool, and click the legend *twice* next to the word *Home Runs* (**Figure 10.12**). This selects the data range for the home runs.

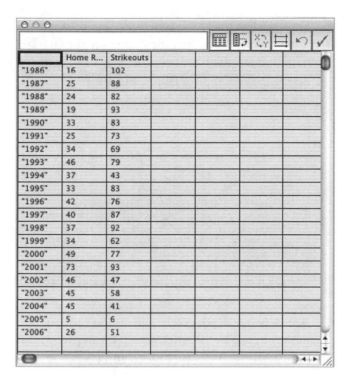

Figure 10.10 The Graph Data window, with the labels and data specified.

	Home R...	Strikeouts
"1986"	16	102
"1987"	25	88
"1988"	24	82
"1989"	19	93
"1990"	33	83
"1991"	25	73
"1992"	34	69
"1993"	46	79
"1994"	37	43
"1995"	33	83
"1996"	42	76
"1997"	40	87
"1998"	37	92
"1999"	34	62
"2000"	49	77
"2001"	73	93
"2002"	46	47
"2003"	45	58
"2004"	45	41
"2005"	5	6
"2006"	26	51

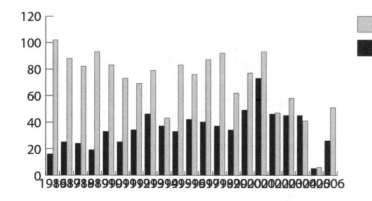

Figure 10.11 Illustrator displays the graph, with the values and the legend.

Figure 10.12 Using the Group Selection tool to click the legend twice will select that entire data series in the graph.

5. Double-click the graph tool in the Tools panel, which opens the Graph Type dialog. Select the Line option for the Graph Type, and click OK. This redraws the home-runs data as a Line graph but keeps the strike-outs data as a Column graph (**Figure 10.13**).

Figure 10.13 The graph now correctly displays each data series with a different graph type.

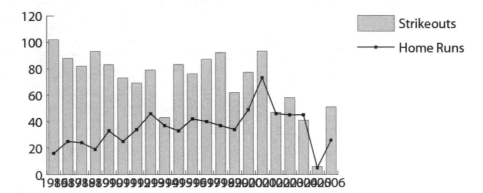

6. At this point, the data is complete and formatted as needed. Using graphic styles and paragraph styles, you can quickly adjust the appearance of the final graph (**Figure 10.14**).

Figure 10.14 With the help of a few graphic styles and paragraph styles, the final graph is complete.

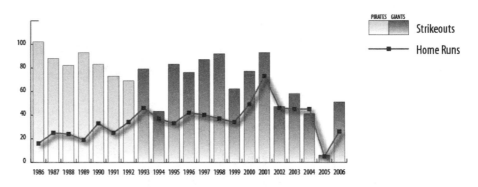

With the graph in final form, the strikeouts and the home runs are easy to observe separately and can be compared to each other as well.

WORKING WITH TOOLS OF MASS DISTORTION

Illustrator has a plethora of tools that can help you create crisp, clean paths with extreme precision. But at times a design calls for something less perfect, and it is also appropriate to bend or stretch artwork to achieve a distorted effect. That's where the distortion tools come into play.

You have already caught a glimpse of Illustrator's Warp effect, which was discussed in Chapter 8, *3D and Other Live Effects*. In addition, Illustrator contains a suite of distortion tools, dubbed the Liquify tools, and a feature called *enveloping*, which allows you to squeeze artwork into a customized shape. Let's take a closer look at these two additional distortion techniques.

Painting with Distortion: The Liquify Tools

In your average box of classic toys, you'd surely find an Etch A Sketch, a Slinky, a collection of Tinkertoy parts, and, undoubtedly, a plastic egg filled with Silly Putty. For those not familiar with the popular toy, Silly Putty is this gooey, plastic substance that looks much like a wad of chewing gum. Once you've flattened the plastic, you can press it firmly on newsprint (we always used the comics section) to transfer the images or text to the plastic surface. Then the fun begins; you can pull and twist and stretch the plastic to distort the pictures or comics.

If you've missed out on all of the fun over the years, fear not—you can perform the same distortion to your artwork using Illustrator's suite of Liquify distortion tools (although your hands won't smell of Silly Putty afterward). The Liquify toolset includes the Warp, Twirl, Pucker, Bloat, Scallop, Crystallize, and Wrinkle tools (**Figure 10.15** on the following page). Each of these tools allows you to "paint" with distortion effects by simply clicking and dragging over vector art. The tools feature a brush size, which helps determine how large of an area is distorted (**Figure 10.16** on the following page). You can change the brush size for any of the Liquify tools interactively by holding the Option (Alt) key while dragging with the tool. Adding the Shift key while dragging constrains the brush size to a perfect circle.

Figure 10.15 The Liquify tools appear grouped together in the Toolbox and offer a wide range of distortion effects.

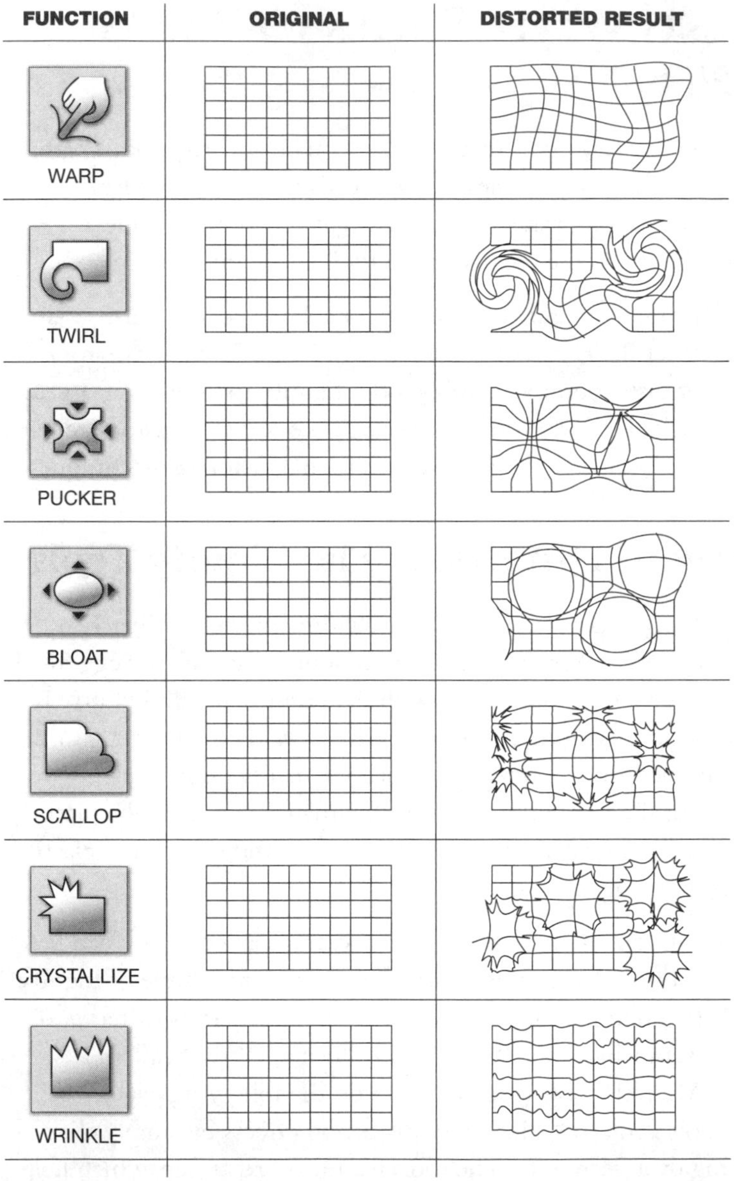

FUNCTION	ORIGINAL	DISTORTED RESULT
WARP		
TWIRL		
PUCKER		
BLOAT		
SCALLOP		
CRYSTALLIZE		
WRINKLE		

Figure 10.16 Changing the size of a Liquify brush allows you to control how much a selection becomes distorted with each drag of the mouse.

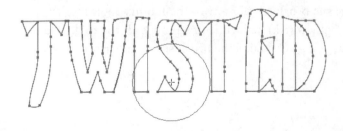

You'll have to be careful when using the Liquify tools, because they exhibit different behavior based on your selection. If you have artwork selected before you start dragging with a Liquify tool, only the selected art becomes distorted. However, if you have not made a selection, clicking and dragging with a Liquify tool distorts any path you touch.

The Liquify tools don't work on live text (you'll need to convert text to outlines first), but the tools do work on embedded images. As you drag a Liquify tool over an embedded image, Illustrator creates a mesh that is used to distort the image beneath it (**Figure 10.17**). In fact, if you've created a gradient mesh object, using the Liquify tools on the mesh object produces interesting effects as well.

Figure 10.17 Although you can't change actual pixels in Illustrator, you can apply Liquify distortions to embedded images.

Double-clicking any of the Liquify tools in the Toolbox opens a dialog offering a variety of settings. The top half of the dialog features Global Brush Dimensions settings, which control the size (width and height), angle, and intensity of the tools. In addition, if you are using a pressure-sensitive tablet, you can choose to control the intensity with pen pressure by checking the Use Pressure Pen check box. Any changes you make to the Global Brush Dimensions settings are applied to all the Liquify tools (**Figure 10.18**).

Figure 10.18 If you have a pressure-sensitive tablet, you can achieve greater control over the Liquify tools.

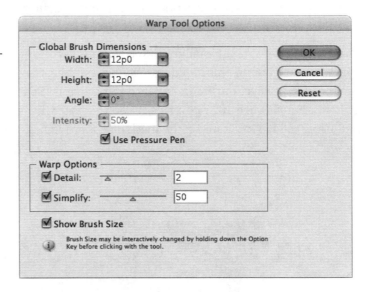

The bottom half of the dialog offers options for the specific tool that you double-clicked. Most tools offer Detail and Simplify settings, although the Wrinkle tool offers many additional options as well. The changes you make to each of these tool-specific settings affect only the tool you double-clicked.

Getting Into Shape: Envelope Distortion

Ever see those cartoons where one of the characters gets his head stuck in a glass jar? And remember that when he pulls his head out of the jar, his head is in the shape of the jar? Wouldn't it be cool if you could do the same thing with your artwork? Well, you can, using Illustrator's enveloping features.

An *envelope* is a regular vector shape that can contain other artwork. And any artwork that is contained inside the envelope becomes distorted to take on the shape of the envelope. As you will soon learn, envelopes use Illustrator's mesh technology to distort artwork. In fact, these envelope meshes, as they are called, are identical to the gradient meshes you created in Chapter 5, *Brushes, Symbols, and Masks.*

You can create an Envelope distortion in Illustrator in three ways, and naturally, each offers a slightly different approach and warrants its own benefits. As you learn about these three different types of envelopes, you will understand when it's best to use them for a specific project or desired result. You can find these three methods in the Object > Envelope Distort menu; they are named Make with Top Object, Make with Mesh, and Make with Warp.

Method One: Make with Top Object

A commonly used Envelope distortion technique in Illustrator is the Make with Top Object method. Creating an Envelope distortion using the Make with Top Object method is similar to creating a mask. A regular vector shape at the top of the stacking order acts as the envelope, and all selected artwork that appears beneath the envelope becomes distorted to fit within the envelope shape. Here are the steps you'll need to follow to perform this technique:

1. Select the shape you will be using as the envelope. You can use any vector object consisting of a single path as an envelope.

2. Choose Object > Arrange > Bring to Front. This ensures that the envelope is at the top of the stacking order.

3. Select both the artwork that you want to distort and the vector shape that will become the envelope.

4. Choose Object > Envelope Distort > Make with Top Object (**Figure 10.19**).

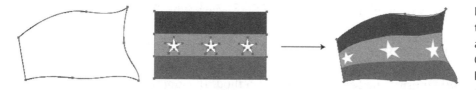

Figure 10.19 On the left, the envelope shape and the artwork appear selected. On the right, after the envelope has been applied, the artwork appears distorted within the envelope shape.

Once you've created an Envelope distortion, you can edit the envelope shape using your Direct Selection tool—just as you'd do with any other vector shape. As you adjust the shape of the envelope, the distorted artwork updates to match the edited shape (**Figure 10.20**). Pay close attention to the position of the control handles that appear on the anchor points of your envelope path, because they also affect how art within the envelope shape is distorted (**Figure 10.21**).

Figure 10.20 Changing the shape of the envelope after you've applied the distortion makes it easy to tweak your distortion to perfection.

Figure 10.21 When you drag one of the control handles on the envelope, you can see that the distortion pulls the artwork toward that point.

Using a distinct custom shape as a distortion envelope is useful for times when you need artwork to fit within the confines of a specific shape. However, you'll notice that although you can easily adjust the outside path to change the overall shape of the distortion, you have little control over how the artwork inside the envelope is distorted. To control distortion across the entire object, not just the edges, you need to employ one of the next two methods: Make with Mesh or Make with Warp.

Method Two: Make with Mesh

When using the Make with Mesh method, Illustrator creates the envelope shape for you, so you don't need to create a shape first. The shape that Illustrator creates is a rectangle, so no immediate distortion is visible when you apply this kind of envelope. Once the envelope is created, you can edit the mesh points to control how the distortion affects the artwork. Editing an envelope mesh is identical to editing a gradient mesh.

To create an Envelope distortion using the Make with Mesh method, perform the following steps:

1. Select any artwork on your artboard. You can select multiple objects, and although you aren't required to group them, you may want to do so to ensure easier editing later.

2. Choose Object > Envelope Distort > Make with Mesh.

3. In the Envelope Mesh dialog, specify how many rows and columns you want the mesh to be initially created with (**Figure 10.22**). It doesn't matter whether you aren't sure of the exact number of rows and columns at this point, because you are able to add mesh points later as needed. Click OK to apply the Envelope distortion.

4. Using the Mesh tool or the Direct Selection tool, move the individual mesh points and their control handles to apply distortion to your artwork (**Figure 10.23**).

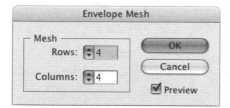

Figure 10.22 The Envelope Mesh dialog gives you the ability to set how many mesh points appear initially in the envelope. Creating more rows and columns gives you additional control over the amount of distortion you can apply.

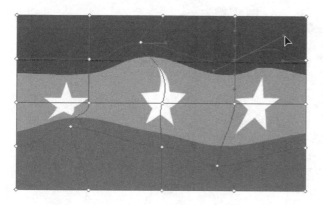

Figure 10.23 Similar to working with a gradient mesh, adjusting the position and control handles of mesh points in an envelope mesh controls the distortion of the artwork.

If you want to add mesh points to your envelope, select the Mesh tool, and click anywhere within the selected envelope. Hold down the Option (Alt) key while clicking with the Mesh tool to remove mesh points.

Although you start with a rectangle mesh shape, moving the individual mesh points on the envelope gives you control over not just the outer edge

You can also use the Mesh tool to add mesh points to envelopes that you created using the Make with Top Object method.

of the distortion but also any points within the envelope shape. However, this method is harder to use only because you aren't starting with a distorted shape, just a grid of mesh points.

Method Three: Make with Warp

The Make with Warp method of applying Envelope distortion is nearly identical to the Make with Mesh method—only with a twist (sorry, couldn't resist). Instead of starting with a rectangular-shaped mesh, Illustrator gives you the option of choosing from several preset shapes. Actually, they are the same presets as those found in the Warp effect.

Follow these steps to apply an Envelope distortion using the Make with Warp method:

➔ When you select art that you've enveloped with a warp, you can adjust the warp settings directly from the Control panel.

1. Select any artwork on your artboard. You can select multiple objects, and although you aren't required to group them, you may want to do so to ensure easier editing later.

2. Choose Object > Envelope Distort > Make with Warp.

3. In the Warp Options dialog that appears, choose a Warp style, and adjust the settings as necessary. Click OK to apply the Envelope distortion (**Figure 10.24**).

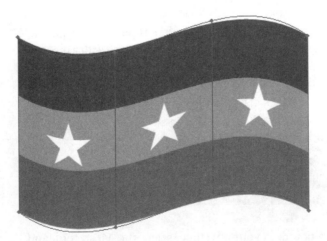

Figure 10.24 Starting an Envelope distortion with a warp gives you a head start in getting the look you need.

4. Using the Mesh tool or the Direct Selection tool, move the individual mesh points and their control handles to apply distortion to your artwork (**Figure 10.25**).

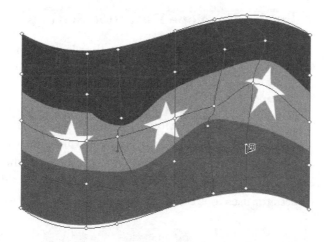

Figure 10.25 Although the envelope starts out as a warp, you can add mesh points as needed to adjust the distortion to your needs.

Overall, this third method of creating an envelope mesh is a combination of the first two. You start with an initial distortion using a warp, and then you complete the distortion by editing the envelope as a mesh object. This method is useful for times when you want to use a warp shape but need the ability to tweak the distortion a bit—something that isn't possible with the Warp effect. Refer to "Featured Matchup: Envelopes vs. the Warp Effect" for an in-depth comparison of the Envelope and Warp effect distortion features.

 When a point type object is selected, you can quickly apply the Envelope Make with Warp function by clicking the icon that appears in the Control panel.

⟨⟩ Featured Matchup: Envelopes vs. the Warp Effect

After learning how to apply some of the Envelope distortion features—especially the Make with Warp method—you may wonder how these kinds of distortions differ from the Warp effect distortions you learned about in Chapter 8, *3D and Other Live Effects*.

Although it's true that both the Warp effect and Envelope distortions are live in that you can edit them after they've been applied, they don't behave the same way. The Warp effect, which appears in the Effect menu, exhibits the same behavior as any other live effect. That means you can apply the Warp effect to any object, to any group, or even to an entire layer. Because live effects appear listed in the Appearance panel, you can apply warps to individual parts of an object (that is, just to the Stroke attribute). In addition, you can save a warp in a graphic style so you can easily apply it to other objects.

On the other hand, Envelope distortions give you complete control over the shape of your overall distortion, and using mesh points, you can even control how the interior artwork is distorted. Overall, envelopes offer a level of control that is simply not possible with the Warp effect. After all, the Warp effect contains only 15 shapes to choose from, and these cannot address every design need. Generally, the Warp effects are great for quick adjustments to artwork, whereas envelopes excel at distortions that require individual attention.

Adjusting Envelope Distortion Settings

By default, Illustrator tries to create Envelope distortions as quickly as possible. Artwork that takes longer to distort, such as live effects, gradients, or patterns, is not distorted at all, and images or other complex artwork may not fit perfectly within the envelope shape. Don't assume that Illustrator's Envelope distortion is below par; rather, select your envelope, and choose Object > Envelope Distort > Envelope Options. Alternatively, you can click the Envelope Options button that appears in the Control panel. This opens the Envelope Options dialog, where you can adjust the settings that Illustrator uses to create Envelope distortions (**Figure 10.26**).

Figure 10.26 The Envelope Options dialog gives you greater control over how Illustrator distorts artwork within envelopes.

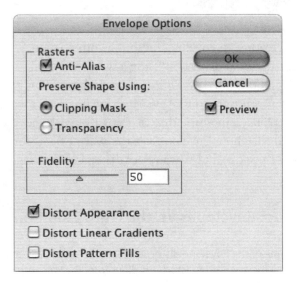

- **Rasters.** If your envelope contains a raster image, you can choose to turn antialiasing on or off. With antialiasing turned on, Illustrator produces smoother and nicer-looking art, at the expense of longer calculations and render times. When nonrectangular shapes are used as an envelope (as is usually the case), you can choose to have any raster art enclosed by a clipping mask or a transparency alpha channel.

- **Fidelity.** When Illustrator performs an Envelope distortion, it has to stretch or squeeze artwork to fit within another shape. During this process, Illustrator may make small adjustments to the art so that it doesn't become overly complex. A higher-fidelity setting forces Illustrator to preserve the integrity of the artwork as much as possible, which may produce more anchor points but results in final distorted art that closely matches the original. A lower-fidelity setting gives Illustrator more wiggle room to create files that print and save faster.

- **Distort Appearance.** If the artwork you're placing into an envelope contains live effects or multiple fill or stroke attributes, those appearances do not become distorted by the envelope shape by default. You must check the Distort Appearance option if you want the Envelope distortion to affect the appearance.

- **Distort Linear Gradients.** If the artwork you're placing into an envelope contains linear gradients, the gradient does not become distorted by the envelope shape by default. You must check the Distort Linear Gradients option if you want the Envelope distortion to affect the gradient fill.

- **Distort Pattern Fills.** If the artwork you're placing into an envelope contains a pattern fill, that fill does not become distorted by the envelope shape by default. You must check the Distort Pattern Fills option if you want the Envelope distortion to affect the pattern.

Editing Envelopes and Their Contents

It is certainly no coincidence that many of Illustrator's features exhibit live functionality, thus allowing you to perform edits without having to re-create art. Live effects, symbols, Live Trace, Live Paint, and Compound Shape modes are all examples of effects that are live and can be edited at any stage of the workflow. Envelope distortion is no exception. Once you apply an Envelope distortion using any of the three methods described earlier, you can continue to adjust either the envelope itself or the artwork that it contains.

Illustrator manages the process of editing envelopes and their contents by giving you two distinct modes in which to work. At any one time, you can work with the envelope shape, or you can change modes and edit the contents of the envelope. Unfortunately, Illustrator doesn't clearly identify the difference between these two modes, so we'll take a closer look at how you can edit Envelope distortions and the artwork within them.

When you first create a new Envelope distortion, Illustrator is in the Edit Envelope mode. In this mode, you can select and edit the shape of the envelope, but you have no way to access the art that is distorted within the envelope. If you look at the Layers panel, you'll notice an object named

Envelope, but you won't find the distorted artwork listed anywhere (**Figure 10.27**).

Figure 10.27 The Layers panel lists only one object on Layer 1—the envelope. The artwork that appears distorted within the envelope doesn't appear listed in the Layers panel at all.

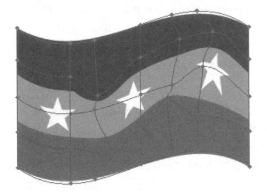 

When you're editing the contents of an envelope, you might find it easier to make edits to your art with Smart Guides turned on. The Object Highlighting feature of Smart Guides allows you to quickly find and see the art you are editing.

To edit the contents of an envelope, select it on your artboard, and choose Object > Envelope Distort > Edit Contents, or press Command- Shift-V (Control-Shift-V). Doing so puts Illustrator into the Edit Contents mode, where you can select the artwork and edit it as normal. In the Edit Contents mode, you cannot adjust, or even select, the envelope. If you look at the Layers panel, you'll see that the Envelope object now contains a triangle to the left of its name, which you can click to reveal the objects contained within the envelope (**Figure 10.28**). This triangle is your only clue in figuring out which mode you are in. If you see the disclosure triangle, you're in Edit Contents mode, and if you don't, then you are in Edit Envelope mode. If you are in Edit Contents mode and want to return to Edit Envelope mode, use the same keyboard shortcut mentioned earlier, or choose Object > Envelope Distort > Edit Envelope.

Figure 10.28 When you're in Edit Contents mode, Illustrator reveals the artwork within the envelope on Layer 1.

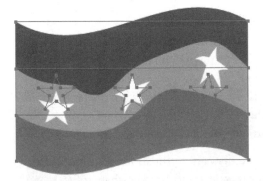 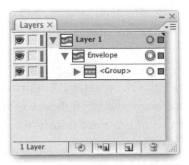

Keep in mind that Illustrator maintains each Envelope distortion in your file as a separate entity. Therefore, it's entirely possible to have one envelope in Edit Envelope mode and have another envelope in Edit Contents mode.

Releasing and Expanding Envelopes

At any time, you can select an existing envelope and choose Object > Envelope Distort > Release, which returns the artwork to an undistorted state. In addition, you can choose Object > Envelope Distort > Expand, which applies the Envelope distortion to the artwork itself. You can then edit the distorted paths freely (**Figure 10.29**), although you won't be able to edit or change the Envelope distortion after this point.

You can also toggle between editing an envelope and its contents by clicking the Edit Envelope and Edit Contents buttons that appear in the Control panel. Alternatively, you can double-click an envelope with the Selection tool to toggle between the two editing modes.

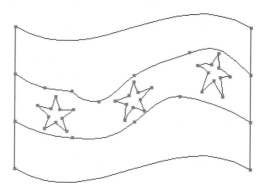

Figure 10.29 When you expand an envelope, the distortion is applied permanently to the artwork, as shown here, in Artwork Preview mode.

CREATING TRANSITIONS WITH BLENDS

By definition, a *blend* is the result of two or more items that are combined. In Illustrator, a blend is a set of at least two objects that morph into each other. In an example where you are blending two objects, Illustrator generates new shapes that appear between the two objects, making it seem like one of the objects is turning into the other. The iterations that are created between the two main objects (also referred to as *key objects*) are called *steps*, and as you'll learn shortly, Illustrator gives you control over how many steps make up each blend (**Figure 10.30**).

Figure 10.30 A blend in Illustrator consists of key objects and blend steps. A straight line, called the *spine*, connects the key objects.

Although at first glance it may seem like creating blends is something reserved for highly specialized tasks, the reality is that you can use blends for many different reasons. In fact, back in the day, before gradients were introduced to Illustrator, blends were the only way you could create color gradations. Here's a list of some other common uses for blends in Illustrator:

- **Creating shading effects.** You can use blends to create photorealistic shading effects. Because blends can be created using any vector shape, you can create customized gradations not only in color but in shape as well (**Figure 10.31**). This gives blends a distinct advantage over gradients.

- **Creating animations.** When creating animations in Illustrator, you can use a blend to *tween* steps between objects, saving you from having to create the necessary keyframes yourself (**Figure 10.32**). Tweening is a term used in animation to define the steps that appear when showing movement or one object morphing into another. In Chapter 11, *Web and Mobile Design,* you will learn how to export animated SWF (Flash) files directly from Illustrator.

- **Distributing objects.** If you need to repeat art across an area or along the curve of a path, you can use a blend to evenly distribute a specific number of steps (**Figure 10.33**).

Figure 10.31 By blending two crescent shapes, you can get realistic shading in a way that is not possible with linear or radial gradients.

Figure 10.32 By blending two symbols with different opacity levels, Illustrator creates the necessary steps to create an animation.

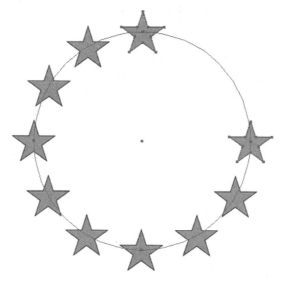

Figure 10.33 If you are creating a blend between identical stars, you can have it follow a specific path. We cover this technique later in the "Replacing the Spine of a Blend" section.

You can't blend images or Area Type objects, but you can blend just about anything else—including symbols and groups. In fact, as we discussed briefly in Chapter 8, *3D and Other Live Effects*, you can blend between objects that have different effect settings; Illustrator blends the settings of those effects as well. Blends are pretty powerful, but don't worry, they are easy to work with.

In case you're ever playing something like the Adobe edition of Trivial Pursuit, you'll find this info helpful: The 3D effect in Illustrator uses blends to create lighting and shading effects.

Creating a Blend

If there were always just one way to perform a particular function in Illustrator, there would be less of a need for books like this one. But as you've seen up to this point in this book, Illustrator offers a variety of ways to perform tasks, each of which offers specific benefits. In the case of blends, Illustrator allows you to generate a blend from a menu item, or you can achieve finer control over the result of your blend using the Blend tool.

Method One: Using the Blend Submenu

Creating a blend using the Make command is the quickest way. You simply select at least two objects and choose Object > Blend > Make. Using this method, Illustrator takes the bottommost object in your selection and creates a blend with the next object up in the stacking order.

Method Two: Using the Blend Tool

Creating a blend using the Blend tool takes a few extra clicks of the mouse but gives you the ability to control the blend in ways that the menu command can't. You begin by selecting the objects that you want to blend, and then you choose the Blend tool from the Toolbox. Then, click an anchor point once in the first object to define where you want the blend to start, and click an anchor point in the second object where you want the blend to end. If you have more than two objects to blend, keep selecting an anchor point from each object until the blend is created.

Unlike the first method where Illustrator created the blend based on stacking order, this method allows you to control in which order key objects appear in the blend. Additionally, if you click an anchor point near the top of one object and then choose an anchor point toward the bottom of the next key object, Illustrator rotates and modifies the intermediate steps of the blend to match the orientation of the anchor points (**Figure 10.34**).

Figure 10.34 When you click with the Blend tool to blend specific points (instead of the entire object), Illustrator twists and rotates the blend steps accordingly.

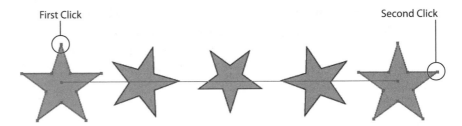

Editing a Blend

Once you've created a blend, you can edit it in a variety of ways. It should come as no surprise to you at this point to learn that blends are live in Illustrator, meaning you can adjust them even after you apply the blend. To do so, using the Direct Selection tool, click a key object, and change its color, shape, position, attributes—whatever. When you do, Illustrator simply redraws the blend to incorporate the change.

You will notice that you can't select or edit the intermediate steps that Illustrator creates to form the blend. This is an attribute of the live functionality of the blend—you can access the steps only by expanding the blend (see "Releasing and Expanding Blends" later in this chapter). However, you can control how Illustrator draws blend steps by selecting a blend and choosing Object > Blend > Blend Options.

In the Blend Options dialog, you have two general settings: Spacing and Orientation:

• **Spacing.** The Spacing setting determines the number of blend steps that are created. When Smooth Color is chosen, Illustrator creates as many steps as are necessary to display a smooth and gradual transition between key objects (**Figure 10.35**). The Specified Steps setting allows you to define exactly how many blend steps Illustrator creates. Using a higher number of steps results in a smoother transition, whereas a lower number allows you to see the individual steps in the blend (**Figure 10.36**). The Specified Distance allows you to specify how far apart each step appears from the next.

Figure 10.35 When you want to create shading techniques using blends, the Smooth Color option provides the best results.

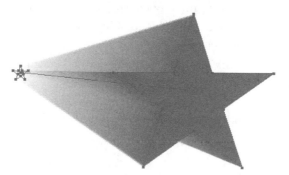

Figure 10.36 By specifying a particular number of blend steps, you can control how visible the individual steps of the blend are.

- **Orientation.** The Orientation setting controls the baseline angle of each step in your blend. With the Align to Page setting, each blend step aligns parallel to the bottom of the page, even if the path is curved or diagonal. With this setting, all blends steps share the same orientation. In contrast, the Align to Path setting aligns the baseline of each blend step to the angle of the path itself. With this setting, you'll see that each blend step has a different orientation (**Figure 10.37**).

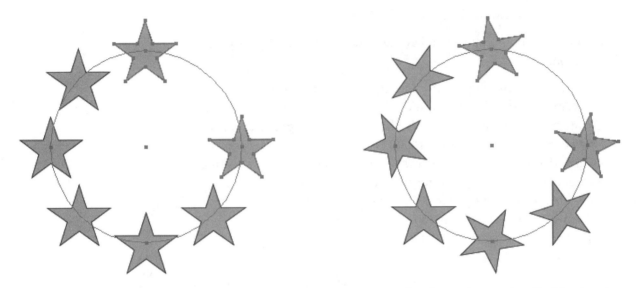

Figure 10.37 On the left, the blend is set to the Align to Page option. The blend on the right is set to the Align to Path orientation option.

Replacing the Spine of a Blend

Illustrator can have a maximum of 256 steps in a blend. The number of steps that appear in a blend has a direct impact on screen redraw speed, print performance, and file size.

As we briefly mentioned earlier, you'll notice a straight path that connects the key objects in a blend. This path is referred to as the *spine* of the blend. The individual steps that are created in a blend follow along the spine as they connect the two outer objects. The spine is an editable path, and you can use the Pen tool and the Direct Selection tool to edit the path if you want to alter the direction of the blend steps. In fact, the position of the control handles on a spine can control how the individual steps are distributed along the spine.

Additionally, you can perform a delicate operation—a spine transplant. You can draw any vector path, open or closed, and use it as the spine for an existing blend. To perform this surgery, select both the blend and the path you've created, and then choose Object > Blend > Replace Spine. Illustrator then uses the path you created as the spine for the blend, allowing you to customize how blend steps appear.

Reversing Blends

With a blend selected, you can choose Object > Blend > Reverse Spine to reverse the order of the key objects in your blend. This function is helpful for when you want to flip the blend so that it travels in the opposite direction.

Additionally, you can reverse the stacking order of the key objects in a blend by selecting the blend and choosing Object > Blend > Reverse Front to Back. This setting is especially useful for when you are using blends to create animations, which always travel in one direction. To have your animation play in reverse, you use this feature.

Releasing and Expanding Blends

As with Envelope distortions, you can select an existing blend and choose Object > Blend > Release, which removes the blend steps and returns the artwork to its original state (just the two original objects). In addition, you can choose Object > Blend > Expand, which applies the blend to the artwork itself, leaving the individual blend steps visible and available for editing. Once a blend has been expanded, it is no longer updated when the original two objects are edited.

There is yet another way to release a blend that is useful, especially when you're creating frames for animations either that will be exported directly from Illustrator as SWF (Flash) files or that will be imported into a video package such as Adobe After Effects, Adobe Premiere Pro, or Apple Final Cut Pro. This method actually expands the blend into its individual steps and then places each step on its own layer. To release a blend in this way, you must follow these steps:

1. If it isn't already open, choose Window > Layers to open your Layers panel.

2. In the Layers panel, highlight the blend object you want to release by clicking it once (**Figure 10.38**).

3. From the Layers panel menu (**Figure 10.39**), choose Release to Layers (Sequence), or choose Release to Layers (Build).

Figure 10.38 The Release to Layers command is a feature of the Layers panel, so selecting the blend on the artboard won't help. You have to highlight the blend in the Layers panel.

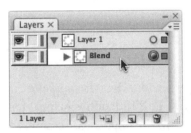

Figure 10.39 Illustrator supports the ability to release artwork to layers using the Sequence or Build method.

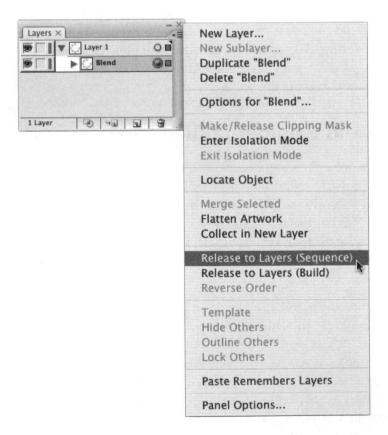

You should use the Sequence option when you want each layer to contain only one step, and you should use the Build option when you want to produce layers that add steps cumulatively to each layer that is created.

ADDING PIZZAZZ WITH THE FLARE TOOL

You may ask yourself, what is the Flare tool doing in a chapter about distortion and blends and graphs? It seems as if it's out of place. In reality, the Flare tool is unlike any of the other tools in Illustrator, so it seems out of place in general.

The Flare tool is really something spectacular, although it's a one-trick pony. The tool is present in Illustrator to create fantastic lens flares of the likes you would normally create in programs such as Adobe Photoshop or After Effects. However, the Flare tool creates these effects using only vector objects, not rasters, and Illustrator keeps them in an editable state, which makes them easy to adjust.

➡ Because vector lens flares utilize a variety of transparency blend modes, you may see odd results when adding flares that overlap areas with no background. Adding a white rectangle that fills your entire artboard and sending it to the back will help.

Drawing a Vector Lens Flare

Drawing a flare with the Flare tool is basically a two-step process. First you define where the highlight will go, and then you define the angle of the light. In reality, though, many other little steps need to happen in between these two. To apply a lens flare with the Flare tool, follow these instructions:

1. Select the Flare tool, which you'll find grouped with the closed-path shape tools (don't ask why it's there—just accept it; **Figure 10.40**).

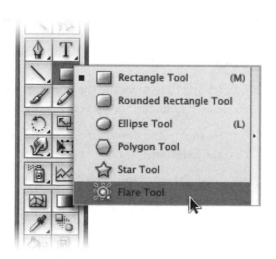

Figure 10.40 The Flare tool is grouped with the closed-path shape tools.

2. Click and drag from the point where you want the center of the highlight to be (**Figure 10.41**). Do not release the mouse button yet.

Figure 10.41 Clicking and dragging with the Flare tool is the first step in creating a vector flare.

3. Press the up and down arrows to add and remove the number of rays in the lens flare.

4. Release the mouse button.

5. Click and drag to define the lighting direction of the flare. Do not release the mouse button yet (**Figure 10.42**).

6. Press the up and down arrows to add and remove the number of rings in the lens flare.

7. Release the mouse to complete the lens flare (**Figure 10.43**).

Figure 10.42 The second click and drag with the Flare tool defines additional options.

Figure 10.43 The Flare creates cool effects, although you should refer to Chapter 12, *Prepress and Printing*, for important information about printing documents with transparency effects.

Editing a Vector Lens Flare

Because of the transparency blend modes that are used by the objects created with the Flare tool, you'll see the best results when you're creating flares over colored backgrounds.

Even though it isn't a live effect, once a flare has been applied, it can still be edited—although not via the Appearance panel. To edit a flare, follow these steps:

1. Select the flare with the Selection tool.

2. Double-click the Flare tool in the Toolbox. The Flare Tool Options dialog opens

3. Specify any changes to the appearance of the flare in the Flare Tool Options dialog.

4. Click the Preview button and you will see the changes happening to the flare as you adjust the settings.

CHAPTER ELEVEN

Web and Mobile Design

There's no question that Adobe Illustrator suffers from schizophrenia. One moment it's a print-based application with spot colors and crop marks, and the next, it's a Web-based application with Web-safe color panels and slices. And that's okay, because as designers living in the 21st century, we all suffer from the same schizophrenia. This is because we are called upon to create art that will be used in many different ways—most notably in print, on the Web, and even now on handheld mobile devices, such as cell phones. Even if you are living in a print- or Web-centric world, others may use and repurpose the art that you create. That's where Illustrator excels—in repurposing artwork for a variety of uses.

In this chapter, we focus on Web and mobile technologies and understanding how Web browsers and mobile devices display graphics. New features in Illustrator CS3 and Flash CS3 Professional make working between these two programs much easier and give designers new options for working between print and Web environments. We'll discuss these features and how you can use your favorite design application—Illustrator—to create quality graphics with ease.

Illustrator's Role in Web Design

Before we dive into the world of Web design, it's important to realize where Illustrator fits in when it comes to creating Web graphics. There's certainly more to creating a Web site than drawing pretty pictures. Programs are dedicated specifically to creating and maintaining Web sites, such as Adobe Dreamweaver and Adobe GoLive, and in no way does Illustrator replace those programs.

You can use Illustrator to design how a Web page looks (by creating a composition), but you wouldn't normally use Illustrator to create an actual HTML-based Web page. Similarly, you wouldn't use Illustrator to manage a multipage Web site because Illustrator lacks the toolset to do so.

Illustrator's strength is in designing Web interfaces or the navigation bars, buttons, individual Web graphics, and general artwork that appear within a Web page. You can place elements such as this that you design in Illustrator into Dreamweaver, GoLive, or any other program you use to create your Web pages. Alternatively, you can create graphics in Illustrator, which you can then bring into Photoshop as well, if your Web workflow requires it.

DESIGNING FOR THE WEB— ATTRIBUTES OF GRAPHICS

Throughout this book, you have been learning how to create vector-based artwork. You've even learned how to use Illustrator's Live Trace feature, which converts pixel-based images into Bézier paths. So, it's with a large spoonful of irony that we inform you how important pixels are in the world of Web graphics.

Unlike printed artwork that is produced with image setters or digital presses that are capable of resolutions upward of 3,000 dots per inch (dpi), artwork that is created for the Web is always viewed on a computer screen, usually at 72 pixels per inch (ppi). Features that a print designer might be used to, such as working with high-resolution images, choosing spot colors, or carefully calculating where fold lines or trim lines will be, are of no concern to someone who is designing a Web site.

However, don't be fooled into thinking that Web designers have it easier than print designers. A Web designer faces plenty of challenges—issues that never cross the minds of print designers. For example, because people view Web sites on computer screens, a designer has no way of knowing what size a viewer's screen is. Especially now, when you have WebTV, Internet kiosks, and Web-capable cell phones, it is important for Web designers to create their art so that it can be displayed on virtually any device.

Although print and Web technologies are different, it's important not to lose sight of your goal as a designer—to communicate a message in an effective manner. The same rules of design that apply to the print world also apply to artwork destined for the Web. If you keep this at the forefront of your mind, and if you follow the advice and techniques revealed throughout the rest of this chapter, you're sure to create effective and compelling Web graphics.

In the business world, there's a saying that goes, "We offer excellent service, exceptional quality, and cheap prices—pick any two out of the three." You can apply a similar saying to Web graphics; it would sound something like, "There's color, quality, and file size—pick any two out of the three." Allow us to explain.

With Web graphics, there's a delicate balance between the way an image looks when viewed on a computer screen and the time it takes to download the image so that the user can view it. No matter how good the image looks, if viewers have to wait too long for a graphic to appear on their screens, their patience runs out, and they click to some other Web site in the blink of an eye. In general, there is a direct correlation between the detail and number of colors in an image and the size of the file. A file with many colors may have a large file size, but an image with a small file size may not have enough colors or detail to look good. As a designer, your job is to find a happy medium—an image that looks good and is small enough that it downloads quickly. Luckily, you have Illustrator on your side, which has the tools you'll need to get results.

Although the argument can be made that file size isn't that important anymore because of the growing population of broadband Internet installations, remember that many people still have slower dialup connections (especially outside the United States). In addition, handheld wireless devices and Web-based cell phones are becoming increasingly popular, and those devices have much slower download capabilities.

Understanding and Using Web-Safe Colors

Most designers have a swatch book by their side—such as a Pantone book—that helps them choose colors to use in a design. And even though color management technologies have been getting better over the years, most people still don't trust the color they see on their computer screens. If you're designing Web graphics, though, you don't have much of a choice because the computer screen is the delivery medium for your artwork. Therefore, it's entirely possible that you can choose a nice yellow color on your screen, but when someone views your Web site on a different computer, that color might appear green or orange. So, what's a designer to do?

With a little bit of information and some simple math, it's possible to narrow the number of colors that you might use to ensure that your color looks decent on someone else's computer screen. Although there are all types of computers and graphics cards out there, the minimum number of colors that all systems support is 256 (also referred to as VGA). However, not all computer systems use the same set of 256 colors. In fact, Windows-based computers use a different system set of colors than Mac-based computers (not surprising). The good news is that of these two mainstream systems, only 40 colors are different, which leaves 216 common colors. This means if a designer were to use one of these 216 colors, referred to as *Web-safe colors*, they would be assured that their artwork would display properly on just about any computer.

Illustrator can help you choose from these Web-safe colors in several ways. First, you can load a custom library that contains all 216 Web-safe colors by choosing Window > Swatch Libraries > Web. Illustrator also features a library called VisiBone2, which displays Web-safe colors in a more intuitive way (**Figure 11.1**). Alternatively, you can choose Web Safe RGB from the Color panel menu, which allows you to choose Web-safe colors by using the color ramp, by using the RGB sliders, or by directly entering their hexadecimal values. If you are using the regular RGB sliders in the Color panel, Illustrator lets you know when a color is not a Web-safe color by displaying a small cube under the color icon. If you click the cube, Illustrator chooses the closest Web-safe color for you (**Figure 11.2**).

As if that weren't enough, you can also take advantage of the Color Guide panel's ability to work within a specific library of colors. Clicking the icon in the lower-left corner of the Color Guide panel, you can choose to limit the Color Guide to only suggest Web-safe colors (**Figure 11.3**).

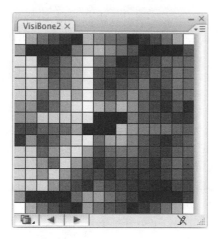

Figure 11.1 When the panel is resized correctly so that there are white swatches in each of the four corners, the VisiBone2 panel displays the 216 Web-safe colors in a way that closely matches a color wheel, making it easier to use when designing.

Cube —

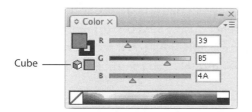

Figure 11.2 A small cube in the Color panel indicates when a chosen color is not a Web-safe color. You can have Illustrator snap to the closest Web-safe color by clicking the cube.

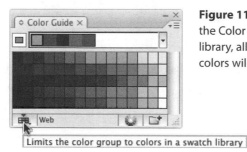

Limits the color group to colors in a swatch library

Figure 11.3 By limiting the Color Guide to the Web library, all recommended colors will be Web-safe ones.

Maximizing Image Quality on the Web

Overall, two issues affect the appearance of Web graphics—dithering and antialiasing. We mentioned earlier how computers display different colors. Higher-end graphics cards allow computers to display many millions of colors, whereas lower-end cards restrict the display to a far smaller number of colors. Therefore, the following question arises: "If you create multicolored artwork on a high-end machine (which most designers use), what happens when that graphic is displayed on a low-end machine that can't display all of those colors?"

Dithering

The answer is *dithering*—a process in which a computer simulates a color that it doesn't have by mixing colors that it does have. For example, if you have a set of paints, you might have only a few colors, but you can create more colors by mixing the paints. Although the dithering concept is nice in theory, the results are not always great. The problem is that a computer can't mix colors within a single pixel, so the dithering process creates a pattern of different-colored pixels in an effort to appear as another color. Many times, this pattern is visible and can give an odd appearance to a graphic (**Figure 11.4**). In fact, the entire concept of using a Web-safe color is to ensure that you'll be using a color that won't dither. As you'll see later in the chapter, Illustrator contains certain settings that can control how dithering is applied to a graphic.

Figure 11.4 The gradient on the left has been enlarged to show the effects of dithering. Notice the pattern of pixels that are visible where colors blend into one another. The same gradient on the right, however, exhibits no dithering.

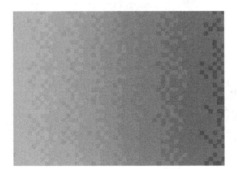

Antialiasing

The second issue that arises with screen-rendered graphics has to do with the low resolution that a monitor uses—in most cases, 72 ppi. At such a low resolution, the eye actually sees pixels, and curved edges display with jagged edges (often referred to as *jaggies*). To make graphics look better onscreen, computers use a method called *antialiasing* to slightly blur the edges of boundaries between colors. The result is an image that looks smooth instead of jagged (**Figure 11.5**).

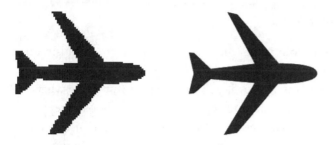

Figure 11.5 Pictured here are identical vector objects. The object on the right has antialiasing turned on, resulting in a smoother appearance onscreen.

Disabling Antialiasing

Although antialiasing is generally a good thing, sometimes it can work against you. The side effect of blurring edges of color is that sometimes doing so makes your graphics unsightly or makes your text illegible. This is especially true when your design contains small text or thin lines. Using Pixel Preview helps you see these issues before you export these graphics (**Figure 11.6**).

You may find that for some artwork, it is even beneficial to turn off antialiasing altogether. To do so, make your selection, and choose Effect > Rasterize. Choose 72 ppi for the Resolution setting, choose None for the Anti-aliasing setting, and click OK. With Pixel Preview turned on, you will clearly see the difference between objects that do and do not have antialiasing disabled (**Figure 11.7**).

Figure 11.6 Although you may have specified a 1-point black stroke for an object, Pixel Preview mode may reveal that antialiasing has produced a 2-point gray stroke instead.

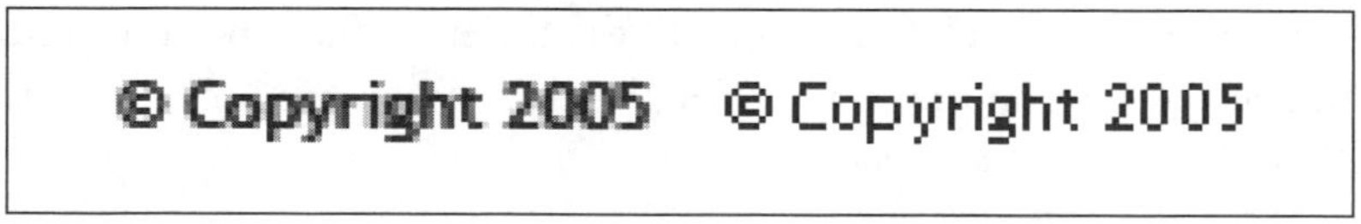

© Copyright 2005   © Copyright 2005

Figure 11.7 Legibility can suffer on small text when antialiasing is used. The text on the right has antialiasing disabled. Although it doesn't look as pretty, at least you can read it.

Using Pixel Preview Mode

When you save or convert your vector graphic to a raster format, Illustrator can apply antialiasing (it does by default). However, when you're viewing your graphic on the Illustrator artboard, you might also want to see what your graphic looks like with antialiasing applied. To do so, choose View > Pixel Preview, which is a special preview mode where your graphics display on your artboard as they would when viewed in a Web browser. You can work and edit graphics in Pixel Preview mode, and you should do so when you're designing graphics for the Web.

Working in Pixel Preview mode is important because antialiasing can cause slight adjustments in the appearance of your graphics, such as thin black lines becoming fat gray lines or text appearing chunky or blurry (see the sidebar entitled "Disabling Antialiasing"). With Pixel Preview on, you can position your artwork and see results instantly.

Using Compression to Reduce File Size

The last—and possibly the most important—attribute of a Web graphic is its file size. Anyone can create great-looking graphics with large, high-resolution images, but a Web designer has to deliver the best possible graphics using low-resolution images that download fast.

For the most part, Web designers can save files in a variety of file formats, each of which utilizes compression techniques to help reduce file size. In general, file formats use one of the following two types of compression: lossless and lossy. *Lossless* compression reduces file size without any loss in image quality or image detail. In contrast, *lossy* compression reduces file size by sacrificing image data, resulting in images that have less detail. As with just about anything else in life, a designer is faced with making decisions based on which attributes are most important on an image-by-image basis. In the next section, you'll learn about all the different file types Illustrator can utilize and the compression techniques these file types use.

OPTIMIZING WEB GRAPHICS

The process of preparing graphics for display on the Web is called *optimization*. This process entails choosing how artwork is exported from Illustrator, what file formats are being used, and what settings are being used for each file type. Illustrator offers several features, such as Web slicing and Save for Web & Devices, which help you create the best-looking Web graphics.

Creating Web Slices

One way to optimize Web graphics is to use a technique called *Web slicing*. In simple terms, Web slicing is the process of cutting a large image into several smaller images, which is desirable for various reasons.

First, there's user perception. If you try to load a Web page that has a single large image on it, the user sits there impatiently waiting for it to download and appear on the page. But when an image is sliced into smaller parts, each smaller image loads faster, and as a result, it seems like the image itself is loading faster.

Second, you can use different file formats for each image slice, which can save some valuable file size space, resulting in a faster-loading graphic overall. As you'll see when we discuss the Save for Web & Devices feature, these settings directly impact the final file size (read: download time) of your total image.

Slicing is also helpful if parts of a graphic need to be updated often. Instead of always creating larger images, you can update just a part of the image. Swapping out a slice or two can be more efficient than having to work with one large, bulky file all the time.

Finally, because each slice is its own image, you can assign a link (a URL) to it, effectively making it a button. When someone clicks a sliced part of an image, they are linked to another Web page. Of course, you can specify other functionality for such a button as well.

Any Way You Slice It...

Illustrator offers two ways to create Web slices. The more traditional way is to draw them yourself, but Illustrator can also create slices from objects automatically using a feature called *object-based slicing*. Let's explore both methods.

Once your artwork is created, you can choose the Slice tool from the Toolbox and click and drag in your document window. When you do, Illustrator draws rectangular regions—slices—and each appears with a number that identifies it (**Figure 11.8**). As you create slices, other dimmed slices might appear automatically in the document. These are called *auto slices*. Slices that you create are called *user slices*. Because the overall image has to be rectangular (for an explanation, see the sidebar "Web Slices = HTML Tables") and all the slices must be rectangles as well, Illustrator creates slices as necessary (**Figure 11.9**). As you continue to create slices, Illustrator updates the auto slices accordingly.

Figure 11.8 Create slices where it makes sense to do so to allow for interactivity or future editing.

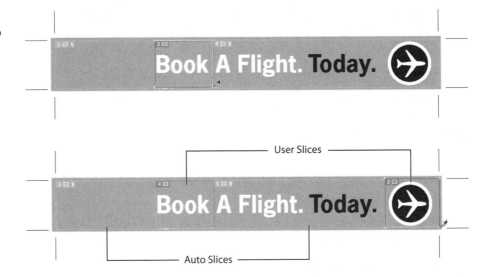

Figure 11.9 As you draw slices with the Slice tool, Illustrator creates other slices to fill out the rest of the document.

Web Slices = HTML Tables

So, what exactly happens when you create a slice? Illustrator splits a single graphic into multiple images. It creates an HTML table, with each cell of the table containing one of these slices, or pieces of the image. In this way, when you display the Web page in a browser, all the sliced-up images appear together, almost like a puzzle. This is an important concept to keep in mind because you can create only rectangular slices.

When you draw a slice with the Slice tool, Illustrator is really drawing a rectangle with no fill and no stroke and making it a slice (**Figure 11.10**). When you want to edit the slice, you can use the Slice Select tool to change the boundaries of the slice.

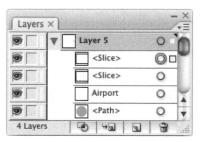

Figure 11.10 Slices you create with the Slice tool appear listed in the Layers panel. They are special rectangles that have their Fill and Stroke attributes set to None.

However, Illustrator also has a different kind of slice. Instead of creating graphics and drawing slices over them, you can apply a slice as an attribute to a selection—something Illustrator calls an *object-based slice*. To apply this kind of slice, make a selection, and then choose Object > Slice > Make. Illustrator uses the bounds of your selected artwork as the area for the object-based slice. Using this method, if you make an edit to your graphic, the slice updates automatically along with it.

If you want to hide all the little squares and numbers that indicate slices on your screen, you can do so by choosing View > Hide Slices.

Editing Slice Attributes

You can specify certain attributes for a slice. Remember that a slice is really a cell in an HTML table. So, for example, a slice can have its own background color or URL link. Once a slice has been defined using either of the two methods described earlier, you can select it with the Slice Select tool. To edit the attributes of a slice, select a slice, and choose Object > Slice > Slice Options to specify a URL and alt text (**Figure 11.11** on the following page). When you specify text as an object-based slice, you can also set the slice to be an HTML slice (rather than an image slice). In that case, Illustrator exports the text as editable HTML instead of as a graphic.

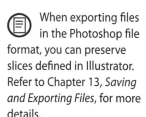 When exporting files in the Photoshop file format, you can preserve slices defined in Illustrator. Refer to Chapter 13, *Saving and Exporting Files*, for more details.

Figure 11.11 The Slice Options dialog gives you the ability to assign specific URLs and additional information for each slice in your document.

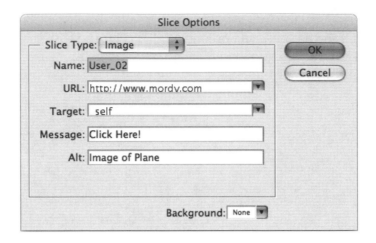

HTML text slices might not show up in a browser exactly as you see them in Illustrator. Although bold or character attributes are preserved, exact fonts and sizing depend on the browser used. Other text features, such as kerning and baseline shift, are ignored in the browser.

Once you have created all your slices, you can choose individual file formats and additional settings by using the Save for Web & Devices feature, which we discuss in detail right about … now.

Using the Save for Web & Devices Feature

At one time, saving a graphic for use on the Web was a difficult task that involved saving an image, opening it in a Web browser, and then repeating that process again and again. Illustrator's Save for Web & Devices feature—which is also found in Photoshop—allows you to speed up the process of optimizing and saving Web graphics.

Once you're ready to export a final version of your Web graphic, choose File > Save for Web & Devices to open the Save for Web & Devices dialog. The dialog, which fills up most of your screen, is split into several different sections (**Figure 11.12**). Along the far left are several tools you can use within the Save for Web & Devices dialog. In the center, a preview pane allows you to view up to four different versions of your art. The upper-right side offers a variety of different export formats and their settings, and the lower-right side offers a trio of panels that control color, image size, and layer settings. Along the bottom of the dialog are zoom controls, color information, and a Preview in Browser button.

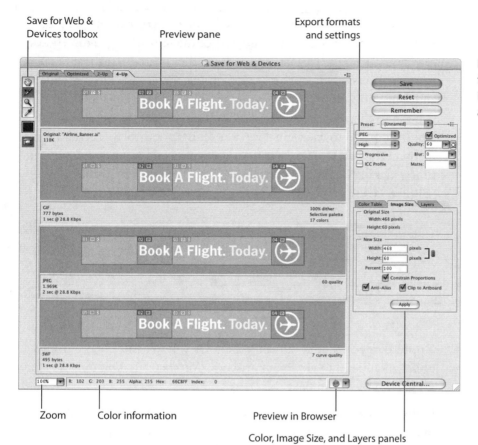

Save for Web &
Devices toolbox

Preview pane

Export formats
and settings

Zoom   Color information

Preview in Browser

Color, Image Size, and Layers panels

Figure 11.12 The Save
for Web & Devices dialog
is almost an entire
application within itself.

Let's take a closer look at each of the individual sections of the Save for Web
& Devices dialog.

- **Save for Web & Devices toolbox.** The Save for Web & Devices dialog has its own toolbox, which is the first indication that this feature
  is above and beyond just a simple dialog. The Hand tool lets you pan
  the view of your artwork; it is especially useful when you are viewing your art at higher zoom levels. The Slice Select tool enables you to
  select a particular slice with which to work. The Zoom tool allows you
  to change the zoom setting of your artwork, and the Eyedropper tool
  allows you to sample color from an image that appears in the preview
  pane. In addition to the icon that indicates the eyedropper color (you
  can click it to get the Color Picker), there's also a button that toggles
  slice visibility on and off.

- **Preview pane.** The preview pane is the main feature of the Save for Web & Devices dialog. By clicking any of the four tabs, you can choose to view your original art (as it appears on the Illustrator artboard), an optimized version of your art (based on the current file settings chosen), and 2-up and 4-up versions of your art. Using the 2-Up and 4-Up tabs, you can easily compare different file settings or how an optimized file looks compared to its original version. Illustrator displays useful information below each preview, including file size and estimated download times, making it easy to find just the right file type for your image (**Figure 11.13**).

Figure 11.13 Besides being able to preview the results of different file and compression settings, you can also view file size and estimated download times.

- **Zoom control.** The zoom control allows you to easily choose from a preset zoom level to view your artwork. Alternatively, you can enter any number in the zoom field.

- **Color information.** As you move your mouse pointer over artwork in the preview pane, the Save for Web & Devices dialog provides feedback for colors in real time. This is helpful if you want to confirm color information or if you want to sample a specific color from an image.

- **Preview in Browser icon.** The Preview in Browser icon is a huge time-saver. Although you get a beautiful preview of your artwork in the preview pane of the Save for Web & Devices dialog, it can be useful at times to see what your artwork looks like in an actual Web browser. This is especially useful for when you want to preview SWF animations, because those do not preview in the Save for Web & Devices dialog. Clicking the icon previews the selected artwork in your computer's default Web browser. Clicking the arrow opens a list of installed browsers that you can choose from (**Figure 11.14**), or you can edit the list of browsers to customize it to your needs.

Figure 11.14 The Preview in Browser feature makes it easy to quickly see what your art will look like when rendered in your favorite Web browser.

The two remaining sections, which feature the group of three panels and the ability to choose from different file types, are covered individually, in the following sections.

Choosing the Right Image File Type

Overall, the main benefit of using the Save for Web & Devices feature is the ability to compare the final results of multiple file formats and choose the one that fits best for a particular use. To make the right decision, you have to understand the differences between each of these file formats and what their strengths and weaknesses are. Let's take a closer look.

Choosing the GIF File Format

A common image file format used on the Web, the Graphics Interchange Format (GIF) was developed by the people at CompuServe, one of the pioneers of the Internet and the Web, though you hardly hear that name mentioned today (it's amazing how fast things change). Recognizing the need to send graphics files across modem connections (which in those days were quite slow), they developed the GIF file format, which can contain a maximum of 256 colors and which uses a lossless method of compression. A GIF tries to save space by looking for large areas of contiguous solid color; this makes the format perfect for logos, backgrounds, text headlines, and the like. However, the 256-color limit and the limited compression for images with a lot of detail make the GIF file format a bad choice for photographic content.

The GIF file format supports other features, including the ability to control the exact number of colors present in the file and the ability to specify transparency for a single color of the file.

To get an exact image size when you're exporting via the Save for Web & Devices dialog, draw a rectangle around your artwork, and choose Object > Crop Area > Make. Alternatively, you can use the Crop Area tool. The Save for Web & Devices feature honors Illustrator's crop area setting when you're exporting graphics. Any artwork that appears outside the crop area is not exported. If you used the Web new document profile to create your document, a crop area is automatically set.

GIF files can also contain multiple images or frames, creating an animation, although Illustrator doesn't support the creation of animated GIF files.

When you choose the GIF file format in the Save for Web & Devices dialog, you have the following settings available:

- **Color settings.** The Color Table settings enable to you to specify exactly how many colors the GIF will contain. Lower numbers of colors result in smaller file sizes but could also result in lower-quality images. Because a GIF can contain a maximum of 256 colors, you can choose from several color-reduction algorithms, including the restrictive option, which chooses only Web-safe colors.

- **Dithering.** The Dither settings control what method of dithering is used when the image calls for a color that isn't available in the reduced set of colors or when the image is displayed on a computer screen that doesn't support enough colors to display the image.

- **Transparency.** The Transparency setting enables to you to define colors that will display as transparent in a browser. For example, if you want to place a logo on a colored background, you can specify the background color of the GIF to be transparent; doing so causes the background color in the browser to show through those transparent areas. The edges where color meets the transparent edge are usually white when displayed in a browser, and specifying a matte color that matches the background ensures that the edges of your art blend seamlessly into the background (**Figure 11.15**).

Figure 11.15 The image on the left was saved with a Matte setting that matched the background on which the art would eventually appear. The image on the right used the default Matte setting of white.

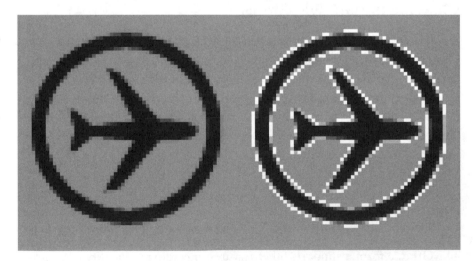

- **Interlacing.** An interlaced image loads gradually in a Web browser, first in a low resolution and then in a higher resolution in a second and third pass. This allows the image to appear in the browser immediately so that viewers can get an idea of what the page will look like, and then after a few seconds, the higher-quality image appears. Turning interlacing off means the image won't display on a Web page until the entire image has been downloaded.

- **Web Snap.** By specifying a value in the Web Snap field, you can have Illustrator ensure that a certain percentage of the colors used in the graphic are actually Web-safe colors.

Choosing the JPEG File Format

JPEG (pronounced "jay-peg") stands for Joint Photographic Experts Group, and it was created to allow photographers to share images using a standard file format. JPEG files can contain millions of colors and use a lossy compression method. Digital images usually contain more color information than the human eye can see or detect, and by throwing out some of that extra information, JPEG images can achieve amazing file size savings. For example, a 10 MB photograph can easily be compressed into a JPEG that's less than 1 MB.

Because the JPEG format supports millions of colors (as opposed to only 256 in a GIF), it's the perfect format to use for photographs or images with complex colors and gradient fills. However, JPEG files do not support transparency as GIF files do.

When you choose the JPEG file format in the Save for Web & Devices dialog, you can choose from the following settings:

- **Compression/Quality.** The Quality settings enable you to specify how much information is thrown out of a file when the file is compressed. The settings are actually a bit confusing in the way they are presented in the dialog. You might think that a setting of Maximum would mean the highest compression with a smaller resulting file size, but that's incorrect. To prevent confusion, it's best to think of these settings as quality settings. A setting of Maximum means the best quality of an image, meaning less information is being tossed from the image

(**Figure 11.16**). The result is a better-looking image that is larger in file size. Alternatively, you can specify numerical values in the Quality field. A setting of 100 is the same as choosing the Maximum setting.

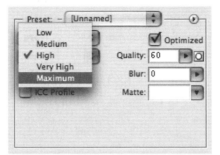

Figure 11.16 Don't be confused by the different settings for JPEG compression. For the best quality, choose Maximum. For the smallest file size, choose Low.

- **Blur.** One of the most noticeable side effects of compression in a JPEG file is artifacts or stray pixels that appear in the image. Specifying a blur amount can help cover up those artifacts.

- **Matte.** The Matte setting enables you to specify a color for the edge of the graphic, thus allowing it to blend smoothly into colored backgrounds.

- **Progressive.** The Progressive setting allows a JPEG image to load gradually in a browser, similar to the interlacing setting we discussed, which is available for GIF images.

Choosing the PNG File Format

The PNG (pronounced "ping") format was developed mainly as an alternative to GIF. Shortly after GIF became popular on the Web, the Unisys corporation, which developed the actual compression algorithm used in GIF, tried to collect royalties on its technology from those who used GIF. To get around the legal issues, an open standard called Portable Network Graphic (PNG) was developed. The PNG format utilizes lossless compression and can support millions of colors. Instead of allowing you to specify a single color as being transparent, the PNG format also supports 256 levels of transparency, similar to alpha channels inside Photoshop.

Older Web browsers require a special plugin to view PNG files, although most newer browsers can display them natively. PNG files also might not be compatible with some PDA devices and cell phones. PNG files come in two varieties, 8 bit and 24 bit. The different optimization settings for PNG-8 are identical to those found for GIF, mentioned previously.

Choosing the SWF File Format

Shockwave Flash (SWF) is a popular Web-based file format that supports both vectors and rasters. This Flash file format has become extremely popular because of its capability to contain interactive or animated content. You can use Illustrator to generate a SWF file that you want to upload directly to a Web site or to create art for import into the Adobe Flash application for further editing.

When you choose the SWF file format in the Save for Web & Devices dialog, you can choose from the following settings:

- **File options.** You can create SWF files in one of two ways: AI File to SWF File, which creates a single SWF file that contains all of your Illustrator artwork, and AI Layers to SWF Frames, where each layer is converted into a keyframe, resulting in a single animated SWF file. Additionally, you can choose the Protect File option to prevent others from opening the resulting SWF file. The Text as Outlines options converts all text to outlines (so no font files are necessary), and you can make the file size smaller by choosing the Compressed option. The Curve Quality setting controls the fidelity of curved paths.

- **Appearance.** When using transparency or other special effects in Illustrator, you can choose to Preserve Appearance, which flattens any effects as necessary, or you can choose the Preserve Editability Where Possible option if you plan on opening the file in Flash in order to edit it. This way you can make additional tweaks to the artwork if you need to do so.

- **Animation settings.** If you choose the AI Layers to SWF Frames option, all layers in your Illustrator file become keyframes and play as an animation when the SWF file is viewed in a Web browser. The Frame Rate setting controls the speed at which the animation plays (you can't control the timing of individual frames like you can in a GIF animation), and the Looping option forces the animation to repeat continuously. More information on creating animated SWF files is covered later in this chapter.

The Flash (SWF) Export dialog offers additional options for creating SWF files that are not present in the Save for Web & Devices dialog. For detailed information about the Flash format and these additional settings, see Chapter 13, *Saving and Exporting Files.*

Choosing the SVG File Format

Scalable Vector Graphics (SVG) is an XML-based file format that is used primarily on the Web and has recently become more popular in creating content for cell phones and handheld wireless devices.

Most Web browsers require a special plugin to view SVG files, although some of the newer versions of browsers, including Firefox and Apple's Safari are beginning to support SVG files natively. Because SVG files are text-based, they can be edited easily, even after they have been exported and uploaded to a Web server. Because of this ability, SVG files are used in data-driven server-based workflows where customized content is a necessity.

When you choose the SVG file format in the Save for Web & Devices dialog, you can choose from the following settings:

You can find more information on SVG at www.svg.org and www. adobe.com/svg.

- **DTD.** The DTD (Document Type Definition) setting is akin to the version of SVG with which your file is compatible. Because SVG is an open standard, additional specifications are revised and approved. If you save an SVG file with a particular DTD, it means your file will be compatible with any device that supports that DTD. Newer specifications usually support more functionality than the older ones did. SVG Tiny (also referred to as SVG-t) is a subset of SVG used for displaying content on SVG-enabled cell phones. SVG Basic is another subset used for displaying content on PDAs.

- **Fonts.** When text is present in your file, you can specify the Adobe CEF type, which results in better-looking text when your file is viewed with the Adobe SVG Viewer, but which may not be supported with other SVG viewers. SVG creates more compatible text, but this text may not be as readable at smaller font sizes. Alternatively, you can convert all text to outlines, which increases file size.

- **Images.** When you save a file in SVG, you have the ability to embed any images within the SVG file (making for larger but self-sufficient files), or you can choose to create smaller SVG files by using the Link option.

- **CSS Properties.** You can format SVG code in a variety of ways, and the CSS Properties settings allows you to determine how object attributes are coded within the file. For the most part, this setting affects the performance of your file when viewed.

- **Decimal Places.** Illustrator allows you to specify how precisely vector paths are drawn. You may choose a value from 1 to 7, where higher numbers result in better-looking paths at the expense of file size and performance.

- **Encoding.** When you save an SVG file that contains text, you can specify a character encoding, including ISO-8859-1 (suitable for European languages) and 8- or 16-bit Unicode (suitable for more complex languages).

- **Optimize for Adobe SVG Viewer.** If people will be using the Adobe SVG Viewer to view your SVG files, you can check this option, which takes advantage of proprietary optimizations that exist in the Adobe SVG Viewer, including faster rendering of SVG filter effects.

Choosing the WBMP File Format

The Wireless Bitmap (WBMP) file format is a format that is optimized for wireless devices that have slow connections and limited display capabilities. These devices are quickly fading because newer phones are being introduced constantly and cell phones are the largest-selling consumer electronic devices worldwide. WBMP files are black-and-white images (color isn't supported) and are optimized via a dithering setting.

Specifying Additional Image Settings

In addition to choosing a file format, Illustrator's Save for Web & Devices feature allows you to control how colors, image sizes, and layers are treated when saving your files. You can find these settings within the three panels that appear at the lower-right side of the Save for Web & Devices dialog.

Color Table

The Color Table panel lists all the colors contained within the selected slice. Colors that appear with little diamond icons are Web-safe colors (**Figure 11.17** on the following page). Using the Eyedropper tool to sample colors, you can click the Maps Selected Colors to Transparent icon beneath the panel to specify a color that will appear as transparent (when saving to file formats that support transparency).

Figure 11.17 Illustrator indicates Web-safe colors in a color table with tiny diamond-shaped icons.

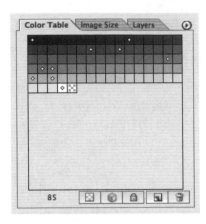

Image Size

The Image Size panel gives you feedback on the actual size of the selected slice, and it also allows you to specify new sizes, although it's always better to make changes to image size on the Illustrator artboard before launching the Save for Web & Devices dialog. Of importance are the Anti-Alias button and Clip to Artboard check box. By default, Illustrator antialiases artwork that is exported from the Save for Web & Devices dialog and exports artwork based on the art's bounding box or your crop area setting. To have the Save for Web & Devices dialog honor the artboard size, you can check the Clip to Artboard setting.

When creating documents using the Web new document profile, Illustrator creates a very large artboard size and sets a crop area at the size you specify. Because of this setting, the Clip to Artboard setting may produce undesirable results. To fix this, use Document Setup to adjust the size of your artboard accordingly.

Layers

If you specified layers in your Illustrator document, you have the option of exporting those layers as CSS layers by checking the Export as CSS Layers option in the Layers panel found in the Save for Web & Devices dialog. CSS, which stands for Cascading Style Sheets, allows you to take advantage of absolute positioning and overlapping objects within a Web page. Although the technical aspects of CSS are outside the scope of this book, it's important to realize that CSS has become a standard, especially when you're generating content that will be displayed on a wide range of devices.

For more information on CSS, refer to *Stylin' with CSS: A Designer's Guide,* by Charles Wyke-Smith (New Riders, 2005).

If you choose to export Illustrator layers as CSS layers, you can choose whether each top-level layer in your document should be exported as being visible or hidden (**Figure 11.18**). Alternatively, you can specify that certain layers aren't exported at all.

Using layers is extremely important when creating SVG graphics because the format relies heavily on object hierarchy.

Figure 11.18 CSS Layers that are exported as hidden can be activated via scripts on the server using Dynamic HTML.

 Featured Matchup: Web Slicing vs. CSS Layers

If you think about it, no matter whether you choose to export Web graphics as a group of slices or as CSS layers, you end up with a single graphic that is broken down into several parts. But there's a big difference between these two approaches. In fact, you can almost categorize Web slicing as yesterday's technology and CSS layers as the way of the future.

As we mentioned earlier, Web slicing is a process of taking a single image and converting it into an HTML table. Each cell in the table contains a different portion of the image, and when the entire table is rendered within a browser, you can see the entire graphic. Although this method of slicing is widespread, HTML tables were never intended to be used in this way. As a result, when these tables are displayed on handheld devices or different browsers, the results can vary. Sometimes, the images may not appear as intended at all. In addition, a limitation in HTML is that images cannot overlap each other, which makes designing with slices an exercise in careful planning.

In contrast, CSS layers are an open standard built on the premise that Web graphics will be displayed on a variety of different devices. When CSS layers are used, there's a good chance your artwork will appear as intended even on smaller devices. In addition, CSS layers support overlapping graphics, and each layer can be programmed with interactivity, meaning you can have layers animate independently and also appear and disappear based on user-defined parameters. To take full advantage of CSS, though, Illustrator alone won't be enough, and you'll want to add functionality on your own by using applications such as Dreamweaver.

Achieving Efficient Web Design

Above and beyond the Web-specific features that we've discussed in this chapter, such as using Web-safe colors and the Pixel Preview mode, you can employ other features and strategies to achieve more efficient Web design.

When you're designing Web graphics that will eventually be exported as PSD files to be edited in Photoshop, be sure to use layers to organize your artwork in a meaningful way. Because layers can be preserved when exporting to Photoshop, you will be able to perform edits and add functionality easily when different elements of your design are easily accessible. Pixel-based applications such as Photoshop rely heavily on the organization of layers and functions such as assigning rollovers or other interactivity and are based on layers as well. Refer to Chapter 9, *Mixing It Up: Working with Vectors and Pixels*, and Chapter 13, *Saving and Exporting Files,* for more information on exporting Illustrator files in the PSD file format.

By using symbols, you can achieve tremendous file size savings when you are creating Web graphics for export in the SWF and SVG file formats. When you use symbols in your artwork, you can repeat a graph many times, but only one original copy of that artwork is stored within the file. When designing maps, creating animations, or using other designs that incorporate repeating graphics, it's well worth the effort to find excuses to use symbols. Refer to Chapter 5, *Brushes, Symbols, and Masks*, for more information on how to create, use, and edit symbols in your artwork.

ADDING INTERACTIVITY AND CREATING ANIMATIONS

Although it's nice to admire graphics on a Web page, nothing is quite like a graphic that invokes action on the viewer's part. It is those images that move with animation or that contain clickable hotspots that can take a viewer to additional content that make the Web such an exciting medium. Although Illustrator isn't a replacement for an application such as Flash, you can still create Web graphics that come to life using your favorite vector graphics application.

Creating Image Maps

On the Web, a designer's job is far more than just creating a pretty graphic. Rather, a graphic must draw a viewer to action. The action could be as simple as switching to a different page or as significant as generating a sale.

In Illustrator, you can assign a URL to an object, which results in an *image map*. An image map is a region or portion of a graphic on which a viewer can click.

To create an image map, follow these steps:

1. Select an object on your artboard, and choose Window > Attributes to open your Attributes panel.

2. Once the panel is open, choose Rectangle or Polygon from the Image Map pop-up menu (**Figure 11.19**). For objects that are rectangular, choose the Rectangle option. For images that fit any other shape, choose the Polygon option.

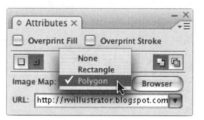

Figure 11.19 Older browsers supported only rectangular image maps, but just about all of today's browsers support polygonal image maps.

3. Once you've chosen an Image Map type, enter a URL in the field below the pop-up menu. For the best results, enter the complete URL, including the **http://**.

    Illustrator keeps track of all the URLs you enter, so if you're applying the same URL to multiple objects in your document, you can choose the correct URL from the URL pop-up (**Figure 11.20**). To test a URL to see whether it is correct, click the Browser button; when you do, Illustrator launches your system's default browser and navigates to the chosen URL.

Figure 11.20 Once you've entered a URL into the Attributes panel, Illustrator remembers it so that you can easily apply it to other objects in your document.

Animation: Making It Move

Animation in SVG is not directly supported within Illustrator. In order to add animation to SVG files, you can add the code by hand once you've exported the SVG from Illustrator, or you can use an SVG animation application, such as Ikivo's Animator (www.ikivo.com).

There's no question that adding motion to Web graphics enhances their appearance and ability to garner the attention of viewers. Illustrator can build frame-based animations quite easily, although if you're looking for a high-end animation tool, you'd best look elsewhere. The techniques we discuss here are indicative of the simple animations you can create quickly and easily with Illustrator. You might still want to look to Flash and Adobe After Effects for more complex work.

The key to creating great animations in Illustrator is to use layers carefully. Illustrator doesn't have an animation panel or a timeline. Rather, Illustrator treats each top-level layer in your document as a frame in your animation. As you build your animation with each new layer, keep in mind the advice you learned throughout this chapter, especially with regard to using symbols (**Figure 11.21**). Illustrator allows you to create blends between symbols, and even objects with live effects applied. Refer to Chapter 10, *Graphs, Distortion, and Blends*, for detailed information on creating blends.

Figure 11.21 In this illustration, the airplane was defined as a symbol and then used in a blend across the width of the banner. The symbol on the far left was then set to 0% opacity, resulting in a blend that makes the plane appear to fade in as it moves from left to right.

Illustrator can generate only SWF animations. If you want to create animations using SVG, GIF, or other file formats, you'll have to export your Illustrator artwork into other applications.

Once you've created the art for your animation, choose File > Export, and choose the Flash (SWF) file format. When you choose the AI Layers to Flash Frames setting, your resulting SWF file plays through each layer sequentially. Setting the animation to loop causes the animation to repeat endlessly (always fun). Refer to Chapter 13, *Saving and Exporting Files*, for information on the settings found in the Flash (SWF) Export dialog.

Designing Specifically for Flash

After reading this chapter, you've undoubtedly realized that you can use Illustrator to create interactive SWF files. However, if you're looking to develop truly interactive Web sites, interfaces, and experiences, you'll quickly find that Illustrator's capabilities top out rather quickly. Flash is the application you want to use to create truly interactive and engaging content.

However, many Flash professionals use Illustrator to design their artwork and then bring that artwork into Flash, where they add the interactivity. Both Illustrator and Flash are vector-based applications, and many designers are familiar with the design environment and powerful design features found in Illustrator. In addition, it's easy to create mock-ups and PDF files to submit to clients for approval from Illustrator. The challenge, however, is finding a way to bring rich Illustrator content into Flash while keeping features such as artwork, text, gradients, masks, and symbols in an editable state.

The good news is, if you're using Illustrator CS3 and Flash CS3 Professional, you can easily move your artwork between the two—all while keeping the fidelity of your content. In fact, if you know that your artwork will end up in Flash, you can save valuable time by taking advantage of certain features in Illustrator CS3. Let's take a look at some of these features.

Working with Symbols

In Chapter 5, *Brushes, Symbols, and Masks,* you learned how to both define and edit symbols. When working with Flash, creating symbols is extremely important because they allow you to easily add interactivity and make global changes, all while keeping files sizes small and manageable.

When you define a new symbol in Illustrator (F8), you're presented with the Symbol Options dialog (**Figure 11.22** on the following page), which offers three settings. These settings don't have any effect on the symbol within Illustrator and are useful only when you bring the symbol into Flash.

Figure 11.22 The Symbol Options dialog gives you the ability to name the symbol and to apply certain Flash-specific settings.

- **Type.** Flash utilizes several types of symbols for different tasks. You can wait until you bring your symbol from Illustrator into Flash to determine what kind of symbol it should be, or to save time, you can specify the symbol type at the time you first define the symbol in Illustrator. A Graphic symbol is used for static artwork, while a Movie Clip symbol can contain interactivity within it.

- **Flash Registration.** The Flash Registration setting allows you to define an origin point for the symbol. This origin point is used when you apply transformations in Flash or when ActionScript commands are applied to the symbol. This setting is similar to what you learned in Chapter 4, *Advanced Vectors*, with the Transform panel.

- **Enable Guides for 9-Slice Scaling.** Flash has the ability to scale symbols in a special way to prevent distortion. For example, you can specify that only parts of a symbol scale, while other parts don't. To control exactly how symbols scale, check the Enable Guide for 9-Slice Scaling option in the Symbol Options dialog box, and then click OK. Then, double-click the symbol to edit it, at which time you'll see a series of guides appear (**Figure 11.23**). Use the Selection tool to position the guides as desired, and the symbol will scale appropriately when transforms are applied to it in Flash.

Figure 11.23 The Enable Guide for 9-Slice Scaling option allows you to control which parts of a symbol scale and which don't. If you think about the artwork as being divided up by a tic-tac-toe board, the corner and center areas don't scale, while the center-top and center-side areas do.

In addition, you can name each symbol instance that you place on your artboard. Giving an instance a name allows you to reference that instance from within an ActionScript in Flash. When any symbol instance is selected on your artboard, you can give it a name in the field that appears in the Control panel (**Figure 11.24**).

Figure 11.24 Applying instance names in Illustrator can save plenty of time later in your workflow, after bringing your art into Flash.

Working with Text

As you learned in Chapter 7, *Typography,* Illustrator has sophisticated type controls and features. However, when developing Flash content, text can also be interactive. Rather than waiting to add that interactivity in Flash, you can specify interactive text for Flash right within Illustrator. Choose Window > Type > Flash Text to define text destined for Flash as either static, dynamic, or input text (**Figure 11.25**). Static text doesn't change within the Flash file, while you can change dynamic text using ActionScript. Input text is used when building things such as Flash forms, where a user would be asked to enter custom information.

Figure 11.25 The Flash Text panel gives you control over how text objects in Illustrator will behave when brought into Flash.

Bringing Your Artwork into Flash

Once you've created your artwork in Illustrator, you need a reliable way to bring your graphics into Flash. In previous versions of both Illustrator and Flash, this was anything *but* easy. However, in the CS3 versions of these applications, it's actually quite easy.

To quickly move individual pieces of art, you can simply copy and paste from Illustrator into Flash. Any defined symbols will be retained, as well as text and other settings. However, you may want to bring an entire Illustrator file into Flash, preserving layers and document structure as well. To do so, save your file as a native Illustrator document (.ai), because Flash CS3 Professional is able to read native Illustrator files. From Flash, choose File > Import to Stage, and choose the Illustrator file you saved. An import dialog box will appear listing each object in your file (**Figure 11.26**). The import dialog offers many options, including the ability to keep text editable and to convert objects to Movie Clip symbols on the fly.

Figure 11.26 When importing native Illustrator CS3 files into Flash, an import dialog provides an incredible amount of control over how the art will appear inside of your Flash project.

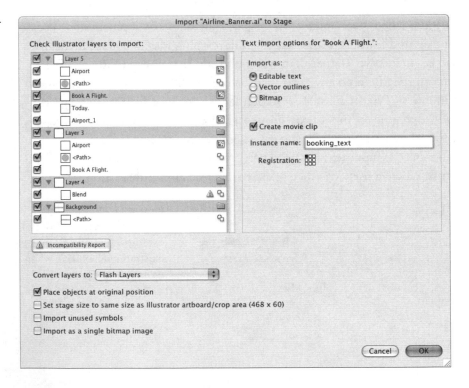

For more information on using Illustrator CS3 and Flash CS3 Professional together, check out the video titled *Illustrator CS3 and Flash CS3 Integration* at http://www.lynda.com.

USING ADOBE DEVICE CENTRAL

Although most Web graphics today are viewed on computer screens, it is becoming more and more popular to view Web content on Web-capable cell phones. Especially with the release of devices such as Apple's iPhone, you can be sure that any graphics you create for the Web will also be viewed on handheld devices. So although the Save for Web & Devices feature is nice on its own, it really doesn't give you a good idea on what your artwork will look like when viewed on a cell phone.

At the lower right of the Save for Web & Devices dialog box, you'll see a button called Device Central, and if you want to see what your Web graphics will look like on a cell phone, clicking that button will launch a separate application called Adobe Device Central.

Adobe Device Central is really a full-blown application on its own and therefore is beyond the scope of this book. But as a basic overview, Adobe Device Central allows you to preview your artwork as it would appear on just about any cell phone or wireless device (**Figure 11.27**). Adobe actually provides quarterly updates, so the list of devices will be current. Not only

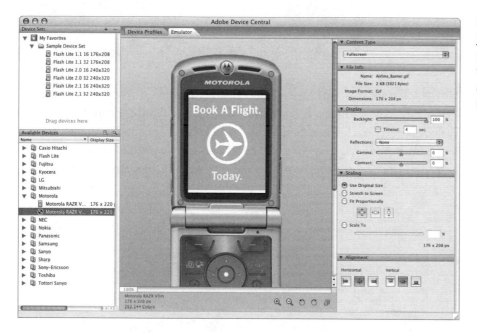

Figure 11.27 More than just a preview, the Emulator panel allows you to click the buttons of the phone and see how your artwork responds to user interaction.

can you preview your artwork on a specific cell phone, you can also simulate specific conditions (such as outdoor lighting, backlighting, low battery power, and so on). Adobe Device Central also provides detailed technical information about each device, including supported resolutions, browsers, and software (**Figure 11.28**).

Figure 11.28 The Device Profiles panel in Adobe Device Central gives you important technical information about most cell phones and wireless Internet devices.

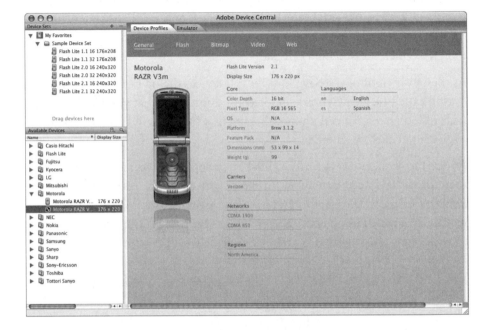

You can also use Adobe Device Central to create new Illustrator documents that are already set to the correct size for a specific device. From the Welcome Screen, clicking the Mobile and Devices new document profile will launch Adobe Device Central. After choosing a profile, click the Create button to have Adobe Device Central create a new Illustrator document at the requested size.

CHAPTER TWELVE
Prepress and Printing

Nothing is more frustrating than spending hours designing the perfect piece of art only to have it come back from the printer not looking the way you expected it to look. Many times, we take printing for granted and assume that whatever we design will reproduce in print the exact way we see it on our computer screens. Achieving consistent color across multiple devices is one challenge (which good color management strategies can help control). Even more challenging are features such as transparency, live effects, and overprint settings; these can turn what seems like an ordinary print job into a weekend-long nightmare.

In reality, you need to think about printing when you first start working on a design. If you work with a printer regularly, the printer will help you figure out things in advance, including spot colors, page settings, folds, and a host of other issues. Although you certainly don't always have the luxury of knowing who the printer is before a job gets started, you can still spend a few moments at the onset of a project carefully reviewing the details; this alone can make a huge difference. Every job has its own specific requirements, and you should always feel comfortable asking an experienced printer or production artist for advice.

Whether you're a designer, a prepress operator, or a printer, this chapter is for you. This chapter discusses everything you need to know about printing files, using transparency, and using overprints—and it leads you to expect the best results every time.

PRINTING FROM ILLUSTRATOR

Printing a file should be a straightforward experience, but it wasn't always that way in Adobe Illustrator. Prior to Illustrator CS, getting a file to print correctly often meant opening the Page Setup dialog, the Document Setup dialog, and the Print dialog. With the release of Illustrator CS, however, Adobe has updated Illustrator's printing engine and interface and modeled them after the Print dialog found in Adobe InDesign. Now, you can go directly to the Print dialog and control all your print specifications in one place.

Because every print job is different and has specific requirements, the contents of this chapter are organized to match the order in which print features appear in the Print dialog. In this way, you can read the chapter and use it as a handy reference as well.

Exploring the General Print Panel

As you're designing a job, printing quick and accurate proofs to your laser or ink-jet printer is just as important as printing final output to an imagesetter. For this reason, you'll find that Adobe put many often-used settings in the General panel of the Print dialog (**Figure 12.1**). This way you can quickly print consistent and accurate files from Illustrator without having to dance between multiple dialogs or settings panels. At the top of the Print dialog you'll find a pop-up to choose from predefined print presets (you'll learn more about print presets later in this chapter), a pop-up to choose which printer you want to print to (extremely useful for those who have several different printers at their disposal), and a pop-up to choose a PostScript Printer Definition (PPD) file.

A PPD file contains specific information about a printer, including media dimensions, color information, and printer-specific settings such as resolution. Illustrator makes an educated guess about the right PPD file for your selected printer, although you can override it and choose your own if you need to do so (however, if you're not familiar with PPD files, it's best to leave this setting alone). You can choose a PPD only when an Adobe PostScript device is selected as your printer.

Along the left side of the Print dialog is a list of all the different panels you can choose from to specify a range of print options. Beneath the list of panels is a print preview, which gives you a better idea of what will print. But

➤ One of the options available in the Printer pop-up is Adobe PostScript File, which allows you to print your document as a Post-Script file that can then be downloaded directly to a printer or converted to PDF using Acrobat Distiller.

this is no ordinary print preview—it's interactive. You can drag the artwork around in the preview to determine which part of the paper the art will print on (**Figure 12.2**). Hold the Shift key while dragging to constrain movement to the X or Y axis, and double-click the preview anywhere to reset the positioning to the default. As you specify changes in the Print dialog, such as adding trim marks, you'll see those appear in the preview as well.

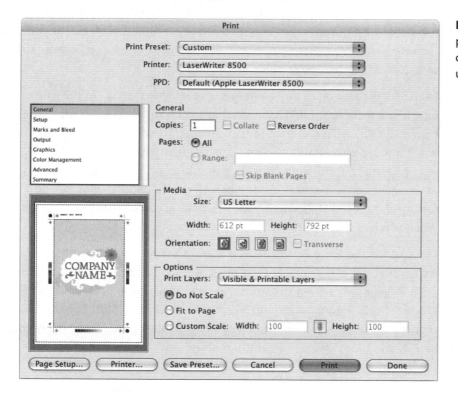

Figure 12.1 The General panel in the Print dialog contains the most often used print settings.

Figure 12.2 If you're an experienced Illustrator user, you may have used the Page tool to print different parts of a page; you can now do this directly from the Print dialog by moving the artwork within the interactive print preview.

Setting Basic Print Options

The items we've dis-
cussed to this point,
which appear across the top
and along the left side of the
Print dialog, are always visible
no matter which panel of the
dialog is active.

As in just about any other program, in the Print dialog, you can specify the number of copies as well as the range of pages you want to print. Although it's true that Illustrator doesn't have multiple pages, when you're using the Page Tiling option (which we'll cover shortly), each tile is assigned a page number, which allows you to specify exactly what will print. When you specify a range of pages, use a comma as a separation device and a hyphen to indicate a continuous string of pages. For example, you can specify a range of 1–3, 6, which will print pages 1, 2, 3, and 6.

In the Media section of the dialog, you can specify the size of the paper on which you want to print. The items that appear in this pop-up are defined by the PPD file that is chosen for your printer. If your printer supports it, you'll also have the ability to define custom media sizes; being able to do so is extremely useful with large-format ink-jet printers or for printing to imagesetters or platesetters. Additionally, you can choose an orientation to flip a page on its side. Changing the orientation can be extremely important when printers want to choose which side of a sheet the press will grip.

You can use the Print Layers pop-up menu to specify which kinds of layers will or won't print: Visible & Printable Layers, Visible Layers, or All Layers. Additionally, you can set a custom scale size at which to print your file. The Do Not Scale option prints your file at actual size, the Fit to Page option reduces or enlarges your artwork so that it fills the entire size of the output media, and the Custom Scale settings allow you to specify any scale size for the height or the width.

Exploring the Setup Print Panel

When you print a file, you can specify which parts of the artwork will print by choosing from the three Crop Artwork settings (**Figure 12.3**):

- **Artboard.** The Artboard setting uses the boundaries of the artboard as the printable area and is the default setting. When you choose this setting, only artwork that appears on the artboard prints.

- **Artwork Bounding Box.** The Artwork Bounding Box setting uses the boundaries of the artwork that appears in the document, no matter whether the artwork appears on or off the artboard. This setting is

valuable when you use it with the Fit to Page option to print a piece
of art that fills an entire page.

- **Crop Area.** The Crop Area setting uses a user-defined area for
  the boundaries of the printable area. To define a crop area, refer to
  Chapter 1, *The Illustrator Environment*. If no crop area is manually
  defined, Illustrator uses the artboard size as the crop area.

Although you can have
multiple crop areas
within a single file, only one
can be active at any one time.

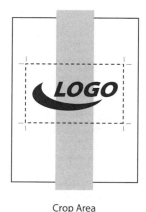

Artboard   Artwork Bounding Box   Crop Area

Figure 12.3 Using the Crop
Artwork settings can make
it easy to print the parts of a
file that you want.

Using Page Tiling

Page tiling was initially added to Illustrator to let users print a single large
file across several smaller pages. This allowed a designer to assemble a large
document at actual size using a printer with smaller media sizes. However,
over the years, designers learned to use this feature to create a single large
artboard, using the tiled areas as a substitute for multiple pages. For example, setting up a document at 11 x 17 inches with page tiling would result in
two 8.5 x 11 inch pages.

You can choose from three page tiling settings (**Figure 12.4** on the following page):

Refer to Chapter 13,
*Saving and Exporting
Files*, for information on how
you can use page tiles to
automatically create a multi-
page PDF file.

- **Single Full Page.** The Single Full Page option turns tiling off and
  treats the entire artboard as a single page.

- **Tile Full Pages.** The Tile Full Pages option divides a single artboard
  into multiple sections, or tiles. Each tile matches the media size you
  choose in the General panel, and Illustrator creates as many of those
  tiles as necessary to cover the entire document. Tile Full Pages also

allows you to specify an Overlap value, in case your printer doesn't print to the edge of each sheet.

- **Tile Imageable Areas.** The Tile Imageable Areas option divides a single artboard into multiple sections, or tiles. Tiles match the media size you choose in the General panel where possible, and Illustrator creates custom-sized tiles as necessary to tile the entire document.

Figure 12.4 You can simulate a multiple page document by setting up a large page with one of the tiling settings.

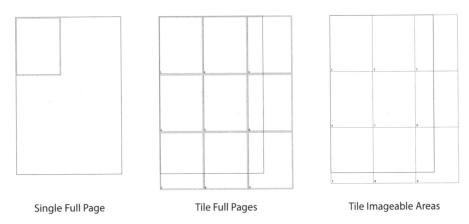

Single Full Page   Tile Full Pages   Tile Imageable Areas

When you're using Tile Full Pages or Tile Imageable Areas, each tile is assigned a number, and you can specify which tiles you want to print by entering a tile number in the Page Range field in the General panel.

Because tiling is something you might want to set in your document before you even start working on your design, be aware of the Done button that appears at the bottom of the Print dialog. Clicking Done keeps the settings you've made in the Print dialog and returns you to the document for further editing and designing without actually printing the file. Although it may seem odd to open the Print dialog to specify tiling settings, remember that the main reason for tiling in Illustrator is specific to printing.

Exploring the Marks and Bleed Print Panel

When printing a page for final output, you need to add page marks and bleeds to help printers print the job correctly on press. *Trim marks* tell a printer where to cut the paper, *registration marks* help a printer align each separated plate correctly, *color bars* help a printer calibrate color correctly on press, and *page information* makes it possible for printers to easily identify each separated plate (**Figure 12.5**).

Of course, you don't always need all this information on each printout, so you choose them individually (for example, on a one-color job, registration marks aren't necessary). Additionally, you can choose between Roman- and Japanese-style trim marks (refer to Appendix B, *Application Preferences*, for examples of these). The trim mark weight determines the width of the strokes used to create trim marks, and the offset determines how far from the page the trim marks will appear.

Trim mark

Page information

Registration marks

Color bars

Figure 12.5 A printer uses a variety of printer marks to help ensure that the job prints correctly.

When you have artwork that extends beyond the boundary of a page, you can specify a bleed setting to ensure that the printable area of the page includes the extra bleed area. When the bleed settings are set to zero, even if you've extended artwork beyond the boundary of the artboard, the art clips to the edge of the artboard. Additionally, if you specify a bleed setting, you'll need to print to a paper size large enough to display the page size and the bleed as well. For more information on bleeds, see the sidebar "Take Heed: Add Bleed."

Page marks print outside the margins of the artboard (or wherever you've defined a crop area), so you need to make sure the media size you've chosen in the General panel is large enough to include the page marks. If you use the Fit to Page option, Illustrator scales the entire document to ensure that the trim marks print on the chosen page.

Take Heed: Add Bleed

To print art all the way to the edge of a sheet, a printer uses a larger-sized sheet than the finish size (trim size), and after printing, the printer cuts the paper down to size. Printers can't print all the way to the edge of a page because a certain amount of space is needed for gripper space (space for the press to "grab" the sheet of paper). Additionally, if this space weren't there, the ink could run off the sheet and onto the press, causing smudging on other sheets.

When a printer trims the paper to the final size, the paper may shift while being cut, and if your image comes only up to the border of the trim size, you might end up seeing a bit of white near the edge of the paper. To avoid this, printers need *bleed*, or extra image space. If the artwork extends beyond the edges of the trim size, even if the cutter is off a bit, you'll still get color all the way to the edge of your sheet.

As a designer, it's important to leave enough room when you're cropping photos or backgrounds to allow for bleed (**Figure 12.6**). You should speak to your printer if you have questions, but most printers ask for anywhere from .125 to .25 inch of bleed. If printers don't have enough image space to add bleed, they may need to trim the paper to a slightly smaller size.

Trim

Bleed

Figure 12.6 If your design calls for artwork that prints to the edge of a page, make sure you add bleed before sending it to the printer.

Exploring the Output Print Panel

The Output panel in the Print dialog is a prepress operator's dream come true. With the ability to specify color separations and control the behavior of inks, a print service provider can output Illustrator files with confidence.

Illustrator supports three printing modes, each of which is used for a different workflow (**Figure 12.7**):

- **Composite.** When you choose the Composite setting, Illustrator sends a single composite of the artwork, with all colors appearing on the same page, to the printer or raster image processor (RIP). This is the setting you would use to create any kind of black-and-white or grayscale printout, as well as any color proof printout.

- **Separations (Host-Based).** When you choose the Separations (Host-Based) setting, Illustrator (the host) separates the artwork into the required number of plates (specified in the Document Ink Options settings mentioned shortly) and sends each plate to the printer or RIP as a separate page. This is the setting you use if you want to proof color-separated artwork. A prepress operator or printer also uses this setting to create final film or plates from your artwork.

- **In-RIP Separations.** When you choose the In-RIP Separations setting, Illustrator sends a single composite of the artwork to the RIP so that the RIP itself can perform the color separation instead of Illustrator. All the Document Ink Options and separation-specific settings become available so that you can still control the inks that will print on the composite. This is the setting you use if you want to take advantage of proprietary trapping, screening, and separations software present in your RIP.

A raster image processor is the software in a printer, imagesetter, or platesetter that converts all art into dots so that it can be printed.

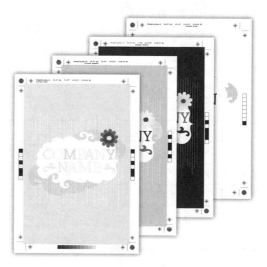

Figure 12.7 Printing a composite is perfect for proofing (left). Printing separations is required for printing colors on a printing press (right).

Specifying Color Separations

If you choose either of the two separations print modes, you can specify additional options for how the color separation will print.

You can choose to print with the Right Reading Emulsion Up or Down option, and you can choose whether to print a positive or negative image. You'll notice that as you choose these settings, the interactive print preview updates to show you how the art will print. You can also choose a printer resolution setting; these settings are specific to the printer to which you've chosen to print. This information comes from the PPD file chosen for your printer or RIP.

If your file contains spot colors, you can convert them all to separate as process colors by choosing the Convert All Spot Colors to Process option. This option is even available when you're printing composite proofs.

When you choose the Overprint Black option, all objects that are colored 100% K overprint. See "Understanding Overprints" later in this chapter for more information on overprinting.

In the Document Ink Options section of the Output panel, you can specify which plates are sent to the printer and which settings each plate uses (**Figure 12.8**). Colors that appear with a printer icon on the far left print. To prevent an ink from printing, click the printer icon to remove it. Inks that appear with a four-color icon separate as process colors. Inks that appear with a solid color icon print to their own plates as a spot (custom) color. Clicking a solid color icon causes just that color to separate as a process color. Additionally, you can specify custom Frequency, Angle, and Dot Shape settings for each ink.

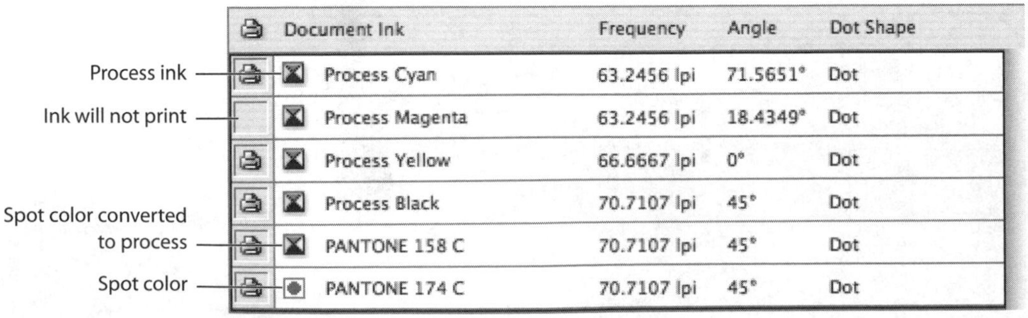

	Document Ink	Frequency	Angle	Dot Shape
Process ink →	Process Cyan	63.2456 lpi	71.5651°	Dot
Ink will not print →	Process Magenta	63.2456 lpi	18.4349°	Dot
	Process Yellow	66.6667 lpi	0°	Dot
	Process Black	70.7107 lpi	45°	Dot
Spot color converted to process →	PANTONE 158 C	70.7107 lpi	45°	Dot
Spot color →	PANTONE 174 C	70.7107 lpi	45°	Dot

Figure 12.8 The different icons that display in the Document Ink Options section of the Output panel indicate how the inks print.

Exploring the Graphics Print Panel

The settings in the Graphics panel of the Print dialog are mainly for specifying options for your print device.

Prior to the release of Illustrator CS, the Document Setup dialog of Illustrator contained a setting called Object Resolution, which determined the flatness setting for Bézier paths at output time. In Illustrator CS, CS2, and CS3, the flatness setting is set by default, based on information from the selected PPD file. You can override this setting and use the slider to sacrifice path quality for print performance (although it's best to leave this setting alone).

By default, Illustrator downloads subsets of fonts to the printer when you print a file. *Downloading a subset* simply means that Illustrator sends only the parts of a font that are required to print the text in your document. For example, if you have the word *me* in your document, Illustrator sends only the letters *m* and *e* to the printer instead of the entire font (this practice speeds up print times). You can override this behavior and choose Complete, which forces Illustrator to download the entire font to the printer at print time. Alternatively, you can choose not to download any fonts at all. You choose this option if you have fonts installed in your printer (some printers can contain hard drives and store fonts internally).

By default, Illustrator chooses a PostScript Language Level that your selected printer will support. Language Level 3 PostScript can print certain documents with transparency more reliably, and it also contains smooth shading technology that helps prevent banding from appearing in gradients. Additionally, you can choose whether to send data to the printer in ASCII or in the default Binary format.

As we discussed in Chapter 8, *3D and Other Live Effects*, the resolution at which live effects are rasterized is determined by the setting in the Document Raster Effects Resolution dialog. Here in the Graphics panel of the Print dialog, Illustrator displays the current setting in that dialog, allowing you to double-check to make sure the setting is indeed correct for printing (**Figure 12.9** on the following page). Illustrator won't allow you to change the setting from the Print dialog because, as you learned in Chapter 8, *3D and Other Live Effects*, changing the resolution setting may change the appearance of your artwork. To change the resolution setting, click the

If you have problems printing Illustrator files to older print devices, try checking the Compatible Gradient and Gradient Mesh Printing options.

Done button in the Print dialog, and choose Effect > Document Raster Effects Settings. You can then return to the Print dialog to print your file.

Figure 12.9 Although you can't change the Document Raster Effects Resolution setting from the Print dialog, the Graphics panel does alert you to the current setting in case you need to make a change.

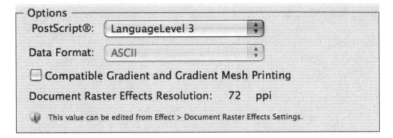

Exploring the Color Management Print Panel

The topic of color management really requires a book of its own. In fact, if you really want to learn everything there is to know about color management, you should check out *Real World Color Management, Second Edition,* by Bruce Fraser, Chris Murphy, and Fred Bunting (Peachpit Press, 2005).

Within the scope of this book (the one you are now reading), however, here are some brief explanations for the settings found in the Color Management panel of the Print dialog:

- **Document Profile.** The Document Profile displays the color profile that is currently embedded (or assumed) in the file. If you didn't manually choose one, the profile you see here is the profile that is chosen in the Color Settings dialog.

- **Color Handling.** The Color Handling setting allows you to determine whether Illustrator will perform any necessary color adjustments (based on the chosen printer profile) or whether your printer will handle any required conversion on its own. Unless you are working within a proprietary workflow system, you should always choose to let Illustrator determine colors, not the printer.

- **Printer Profile.** When the Color Handling option is set to Let Illustrator Determine Colors, the Printer Profile setting allows you to specify a profile for your printer. This gives Illustrator the information it needs to change colors so they look correct on your printer. If the Color Handling option is set to Let PostScript Printer Determine Colors, the Printer Profile setting is not applicable.

- **Rendering Intent.** If some colors in your document cannot be reproduced on the chosen output device, those colors are considered *out of gamut* and must be converted to colors that will reproduce on the output device. There are different methods for converting these colors, and the Rendering Intent setting determines the method used. The most commonly used method, Relative Colorimetric, moves out-of-gamut colors to the closest possible color that will print on the device. It also adjusts other colors so that colors appear to be accurate. The Absolute Colorimetric setting adjusts only out-of-gamut colors and may result in *posterization*, where many shades of similar colors are used. The Perceptual method shifts colors so that they appear correct relative to each other, but it may not represent colors as being the most accurate match to the original values. The Saturation method enhances colors and makes them more vibrant and most suitable for business presentations where bright colors are more important than accurate colors.

- **Preserve CMYK Numbers.** The Preserve CMYK Numbers setting is active only when Color Handling is set to the Let PostScript Printer Determine Colors option. With Preserve CMYK Numbers active, color values will remain untouched in native artwork and text components of your file.

Exploring the Advanced Print Panel

The Advanced panel in the Print dialog gives you control over important settings such as overprinting and transparency flattening.

If your document contains overprint settings, you can choose from one of three settings to control overprint behavior:

- **Preserve.** The Preserve option leaves all overprints intact in your file.

- **Discard.** The Discard option strips your file of any overprint commands. Those who have proprietary production systems or advanced trapping software in their RIPs will find this option useful. Rather than use a designer's overprint settings, the trapping software applies and determines all overprint behavior instead.

- **Simulate.** The Simulate option, available only when printing composite proofs, simulates overprints in the printout, giving the correct appearance of the final output in the proof.

The Print as Bitmap option is available for non-PostScript printers only and rasterizes all artwork in your file for printing.

See "Understanding Overprints" later in the chapter to learn more about overprints.

If your document contains transparency, you can choose from a list of pre-defined transparency flattener presets. Illustrator ships with three presets called Low Resolution, Medium Resolution, and High Resolution, but you can also define your own by choosing Edit > Transparency Flattener Presets. For detailed information about what these settings are used for and what the differences between them are, see "Learning the Truth About Transparency" later in this chapter.

Defining Print Presets

If you delete your application prefer-ences, you won't lose your saved print presets.

As you've undoubtedly seen, Illustrator's Print dialog contains a plethora of settings, and going through each panel to make sure the settings are correct is an exercise in patience. *Print presets* allow you to capture all the options set in the different Print dialog panels so that you can easily retrieve those set-tings at any time. To create a print preset, either click the Save Preset button at the bottom of the Print dialog; to manage your presets, choose Edit > Print Presets. Print presets are saved in XML and are cross-platform, so you can import and export them and distribute them among others.

LEARNING THE TRUTH ABOUT TRANSPARENCY

Illustrator contains several features that use transparency, including the abil-ity to specify blend modes and opacity masks with the Transparency panel and via effects such as Feather and Drop Shadow. Transparency as a feature in Illustrator (and InDesign as well) requires closer attention when it comes to printing documents. In fact, Illustrator CS3, InDesign CS3, and Adobe Acrobat 8.0 all use the same methods to print with transparency, so the concepts you learn here apply to all those applications as well.

Although you may have heard that printing with transparency is problematic, the reality is that a lot has changed since transparency was first introduced in Illustrator 9. Once you understand what happens to a file with transparency and you learn about a few simple settings, you won't have to worry about running into printing issues when you're using transparency features.

In truth, transparency has always been around—in raster form—in Adobe Photoshop. The only difference now is that you can apply these effects in vector form and still edit them late in your workflow. At the end of the day, these transparency effects will become rasterized, leaving you with the same result as if you had done everything in Photoshop. In any case, let's take a closer look at what transparency is and how it works.

Understanding Transparency Flattening

Let's start with a simple fact: PostScript doesn't understand transparency. As you probably know, PostScript is the language that printers and RIPs speak. Native transparency is understood only by PDF language version 1.4 or newer (first present in Acrobat 5 and Illustrator 9).

To print objects with transparency, Illustrator must "translate" any transparent artwork into a language that PostScript understands. This translation process is called *transparency flattening*.

The process of flattening is simple, and Illustrator follows two cardinal rules when performing flattening on a file:

1. All transparency in the file must be removed.

2. In the process of performing rule #1, the appearance of the file cannot change.

Both of these rules are followed during the flattening process, with no exception. Obviously, all transparency has to be removed because PostScript doesn't know what transparency is. Additionally, if removing the transparency would result in your file changing in appearance, that would mean you could design something in Illustrator that couldn't be printed, which doesn't make sense either. If you think about it, if you're removing transparency from the file and you're also keeping the visual appearance of the object, something has to give, and that something is the editability of your file. Let's take a look at an example of this.

If you've used Photoshop before, you may be familiar with the term *flattening*, which combines all layers in a document. Although similar in concept, transparency flattening is different.

Seeing an Example of Flattening

We'll draw two different-colored circles, one overlapping the other, and we'll set the top circle to Multiply (**Figure 12.10** on the following page). The nice feature of transparency is that you can move the top circle around or change its color, and any overlapping areas will simply multiply. The problem is that PostScript doesn't know what transparency is and doesn't know how to print that overlapping area, so transparency flattening is required.

Figure 12.10 By setting the top circle to the Multiply blend mode, you can see through it to the circle below, even with Opacity set to 100%.

Select both circles, choose Object > Flatten Transparency, and click OK (don't worry about the dialog, which we'll get to later). The file is now flattened. Does it look any different? It can't, because of rule #2, but the file now no longer contains any transparency and can be printed on a PostScript device. The difference is that the file is no longer editable as it was before it was flattened. Upon selecting the circles, you'll find that the two transparent circles have now been broken up into three individual opaque shapes (**Figure 12.11**).

Figure 12.11 Once the objects are flattened, the artwork is split up into individual opaque pieces, called *atomic regions*.

This flattening process happens every time you print something with transparency. However, the flattening happens in the print stream, not to your actual Illustrator file. When you choose to print a file, Illustrator flattens a copy of your file and sends the flattened file to the printer, while leaving your document intact. It wouldn't be good if simply printing a file rendered it uneditable. In our example, we specifically flattened the file using the flatten transparency function to see the results, but under normal circumstances, you would not flatten the transparency manually—Illustrator would do that for you automatically at print time.

So we can now understand that when you print a file with transparency, this flattening process occurs so that a PostScript printer can print the file correctly, and this process happens on the way to the printer, so your Illustrator file is not affected in any way.

This example of the two overlapping circles is a simple case of flattening. However, other examples can display certain side effects. Let's explore such a case.

Flattening also happens whenever you save or export your file to a format that doesn't understand transparency. For example, EPS (which is PostScript) and PDF 1.3 do not support transparency.

Flattening with Rasterization

As in the previous example, create two overlapping circles, and set the top circle to Multiply. Fill each circle with a linear gradient, but in one of the circles, apply the gradient on a 45-degree angle. The result is two circles with gradients, but the area in which these two shapes overlap appears as two gradients traveling in different directions (**Figure 12.12**).

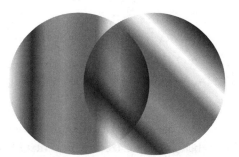

Figure 12.12 This figure shows two overlapping circles, each filled with a gradient on a different angle.

When this file is flattened, you know that the result will be three separate shapes as in the previous example; however, this example is a bit different. Although gradients can be preserved in vector form, there's no way to describe a crisscross gradient, like you see in the overlapping area, as a vector. Because of rule #2, Illustrator is not allowed to change the appearance of your file during flattening, so Illustrator's only course of action is to turn that overlapping area into a raster image.

Select both circles, choose Object > Flatten Transparency, and click OK. You'll find that although the file looks the same, it now consists of two vector shapes and a raster image in the middle. Illustrator creates a vector mask for the middle shape so that the file will print correctly (raster images are always rectangular in shape). It's important to point out that Illustrator didn't raster the entire file; it merely rasterized the portion of the file that could not be preserved in vector form (**Figure 12.13**).

Figure 12.13 Where appearance can't be preserved in vector form, Illustrator converts parts of a file into a raster.

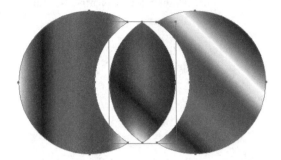

At this point, a question should be forming in your brain: If part of the file is now a raster image, what is the resolution of that raster? Patience, my young Padawan; we'll get to that soon. Here's a review of what you've learned to this point:

- Transparency flattening is required to correctly print a file with transparency to a PostScript device.

- Transparency flattening happens automatically, in the print stream, when you print a file with transparency from Illustrator, InDesign, Acrobat, or Adobe Reader.

- Transparency flattening may cause certain parts of a vector file to become rasterized to prevent a file from changing in appearance.

Printing Files with Transparency from QuarkXPress

You can now begin to understand at a basic level why some people have problems printing files with transparency from QuarkXPress (versions prior to version 7). If you save a PDF from Illustrator and place that file into QuarkXPress, that file still contains native transparency. Although QuarkXPress can place PDF files, QuarkXPress doesn't translate the file when sending the page to the printer, so the transparency flattening never occurs. The result is transparency commands being sent to a PostScript printer that doesn't understand them, and what shows up on the printed page is anyone's guess.

As this book is going to press, the latest version of QuarkXPress is version 7.2, which does have the ability to place PDF 1.5 files that contain transparency, although there are no user-based settings to control how the transparency will be flattened. Tests that we've performed show that the results are less than desirable when placing PDF files with transparent objects in QuarkXPress 7.2. In these workflows, it is still best to save PDF/X-1a or EPS files from Illustrator for placement into any version of QuarkXPress. You can find more details on specific file formats in Chapter 13, *Saving and Exporting Files*.

Using the Two Levels of Rasterization

In the previous example, where two vector shapes resulted in a portion of that file becoming rasterized, Illustrator had no choice but to rasterize the middle region because there was simply no other way to preserve the appearance in vector form. This is one level of rasterization.

However, in some cases a second level of rasterization may occur, even if the appearance of a file could be preserved in vector form. Before printing a file, Illustrator analyzes the entire document and looks for *complex regions* containing many overlapping objects (which would result in a large number of atomic regions). Illustrator may then choose to rasterize those complex regions for performance reasons. Although we've been trained to think vector objects are simpler than their bitmapped counterparts, try to imagine an Illustrator graphic filled with many overlapping objects with transparency applied (**Figure 12.14**). Although it may seem like only several objects at first glance, once those objects are broken up into atomic regions, we may be looking at thousands of vector shapes, which can take a long time to process and print (**Figure 12.15**). In those cases, Illustrator can save precious RIP and processing time by rasterizing these complex regions.

Figure 12.14 Using the Symbol Sprayer tool, you can easily create a file that contains many overlapping shapes. Using the Symbol Screener tool, you can also make some of these symbols transparent.

Figure 12.15 Even though you may have started with a small number of objects, the resulting number of atomic regions due to flattening can be extremely large.

As far as the first level of rasterization goes, we really have no choice but to allow Illustrator to rasterize objects where it needs to do so. What we *can* do, however, is learn how to build files that work around this issue (see "Understanding Object Stacking Order and Transparency Flattening" later in this section). With regard to the second level of rasterization, we can control how liberal Illustrator is when looking for complex regions. In fact, we can even disable this second level of rasterization altogether. Finally, with either level of rasterization, Illustrator always gives us total control over *how* these areas are rasterized.

Understanding the Transparency Flattener Settings

As mentioned earlier in this chapter, Illustrator has three transparency flattener presets that you can choose from in the Advanced panel of the Print dialog. These settings control how files with transparency are flattened at print time. To access these settings, choose Edit > Transparency Flattener Presets, and click the New button to define a new preset. Let's explore the settings in the Transparency Flattener Preset Options dialog (**Figure 12.16**).

Figure 12.16 You can define your own custom flattener settings, or your printer or service provider can define them for you.

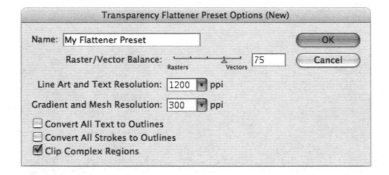

- **Raster/Vector Balance.** This slider is what controls how liberal Illustrator is when looking for complex regions to rasterize (what we've defined previously as the second level of rasterization). A number closer to zero (0) gives Illustrator more freedom to rasterize at will, resulting in faster print times. Moving the slider closer to 100 results in fewer rasterized areas but longer print times. At the 100 setting itself, Illustrator does not rasterize *any* parts of the file for performance reasons, effectively disabling the second level of rasterization. The High Resolution flattener preset uses this setting. In cases where files are taking extremely long to print (or crashing the RIP altogether), adjusting this slider to a slightly lower setting helps.

- **Line Art and Text Resolution.** In cases where Illustrator is going to rasterize line art or text, you can specify a resolution that results in good-looking, sharp output. You'll notice that the High Resolution flattener setting specifies a resolution of 1200 ppi, ensuring that text elements and vector objects still have nice, clean, sharp edges in final output.

- **Gradient and Mesh Resolution.** Because gradients and meshes are continuous tones in nature, they don't require a resolution as high as line art or text. In fact, anything twice your line screen is probably getting thrown out anyway. Therefore, Illustrator uses this setting to rasterize elements that can afford to be set at a lower resolution. You'll notice that the High Resolution flattener preset uses a value of 300 ppi.

- **Convert All Text to Outlines.** In cases where text is going to be rasterized, chances are that the rasterized text looks a bit chunkier than regular vector text. To compensate for this, you can turn on this option to convert all text to outlines, giving a consistent chunkier look to all of your text. If you use the method described later in this chapter to move text onto its own layer, you'll rarely need to concern yourself with this setting.

- **Convert All Strokes to Outlines.** Similar to the previous setting, this compensates for disparity between vector and rasterized strokes by converting all strokes to outlines.

- **Clip Complex Regions.** We mentioned that Illustrator can look for complex areas of a file and rasterize them for performance reasons. However, we know that raster images are always rectangular in shape, which means it's possible for "innocent" parts of your file to become rasterized simply because they fall into the rectangular bounding box of the area that is complex. More often than not, this results in *stitching*, or noticeable boxes and color shifts. The Clip Complex Regions option avoids this issue by creating a clipping mask around any rasterized complex region (so the rectangular-shaped raster is masked by the vector outline of the object). As you can probably understand, this makes for even more complex files and can result in longer print times as well. This option is turned on by default but isn't applicable in the High Resolution preset because no complex regions are rasterized at all with that setting (because it has a Raster/Vector Balance setting of 100).

The two resolution settings in the flattener controls are used whenever vector objects are forced to become rasters during the flattening process. However, live effects, such as Feather and Drop Shadow, use the Document Raster Effects Resolution setting to determine their resolutions.

Understanding Object Stacking Order and Transparency Flattening

When rasterization occurs during transparency flattening, the last thing you want to see turning into a raster is text. That's because you always want text to be clean and sharp in your printouts. Even at the High Resolution setting, where text is rasterized at 1200 ppi, that resolution is still less than half of what most imagesetters set text with—usually upward of 2400 ppi.

Although it's true that under certain circumstances rasterization must occur in order to print a file and maintain its appearance, the way you build your files can affect how often this happens. Let's look at a simple example that clarifies this.

Draw a circle and add a drop shadow to it by choosing Effect > Stylize > Drop Shadow. As you learned in Chapter 7, *Typography*, the Drop Shadow effect is a raster-based effect, and when transparency is flattened, the drop shadow becomes rasterized. Switch to the Type tool, create some text, and position the text near the drop shadow (**Figure 12.17**). With the text still selected, choose Object > Arrange > Send to Back.

Figure 12.17 Placing text near an object is common, especially when you're adding captions or credit text near photographs.

Now select both the circle and the text, choose Object > Flatten Transparency, and click OK. Upon close inspection, you'll see that a portion of the text was rasterized. This happened because the text was below the drop shadow in the stacking order, and to maintain the file's appearance when the drop shadow was rasterized, Illustrator had to include part of the text in the drop shadow's bounding area (**Figure 12.18**).

Figure 12.18 To maintain the appearance of the file, Illustrator rasterized the text that was behind the drop shadow.

Choose Edit > Undo to go back before you applied the Flatten Transparency function, and select the text object. Choose Object > Arrange > Bring to Front. Select both the circle and the text, choose Object > Flatten Transparency, and click OK. In this case, the text, which was above the drop shadow in the stacking order, was not affected at all and was not rasterized (**Figure 12.19**).

Figure 12.19 If the text appears above the shadow in the stacking order, the text is not rasterized during flattening.

When using transparency features in Illustrator (or InDesign, for that matter), it's important to make sure that text always appears *above* objects with transparency to avoid unwanted rasterized text issues. Of course, some designs call for text to appear beneath transparent objects, and in those cases, you don't have much of a choice.

Does My File Contain Transparency?

Not every document needs flattening—only those with transparency in them. The tricky part is that transparency can be introduced into an Illustrator document in several ways:

- You apply a blend mode or an Opacity value other than 100% in the Transparency panel.

- You apply the Effect > Stylize > Drop Shadow feature.

- You apply the Effect > Stylize > Feather feature.

- You apply the Effect > Stylize > Outer Glow feature.

- You apply the Effect > Stylize > Inner Glow feature.

- You apply any "below-the-line" Photoshop effect from the Effect menu.

- You place a PDF file that contains transparency.

- You place a native Photoshop file that contains transparency.

It would be helpful to know whether the document you're working on uses transparency or is even going to require any of the two levels of rasterization we spoke of earlier. You can use the Flattener Preview panel (Window > Flattener Preview) to tell whether a document has transparency effects in it, as well as to preview areas that will become rasterized in the flattening process.

By clicking the Refresh button in the panel, Illustrator highlights specific areas in your file in red, indicating where rasterization will occur. You can enlarge the panel to see a larger image, and you can also click inside the preview area of the panel to zoom in closer to see more detail. From the Highlight pop-up menu, you can choose from a variety of items that Illustrator will preview. If all the items listed in your Highlight pop-up are dim, that indicates your file doesn't have transparency present, and no flattening is necessary to print your file (**Figure 12.20**). For example, when you choose Transparent Objects, Illustrator shows you where all objects that use transparency are on your page—although those regions may not necessarily become rasterized. We also mentioned earlier that Illustrator looks for complex areas of a document; you can see where those areas are by choosing Rasterized Complex Regions in the pop-up (**Figure 12.21**). Additionally, the All Affected Objects option shows you all the objects that may not be transparent themselves but that interact with transparency in some way (like the example we mentioned earlier with the drop shadow and the text: The text itself doesn't have transparency applied to it, but if the text appears below the drop shadow, the text must become rasterized to preserve the appearance).

Figure 12.20 If your file contains no transparency, you don't have to worry about the effects of flattening.

Figure 12.21 You can use the Flattener Preview panel to identify areas that Illustrator deems as complex regions, giving you a heads up for what areas will become rasterized.

To take advantage of all that the Flattener Preview panel can offer, adjust the different flattener settings, and preview the results—making changes or adjustments where necessary—all before you actually print the file. As an aside, InDesign and Acrobat Professional also contain a similar Flattener Preview panel and identical flattener settings (in fact, it's the same underlying code).

What Kind of RIP Are You Using?

To throw yet another variable into the mix, the kind of printer or RIP that you use can also render different results. For the most part, any Adobe PostScript Language Level 3 device should be able to handle transparency without issue. Specifically, PostScript version 3015 (which appears in the latest versions of RIPs) has enhanced functionality to process files that have been flattened. It's important to remember that flattening has to occur for any RIP to understand how to print transparency. If your RIP can process PDF files, that doesn't necessarily mean it can process PDF files with transparency in them. If you're in doubt, check with your RIP manufacturer to find out whether transparency flattening can occur inside the RIP or whether you need to print files from an Adobe application to flatten them.

Some older print devices are confused by the effects of flattening. For example, a Scitex Brisque RIP (since acquired by Creo and now Kodak) looks at jobs that are printing and splits up the vector and raster elements onto two "layers." The rasterized content prints on a continuous tone (CT) layer at a lower resolution (such as 300 dpi), and line art prints on a separate vector layer at a much higher resolution (such as 2400 dpi). Because flattening could cause a vector object to be rasterized, the RIP sees that raster only as a CT image and prints it at the lower resolution. This might cause text that is rasterized to print with noticeably jagged edges. There's an update available for Brisque RIPs to address this issue, but that doesn't automatically mean everyone who owns a Brisque has installed the update (or knows it exists).

Rampage RIPs also experience similar issues, although turning off the dual-mode setting easily addresses the problem.

The best advice in any case is to talk with your printer. For any big job, most printers will be happy to run a test file for you to make sure everything will print correctly. Taking advantage of these opportunities will surely save you headaches when press deadlines loom. Adobe also has free specialized training materials for print service providers if your printer needs more information (located online at http://partners.adobe.com/public/asn/psp/detail.html).

Printing with Confidence

You can avoid accidents by learning to anticipate possible problems. Now that you're aware of how transparency works, here are a few ways to ensure that you get the results you expect when you're printing from Illustrator:

- Use the right flattener presets—Low Resolution, Medium Resolution, and High Resolution. For quick proofs to your laser printer, you can use the Low Resolution or Medium Resolution setting, but when you're printing to a high-end proofer or imagesetter, use the High Resolution setting. You'll find the Transparency Flattener settings in the Advanced panel of the Print dialog.

- To avoid text becoming rasterized, create a new layer in your Illustrator file, and place all your text on that layer. As long as you keep that text layer as the top layer in your document, you won't have to worry about chunky or pixelated text due to rasterization.

- A potential problem is that even if you, as a designer, are aware of transparency, plenty of printers are out there that aren't. If you are sending a file and aren't sure who will be printing it or what they will be using to print it, you might consider sending the file as a PDF/X-1a file. See Chapter 13, *Saving and Exporting Files*, for more information on PDF/X.

If you'd like an easy way to remember the important steps to get great results when printing, you can find a small transparency checklist (**Figure 12.22** on the following page, courtesy of Design Responsibly), available when you register at www.peachpit.com/rwillcs3.

Designing with transparency allows you to design creations that were previously prohibitive and difficult to implement, thus allowing you to save valuable time while being even more creative. Now that you know how transparency works and what's necessary to use it in your workflow, give it a test drive. You'll be happy you did.

Figure 12.22 The transparency checklist offers a few quick reminders to help ensure your file prints correctly.

UNDERSTANDING OVERPRINTS

Hang around a print shop long enough, and you'll hear the term *overprint*. In the world of prepress, overprinting is a way to control how color-separated plates interact with each other. A printing press imprints each color on a piece of paper, one after the other, as it runs through the press. Because of this process, you need to consider certain issues when making color separations.

For example, say you design some blue text over a yellow background. When those colors are separated and printed on press, the blue and yellow mix, resulting in green text on a yellow background. Therefore, under normal conditions, when pages are separated, color that appears underneath other objects is removed so that the color on top is unaffected. In the preceding example, the blue text removes, or *knocks out*, the yellow background underneath it, allowing the blue to appear correctly when printed.

Overprinting, on the other hand, is a method of overriding a knockout and forcing overlapping colors to mix on press. In our example, setting the blue text to overprint means that the yellow background still appears behind it, and the result on press is green text on a yellow background (**Figure 12.23**).

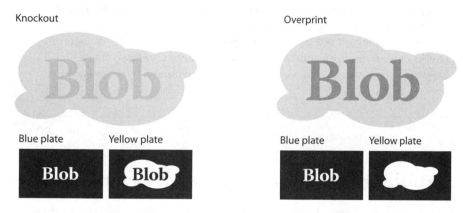

Figure 12.23 The text on the left, by default, knocks out the background behind it. The text on the right is set to overprint, and the background behind it is unaffected.

Why Overprint?

You'd want to apply an overprint when you specifically want to mix colors on press. Some designers who work with low-budget jobs that print in two or three spot colors can simulate other colors by mixing those spot colors. Before transparency rolled around, designers would also specify overprints to simulate objects being transparent; you could also simulate shadows or shading by overprinting with black over other elements.

Overprinting is also essential when you're creating plates for custom dyes and varnishes. For example, if you want to create a spot varnish for a particular photo, you need to create a color called Varnish and set it to overprint, because this allows the photo that appears beneath it to print (otherwise, the varnish knocks out the photo).

You can easily specify overprinting from the Attributes panel (Window > Attributes). With an object selected, you can force the fill, the stroke, or both to overprint. Remember that Illustrator also allows you to specify whether a stroke is painted in the centerline, inside, or outside a path, and you should be aware that if you overprint a stroke that's on the inside or the centerline of a path, the stroke also overprints the fill of that object.

Trapped into a Corner

Those who work in packaging rely on using overprints all the time for creating *traps*—colors that share borders with other colors that overlap slightly. This is because the materials that are used for many packages and the printing processes used (called *flexographic printing*, or *flexo* for short) don't always result in perfect printing. Remember that the requirements for printing 1,000 brochures and printing several million containers of milk can be quite different. The next time you see a bag of potato chips or a bottle of soda, take a close look at the label; you'll be able to see the overprint traps. These are usually created in Illustrator by setting just the stroke set to overprint.

Handling the Limitations with Overprints

Let's get technical for a moment. You'll encounter some limitations when it comes to using overprints. First, whereas one color plate can overprint another, an overprint cannot overprint its own plate. For example, if you have a color that contains cyan and you set it to overprint over a background that contains cyan, you won't get an overprint on the cyan plate.

Second, sometimes users specify overprinting for objects colored white. Usually, white is always a knockout (because it lets the white paper show through), and setting a white object to overprint would kind of defeat the purpose. However, these things do happen accidentally. You might have a logo that you created that's colored black and that you've set to overprint. Then you might come upon a situation where you need a reverse (white) version of the logo, so you might just open the file, color it white, and save it with a different name, forgetting that you had set the fill to overprint. This would most likely result in the file not printing properly, because either the white overprints (making it entirely transparent) or the RIP doesn't process the file correctly.

Previewing Overprints

Because overprints are really PostScript commands that you use when you're printing color separations, you'll always have a problem with displaying overprints onscreen or when you're printing composite proofs to show a client. In the past, the only real way to proof overprints was by printing separations and creating a Matchprint proof or by investing in expensive prepress plugins. More often than not, a designer would show a proof to a client and say, "It won't look like this when it's actually printed." If only there were a better way…

Illustrator offers that better way. By choosing View > Overprint Preview, you can actually see on your monitor what the effects of overprint commands are. Additionally, in the Output panel of the Print dialog, the Simulate Overprint option, when activated, prints composites as they will look with overprints applied. This is perfect for showing clients exactly what they are going to get. The Simulate Overprint option is also available in the Advanced panel of the PDF dialog, so you can even show your client an accurate proof via PDF. You disable Simulate Overprint when you choose to print separations—it's available only when you're printing composites.

Although overprints are useful (and essential in some workflows), our advice is to talk to your printer before you use them, because some printers prefer to specify overprints themselves.

Handling Transparency Effects That Disappear or Print as White Boxes

Has the following scenario ever happened to you?

You create some artwork that contains two spot colors (let's say Pantone Blue 072 and Red 032). The logo has a drop shadow behind it, and you've correctly set Illustrator's Drop Shadow effect to use the Blue 072 spot color, not black. On Illustrator's artboard, the logo appears correctly against the spot color background (**Figure 12.24**).

Figure 12.24 In Illustrator, the Drop Shadow effect appears correctly against the spot color background.

Then you save the art as a PDF/X-1a file because it will be used in an ad and you want to make sure it will print correctly. Or you save your document using Acrobat 4 (PDF 1.3) compatibility. Alternatively, you save your file as an EPS file because maybe you're required to place this logo into a QuarkXPress document. The point here to focus on is that you're saving your file to a flattened format.

The "problem" is that when you open the PDF in Acrobat or Reader, or when you place the file into QuarkXPress or InDesign and print the file to your laser or ink-jet printer, it comes out looking incorrect—either the drop shadow disappears completely (**Figure 12.25**) or a white box appears where the transparent effect should blend into the background (**Figure 12.26**).

Figure 12.25 When saving the file from Illustrator CS3 and viewing or printing the art outside of Illustrator, the transparency effect seems to disappear.

Figure 12.26 When saving the file from Illustrator CS2 and viewing or printing the art outside of Illustrator, a white box appears around the transparency effect.

The key items to focus on here are that you have used a transparent effect and you've used a spot color. You'll know what's happening and what the solution is.

When you have a transparent effect, the result is a mixture of the inks. In this case, the shadow, which is Pantone Blue 072, blends right into the Red 032 background. By default, when one color sits on top of another color, a knockout occurs, as we discussed earlier in this chapter. In other words, the area beneath the top shape is removed from the lower object. Otherwise, the top color will print on top of the bottom color when the paper is run through the printing press, causing the two inks to mix. In our case of the red and blue colors, the result would be purple in appearance. However, in this case, where you *want* the drop shadow to blend into the background on press, you have to override that knockout by specifying an overprint.

The thing is, Illustrator already knows this, so no action is required on your part. When you print your file from Illustrator, all these settings are done automatically, so your file looks great when you print it—either as a composite or as separations. The same applies when you save your file from Illustrator as a native Illustrator file and place it into InDesign, or when you create a PDF with Acrobat 5 compatibility (PDF 1.4) or newer.

But when you save your file to a format that doesn't support transparency, Illustrator has to flatten the transparency. And in that process, Illustrator realizes that in order to preserve the spot colors so that they print in separations correctly, the drop shadow must be set to overprint the background color (in Illustrator CS3, the spot color is set to overprint instead).

The problem is that overprint commands are honored only when you print your file as separations. When you are previewing your document onscreen or when you are printing a composite proof of your file, the overprint commands aren't used, and either the result will be white where overprinting should occur or the transparency effect will simply disappear (see note). The file will print correctly when you print as separations, because at that time, the overprints are honored (as they should be).

The good news is that this issue is easy to solve when using InDesign, Acrobat, or Reader:

- In InDesign, choose View > Overprint Preview. This will allow you to view overprints on your screen. When printing composite proofs, check the Simulate Overprints box in the Output panel of the Print dialog to get the correct appearance in your printouts.

- In Acrobat or Reader, check the Overprint Preview button in the Page Display panel in Preferences to view the file correctly on your screen. When printing composite proofs, choose Print, and then click the Advanced button. Then check the Simulate Overprinting box in the Output section of the dialog. The file will then print with the correct appearance.

A key change occurred with the release of Illustrator CS3: the order of the plates on output have been reversed. In Illustrator CS2, the spot channels were painted first, so the process colors were set to overprint above them. In Illustrator CS3, the process colors are painted first, resulting in the spot colors getting the overprint commands set to them. This is why you see the white boxes when saving these files from CS2 and why you see the transparency effect disappear when saving those same files from CS3. The solution, however, is the same, in that using Overprint Preview or Simulate Overprint solves the issue. As a side note, these behaviors are identical to those found in InDesign CS2 and CS3.

Some RIPs have built-in settings to ignore overprints in files and instead use their own settings for overprints. This often results in output that isn't desirable. You can easily fix these issues by instructing the RIP to honor the overprints in your files. For example, Rampage RIPs have a setting called Preserve Application Overprint that, when activated, results in perfect output.

If you're using QuarkXPress, though, you really don't have an option, because that program doesn't allow you to simulate overprint commands when printing composite proofs. One workaround is to create two versions of your file: one that uses spot colors that will separate correctly when you print separations, and one version where you've converted your spot colors to process colors. When you convert to process colors, you don't need the overprints, and the file will print with the correct appearance on a composite proof.

CHAPTER THIRTEEN
Saving and Exporting Files

Saving and exporting your Adobe Illustrator files is obviously very important. Illustrator is a fantastic utility that can open a wide variety of file types, including EPS and PDF. Additionally, you can also use Illustrator to save and export files in just about any format that you need, including SWF and SVG. If you aren't familiar with these file types, it's okay, because that's what this entire chapter is about.

With so many file formats to work with, how do you know which format to use when you're saving or exporting a file? How do you know what each file format supports and what they are each used for? Throughout this chapter, you will learn the strengths and weaknesses of each file format and see examples of when to use or not use each.

Saving Files from Illustrator

When you save a document from Illustrator using any of the file formats found in the Save or Save As dialog, you are able to reopen that file and edit it as needed. When you do, all native information, by default, is preserved in the file. For example, if you save a file as an EPS document, you can reopen the EPS file in Illustrator and make edits to the file with no loss of functionality or editability. Adobe calls this *round-tripping*, and working in this way has many benefits.

If you create a file in Illustrator but you need to place it into a QuarkXPress document, you'll learn that you need to create an EPS file. Because an Illustrator EPS file is round-trippable, you can place the EPS file into your QuarkXPress layout, yet you can edit that same EPS file in Illustrator if you need to make changes.

As you will find out, Illustrator accomplishes this by using what engineers call *dual-path* files. This means a single file contains two parts in it: One part contains the EPS data that QuarkXPress needs; the other contains the native Illustrator information that Illustrator needs. As we explore the different formats and their settings, this dual-path concept will become clear.

The Native Illustrator (.ai) Format

By default, when you choose to save a new file, the Adobe Illustrator Document setting is chosen as the file format. Whenever you create documents, it's best to save them as native Illustrator files, because they will *always* contain rich and editable information.

When creating documents that you plan to use as a base for other files, you may choose to save your file as an Illustrator Template (.ait). Details on this format appear in Chapter 1, *The Illustrator Environment*.

Up until version 8, Illustrator's native file format was PostScript (EPS), but for a variety of reasons, with the release of version 9, Adobe changed Illustrator's native file format to use the PDF language. In fact, Adobe is quick to tell you that a native Illustrator file can be opened and viewed in Adobe Acrobat or the free Adobe Reader. Adobe also advertises that you can place native Illustrator files directly into Adobe InDesign layouts. It makes sense when you think about it, because if Illustrator's native file format is using the PDF language, then placing it in InDesign is similar to placing a PDF file in InDesign.

In reality, though, Illustrator's native file format is a special flavor of the PDF language—a flavor that only Illustrator can understand. Certain constructs exist in Illustrator but do not exist in the PDF language, such as live blends, Live Paint effects, and live effects (these effects are all expanded when printed or translated to regular PDF). You can think of Illustrator's native file format as a superset of the PDF language. If this is the case, however, how is InDesign or Acrobat able to import and display native Illustrator files? That's where the dual-path concept comes in.

When you save a native file, Illustrator embeds two files—a native Illustrator file (.ai) and a standard PDF file (**Figure 13.1**). When you place the native Illustrator file into InDesign, the application sees the PDF portion of the file and uses that for display and printing. When you reopen the file in Illustrator, the application sees the native Illustrator portion and uses that for editing. In the end, everyone is happy, and you get to work with a single file.

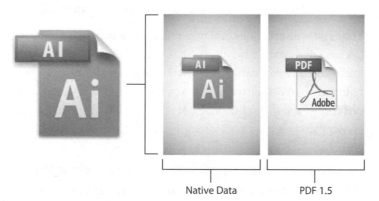

Native Data   PDF 1.5

Figure 13.1 When you save a native Illustrator file, you're really saving two files. The PDF file that is created with the native Illustrator file is PDF 1.5, which preserves transparency.

To save your file as a native Illustrator file, choose File > Save, and select Adobe Illustrator Document from the pop-up menu. When you click Save, you are presented with the Illustrator Options dialog where you can specify settings for how your file should be saved. These are described in the section "Native Illustrator File Format Settings."

The two files within an Illustrator file print and display the same and are identical except the native Illustrator version maintains more editability within the Illustrator environment.

Legacy Illustrator Formats

Illustrator CS3 allows you to save your file so that it is compatible with a variety of previous versions of Illustrator. Obviously, the older the version you specify, the less editable your file will be. Specifically, you should be aware of two distinctions:

- Adobe introduced a new text engine in Illustrator CS. If you save your file to any version prior to Illustrator CS, your text is either broken apart or converted to outlines. For more details, see "Saving Illustrator CS3 Files to Illustrator Legacy Versions" in Chapter 7, *Typography*.

- Adobe introduced transparency features in Illustrator 9. If you save your file to any version prior to Illustrator 9, transparency flattening will occur, resulting in a document that may be extremely difficult, or even impossible, to edit. For more details, see "Learning the Truth About Transparency" in Chapter 12, *Prepress and Printing.*

Your file will print or display correctly when you're saving to older versions because appearance is always maintained. However, you are limited in what kinds of edits you can make in your file. For this reason, we recommend you *always* save a native CS3 version of your file to keep on your computer or server for editing purposes. If someone else requests a file from you that is compatible with a previous version of Illustrator, send them a *copy* of your file.

Native Illustrator File Format Settings

A variety of settings are available in the Illustrator Options dialog (**Figure 13.2**), and depending on your needs for each particular workflow, you can adjust these settings.

- **Version.** The Version pop-up menu allows you to choose which version of Illustrator you want your file to be compatible with. See "Legacy Illustrator Formats" earlier in this chapter for more information.

- **Fonts.** When you're saving a file, any fonts you use are embedded in the PDF portion of the file. This allows other applications to print the file without requiring the fonts. However, you still need the fonts installed if you are going to reopen the file within Illustrator. This setting is disabled when the Create PDF Compatible File option is unchecked (see the following description). At the 100% setting, Illustrator embeds only those characters of a font that are necessary to print the text in your document. Using a setting much lower (such as to 0%) embeds the entire font, resulting in a larger file. Fonts with permission bits turned on cannot be embedded (see the sidebar "Font Embedding and Permissions" later in this chapter).

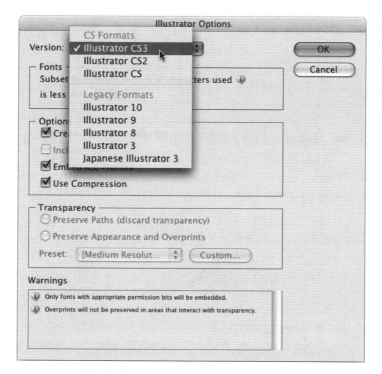

Figure 13.2 The Illustrator Options dialog allows you to specify which version of Illustrator you want your file to be compatible with, among other settings.

- **Create PDF Compatible File.** The Create PDF Compatible File option embeds a full standard PDF 1.5 file within your Illustrator document. As just mentioned, this allows applications such as Acrobat or InDesign to read and place native Illustrator files. Turning this option *off* effectively cuts your file size in half and also reduces how long it takes to save an Illustrator file (**Figure 13.3** on the following page). If you use Illustrator for all your work and print directly from Illustrator, you can turn this option off to enhance performance and to create smaller file sizes, but be aware that you won't be able to place your file into an InDesign layout. Even if you do turn this option off, you can always reopen the file in Illustrator and resave the file with the option turned back on.

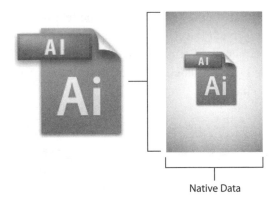

Figure 13.3 When you have the Create PDF Compatible File option unchecked, only the native Illustrator portion is saved with the file, cutting save time and file size in half. The result, however, is a native file that cannot be placed into another application.

Native Data

- **Include Linked Files.** When you choose the Include Linked Files option, any place-linked files are embedded in your document. Although this means you can send the file to someone without requiring any external links, it also means you can't easily update linked graphics anymore. This option also increases file size because the images are now included within the file.

- **Embed ICC Profiles.** The Embed ICC Profiles option includes any color profiles (including those from placed images) within your document.

- **Use Compression.** The Use Compression option employs compression algorithms to your file to try to reduce file size.

- **Transparency.** When you're saving to an Illustrator 8 or Illustrator 3 format, transparency flattening must occur in documents that contain transparency effects. You can choose to discard the transparency effects completely (which preserves path geometry), or you can choose to preserve the appearance of your file. You can also choose from the list of available transparency flattener presets. For more information on which flattener preset to use, refer to Chapter 12, *Prepress and Printing*.

The Encapsulated PostScript (.eps) Format

When Adobe introduced PostScript to the world, it forever changed the face of design and publishing. Since desktop publishing became a buzzword, the format in which designers and printers exchanged file information was always EPS. To this day, EPS is a reliable, universal format that can be used to reproduce graphics from just about any professional (and even some non-professional) graphics applications. You can even use EPS files with video applications such as Adobe After Effects.

As you learned in Chapter 12, *Prepress and Printing*, PostScript doesn't support transparency, so if your file contains any transparency effects, those effects are flattened when the document is saved as EPS. However, you can still reopen and edit the native transparency in Illustrator CS3 because Illustrator also uses a dual path when saving EPS files. An Illustrator CS3 EPS file has two portions within it: a native version for editing within Illustrator and an EPS version that other applications, such as QuarkXPress, use (**Figure 13.4**).

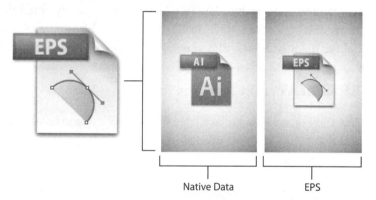

Native Data   EPS

Figure 13.4 When you save a document as an EPS file, Illustrator also embeds a native version of the file so that you can reopen and edit the file in Illustrator with no loss in editability.

To save your file as an EPS file, choose File > Save, and select Illustrator EPS from the pop-up menu. When you click Save, you are presented with the EPS Options dialog where you can specify settings for how your file should be saved, as described later in the section "EPS File Format Settings."

Legacy EPS Formats

As with native files, Illustrator allows you to save your file so that it is compatible with a variety of versions of Illustrator EPS. This setting affects both the native portion and the EPS portion of the file. When you save a file that is compatible with an older version of Illustrator, both the native data and the PostScript are written so they are compatible with that version (**Figure 13.5** on the following page). Obviously, the older the version you specify, the less editable your file is.

Figure 13.5 When you save a file in Illustrator 8 EPS format, the native portion of the file is also saved in Illustrator 8 format, which doesn't support transparency. Even if you reopen the file in Illustrator CS3, any transparency that was in the file is flattened.

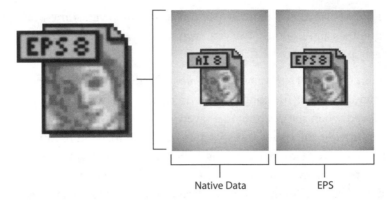

Native Data   EPS

The same rules mentioned for native Illustrator files apply here (with regard to versions that result in loss in text and transparency editability), and it always makes sense to save an Illustrator CS3 EPS for your own needs and deliver older or legacy EPS versions for others, as needed.

EPS File Format Settings

A variety of settings are available in the EPS Options dialog (**Figure 13.6**), and depending on your needs for each particular workflow, you can adjust these settings.

Figure 13.6 The EPS Options dialog offers a variety of settings to choose from when you're saving an EPS file, including the type of preview that you want saved within the file.

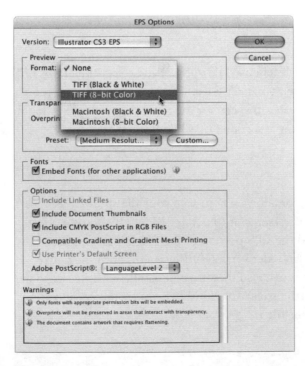

- **Version.** The Version pop-up menu allows you to choose which version of Illustrator EPS you want your file to be compatible with. See the preceding section "Legacy EPS Formats" for more information.

- **Preview.** The Preview setting lets you choose from different options for embedding a preview in your EPS file. Because most programs can't display PostScript on your computer screen, a low-resolution preview is stored along with the file so that programs such as QuarkXPress or Microsoft Word can give you a visual representation of what the file will look like in your layout.

- **Transparency.** If your file contains transparency, your file must be flattened so that it can be saved in PostScript and printed from another application (remember, the version you choose determines whether the native portion of the file, which Illustrator reads when it reopens the file, still contains editable, unflattened data). Although you can choose different transparency flattener presets from the pop-up menu, it almost always makes sense to choose the High Resolution setting, because you'll always want to get the best possible results when printing the EPS file from other applications (see "Choosing File Formats Based on Workflow" later in this chapter).

- **Embed Fonts.** When this option is checked, any fonts used are embedded in the EPS portion of the file. This allows other applications to print the file without requiring the fonts. However, even with the setting turned on, you still need the fonts installed if you are going to reopen the file within Illustrator. Fonts with permission bits turned on can't be embedded (see the sidebar "Font Embedding and Permissions" later in this chapter).

- **Include Linked Files.** Choosing the Include Linked Files option embeds any place-linked files in your document. Although this means you can send the file to someone without requiring any external links, it also means you can't easily update linked graphics anymore. This option also increases file size because the images will now be included within the file.

- **Include Document Thumbnails.** Use this option if you want to be able to see a preview of your file in the Open and Place dialogs in Illustrator.

- **Include CMYK PostScript in RGB Files.** This setting allows you to maintain RGB colors in your Illustrator file but have the EPS portion of the file converted to CMYK so other applications that don't support RGB can still print the file correctly.

- **Compatible Gradient and Gradient Mesh Printing.** If you experience problems printing EPS files saved from Illustrator on older print devices, try turning on this option.

- **Use Printer's Default Screen.** This instructs the PostScript to use the line screen of the default setting of the printer.

- **Adobe PostScript Level.** Use this pop-up menu to write the EPS file as PostScript Language Level 2 or Language Level 3. Illustrator uses Level 2 as the default setting in order to create a file that is compatible with a wider range of devices, but Level 3 PostScript offers certain benefits such as smooth shading technology to prevent banding in gradients.

The Portable Document Format (.pdf)

Walk up to just about anyone on the street these days and ask them about Adobe. Most will reply, "Oh, sure, I have Adobe on my computer." What they are probably referring to is the free Reader file viewer, which enables just about anyone to view and print PDF files. Now that Reader is nearing a billion downloads worldwide, PDF files are ubiquitous and are quickly becoming a standard format used not only by designers and printers but also by governments and enterprise corporations.

Over the past few years, PDF has become the format of choice for both printers and designers, replacing EPS and other formats. There are several reasons for this, including the following:

You can instruct clients or users to download the free Reader at www. adobe.com/ products/ acrobat/ readstep2.html. Reader is available for Mac, Windows, Unix, and a variety of mobile platforms.

- **Smaller file sizes.** PDF supports a variety of image compression techniques, resulting in smaller file sizes. In addition, users can easily create low-resolution files to send to clients for review and can create high-resolution files to send to printers for high-quality output.

- **A free universal viewer.** Adobe Reader is free and available for nearly every computer platform, including Palm-based handheld devices. This means a designer can deliver a PDF file and be assured that anyone can view the file correctly.

- **Ability to embed fonts.** A PDF file is a single, self-contained file that includes all necessary images and fonts. This makes it easier to distribute and reduces the chance of error.

- **Easy to create.** Designers can easily create PDF files from any Adobe application. Additionally, Adobe supplies free utilities, such as PDF-Maker, that enable users to instantly create PDF files from Microsoft Office documents or AutoCAD files. A PDF virtual printer also enables a user to create a PDF file simply by printing a file from any application.

- **Security.** PDF files can contain multiple levels of security that can restrict functionality such as printing or editing. This ensures the integrity of a file and gives a designer the ability to protect his or her work.

By default, a PDF saved from Illustrator is also a dual-path file, containing both PDF data and native Illustrator data (**Figure 13.7**). In fact, if you think about it, saving a native Illustrator file and an Adobe PDF file is quite similar. When you save a PDF file from Illustrator, though, you can control a variety of settings in the resulting PDF data of the file.

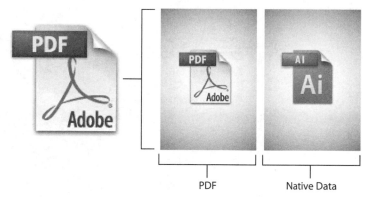

Figure 13.7 If you've ever heard that Illustrator creates large PDF files, it's probably because by default, Illustrator embeds a native version of the file along with the PDF data, resulting in a PDF file that appears twice as large.

PDF   Native Data

To save your file as a PDF file, choose File > Save, and select Adobe PDF from the pop-up menu. When you click Save, you are presented with the Save Adobe PDF dialog where you can specify settings for how your file should be saved.

Different Uses of PDF Files

Before we discuss all the different options you have available when saving a PDF file, it's important to realize that PDF files have many uses. For example, you might create a PDF file to send to a client so that they can approve a design, or you might create a PDF file to send to a printer for final output. Alternatively, you might even create a PDF file to upload to a Web site so that anyone can view the content. Each of these PDF files serves a different purpose, and therefore each can have very different settings. Just because you create a PDF file doesn't mean you can use it for any and all purposes.

PDF presets are similar to Distiller Job Options, which are simply a captured set of PDF settings.

Instead of having to manually specify PDF settings each time you want to create a file for a specific purpose, Illustrator offers to let you create Adobe PDF presets, which capture all the settings a PDF can have. At the top of the Save Adobe PDF dialog, a pop-up menu lets you choose from some presets that ship with Illustrator (**Figure 13.8**), or you can define your own by clicking the Save Preset button at the bottom left of the dialog.

Figure 13.8 Illustrator ships with several predefined PDF presets. If you're using other Adobe CS3 applications, any PDF preset you save in Illustrator also becomes available in all the other applications.

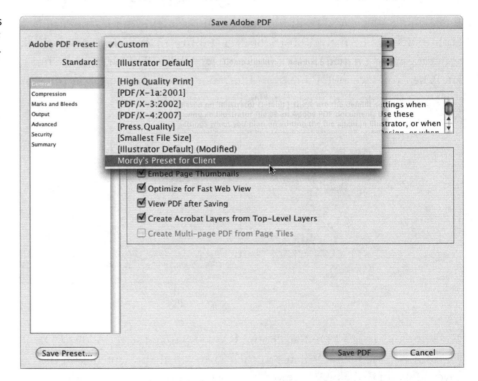

Acrobat Version Compatibility

When PDF was first introduced, it had limited support (spot colors weren't supported until version 1.2), but as each new version of Acrobat has been introduced, Adobe has updated the PDF language specification (called

PDFL for short) to include more advanced functions and to feature new capabilities.

Adobe released PDFL version 1.3 when it introduced Adobe Acrobat 4.0, which was the first mainstream version of Acrobat and the free Acrobat Reader. With each new version of Acrobat, Adobe has also revised the PDFL version (Acrobat 5 = PDF 1.4, Acrobat 6 = PDF 1.5, and so on), although trying to remember all of these different numbers can prove quite confusing. An easy way to figure it out is to remember that if you add up the numbers in the PDFL version, it equals the corresponding version of Acrobat (1+4 = 5).

In any case, when you save a PDF file from Illustrator, you can specify which version of Acrobat you want your file to be compatible with in the Save Adobe PDF dialog (**Figure 13.9**). Although saving a file using a newer version compatibility setting offers more options when saving, anyone who wants to view that PDF file needs to use a newer version of Acrobat or Reader to see and print the file correctly.

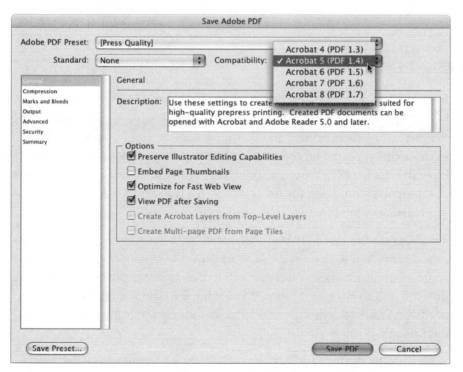

Figure 13.9 The Save Adobe PDF dialog offers a plethora of settings for creating PDF files for a wide variety of purposes. The Compatibility setting determines the version of Acrobat that the resulting PDF file needs in order to display and print correctly.

The most important point to remember is that from a print perspective, there's a line in the sand between PDF 1.3, which doesn't support transparency, and all later PDF versions, which do support live transparency (**Table 13.1**). See "Choosing File Formats Based on Workflow" later in this chapter to learn when to use each version.

Table 13.1 Acrobat Version Compatibility

Version of Acrobat	PDFL Version	Transparency Support	Main Features Introduced
Acrobat 4	PDF 1.3	No	SmoothShading, digital signatures
Acrobat 5	PDF 1.4	Yes	Transparency, XML tagging, and metadata
Acrobat 6	PDF 1.5	Yes	Layers, JPEG2000 compression
Acrobat 7	PDF 1.6	Yes	Object-level metadata, AES encryption
Acrobat 8	PDF 1.7	Yes	Enhanced 3D support, PDF packages

The PDF/X Standard

Imagine the following scenario: A designer submits a PDF file to a printer for final printing. When the job is complete, the designer is horrified to find that the wrong fonts printed and that the colors weren't anywhere near close to those that appeared on the screen when the designer designed the job. How did this happen? After all, didn't the printer say they accept PDF files? For designers, and especially for printers, this is a scenario that unfortunately happens too often.

This happens because PDF is a "garbage in, garbage out" file format. Whatever you put into it, that's what you can expect to get out of it. If you don't embed your fonts when you create a PDF file, a printer can't print your file unless they also have your fonts. If you embed RGB images when a printer needs CMYK, you will see color shifts in your output (some devices may not print RGB images at all).

With so many other possible things that could go wrong with a PDF file, printers and publishers realized that they needed a way to ensure that a PDF file meets certain requirements before it is submitted for final printing or publication.

Understanding Illustrator's Supported PDF Standards

Because PDF files have so many uses and because each workflow is different, many PDF standards exist. The following is an explanation of what each standard is and what each is best used for:

- **PDF/X-1a:2001.** The PDF/X-1a standard was defined to allow for the reliable exchange of files between designers and printers or publishers. The standard, which was first defined in 2001 (which is where it gets its name), is based on PDF 1.3 and therefore doesn't support transparency. When you save a PDF/X-1a file from Illustrator, a transparency flattener preset is used to flatten the transparency in the file. A PDF/X-1a-compliant file must also have all fonts embedded within the file. If your file uses a protected font that cannot be embedded (see the sidebar "Font Embedding and Permissions" later in this chapter), Illustrator can't create a valid PDF/X-1a file. Additionally, PDF/X-1a files are CMYK and spot only (any RGB information is converted to CMYK). For ad submission or for sending final files to a printer for offset printing, PDF/X-1a:2001 is the preferred choice.

- **PDF/X-3:2002.** In recent years, print service providers have been adopting color management technologies to offer better color matching. Rather than converting images to CMYK early in the process, in a color-managed workflow you can have images remain in RGB and tag them with profiles that allow color integrity to be preserved from proof to final print. Because PDF/X-1a doesn't support RGB or embedded color profiles, PDF/X-3:2002 was created to allow for these variables. If you or your printer are using a color-management workflow, you might consider using PDF/X-3:2002.

- **PDF/X-4:2007.** Once a file has been flattened, a printer can't do much in the way of making changes to that file. More important, a printer can't trap files that have already been flattened. Although PDF/X-1a and PDF/X-3 don't allow transparency constructs within the file, the PDF/X-4 standard is based on PDF 1.5 and allows transparency. This gives the printer the ability to choose a flattener setting and to make late-stage edits. In any case, it's best to speak with your printer before using the newer PDF/X-4:2007 standard.

See "File Formats and Workflow" later in this chapter for additional examples of when you would want to submit a PDF file using one the standards listed here. You can find more information on PDF/X-1a at www.pdf-x.com.

One way to do that was by providing designers with a detailed list of the settings they needed to use whenever they created a PDF file. Although this was a nice idea in concept, printers and publishers soon realized that designers use a variety of different programs, and each has a different ways of creating PDF files. They also realized this meant that each time a new version of software was introduced, a designer would need to learn new settings.

Instead, an International Organization for Standardization (ISO) standard was created, called *PDF/X*. A PDF/X file is not a new kind of file format but rather a regular PDF file that simply meets a list of predefined criteria. Now, when a designer submits a PDF/X file for final printing, a printer can assume that the file meets the minimum requirements to reproduce it correctly.

By choosing a standard from the Standard pop-up menu in the Save Adobe PDF dialog, you are embedding an identifier within the PDF file that says, "I am a PDF/X-compliant file." Certain scripts and preflight utilities can read these identifiers and validate PDF/X-compliant files in a prepress or publishing workflow. See the sidebar "Understanding Illustrator's Supported PDF Standards" for an explanation of the different kinds of PDF/X versions.

General PDF Settings

The General panel of the Save Adobe PDF dialog contains several important settings that determine how your PDF file is saved:

- **Preserve Illustrator Editing Capabilities.** The Preserve Illustrator Editing Capabilities option embeds a full native Illustrator file within your PDF file. This allows Illustrator to reopen and edit the file with no loss in editability. This option is turned on in the default preset, but turning this option off effectively cuts your file size in half and also reduces how long it takes to save a PDF file (**Figure 13.10**). If you want to send a file to a client for approval, for example, you can turn this option off to create a smaller PDF file (which is also not as editable should they try to open it in Illustrator). If you do turn this option off, make sure to always save a copy of your file, because you won't be able to reopen the smaller PDF and edit it as a fully editable file.

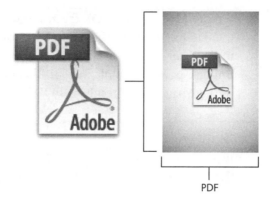

Figure 13.10 By turning off the Preserve Illustrator Editing Capabilities option, you can create a PDF file that is smaller and suitable for posting to the Web or sending via email.

PDF

- **Embed Page Thumbnails.** With the Embed Page Thumbnails option turned on, Illustrator creates thumbnails for each page. You can display these in Acrobat by choosing to view the Pages tab. Be aware that the thumbnails do increase the file size somewhat, however.

- **Optimize for Fast Web View.** Choosing the Optimize for Fast Web View option enables streaming, allowing those who view the file online to view parts of the document while other parts are still loading.

- **View PDF after Saving.** It's always a good idea to take a look at a PDF on your screen to make sure it's okay before you release it to a printer or to a client. Checking the View PDF After Saving option launches Acrobat and opens the file after the PDF file is created.

- **Create Acrobat Layers from Top-Level Layers.** If you choose to save your file with Acrobat 6 (PDF 1.5), Acrobat 7 (PDF 1.6), or Acrobat 8 (PDF 1.7) compatibility, you can have Illustrator convert all top-level layers to PDF layers. You can view a document with PDF layers in either Acrobat or the free Reader, versions 6.0 and newer (**Figure 13.11**). In addition, Acrobat layers can be turned on and off when the PDF is placed within an InDesign CS2 or CS3 document.

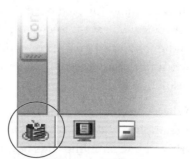

Figure 13.11 When a file is opened in Acrobat or Reader, a layer cake icon indicates that the document contains PDF layers.

- **Create Multi-page PDF from Page Tiles.** If you set up your document to use either the Tile Full Pages or Tile Imageable Areas option in the Print dialog, checking this option creates a single PDF file with multiple pages. Each tile in your Illustrator document appears as a separate page in the resulting PDF file (**Figure 13.12**).

Figure 13.12 A document set up with Tile Full Pages (left) can be saved directly as a multipage PDF file (right).

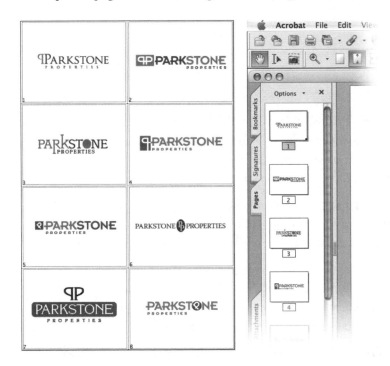

PDF Compression Settings

The Compression panel of the Save Adobe PDF dialog offers a variety of settings for compressing the images and art that appear in your file (**Figure 13.13**). One of the benefits of using PDF is that you can specify a variety of image settings for each need. For example, when you send a file to a client for review, you want to create a small file that transmits quickly via email and might set all images to resample at 72 ppi. However, that same file, when transmitted to the printer for final output, needs to contain high-resolution images, which you might set to at least 300 ppi.

When you create a PDF, Illustrator has the ability to resample an image. Resampling is a method used to change the resolution of a raster image. Although upsampling adds new pixels to a file, downsampling removes pixels from a file, resulting in a lower resolution and a smaller file size. Obviously, downsampling an image results in loss in image detail and is therefore inappropriate for final output to a printer.

- **Resampling settings.** Illustrator can apply different settings to raster images that appear in your file, according to image type and resolution. You can specify these settings for color, grayscale, and monochrome bitmap images. More important, you can define a threshold for when images will be resampled. The Do Not Downsample option leaves images at their native resolutions. Alternatively, you can choose from three different types of downsampling (Average, Bicubic, and Subsampling), which reduce the resolution of any raster images within your file according to the threshold settings. The first value is for the resolution to which you want images to be downsampled. The second value determines which images in your file get downsampled. For example, if you set the first value to 72 ppi and the second value to 150 ppi, then any image in your file that exceeds 150 ppi is downsampled to 72 ppi. However, if your file contains an image that's set to 100 ppi, that image is not downsampled and remains at 100 ppi because it falls below the threshold.

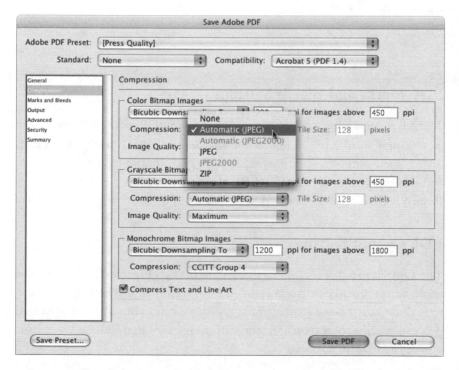

Figure 13.13 The Compression panel of the Save Adobe PDF dialog lets you determine which image types will be resampled, as well as choose the compression method in which to do so.

- **Compression and Image Quality.** In addition to resampling raster images, PDF also uses compression techniques to further reduce the size of a file. Different methods are used for compression, or you can choose None to disable compression completely (see the sidebar "Compress This").

- **Compress Text and Line Art.** To achieve smaller file sizes, check the option to compress text and line art. This uses a lossless method of compression and doesn't sacrifice quality in your file.

Compress This

Getting smaller file sizes comes at a cost. That cost is the quality of the image after it has been compressed. As we discussed in Chapter 11, *Web and Mobile Design*, there are two types of compression algorithms: lossy compression, which results in smaller files at the expense of image detail, and lossless compression, which doesn't make files quite as small but loses no information in the process.

When saving PDF files from Illustrator, you can choose no compression, JPEG compression, JPEG2000 compression (both JPEG compression types are lossy), or the lossless zip compression method. When using lossy compression, you can also choose an image quality setting to control how much information or detail is lost in the compression process. The Maximum setting preserves the most information in the file, while the Minimum setting sacrifices quality for a smaller file size.

PDF Marks and Bleeds Settings

The Bleeds settings you specify here in the Marks and Bleeds panel define the bleed box values in the resulting PDF.

The Marks and Bleeds panel of the Save Adobe PDF dialog (**Figure 13.14**) is strikingly similar to the Marks and Bleeds panel you'll find in the Print dialog. Here you can specify whether your PDF should have printer's marks and whether the document will have bleed space added. See Chapter 12, *Prepress and Printing*, for detailed descriptions of these settings.

PDF Output Settings

The Output panel of the Save Adobe PDF dialog (**Figure 13.15**) gives you control over what color space your PDF is saved in and whether you want to include image color management profiles within your PDF. Additionally, you can specify color management settings for files that will be saved using one of the PDF/X standards.

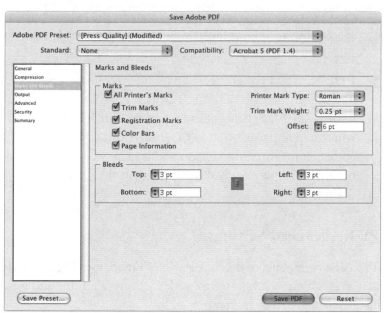

Figure 13.14 The Marks and Bleeds panel of the Save Adobe PDF dialog lets you create PDF files with crop marks automatically. Additionally, the Bleeds settings make it easy to turn bleed on or off depending on to whom you are sending the PDF file.

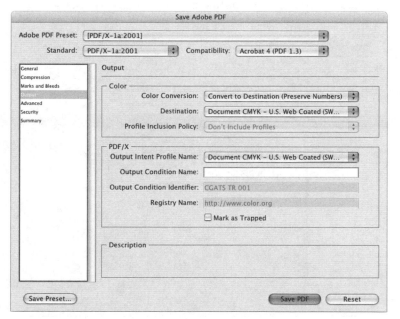

Figure 13.15 The Output panel of the Save Adobe PDF dialog gives you the ability to convert all objects to a specific color space. For example, when saving a PDF/X-1a file, any linked RGB images are converted to CMYK automatically.

- **Color.** When you create a PDF file, you can specify a color conversion for the file. In the Color Conversion pop-up, you can choose No Conversion, in which case the color values and color space will remain untouched, or you can choose Convert to Destination and choose from the Destination pop-up options to convert the color values or color space using a color profile of your choice. You can also specify when Illustrator will include color profiles in the PDF file.

- **PDF/X.** When you create a PDF/X file, you must specify a color profile intent; with PDF/X-1a, this is usually set to SWOP. You can also choose to mark the file as being already trapped, which is useful in workflows where trapping may occur in the RIP. If you trapped a file in Illustrator (either manually or via a plugin such as Esko-Graphics' DeskPack), identifying the file as already trapped prevents the file from being trapped again in the RIP.

PDF Advanced Settings

The Advanced panel of the Save Adobe PDF dialog (**Figure 13.16**) allows you to specify how fonts are embedded in your PDF file and how transparency is flattened, if necessary.

Figure 13.16 The Advanced panel of the Save Adobe PDF dialog allows you to specify a transparency flattener preset when saving to PDF 1.3 (all other versions support live transparency).

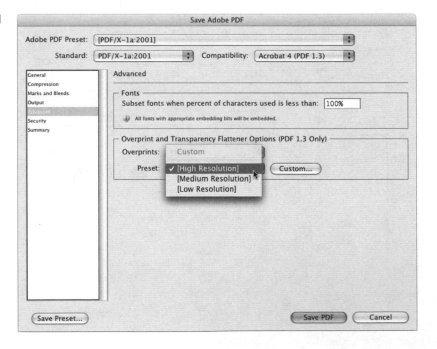

- **Fonts.** By default, Illustrator embeds subsets of fonts when saving a PDF file. A subset simply means that Illustrator includes only the parts of a font that are required to view and print the text you have in your document. If a font is protected, however, Illustrator does not embed the font. See the sidebar "Font Embedding and Permissions" for more information.

- **Overprint and Transparency Flattener Options.** If your document contains overprint settings, you can choose to preserve or discard them. Additionally, if your file contains transparency, you can choose a transparency flattener preset to control how the transparency is flattened. For more information on both overprinting and transparency, see Chapter 12, *Prepress and Printing*. It's important to note that these two settings are applicable only when you're saving a PDF file with Acrobat 4 (PDF 1.3) compatibility because all other versions support transparency and don't require flattening.

Font Embedding and Permissions

Using fonts these days isn't the same as it was several years ago. Designer, meet lawyer. Lawyer, meet designer. There are some legal restrictions when it comes to using fonts, and depending on the licensing agreement that comes along with the fonts you own, you may be limited in how you can use your fonts.

Generally, a font can have two kinds of embedding permissions. *Preview and Printing* permissions give the owner of the font the rights to use the font in a design and distribute the file with the font embedded so that others can view and print the document as well. *Editing* permissions give the owner the same rights as Preview and Printing permissions, but others who receive the file with the fonts embedded may also make edits and changes to the file.

Even though most fonts possess one of these two permissions (which are specified in the font licensing agreement), they usually aren't enforced in any way. A font vendor expects a user to abide by the terms specified in its license agreement. For example, a font may have Preview and Printing permissions (the more stringent of the two settings), but you may still be able to embed that font in a PDF file. This means someone using Acrobat Professional, or another product that can edit PDF files (including Illustrator), can make changes to the document, which would violate the license agreement.

To prevent unauthorized use, some font vendors protect their fonts by specifying that their fonts can't be embedded at all. These fonts are referred to as *protected fonts*. If an Adobe application encounters such a font, the application does not embed the font within a PDF file, honoring the rights of the font vendor. Obviously, if a designer is using a protected font and wants to send a PDF file with the fonts embedded to a publication, this can pose a problem. The only solution is for the designer to contact the font vendor and request an extended license that allows the font to be embedded. Alternatively, you may be able to convert the text to outlines before saving the file.

Unfortunately, Illustrator doesn't offer any way to easily tell whether a font is protected (InDesign does). Once you create a PDF, you can open the file in Acrobat and use the Document Properties setting to make sure your fonts are embedded.

PDF Security Settings

In today's world, security has become a priority—not only in airports but with regard to electronic communications and documentation as well. One of the benefits of using PDF files is the ability to password-protect them so that you can control who can view or edit your file.

The Security panel of the Save Adobe PDF dialog (**Figure 13.17**) allows you to specify two kinds of passwords to protect the content of your PDF file.

Figure 13.17 The Security panel of the Save Adobe PDF dialog allows you to choose a password that will restrict how your PDF file can be viewed or printed.

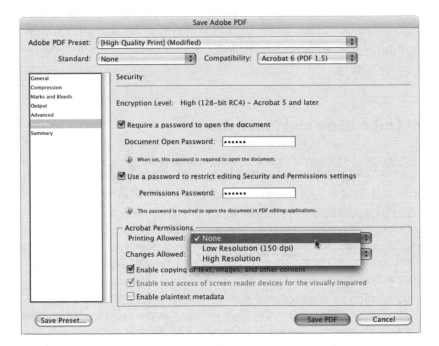

- **Document Open Password.** A document open password, also referred to as a *master password*, controls who can open your PDF file. If a user attempts to view the PDF, they are prompted for a password. Upon entering the password, the user is able to view the file. The file will not open if the password is incorrect.

- **Permissions Password.** A permissions password controls what a user can do with a PDF file once it is open on their screen. For example, a user who has the Professional version of Acrobat or a variety of Acrobat plugins, such as Enfocus PitStop, has the ability to edit a PDF file. Even if a file has a master password, once a user opens the file, they are free to do with the file as they please. By specifying a permissions password, you can restrict what a user can do with a file, even once they've opened the file in Acrobat Professional. For a detailed explanation of the different permissions settings, see the sidebar "Did You Ask for Permission?"

Did You Ask for Permission?

Illustrator provides a range of permissions settings that give you control over the kinds of actions a user can take with your PDF file once they've opened it. You can find these options in the lower portion of the Security panel in the Save Adobe PDF dialog.

- **Printing.** Choosing None disallows the printing of your file. Users are able to view the file in its entirety on their computer screens, but their Print command is grayed out (**Figure 13.18**). Choosing High Resolution enables full printing of the file. When using a compatibility setting of Acrobat 6 or higher, you can also choose the Low Resolution setting, which forces all pages to print only as raster images at 150 dpi.

- **Changing/Editing.** Choosing None disallows all editing of your file. Users are able to view the file in its entirety on their computer screens, but all of Acrobat's editing tools are disabled. You can choose from four additional settings to restrict specific types of edits. For example, by choosing the Filling in Form Fields and Signing setting, you allow users to fill out PDF form fields and to digitally sign the file, but this setting disables all other editing features.

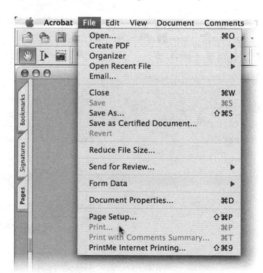

- **Copying.** If you want to prevent users from copying content from your PDF file and pasting that data into other applications, uncheck the option marked Enable Copying of Text, Images, and Other Content. However, realize that by doing so, you may affect the accessibility of your document, especially for users who are visually impaired—those who rely on screen readers to speak the content of files. These screen readers copy the text and paste the data into an application that reads the words to the user. When you check the option to enable text access to screen readers, Acrobat allows the copying of text if it senses that the application that's copying the data is a screen reader application. Additionally, you can enable a user to copy the metadata from a file.

Figure 13.18 If you use a permissions password to restrict printing, a user without the password is able to view the document but is not able to print the PDF file.

The Scalable Vector Graphics (.svg, .svgz) Format

SVG is an XML-based file format that is used primarily on the Web and has recently become more popular in creating content for cell phones and handheld wireless devices. For more information about how SVG is used, refer to Chapter 11, *Web and Mobile Design*. The SVGZ format is simply SVG that is zipped (compressed).

A variety of settings are available in the SVG Options dialog, and depending on your needs for each particular workflow, you can adjust these settings. Click the More Options button in the SVG Options dialog to see the full list of available settings (**Figure 13.19**).

Figure 13.19 Illustrator's SVG Options dialog offers a variety of settings that allow you to fine-tune SVG files, including a button that launches Adobe Device Central CS3, which allows you to preview your file on a variety of handheld devices and cell phones.

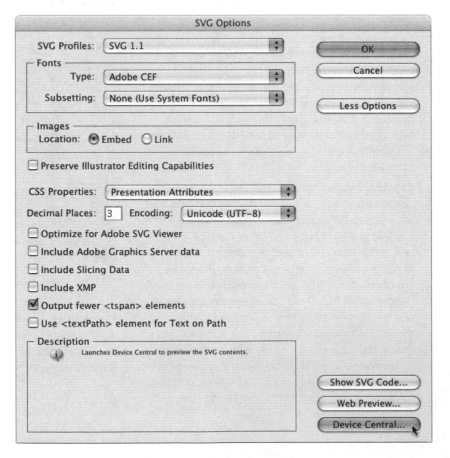

- **DTD.** The DTD (Document Type Definition) setting is akin to the version of SVG that your file is compatible with. Because SVG is an open standard, additional specifications are revised and approved. If you save an SVG file with a particular DTD, it means your file will be compatible with any device that supports that DTD. Newer specifications usually support additional functionality than the older ones did. SVG Tiny (also referred to as SVG-t) is a subset of SVG used for displaying content on SVG-enabled cell phones. SVG Basic is a subset of SVG used for displaying content on PDAs.

- **Fonts.** When text is present in your file, you can specify the Adobe CEF type, which results in better-looking text when your file is viewed with the Adobe SVG Viewer but may not be supported with other SVG viewers. The SVG creates more compatible text, but it's text that may not be as readable at smaller font sizes. Alternatively, you can convert all text to outlines, which increases file size.

- **Images.** When you save a file in SVG, you have the ability to embed any images within the SVG file (making for larger but self-sufficient files), or you can choose to create smaller SVG files by using the Link option.

- **Preserve Illustrator Editing Capabilities.** The Preserve Illustrator Editing Capabilities option embeds a full native Illustrator file within your SVG file (**Figure 13.20**). This allows Illustrator to reopen and edit the file with no loss in editability. This option is unchecked by default, but turning this option on effectively doubles your file size. If you do leave this option off, make sure to always save a copy of your file because you won't be able to reopen the SVG file and edit it as a fully editable file.

For more information on the SVG specification and SVG-enabled cell phones, visit www.svg.org.

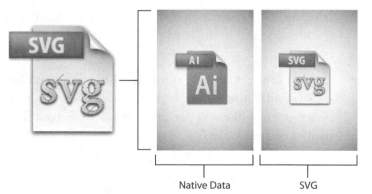

Native Data   SVG

Figure 13.20 Similar to a PDF file, Illustrator can embed a native version of the file within an SVG document to assure editability when the SVG is reopened in Illustrator.

- **CSS Properties.** You can format SVG code in a variety of ways, and the CSS Properties options allows you to determine how object attributes are coded within the file. For the most part, these options affect the performance of your file when viewed.

- **Decimal Places.** Illustrator allows you to specify how precisely vector paths are drawn. You can choose a value from 1 to 7, where higher numbers result in better-looking paths at the expense of file size and performance.

- **Encoding.** When you save an SVG file that contains text, you can specify a character encoding, including ISO-8859-1 (suitable for European languages), and 8- or 16-bit Unicode (suitable for more complex languages).

- **Optimize for Adobe SVG Viewer.** If people will be using the Adobe SVG Viewer to view your SVG files, you can check this option, which will take advantage of proprietary optimizations that exist in the Adobe SVG Viewer, including faster rendering of SVG filter effects.

For more information on Adobe Graphics Server, visit www.adobe.com/products/server/graphics/main.html.

- **Include Adobe Graphics Server data.** If you've defined variables within your Illustrator file (using the Variables panel), checking this option includes those variables within the file. This enables access to variable content when the SVG file is used as a template with Adobe Graphics Server or via Java or ECMAScript otherwise.

- **Include Slicing Data.** If you've specified Web slices and optimization settings in your Illustrator document (using the Slice tool or the Object > Slice > Make function), checking this option preserves the slice information in the file, making it available to other applications, such as Adobe GoLive CS2.

- **Include XMP.** Checking this option includes XMP metadata with the file, specified in the File > File Info dialog. This results in a larger file size.

- **Output fewer <tspan> elements.** This option, on by default, helps create smaller files, although at the risk of text shifting slightly. If you notice errors in the way the text is displayed in your final SVG file, try turning this option off.

- **Use <textPath> element for Text on Path.** If your document contains text on a path, you can turn this option on to use the <textPath> function in SVG to display that text. Otherwise, Illustrator writes each character as a separate <text> element in your file, making for a larger (although more precise) SVG file.

- **Show SVG Code/Preview.** Clicking either of these buttons launches a Web browser and allows you to preview the code and the file itself before you save the file.

EXPORTING FILES FROM ILLUSTRATOR

Illustrator is a robust application that supports a wide range of file formats. Although Illustrator does a great job in opening just about any graphic file format, it can also export files in different file formats for a plethora of uses. To export a file from Illustrator, choose File > Export, and then choose from one of the many formats listed in the pop-up in the Export dialog. Each of these formats is listed in the following pages, with descriptions of their settings as well as when you might want to use them.

Remember that when exporting, it is expected that some level of formatting or editability will be lost, so always save a native Illustrator version of your file before you export to another format.

The Bitmap (.bmp) Format

Bitmaps are raster-based files and are often used in older computer applications. The bitmap format is also used by some applications for displaying logos or bar codes.

When exporting a bitmap, you can choose one of three different color models: RGB, Grayscale, or Bitmap, which creates a file that contains only black-and-white pixels (**Figure 13.21** on the following page). Additionally, you can specify the resolution for your image and choose whether to anti-alias the art.

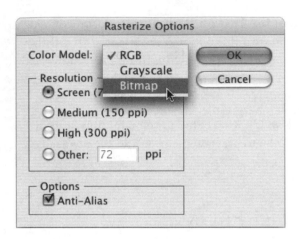

Figure 13.21 Many applications (including Illustrator and QuarkXPress) allow you to change the color of a bitmap file that uses the Bitmap color model.

The Targa (.tga) Format

The Targa file format is a raster-based image format used mainly in video applications. For example, you might use the Targa file format to add Illustrator artwork as masks in Adobe Premiere.

When exporting a Targa file, you can choose one of two color models: RGB or Grayscale. Additionally, you can specify the resolution for your image and choose whether to antialias the art.

The Portable Network Graphic (.png) Format

The PNG file format (pronounced "ping") was originally formed as an open standard format to replace the need for the GIF image file format, because of legal complications with those who developed the compression technology used in the GIF format.

As you learned in Chapter 11, *Web and Mobile Design*, you can also create PNG files from Illustrator using the Save for Web & Devices feature. However, the PNG format also appears as an export format because the Save for Web & Devices feature is hardwired at 72 ppi. To export a PNG file at any other resolution, you need to use the PNG export function.

The PNG format is a raster-based image format and is used for Web design, for icon and interface design, and as a general image exchange format. In fact, Apple's Tiger operating system (Mac OS X version 10.4) creates a PNG file when you take a screen shot. PNG files can support 24-bit color, but more important, the format also supports 256-level alpha channels for transparency, meaning you can give images soft edges that fade to transparent (unlike the GIF format, which supports one-color transparency only).

When exporting a PNG file, you can specify the resolution for your image as well as the background color. You can choose a transparent background, or you can choose Other to select a color from the Color Picker (**Figure 13.22**). Additionally, you can choose to turn on antialiasing and interlacing.

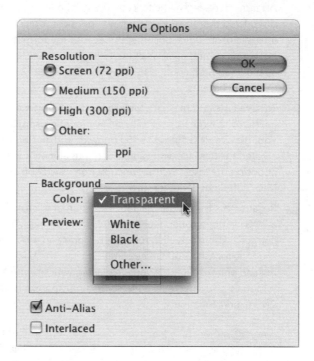

Figure 13.22 You can specify any color as a background color for a PNG file, including transparency.

The AutoCAD Drawing (.dwg) and AutoCAD Interchange File (.dxf) Formats

The DWG and the DXF file formats are both used for exchanging files with computer-aided design (CAD) applications. These formats can be especially helpful when you want to send Illustrator artwork to architects, interior designers, or industrial designers. Both formats support vector and raster elements.

If you need some of the functionality that CAD applications have, you might look into the CAD tools plugin from Hot Door, available at www.hotdoor.com.

Exporting Art for Use in Microsoft Office Applications

One of the most difficult things to do is create artwork in a professional design application (such as Illustrator) and have that same artwork display and print reliably in a business application such as Microsoft PowerPoint. Finding the right file format for this workflow is difficult because JPEG images don't support transparent backgrounds and EPS files don't display well onscreen. In addition, EPS files require the use of a PostScript printer, which most business professionals do not have.

After much research, the folks on the Adobe Illustrator development team discovered that the PNG format was perfect for placing art from Illustrator into Microsoft Office documents. Because the format supports transparent backgrounds and displays beautifully on computer screens, a PNG file set to a resolution high enough to also print well results in great-looking art in Office documents.

To save time and make it easier to quickly export a file from Illustrator to use in Microsoft Office, choose File > Save for Microsoft Office. Illustrator saves your file as a PNG file set to 150 ppi with antialiasing turned on. Once you've created the PNG file, you can place it into any Microsoft Office application by choosing the Insert Picture function from Microsoft Word, Microsoft Excel, or Microsoft PowerPoint (**Figure 13.23**).

Because of a bug in the Macintosh version of Microsoft Office, transparency in a PNG file does not appear correctly at the default view setting (it does appear correctly when viewed in full-screen mode and when printed). For this reason, the Save for Microsoft Office command sets the background color to white instead of transparent. If you are placing your art into Microsoft Office for Windows, you can create a PNG with a transparent background by using the PNG Export function.

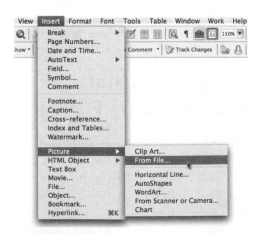

Figure 13.23 To place a PNG file into a Microsoft Office document, choose Insert > Picture > from File, and locate the file on your computer or server.

When exporting a DXF or a DWG file (they both use the same export dialog; **Figure 13.24**), you can specify the version of AutoCAD you want your file to be compatible with and the number of colors in the resulting file. If your file contains raster elements (or if vector elements need to be rasterized), you can choose to have them embedded as either bitmap or JPEG files.

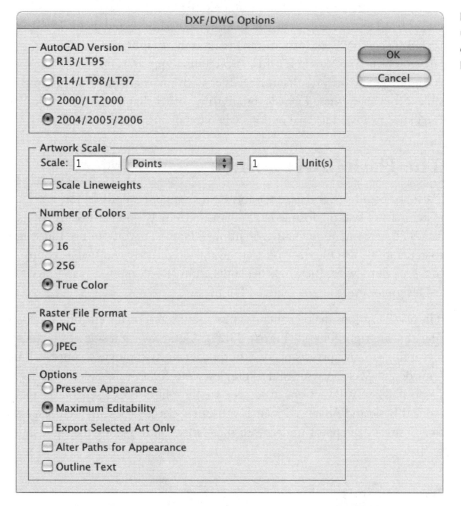

Figure 13.24 Illustrator uses the same export options dialog for both DWG and DXF formats.

Additionally, you can choose to export only the artwork that you currently have selected on the artboard. Choosing Alter Paths for Appearance modifies paths, if necessary, so that they appear when opened in a CAD application. Additionally, you can outline all text to avoid the need to send fonts.

The Windows Metafile (.wmf) and Enhanced Metafile (.emf) Formats

The Windows Metafile and Enhanced Metafile formats were developed to move graphics between applications on the Windows platform. These two formats support both vector and raster elements but are severely limited with regard to the kinds of art they can reliably display and print (EMF is slightly better). Both formats can create only straight vector lines, not curved ones. To make up for this, curved lines appear as numerous tiny straight paths, which results in large files with many anchor points. If possible, avoid using these formats for anything other than simple artwork. You can't specify any additional options when exporting WMF or EMF files.

The Flash (.swf) Format

SWF is a popular Web-based file format that supports both vectors and rasters. The Flash file format has become extremely popular because of its capability to contain interactive or animated content. You can use Illustrator to generate a SWF file that you want to upload directly to a Web site, use in a Flex framework Rich Internet application (RIA), or even place into InDesign for creating interactive PDF files.

The SWF Options dialog contains "just a few" options for creating the SWF files that are right for you (**Figure 13.25**). Along the right side of the dialog are options to save presets of SWF output settings, to preview your SWF in your default Web browser, and to preview your SWF using Adobe Device Central. The SWF Options dialog is actually split into two separate "panels" labeled Basic and Advanced, which you can access by clicking their respective buttons that appear underneath the Cancel button along the right side of dialog.

Basic Options

The options in the Basic panel of the SWF Options dialog are general settings that apply to most SWF files:

- **Export As.** You can export Illustrator files in one of four ways: AI File to SWF File, which creates a single SWF file that contains all of your Illustrator artwork; AI Layers to SWF Frames, where each layer is

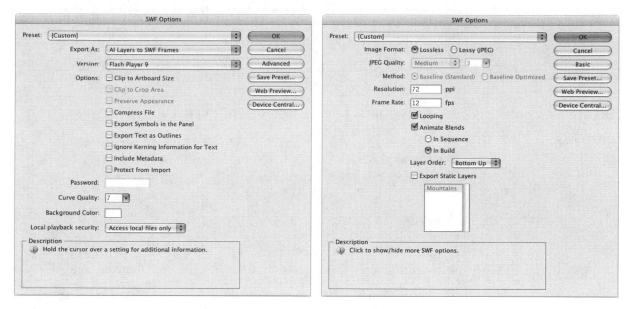

Figure 13.25 The Flash export dialog in Illustrator CS3 has so many options that there's a Basic button and an Advanced button that are used to toggle between two full panels.

converted into a key frame, resulting in a single animated SWF file; AI Layers to SWF Files, where each layer in your Illustrator document is exported as a separate SWF file (useful when you are creating Flash scenes); and AI Layers to SWF Symbols.

- **Version.** You can export a SWF that is compatible with any available version of the Flash Player. The default is Flash Player 9, which many believe is present on more than 90 percent of computers that access the Internet.

- **Options.** A variety of general settings appear in this section. You can choose to export your SWF at the exact size of your artboard or active crop area. If your file contains artwork that may not translate to the SWF format perfectly, you can choose Preserve Appearance to expand or rasterize those areas to ensure the integrity of the appearance of your art. Compressing a file will result in a smaller SWF. You can choose to include all symbols in your resulting SWF (even if they aren't used on the artboard), have your text converted to outlines, and ignore kerning that you may have applied to text. You can also choose to enclose metadata (from information you've entered using the File > File Info function) and protect the resulting SWF file from being opened in Adobe Flash by applying a password.

- **Curve Quality.** This setting controls the quality level for curved paths in the resulting SWF file.

- **Background Color.** This setting allows you to specify a background color for the SWF file.

- **Local playback security.** You can choose whether the SWF file can access local or network files only.

Advanced Options

The options found in the Advanced panel of the SWF Options dialog are settings that apply to rasterized portions of a file and animated content.

- **Image Format.** If there is raster content in your file (or if flattening requires that content becomes rasterized), you can choose how those images are stored in your SWF file—either using a lossless format or a lossy format. If you choose the lossy format, which is JPEG, you can choose a JPEG quality and the Baseline setting. You can also choose at what resolution you want your raster content to use (usually 72 ppi).

The remainder of the options present in the Advanced panel of the SWF Options dialog are specific to animated SWF content. Therefore, they are available only when choosing the AI Layers to SWF Frames option in the Export As pop-up menu in the Basic panel of the dialog.

- **Frame Rate.** This setting controls how fast the animation plays and is measured in frames per second (although in the context of Illustrator, they are actually layers per second). A lower value will slow down the animation, while a higher value will cause the animation to play back faster.

- **Looping.** Checking this option causes the animation to repeat itself endlessly.

- **Animate Blends.** If your Illustrator file contains any blends, checking this option will automatically animate those blends in the resulting SWF file. This setting allows you to keep blends live and editable within your Illustrator file and still get the desired animated result. Otherwise, you would have to use the Release to Layers function in your Illustrator file to manually create the content necessary to create an animation. You can choose to have blends animate either as a sequence (each frame appears individually, one after the other) or as a build (each frame appears successively, adding to the previous one).

- **Layer Order.** By default, Illustrator animates layers from the bottom up, but you can alternatively choose the Top Down option.

- **Export Static Layers.** Static layers are those that appear in every frame of the animation. If you check this option, you can Command-click (Control-click) any layers that you want visible throughout the entire animation. For example, if you had an animation of a bird flying across a cloudy sky, you might set the layers that contain the sky and cloud elements to export as static layers.

For an in-depth discussion of how you can create great-looking SWF files, including adding interactive hotspots and animations, refer to Chapter 11, *Web and Mobile Design*.

The Joint Photographic Experts Group (.jpg) Format

An extremely popular raster-based format, JPEG files are used mainly for exchanging photographic content and artwork. Although the JPEG format is used heavily in Web design, it is also the format of choice for the electronic delivery of stock photographs and for digital cameras. One of the reasons why JPEG is used for these tasks is because the JPEG format can take advantage of compression algorithms that can dramatically reduce file size. For example, a high-resolution image that is normally 10 MB in size might be only 1 MB in size when saved as a JPEG.

However, the JPEG format utilizes a lossy compression algorithm, and sometimes a JPEG file may exhibit artifacts or loss in detail because of this compression (**Figure 13.26**). A lower compression setting enhances image detail, at the cost of a larger file size.

Figure 13.26 When saving a file as a JPEG, using the Maximum setting results in a file with fewer artifacts, but doing so also results in a larger file size.

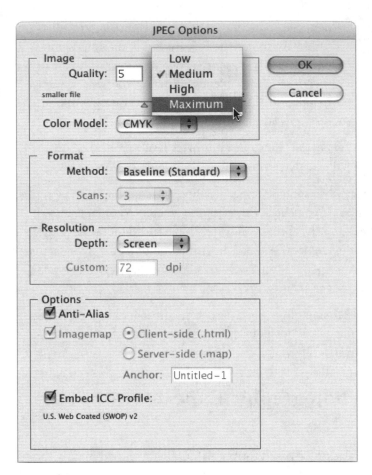

Although you can save JPEG files from Illustrator's Save for Web & Devices feature, you can only do so at 72 ppi. Using the JPEG Export function, you can specify a custom resolution for your file, which allows you to create high-resolution files.

Besides choosing an image compression level for your file, you can also specify the RGB, CMYK, or grayscale color model. Format methods determine how the image appears when viewed in a Web browser. If you choose the Baseline setting, the image loads completely and is then displayed at full resolution. The Progressive setting (similar to interlacing) allows the image to appear immediately at a lower-quality setting; it then appears in full quality once the entire image is loaded (the number of scans determines how many passes are done until the final image is previewed).

Illustrator also gives you the options of antialiasing the art, embedding a color profile, and including a client-side or server-side image map. Refer to Chapter 11, *Web and Mobile Design*, for more information on how to define image maps and the differences between client-side and server-side image maps.

The Macintosh PICT (.pct) Format

Much like the WMF and EMF formats, the PICT format was developed to move files between applications on the Macintosh platform. The format supports both vector and raster elements. You can't specify any additional options when exporting a PICT file.

The Adobe Photoshop (.psd) Format

As you learned in Chapter 9, *Mixing It Up: Working with Vectors and Pixels*, you can export an Illustrator file as an Adobe Photoshop file and preserve vital information in the file. This makes it easy to start work on a design piece in Illustrator and then bring it into Photoshop to add the finishing touches. Bringing Illustrator art into Photoshop is also useful when you're creating art that you plan to use for Web sites. In this way, you have high-quality artwork in Illustrator that can easily be repurposed for print, and you can add rollovers and interactivity using Photoshop or even Adobe Fireworks or Flash for the Web site.

When exporting a PSD file, you can choose between the CMYK, RGB, and grayscale color models, and you can specify a resolution for your file. If you choose to export a flat image, all Illustrator layers are flattened into a single nontransparent layer (what Photoshop calls the Background layer). Alternatively, you can choose the Write Layers option, which preserves Illustrator's layering where possible (**Figure 13.27** on the following page). You can also choose to preserve text and other native elements, such as compound shapes and Web slices (see Chapter 9, *Mixing It Up: Working with Vectors and Pixels*, for a complete list of the attributes that can be preserved between Illustrator and Photoshop).

Figure 13.27 By choosing to write layers, you gain the ability to export a file that preserves live text, layers, transparency and mask effects, and more.

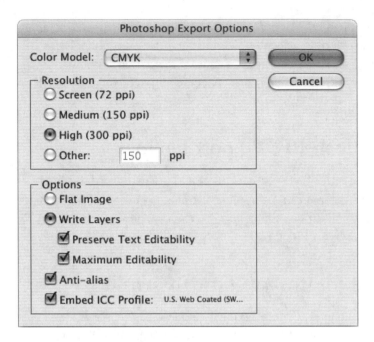

The Tagged Image File Format (.tif)

The TIFF format is widely used in graphics applications. Completely raster-based, a TIFF is a lossless image format. High-resolution files can be quite large, but image integrity is maintained. TIFF files are generally supported by print, video, and 3D rendering applications.

When exporting a TIFF, you can choose one of three different color models: RGB, CMYK, or grayscale. Additionally, you can specify the resolution for your image and choose whether to antialias the art. Checking the LZW Compression option results in a smaller file (the compression is lossless). You can also specify a platform-specific byte order (for better compatibility with Windows systems), and you have the ability to embed color profiles when you're working in a color-managed workflow.

Text Format (.txt)

Sometimes you just need to export the text in a file so you can use it in another application or for another purpose that Illustrator can't handle. You can export text to be compatible with a specific platform, or you can export text in Unicode, which is platform independent.

CHOOSING FILE FORMATS BASED ON WORKFLOW

So many different file formats exist that it's often difficult to know which one to use for each situation. Of course, every workflow demands special attention, and there are always exceptions and special cases. However, for the most part, you can follow certain rules, now that you really understand what each file format is capable of doing.

Print Workflows

When working in print workflows, designers traditionally use page layout applications such as QuarkXPress or InDesign, utilizing file formats such as EPS and PDF.

Traditionally, EPS is used for moving files from Illustrator into page layout applications. However, with the ability to use transparency effects in your Illustrator files, the limitations of EPS become apparent. For example, as a designer, you know that Illustrator creates vector-based files that can be scaled infinitely because they are resolution independent. You have always been able to save a file as an EPS from Illustrator, place it into an application such as QuarkXPress, scale that artwork at will, and never worry about resolution or the quality of the resulting printout.

However, as you learned in Chapter 12, *Prepress and Printing*, the process of transparency flattening may convert some vector content in your file into raster images, which are resolution dependent. Because an EPS contains flattened information, you can't assume that an EPS file can be scaled infinitely in a QuarkXPress layout anymore. In fact, you have to think of an EPS file from Illustrator as you would an EPS file saved from Photoshop—you need to limit how much you can enlarge a graphic.

Although this is a concern only when your file contains transparency effects, keep in mind that many effects in Illustrator introduce the need for flattening (these are discussed in detail in Chapter 12, *Prepress and Printing*).

On the other hand, native Illustrator files (which contain PDF 1.5 by default) have the ability to preserve live transparency, and therefore, flattening doesn't occur. When you save your file as a native Illustrator file, you can still scale that file infinitely, after it has been placed into a page layout

Although QuarkXPress can place PDF files, it can't correctly process PDF files that contain transparency. To avoid nasty printing issues, always place PDF/X-1a files, never native Illustrator or PDF 1.4 files, into QuarkXPress.

application. But this has a catch—you need a page layout application that can flatten that transparency when it prints your file. That means InDesign. Refer to **Table 13.2** for a list of suggested file formats, based on the page layout application you're using.

Table 13.2 Suggested File Formats

Application	When Transparency Is Present	When Transparency Is Not Present
QuarkXPress	EPS, PDF/X-1a (PDF 1.3)	EPS, PDF/X-1a (PDF 1.3)
InDesign	Native AI, PDF 1.4	EPS, Native AI, PDF 1.4

Web Workflows

The choices are much easier to make for Web designers. This is not because there are any fewer file types to choose from but mainly because the use of file types is usually dictated by the technology being used. For example, if you want to create animated content, you know you're using a GIF file or a Flash file. Some sites are restricted as to what kinds of formats are supported (for example, not every Web browser can display SVG files), so a designer is usually at the mercy of technology when it comes to deciding on a file format.

However, much can be done to a file before a final GIF or JPG is created. Therefore, you may find it beneficial to create your artwork in Illustrator and then export it as a Photoshop file, which you can then edit and work on in other applications, such as Photoshop or even Fireworks, Flash, or Dreamweaver.

Other Workflows

Of course, other workflows exist, including video, industrial design, architecture and engineering, fashion design, environmental design—the list goes on. With the information you now have about what each file format is used for, you should be able to develop a workflow that works for you.

APPENDIX A

Automation with Illustrator

With today's "need it now" mentality, we've been thrust into an era where deadlines and delivery dates are shorter than ever—at the same time, we're being asked to perform twice as much work. If you take a moment to read just about every press release and marketing document produced by companies in the high-tech industry, you'll find promises of faster performance and higher productivity with each new software release. Even hardware items such as the TiVo and the Apple iPod speak of our need for on-demand content.

The good news is that Adobe Illustrator supports several techniques for streamlining workflow through automation—in essence, you can have Illustrator do all the hard work for you while you take a few moments to grab some lunch (but who takes lunch anymore?).

TAKING ADVANTAGE OF AUTOMATION IN ILLUSTRATOR

Although automation may sound like a scary technical word, it doesn't have to be. Illustrator supports automation via two methods:

- **Actions.** This feature allows you to record specific steps that you can then reproduce by simply clicking a button. For example, an action may contain the steps necessary to select all text objects in an open document and rasterize them at a specific resolution. Actions are simple to record and don't require any code-writing knowledge. However, not every feature in Illustrator is actionable, so there's a limit to what an action can do.

- **Scripting.** Scripting is essentially a programmatic way to interact with an application. Instead of clicking with a mouse or punching a few keys on your keyboard to control Illustrator, you use a script—a set of commands instructing Illustrator what to do. Because these commands can contain math and logic, a script can create artwork based on variables. For example, a script might draw a graph in which numbers greater than a certain amount appear in black and numbers less than that appear in red. Most of Illustrator's functionality is available through scripting (significantly more so than with actions), but to write a script, you need to know a scripting language. Illustrator supports the AppleScript (Mac), Visual Basic (Windows), and JavaScript (cross-platform) languages. The good news is that you don't need to know how to write scripts in order to use them (that is, you can have someone write a script for you).

In this appendix, we'll explore these two automation methods as they pertain to Illustrator, and we hope this will serve as inspiration for you to learn more about automation.

Recording and Playing Actions

Recording an action is very simple and straightforward in Illustrator; playing back an action is even easier. To access the list of preset actions via the Actions panel, choose Window > Actions. The 22 actions in Illustrator are grouped within the Default Actions set. In addition, you can also create your own sets and actions.

To create a new set and an action within it, follow these steps:

1. Choose Window > Actions to open the Actions panel (**Figure A.1**).

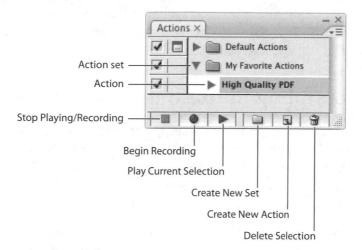

Action set

Action

Stop Playing/Recording

Begin Recording

Play Current Selection

Create New Set

Create New Action

Delete Selection

Figure A.1 You'll find the Default Actions set in the Actions panel. You can create your own sets as well.

2. Click the Create New Set icon at the bottom of the Actions panel. Give your set a unique name, and click OK.

3. Click the Create New Action icon at the bottom of the Actions panel. When you do, Illustrator prompts you to name the action you're about to record. Choose the set you just created, and if you'd like, choose a function key so that later you can perform the action using a keystroke. When you're done, click OK.

4. At this point, you'll notice that the red recording icon at the bottom of the Actions panel is highlighted, indicating that recording has begun. Perform the steps that you want to record in Illustrator.

    You can see each step being added as a line item to your action as you perform it. If a step doesn't appear in your action, it is probably because the function you performed is not actionable.

5. Once you have completed the steps for your action, click the Stop Recording button. At this point, the action is complete.

To play back your action—or any other one—highlight it in the Actions panel, and click the Play Current Selection button. If you assigned a keystroke to your action, you can play it back by pressing the correct key combination on your keyboard.

To apply actions with a single click, you can activate Button mode in the Actions panel. Choose Button Mode from the Actions panel menu.

Once you've recorded an action, you can also modify individual steps by double-clicking them, or you can delete those steps by dragging them to the trash can icon. Highlight a specific item by clicking it in the Actions panel, and choose any of the Insert commands in the Actions panel flyout menu to add specific menu commands, stops, or paths to your action as well. You can also save and load entire sets of actions from the Actions panel flyout menu.

Scripting in Illustrator

In the Adobe Illustrator CS3/Scripting/Documentation folder, you can find a PDF entitled Adobe Intro to Scripting.pdf, which is a wonderful resource for those of you who want to learn more about scripting in Illustrator.

You can script in Illustrator using AppleScript, Visual Basic Scripting Edition (VBScript), or JavaScript. Actually, Illustrator uses a language called ExtendScript, which is an Adobe flavor of JavaScript. You can find resources for this language, such as scripting dictionaries and sample scripts, in the Adobe Illustrator CS3/Scripting folder.

In general, ExtendScript is used to drive functionality within Illustrator. For example, you might use an ExtendScript script to reverse the direction of a selected vector path. In contrast, AppleScript or VBScript can drive functionality that uses different applications. For example, an AppleScript script might pull data from an external file or from the Web, use that data to generate a graphic, and then export that graphic in a specified format and email it.

Scripts that you place in the Adobe Illustrator CS3/Presets/Scripts folder will appear in the File>Scripts menu within Illustrator for easy access.

Each sample script included with Illustrator either contains separate PDF files describing how the script works or comments embedded directly in the script. You can open and view a script using a script editor or any text editing applications, such as BBEdit, TextEdit, or TextPad.

USING AUTOMATION WHEN RELEASING FINAL FILES

Sending a file off to a print service provider for final printing comes with the anxiety of not knowing whether everything in the file is okay and whether the printed results will come back as you envision them. A good designer knows that sending a file that's free of problems, and that includes all the necessary support files, is critical to success.

Using some of the automation features we mentioned earlier in this appendix, along with some sample actions and scripts that ship with Illustrator, you can make it a whole lot easier to release final files.

Cleaning Up Messy Files

When you create a new Illustrator file, any swatches, brushes, symbols, and graphic styles that are present in the New Document Profile used to create the file are added to the new file. Even if you never use these items to create artwork, your file contains this extraneous material. It's also normal for you to add and remove elements as you are working on a design concept. When it comes time to release a final version of your artwork, all these extra elements are still present.

Although in theory there's nothing wrong with having extra items in a file, experience tells a different story. In such cases, files can become corrupt, or art elements can be accidentally changed. In addition, a file with unused swatches or symbols can add to confusion if a printer needs to edit the file as it goes to press. These extra and unnecessary elements also bloat file size, causing longer save and open times.

Once a file has been deemed final, you can quickly remove all unused items using one of Illustrator's preset actions. With the Illustrator document open, choose Window > Actions to open the Actions panel. From the Default Actions set, click the one named Delete Unused Panel Items, and then click the Play button at the bottom of the panel.

Generating a List of Used Items

It's always helpful to provide your print service provider with as much information as possible about any file you are sending. Some designers print a list of all the files used; others mark up printouts with callouts and swatch chips.

Illustrator can help save time with a script called Analyze Documents, which is installed by default in the Scripting/Sample Scripts/AppleScript (Sample Scripts/Visual Basic Scripts) folder. You can run the script by simply double-clicking it. The script prompts you with a dialog asking you to identify a folder that contains Illustrator files. The script works on multiple files at one time. The Analyze Documents script then opens each file in the selected folder and generates a new document that lists every font, gradient, spot color, and placed image used in all the files.

The new file that is created is called DocumentReporter.ai, and you can format to your specifications once the script has finished running.

If you do spend a lot of time manually marking up documents, you may want to look at a plugin called Mechanical Cubed, produced by the fine folks at Triple Triangle. To download a free trial, visit www.tripletriangle.com.

Collecting Necessary Support Files

One of the most requested features for Illustrator is a command that collects all place-linked images and fonts, making it easy to send a file and all necessary support files so that someone else can work on or print the file.

Although Illustrator doesn't have a Collect for Output feature like QuarkXPress does or a robust Package command similar to that found in Adobe InDesign, Illustrator does ship with a script called Collect for Output, which you can find in the Scripting/Sample Scripts/AppleScript (Sample Scripts/Visual Basic Scripts) folder. If you think you will use this script often, you might consider placing a copy in the Adobe Illustrator CS3/Presets/Scripts folder. That way, the script will appear in the File > Scripts menu within the Illustrator application.

For a much better solution around collecting files for output, take a look at Worker72a's Scoop CS3 (www.worker72a.com) and Code Line Communications' ArtFiles (www.code-line.com).

Upon running the Collect for Output script, Illustrator copies the open Illustrator file and all place-linked images and places them in a new folder on your desktop. Unfortunately, the script won't collect fonts, although you can use the Analyze Documents script mentioned earlier to generate a list of fonts that are used in your document to assist in collecting the fonts you need manually.

APPENDIX B
Application Preferences

Adobe Illustrator has many different settings, or *preferences*, that control the program's behavior. Illustrator CS3 actually has 11 different panels of preferences. On Mac OS, you'll find the Preferences dialog by choosing Application > Preferences or by pressing Command-K. On Windows, you'll find the Preferences dialog by choosing Edit > Preferences or by pressing Control-K.

THE GENERAL PANEL

The General panel of Preferences is pretty much a melting pot of settings (**Figure B.1**). These settings are also the ones that alter the behavior of features the most.

Figure B.1 The General panel in Preferences offers quick access to settings such as Keyboard Increment.

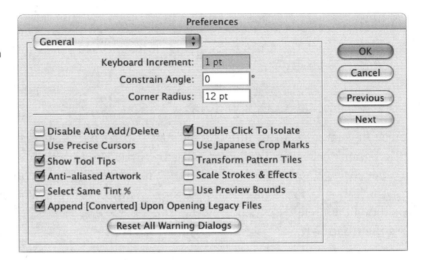

In general, the preferences in Illustrator are application-based, meaning they aren't saved in the file, but rather in Illustrator's application preferences file. This also means that if you open a file that was created on another computer, your preferences don't change.

- **Keyboard Increment.** When moving artwork around on your screen, using the mouse or even a pressure-sensitive pen doesn't always give you the control you need. The Keyboard Increment setting determines the distance a selected object moves when you tap any of the four arrow keys on your keyboard. Some call this the *nudge amount*. Don't be fooled into thinking that this setting should always be as small as possible. When you're working with a grid or in scale (designing floor plans, schematics, and so on), it can be extremely helpful to set your keyboard increment to a specific value (such as .25 inch). In this way, you can easily tap an arrow two times and know you've moved the object exactly .5 inch. It's no coincidence that when you open the Preferences dialog box, the Keyboard Increment value is highlighted. Power users know they can quickly press Command-K (Control-K), enter a value, press Enter, and then nudge their objects precisely.

- **Constrain Angle.** When you draw objects in Illustrator, the objects are aligned to the Constrain Angle setting, which is normally set to 0 degrees. However, sometimes you want to draw your document on a specific angle, and changing the constrain angle affects all tools and modifier keys in Illustrator.

- **Corner Radius.** When you're creating a shape with the Rounded Rectangle tool, this setting defines the default corner radius for the rounded corners. Note that this preference sets the default behavior, which you can easily override on a per-object basis in the Rounded Rectangle tool dialog.

- **Disable Auto Add/Delete.** Illustrator tries its best to help you get your work done, but sometimes its overzealousness gets in the way. By default, when you move your pointer over an existing path with the Pen tool, Illustrator thinks you want to add a point to the existing path and conveniently switches to the Add Anchor Point tool. This is great, unless, of course, you wanted to start drawing a new path with the Pen tool. Turning this preference on politely tells Illustrator, "Thanks but no thanks."

- **Use Precise Cursors.** Some of Illustrator's tool icons are cute, such as the Symbol Sprayer and Smudge tools, but they can be hard to position precisely. Even with the Pen tool, it can be hard to know exactly where the real tip of the pointer is. When Use Precise Cursors is active, all pointers are replaced by a simple X icon, which clearly defines the spot you're clicking (**Figure B.2**). You can also toggle this setting by pressing the Caps Lock key on your keyboard.

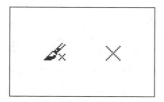

Figure B.2 The normal Paintbrush pointer (left) can be difficult to use, while the Paintbrush pointer with Precise Cursors turned on (right) is far easier to position.

- **Show Tool Tips.** Illustrator has a lot of icons—tiny chicklet icons, as we like to call them. Sometimes it's hard to know what a tool or button is just by looking at it, so if you hold your pointer over the icon for a second, a little window pops up identifying the name of the feature. These are called *tool tips*, and they are turned on by default. Although they are helpful, some people may think that they get in the way, which is why this preference exists.

- **Anti-aliased Artwork.** Computer screens are low-resolution devices (generally between 72 and 130 ppi), and artwork may appear jagged onscreen. This is especially true with the sharp vector shapes you create with Illustrator. Although the files print fine, looking at jagged artwork

The preferences are saved in a text file called Adobe Illustrator Prefs, and if you're brave, you can edit this file in a text editor. If Illustrator's behavior seems odd for any reason, such as tools gone missing from the Toolbox or frequent crashes occurring, you can try to delete your preferences file (Illustrator automatically creates a new one the next time you quit the application).

You can delete the preferences files at launch by pressing Command-Option-Shift (Control-Alt-Shift) while launching Illustrator. Keep the keys pressed until you see the splash screen appear.

all day may cause eyestrain and doesn't accurately display the way the graphics will eventually print. This option (on by default) applies anti-aliasing to Illustrator's Preview mode so your art onscreen appears clean and smooth. Antialiasing is always turned off in Outline view mode. Note that this setting affects how the art appears onscreen only and does not in any way affect how the art prints.

- **Select Same Tint %.** Illustrator has a feature that allows you to select all objects that are filled or stroked with the same color. When you use this feature, all objects that are filled with tint percentages of that same color are also selected. This preference setting selects only those objects that are filled with the same tint percentages of that color (resulting in fewer objects being selected).

- **Append [Converted] Upon Opening Legacy Files.** When you open files that were created in previous versions of Illustrator (what Illustrator refers to as *legacy files*), you may have to adjust text objects. To prevent you from accidentally overwriting your original files, Illustrator tacks on the word *[converted]* to your file name when it opens legacy files. For more information about text and legacy files, see Chapter 7, *Typography*.

- **Double Click to Isolate.** On by default, this option makes it possible to double-click a group to isolate that group for editing. With this option turned off, you can still isolate a group, but you have to select the group and then click the Isolate Selected Group icon on the Control panel.

- **Use Japanese Crop Marks.** Illustrator allows you to create simple crop marks automatically by choosing Object > Crop Area > Make. If you want something more than the standard eight paths, you can turn on this preference. At the very least, people who see your files will know that you're serious about crop marks (**Figure B.3**).

Figure B.3 Regular crop marks (left) use 8 straight lines, while Japanese crop marks (right) are more complex.

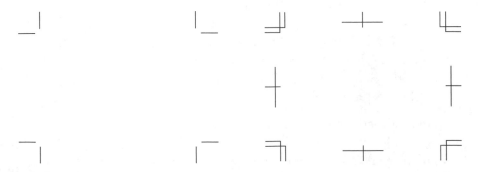

- **Transform Pattern Tiles.** When you apply transformations (such as Scale or Rotate) to objects that are filled with patterns, the default behavior is that only the shape is transformed, not the pattern fill. Turning this preference on changes the default behavior so that pattern fills are transformed as well. Note that this preference sets the default behavior, which you can easily override as you need to by using the setting in the Scale tool dialog or by pressing the tilde key (~) during a manual transform function.

- **Scale Strokes & Effects.** Similar to patterns, when you apply scale transformations to objects that have strokes or effects applied, the default behavior is that only the shape is transformed, not the strokes or the effects. Turning this preference on changes the default behavior so that strokes and effects are transformed as well. Note that this preference sets the default behavior, which you can easily override as you need to by using the setting in the Scale tool dialog.

- **Use Preview Bounds.** One of the benefits of using Illustrator is that you can be extremely precise when drawing objects. Illustrator's Control, Transform, and Info panels all provide exact feedback on coordinates, positioning, sizing, and more. By default, these panels use the actual vector path to determine these numbers, not the visual boundaries of the object. For example, you may have a shape that has a thick stroke or a scale effect applied to it, which is not represented in the value you see in the Transform panel. With the Use Preview Bounds preference activated, all panels use the visual boundary of a file as the value, not the underlying vector path.

- **Reset All Warning Dialogs.** Throughout the daily use of Illustrator, you'll no doubt meet a variety of warning dialogs. Sometimes these are helpful, and sometimes they can be quite annoying and you'll wish bad things upon them. You'll find that most of these dialogs contain a Don't Show Again button, which you can use to tell Illustrator that a simple beep would be just fine, thank you. Clicking Reset All Warning Dialogs brings back any warning dialogs that you asked Illustrator not to show again.

THE SELECTION & ANCHOR DISPLAY PANEL

If you're having trouble selecting individual anchor points or if you are coming from FreeHand and are used to seeing anchor points and control handles displayed a bit differently, the Selection & Anchor Display panel in Preferences is for you (**Figure B.4**). The Object Selection by Path Only setting, which used to appear in the General panel, now appears here.

Figure B.4 The Selection & Anchor Display panel in Preferences enables you to control settings used when you select and edit paths.

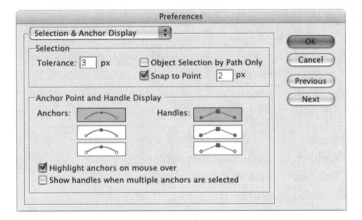

- **Tolerance.** The Tolerance setting determines how close your pointer has to be to an object in order to select it. Using a lower number will mean you'll have to position your pointer perfectly in order to make a selection (good for very precise work where there are many anchor points within a small area), while higher numbers allow for faster and easier selections.

- **Object Selection by Path Only.** When working in Preview mode, Illustrator allows you to select an object by clicking its path or anywhere within its fill area (if it has a fill attribute applied). Although this is convenient, sometimes, especially when you're working with complex artwork, this behavior makes it difficult to select objects. Turning this preference on allows you to select objects only by clicking their paths, not their fills.

- **Snap to Point.** As you drag objects around the page, you'll notice that your pointer snaps to the anchor points of other objects and to guides as well. The Snap to Point value determines how close your pointer has to be to another object in order for it to snap to it.

- **Anchors.** Illustrator offers three different ways to display anchor points. The difference between each size may be subtle here, but this setting can help make Illustrator seem more familiar to FreeHand users.

- **Handles.** Illustrator offers three different ways to display control handles. The difference between each of the three may be subtle, but this setting can mean all the difference to those who might be used to seeing handles in a different way, as in FreeHand.

- **Highlight Anchors on Mouse Over.** On by default, this setting highlights anchor points as you mouse over them. This happens even if the objects are not selected. They can be either very helpful, such as when you're editing paths, or very annoying. This is why this is a preference.

- **Show Handles When Multiple Anchors Are Selected.** In previous versions of Illustrator, you were able to see only the control handles of one anchor point or path segment at a time. With this preference turned on, you can view control handles even with multiple anchor points selected.

THE TYPE PANEL

Illustrator has a variety of preference settings that apply specifically to working with type (**Figure B.5**).

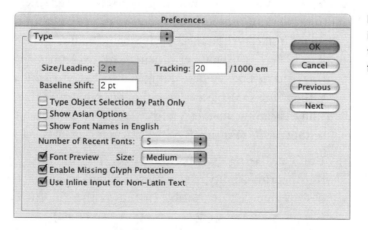

Figure B.5 The Type panel in Preferences enables you to activate the WYSIWYG font menu.

- **Keyboard shortcut increments.** Keyboard shortcut junkies know that they can perform a variety of tasks without ever reaching for the mouse. This is never more true than when you are working with type, when your hands are already on the keyboard. Therefore, you can set the keyboard increments for changing Size/Leading, Baseline Shift, and Tracking here.

- **Type Object Selection by Path Only.** Similar to the Object Selection by Path Only setting, this one refers to text objects only. With this preference enabled, you can select a text object by clicking only its baseline.

- **Show Asian Options.** Illustrator is extremely popular in Japan and in other Asian countries; therefore, it has some features, such as Warichu, Kinsoku, Mojikumi, Tsume, Aki, and composite fonts, that are used specifically in those locales. These features are hidden from view by default, but turning this preference on makes them visible in the user interface.

- **Show Font Names in English.** When working with foreign or non-English fonts, you can use this option to specify that the fonts are listed in the font menu using their English names.

- **Number of Recent Fonts.** As you work, Illustrator takes note of the fonts you use and puts copies of them at the top of your font menu. Especially when you've got hundreds of fonts installed, this can make it easier than scrolling through an entire list to find a particular one. You can have Illustrator track anywhere from 1 to 15 of the most recent fonts you've used. If you need more than 15 recent fonts, you might want to look into taking a course in graphic design.

- **Font Preview.** Illustrator has a WYSIWYG font menu that allows you to preview what each font looks like, directly within the scrolling font menu. You can choose between Small, Medium, and Large preview sizes. There is a slight performance hit that comes with using this feature, and this preference setting can enable or disable the preview altogether. One valuable aspect of the font preview is that it also displays an icon indicating whether a font is TrueType, PostScript, Multiple Master, or OpenType (**Figure B.6**).

- **Enable Missing Glyph Protection.** Turning this setting on gives Illustrator the ability to substitute a glyph or a character where the desired glyph is not available (because either the current font or the font you just switched to doesn't support that glyph).

- **Use Inline Input for Non-Latin Text.** Some operating systems support non-Latin languages by forcing you to enter text into a separate system-level dialog. Turning this option on will allow you to set such text directly within Illustrator.

Figure B.6 The icons on the left side of the WYSIWYG font menu indicate the font type.

THE UNITS & DISPLAY PERFORMANCE PANEL

How do you measure performance? You won't find the answer here, but you will find settings for how your rulers appear and how to speed up screen redraw (**Figure B.7**).

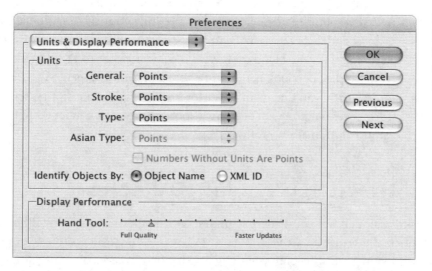

Figure B.7 The Units & Display Performance panel in Preferences lets you easily switch between a variety of measurement settings.

- **Units.** Illustrator can utilize different measurement systems for different uses. These preferences allow you to specify default measurements for general items (rulers and coordinates, sizes and values for objects and drawing tools, and so on), stroke width and dash settings, and Roman and Asian type specifications (size, leading, and so on). Note that these are all used to set the default measurements in Illustrator, but at any time, you can always enter a value and Illustrator does the conversion for you. So if your document is set to inches, you can still specify a 4p9 rectangle (see the next paragraph for information about such measurements).

- **Numbers Without Units Are Points.** When you're using picas and points, the standard notation is to enter the number of picas, the letter *p*, and the number of points (such as 12p6). If your value is only points, you enter something like **p6** to indicate 6 points instead. With this option turned on, simply typing **6** means 6 points (as opposed to 6 picas).

- **Identify Objects By.** Illustrator has the ability to generate templates with XML-based variables, which are useful for generating graphics files automatically using scripts or the Adobe Graphics Server. Some of these templates require that all variables are defined using valid XML names. By default, Illustrator uses the object name to define variables, but you can specify that Illustrator use valid XML IDs instead.

- **Display Performance.** Do you have an ancient video card in your computer? Or are your files so complex that even the fastest of computers begs for mercy when trying to redraw your screen? The Hand Tool slider allows you to dial in the performance that you need when scrolling with the Hand tool. With the slider closer to Full Quality, your graphics do look better while scrolling, at the expense of a slower redraw. You can drag your slider toward Faster Updates for better performance, but you won't get great-looking art until you let go of the mouse button after scrolling.

THE GUIDES & GRID PANEL

Illustrator allows you to define guides, which you drag out from either the horizontal ruler or the vertical ruler (View > Show Rulers). These guides act like magnets, helping you draw or position elements on your page. In reality, you can turn any vector shape into a guide by selecting it and choosing View > Guides > Make Guides. Additionally, Illustrator has a grid feature that makes your artboard appear almost as if it were a sheet of graph paper. Objects can snap to this grid, making it easy to visually align items in a layout.

You set the appearance of guides and the grid using the Guides & Grid panel in Preferences (**Figure B.8**). Some people prefer solid lines for guides whereas others prefer dotted lines. You can also choose the color used for the guides. Additionally, you can set the number of grid lines that appear in the grid and how many subdivisions each has. For example, a Web designer might specify a grid line at every 10 pixels with 10 subdivisions, which would make it possible to zoom in and see artwork on a pixel-by-pixel basis.

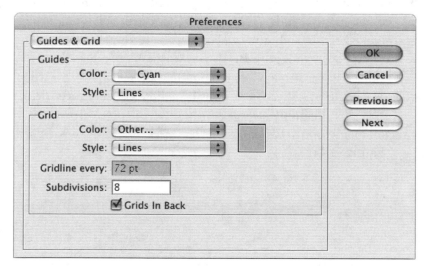

Figure B.8 The Guides & Grid panel in Preferences lets you change the color and appearance of grid lines.

THE SMART GUIDES & SLICES PANEL

In addition to normal guides, Illustrator has a useful feature called *Smart Guides*; these guides offer a variety of pointer feedback options while you work. You can activate this feature by choosing View > Smart Guides. The Smart Guides preferences allow you to control the behavior of this feature (**Figure B.9** on the following page).

Figure B.9 The Smart Guides & Slices panel in Preferences.

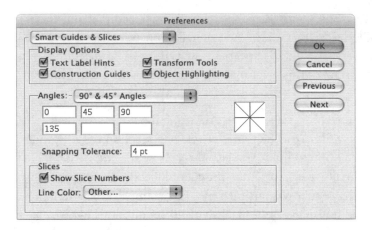

- **Display Options.** Text Label Hints identify items on your screen as you mouse over them (**Figure B.10**); Construction Guides help you align objects by indicating when they are on similar planes or angles as other objects (**Figure B.11**); Transform Tools offer similar functionality to construction guides but they are specifically for when you are using any of Illustrator's transformation tools (**Figure B.12**); and Object Highlighting identifies the underlying original artwork when you mouse over artwork that has had effects or envelopes applied to it (**Figure B.13**).

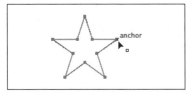

Figure B.10 A Text Label smart guide quickly identifies elements on your screen.

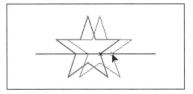

Figure B.11 A Construction Guides smart guide makes it easy to position objects.

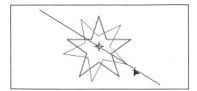

Figure B.12 A Transform Tools smart guide helps when performing transformations.

Figure B.13 An Object Highlighting smart guide makes it easy to quickly find and edit objects.

- **Angles.** The Angles settings allow you to specify at what angles Smart Guides appear when you're using any of the just-mentioned display options.

- **Snapping Tolerance.** The Snapping Tolerance setting specifies the distance to the original pixel from when a Smart Guide is activated.

- **Slices.** Slices are regions that you define to better optimize Web graphics. In Preferences, you can define how these slices are indicated on the Illustrator artboard.

THE HYPHENATION PANEL

Straightforward in its implementation, the Hyphenation panel in Preferences allows you to choose the default language (which you can override by using the pop-up menu in the Character panel) and hyphenation exceptions and to add new words to the dictionary (**Figure B.14**).

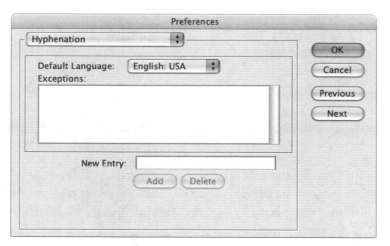

Figure B.14 The Hyphenation panel in Preferences lets you add new words to the dictionary in Illustrator for better hyphenation.

THE PLUG-INS & SCRATCH DISKS PANEL

From an architectural standpoint, Illustrator has a core engine, and the rest of the application is built using plugins. Illustrator's Plug-ins folder contains all of these features plus additional files, including one that contains bevels for the 3D feature in Illustrator (covered in Chapter 8, *3D and Other Live Effects*). Additionally, third-party plugins such as MAPublisher and CAD-tools are stored in this folder. The Plug-ins preference allows you to also specify additional folders where plugins might be stored (**Figure B.15**).

Figure B.15 The Plug-ins & Scratch Disks panel in Preferences lets you specify multiple disks for memory-intensive operations.

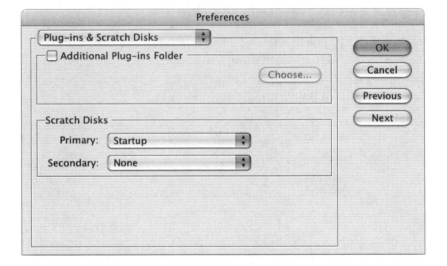

Just as you did in math class, Illustrator uses a scratch pad to save work while performing normal functions. Sometimes, in really complex files, Illustrator may need a lot of space. You can specify a hard drive or volume that Illustrator should use as a scratch disk to perform these functions. By default, your startup disk is your scratch disk, but you can change to a disk with more free space if you'd like. You can also specify a second scratch disk should Illustrator ever run out of room on the first one.

THE USER INTERFACE PANEL

Illustrator CS3 contains a new panel-based user interface that is consistent with other applications found in Adobe Creative Suite 3. The User Interface panel in Preferences allows you to configure how the user interface looks and how it works when you use it (**Figure B.16**).

- **Brightness.** Some people work in a brightly lit studio, while others work in dark or dimly lit rooms. People who do certain types of work, such as video or prepress production, may also prefer to work in darker environments so that they can better focus on their work. In these dark environments, the panels in the interface can be bright enough to be a distraction. To allow these users to better focus on the art on their screens, the user interface has a Brightness slider. Sliding the triangle to the right will make the backgrounds in the panels brighter; sliding the triangle to the left will result in a dark gray background within the panels.

- **Auto-Collapse Icon Panels.** When a panel is in a collapsed state, you can click the icons of the panels, opening them as you need them. With the Auto-Collapse Icon Panels setting turned on, panels will return to their iconic state after you've clicked elsewhere on your screen. Turning the setting off means that a panel will stay open and return to an iconic state only if you click its icon again.

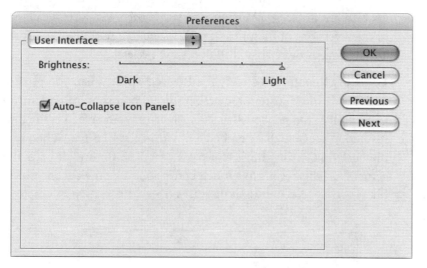

Figure B.16 The User Interface panel in Preferences lets you control settings for how the new CS3 interface looks and works.

The File Handling & Clipboard Panel

This preference panel includes settings for how Illustrator handles certain files as well as settings for how art is copied to the clipboard for pasting into other applications (**Figure B.17**).

Figure B.17 The File Handling & Clipboard panel in Preferences allows you to determine how graphics are copied and pasted into other applications.

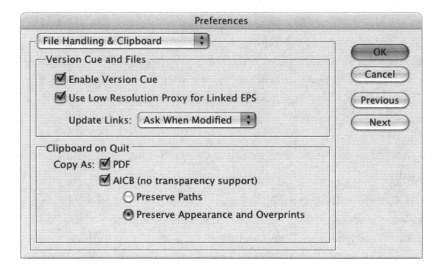

- **Enable Version Cue.** If you own Adobe Creative Suite and are using Version Cue or if someone in your group owns Version Cue, this option enables you to access a Version Cue workspace. Version Cue allows you to track versions of files, manage file usage in a multiuser environment, and manage browser-based PDF review cycles.

- **Use Low Resolution Proxy for Linked EPS.** When you place-link an EPS file into Illustrator, whether it is a Photoshop EPS or any other generic EPS, the preview that's displayed on your screen is the low-resolution preview that's embedded within the EPS file. When you uncheck this setting, Illustrator parses the EPS file and displays the actual file. This results in a much better-looking preview on your screen, but it also slows redraw and increases file size. On a separate note, when you're using the Live Trace feature with place-linked EPS files, the resolution of the image that Live Trace can detect depends on this setting as well. When the option is checked, Live Trace sees the 72 ppi preview file and traces that. By turning this setting off, Live Trace can detect the full resolution of the file and use it to trace the image.

- **Update Links.** When you place-link a file into Illustrator, the Links panel maintains the link information about that file. Because the file is external, you can edit that file easily by using the Edit Original feature, found in either the Links panel or the Control panel. When the default Ask When Modified setting is used, if you edit a linked file outside Illustrator and return to the Illustrator document, you'll get a dialog alerting you to the fact that the file was updated, with an option to update the link. Alternatively, you can choose to manually update links yourself through the Links panel, or you can set Illustrator to automatically update all links as they happen.

- **Clipboard on Quit.** Today's modern operating systems use an efficient method to copy and paste data using the system's clipboard, called *promising*. Rather than copy art in a variety of formats to the clipboard (which would take time), applications promise to deliver art when pasted. Then, when you paste the art, the operating system goes back to the application you copied from and gets the data. The problem is, if you've quit the program since you performed the copy function, the operating system can't fulfill its promise. So when you quit an application, it copies whatever was promised to the clipboard (which explains why sometimes it takes a while for an application to actually quit). The Clipboard on Quit preference allows you to determine which file formats are used to copy art to the clipboard when you quit Illustrator. By default, both the PDF and the AICB (Adobe Illustrator Clip Board) options are checked, which gives you the most options. Unless you have a specific reason, we suggest that you leave both of these checked at all times. In general, the PDF option supports native transparency and is PDF 1.5, whereas the AICB is flattened data and is PostScript.

THE APPEARANCE OF BLACK PANEL

In an effort to display graphics on your screen or proofs that closely match what you will see on an actual printed sheet, Illustrator includes a setting specifically for how the color black is displayed or printed (**Figure B.18**). You can choose to have your blacks display accurately, in which case black will appear closer to a dark gray color (closer to what you might see on press), or you can choose to display rich blacks, in which case your blacks will be much darker. Note that these settings are not color management settings and don't affect your final separated output. These settings affect only your screen display or output to an RGB device.

Figure B.18 The Appearance of Black panel in Preferences allows you to achieve better color results on your screen.

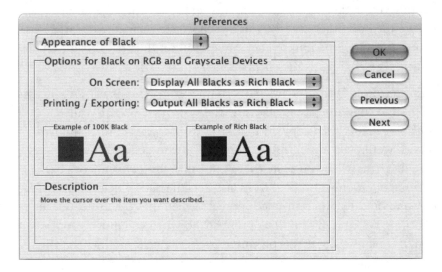

INDEX